Praise for *Bending toward Jus...*

"*Bending toward Justice* is a book of the classical phase [of the Civil Rights Movement], a lively and unabashedly partisan account of Selma and the Voting Rights Act. . . . May tells the story in his own way, and he is able to add many details." — Louis Menand, *The New Yorker*

"Have we — at long last — overcome? Not yet, University of Delaware historian Gary May makes clear in his exemplary account of the landmark law." — Kevin Boyle, *Washington Post*

"May accomplishes what he set out to do, rendering 'a dramatic account of the struggle that finally won African Americans the ballot.' It's a story that is chilling in many ways and inspiring in others. . . . May explores the testy relationship between the Rev. Dr. Martin Luther King Jr. and President Lyndon B. Johnson with nuance and detail. . . . And May's account of Johnson facing down Alabama Gov. George Wallace over Wallace's refusal to force county registrars to register black voters is one of the best descriptions anywhere of the fabled 'LBJ Treatment.'" — Paul Jablow, *Philadelphia Inquirer*

"May's book is a great introduction to voting rights at a moment when the subject is drawing more attention than any time since 1965." — Ari Berman, *The Nation*

"[May] presents a dramatic, highly readable account of the history of the movement for the Voting Rights Act that is suitable for educating students, nonspecialist scholars, and the reading public. . . . Twenty-six years after Henry Hampton's *Eyes on the Prize* documentary — which is shown to classes, repeated on PBS, and has an accompanying reader — May has produced a book written in a deeply moving way that brings to life the people and their deeds and suffering as graphically as Hampton's documentary. That is no easy feat." — Mary Frances Berry, *Reviews in American History*

"May's lively and cogent history of the Voting Rights Act is indispensable reading for anyone concerned about the erosion of voting rights that has accompanied the election of Barack Obama, America's first black president, especially as the issue is still up for debate. . . . May has constructed a vivid, fast-paced morality tale. . . . By focusing on Selma, May pays tribute to the courage of otherwise ordinary people and makes a case for the continued relevance of this legislation." — *Publishers Weekly*

"Gary May's compelling history of why and how the Voting Rights Act advanced the promise of American life could not be more timely. Every member of the Supreme Court and every citizen interested in the widest possible access to the ballot box will want to read May's book. It should be recognized as the standard work on this most important subject." — Robert Dallek, author of *An Unfinished Life: John F. Kennedy, 1917–1963*

"In this vivid and beautifully written page-turner, May brings the story of the Voting Rights Act to life in an altogether new way by deftly drawing out the personal stories and voices of this epoch-making statute. At a time when the future of the Voting Rights Act is uncertain and up for debate, May's book could not be more timely—or more readable."—Richard M. Valelly, author of *The Two Reconstructions: The Struggle for Black Enfranchisement*

"Gary May's dramatic *Bending toward Justice* brings alive the critical dynamic between grass roots advocacy and political leadership which produced the most significant advance in civil rights since the Emancipation Proclamation. How this victory was achieved provides vital lessons to any citizen concerned about the importance of voting rights protections and the dangers and challenges to those rights today."—Nick Kotz, author of *Judgment Days: Lyndon Baines Johnson, Martin Luther King Jr., and the Laws That Changed America*

"It's hard to believe that a pivot in American history as transformative as the Voting Rights Act of 1965 is only now getting its first book-length treatment, but Gary May is the ideal historian for the job. With confidence and concision, he navigates between a landmark bridge in Selma, Alabama, and the also highly contended committees of Congress to produce a compelling narrative of the civil rights movement's ultimate triumph: the Selma-to-Montgomery March and the ensuing federal legislation guaranteeing universal suffrage. By following the struggle over voting rights into the present day, May's fine book provides vivid proof that history is never history."—Diane McWhorter, author of *Carry Me Home: Birmingham, Alabama: The Climactic Battle of the Civil Rights Revolution*

"An illuminating history of a law that remains all too relevant."—*Booklist*

"Compelling. . . . This lucid investigation of the [Voting Rights Act's] history relates its critical importance to American democracy."—*Library Journal*

"Anyone interested in understanding the extent of the damage, actual and symbolic, to the voting rights of racial and ethnic minorities caused by this monumental decision [*Shelby County v. Holder*] would do well to read May's book. . . . Once the reader has finished the book, she will have a good grasp of the long, hard, often dangerous battle Blacks and their allies have fought since the end of Reconstruction to achieve equal voting rights, the terrible sacrifices champions of voting rights—particularly southern Blacks—have made in behalf of this goal, and the importance the VRA has had in partially achieving the goal."—Chandler Davidson, *African American Review*

BENDING
TOWARD
JUSTICE

Also by Gary May:_____

*China Scapegoat: The Diplomatic Ordeal
of John Carter Vincent*

*Un-American Activities: The Trials of
William Remington*

*The Informant: The FBI, the Ku Klux Klan
and the Murder of Viola Liuzzo*

John Tyler

BENDING
TOWARD
JUSTICE

The Voting Rights Act *and the*
Transformation *of* American Democracy

....

GARY MAY

Duke University Press
Durham and London
2015

First published as a paperback edition by Duke University Press, 2015

Designed by Trish Wilkinson
Set in 11-point Minion Pro

Library of Congress Cataloging-in-Publication Data
May, Gary, 1944–
Bending toward justice : the Voting Rights Act and the transformation
of American democracy / Gary May.
pages cm
Includes bibliographical references and index.
ISBN 978-0-8223-5927-2 (pbk. : alk. paper)
1. United States. Voting Rights Act of 1965.
2. African Americans—Suffrage—History.
3. Minorities—Suffrage—United States—History.
4. Election law—United States—History.
5. United States—Politics and government—1861–1865.
6. United States—Politics and government—1865–1933. I. Title.
KF4893.M39 2014
342.73′072—dc23

Cover art: Young Man Waving American Flag during Selma to
Montgomery Civil Rights March. © Steve Schapiro/Corbis

*For Gail and William Aaron May, with love,
and to the thousands of men and women, lost to history,
who fought and died to make America a better country.*

Contents

Hattiesburg, Mississippi, 1964. Two African Americans attempt to register to vote while white officials look on. The sign on the wall informs them that in ten days everyone will know. Their names and addresses will be published in the local newspaper, giving opponents of black suffrage a chance to retaliate against them. © 1976 MATT HERRON/TAKE STOCK/THE IMAGE WORKS

Prologue
The Most Powerful Instrument

AN AMERICAN CITIZEN VOTING—SURELY THERE IS NOTHING REMARKABLE about that. But for an African American living in the Deep South in the 1960s, it was a forbidden act, a dangerous act. There were nearly impossible obstacles to overcome: poll taxes, literacy tests, and hostile registrars. If a person succeeded and was allowed to vote, his name was published in the local newspaper, alerting his employers and others equally determined to stop him. The black men and women who dared to vote lost their jobs, their homes, and often, their lives.

And yet they persevered. They marched on county courthouses, confronted sheriffs, and went to jail. In Selma, Alabama, on March 7, 1965, a day remembered as "Bloody Sunday," they endured a brutal attack from state troopers and local vigilantes. That event touched the conscience of the nation, forcing President Lyndon B. Johnson to place a voting rights bill at the forefront of his political agenda. Its passage permitted millions of African Americans to vote in Alabama and elsewhere in the South. The Voting Rights Act transformed American democracy and in many ways was the last act of emancipation, a process Abraham Lincoln began in 1863.

This book tells the story of the struggles of ordinary people, many unknown to most Americans, who were, in fact, quite extraordinary. They risked all to obtain a fundamental American right that had been codified in the Constitution's Fifteenth Amendment, though it was not fulfilled until

1965. Since then the Voting Rights Act has been repeatedly challenged. Not only has it survived, but it has also been expanded to protect other minorities facing similar obstacles. Those challenges, however, persist, and the Act's most potent provision may soon face its ultimate test before the US Supreme Court, which may well strike it down. But if that should occur, it will not deter those who fought for its creation, battled to expand it, and struggled to maintain it. The fight will go on in courtrooms and, perhaps again, in the streets. The essence of the Voting Rights Act can never be destroyed, for as Martin Luther King Jr. wrote in 1963 while imprisoned in a Birmingham jail, "I have no despair about the future. . . . We will reach the goal of freedom . . . all over the nation, because the goal of America is freedom." And we can also take comfort from the nineteenth-century abolitionist Theodore Parker's words that King famously quoted at the conclusion of the historic Voting Rights march: "The arc of the moral universe is long but it bends toward justice."[1]

THE SIGNING INTO LAW OF THE 1965 VOTING RIGHTS ACT WAS THE culmination of a struggle almost one hundred years in the making. Prior to Lincoln's Emancipation Proclamation in 1863, only five states—all in New England—allowed black men to vote, and when New York joined their ranks, it required that they own property. In the South almost all blacks were *considered* property and, as slaves, were prohibited from voting. Immediately after the Civil War ended former slaves and free black men began demanding the right to vote throughout the South. Meetings and rallies were held in Virginia, North Carolina, Kentucky, Georgia, Alabama, and Washington, DC, where, in January 1866, the National Convention of Colored Men, with delegates from twelve states, both north and south, demanded "the right of impartial suffrage." They hoped that President Andrew Johnson would come to their aid.[2]

He did not. In a stormy meeting with Johnson that February, the new president, a Tennessee racist more sympathetic to poor southern whites than to slavery's victims, told a delegation headed by Frederick Douglass that black voting was a "hollow, unpractical idea" that would "cause great injury to the white and colored man." Johnson despised Douglass, the former slave whose brilliance as a writer and orator had made him an international celebrity. "I know that damned Douglass," Johnson later told an aide. "He's just like any other nigger and he would sooner cut a man's throat than not." Under Johnson, "Presidential Reconstruction" permitted the former rebellious South to rejoin the Union easily and resume their political—if not personal—subjugation of its black population. It was left to the Republican-dominated Congress to assist the former slaves.[3]

During the period later known as "Radical Reconstruction" Congress, in 1866, passed and sent to the states the Fourteenth Amendment to the Constitution, providing black people with the rights of citizenship and legal equality but not the right to vote. Because Johnson resisted all these efforts, Congress's Reconstruction Act, passed over Johnson's veto in 1867, divided the South into military districts occupied by federal troops and prohibited the former confederate states from returning to the Union until they ratified the new amendment. The Fifteenth Amendment, passed in 1869 and ratified in 1870, prohibited the federal or state governments from denying any American his voting rights "on account of race, color, or previous condition of servitude," thereby granting an entire generation of black men—many of them former slaves—the right to vote and, with it, the chance of winning political office. (Their wives and daughters would not receive that right until the Nineteenth Amendment was adopted in 1920, but they too were politically active, organizing meetings and often acting as armed guards protecting those who gathered to discuss the issues of the day.)[4]

Radical Reconstruction brought southern blacks political freedom, and they embraced it enthusiastically. As many as two thousand served as state legislators, city councilmen, tax assessors, justices of the peace, jurors, sheriffs, and US marshals; fourteen black politicians entered the House of Representatives; and two became US senators. But the new era of black activism did not last long: northern support declined, a conservative Supreme Court abolished many of the laws designed to assist black citizens, and terrorist groups like the Ku Klux Klan and the Knights of the White Camellia destroyed black schools and churches and murdered at will.[5]

By 1877 southern white Democrats had overthrown every new state government and established state constitutions that stripped black citizens of their political rights. To circumvent the Fourteenth and Fifteenth Amendments, legislators created clever devices that would disenfranchise black citizens for the next eighty years. These included literacy and "understanding" tests, poll taxes, and residency and property requirements; among these devices was also a "grandfather clause" that exempted white men and their male descendants from literacy tests and property qualifications if they had voted prior to January 1, 1867. That date was important because it was three years before the Fifteenth Amendment guaranteed black citizens that right and just before the all-white Democratic Party primary barred black candidates from political participation. The new laws gave the greatest power to local registrars, usually appointed by state governors, who would choose which applicant succeeded or failed. The intent of the laws was explicit: "The plan," said one Mississippi official in 1890, "is to invest permanently the powers of government in the hands of the people who ought to have them — the white people."[6]

The laws were disastrous for newly empowered black citizens. In Louisiana 130,000 had been registered to vote in 1896. By 1904 only 1,342 remained to exercise the franchise, if whites permitted it. Virginia's 147,000 black voters were reduced to 21,000. Eighty-three percent of Alabama's electorate was again white in 1906, compared to only 2 percent of theoretically eligible black adults. "At first we used to kill them to keep them from voting," declared an Alabamian, but "when we got sick of doing that we began to steal their ballots; and when stealing their ballots began troubling our consciences, we decided to handle the matter legally, fixing it so they couldn't vote." By the early twentieth century black disenfranchisement, like economic and social segregation, was complete throughout the South, and it remained almost unchanged for the next sixty years.[7]

THE DIGNITARIES WHO CROWDED INTO THE US CAPITOL'S STATUARY HALL on August 6, 1965, to witness the signing of the Voting Rights Act were well aware of the injustices that the new legislation was intended to redress, though most had never experienced them directly. The attendees included US senators and representatives, military officers and diplomats, business and labor leaders, clergy and educators, cabinet members and Supreme Court justices, and even a US president's daughter, Luci Baines Johnson. Almost lost in that crowd was a special group who had experienced these injustices directly and had long fought for voting rights. So for these guests, seeing the president of the United States create a law that would at last put the federal government decisively on the side of African Americans as they registered and voted made this day especially exciting.[8]

Among the witnesses was Rosa Parks, the fifty-two-year-old former seamstress best known as the woman whose defiance touched off the first modern mass African American revolt in December 1955 after she refused to give up her seat on an Alabama bus. Her friends knew this was no accident of history. She was a long-time, committed activist and NAACP official who, since the early 1940s, had secretly organized meetings of Montgomery's Voters League, preparing black citizens to register and vote, an effort that might cost them their jobs or even their lives. She quickly came to symbolize a woman who not only encouraged black people to register but also possessed the courage to try to do so herself. Her first attempt ended in failure, as did the second. Taking the exam a third time, she copied her answers to use as evidence in a lawsuit if the Board flunked her again. Perhaps the three registrars realized who they were dealing with, because this time, in 1945, she passed. The next obstacle was paying the $1.50 poll tax. It didn't seem like much, but black voters were required to pay it retroactively, so Parks, at forty-two, paid $16.50, "a considerable amount of money," she later noted. Following the bus boycott she continued working to register black citizens who were still denied the right to vote.[9]

Thurgood Marshall was there. Just three weeks earlier President Johnson appointed him Solicitor General of the United States, the first African American to be so honored. Marshall was already a legendary figure in the civil rights community. As the NAACP's premier lawyer, on numerous occasions he had rushed south to aid black prisoners languishing in jail cells on trumped-up charges. At the same time that he appeared before local magistrates who considered him unqualified to be a member of the Bar, he argued cases before the Supreme Court of the United States. During one such case, in 1944, he argued that a Texas white-only primary was unconstitutional. In *Smith v. Allwright*, eight of the justices agreed. When other southern states refused to accept the decision on the grounds that it covered only Texas, federal judges ruled against them. These successes encouraged thousands of black southerners to try to register. Although he would later be celebrated for winning the case of *Brown v. Board of Education of Topeka*, it was his victory in *Smith v. Allwright*, he told one interviewer, that gave him the greatest pride. "Without the ballot," he often said, "you have no citizenship, no status, no power in this country." With it, anything was possible.[10]

Charles Evers was also waiting for President Johnson that day. Nearly twenty years earlier *Smith v. Allwright* gave him and his younger brother Medgar, both Mississippi veterans of World War II, a chance to vote against a man they despised, Senator Theodore Bilbo, who was seeking renomination in the July 2, 1946, Democratic primary. Bilbo, a virulent racist, wanted blacks deported to Africa, supported the poll tax, fought antilynching legislation, and, above all, opposed black suffrage. "If you let a handful go to the polls, . . . there will be two handfuls in 1947, and from there on it will grow into a mighty surge," he warned his supporters. "The white people are sitting on a volcano, and it is up to you red-blooded men to do something about it." The *Jackson Daily News*, which had endorsed Bilbo, told black voters: "DON'T TRY IT. . . . Staying away from the polls . . . will be the best way to prevent unhealthy and unhappy results."

The Evers brothers managed to register in Decatur, their hometown (the state legislature had exempted all veterans from paying recent poll taxes), and accompanied by a group of fellow black veterans, they went to the courthouse to vote that July morning. There they found twenty armed men barring their way. One yelled, "You niggers are going to wind up getting yourselves killed and everyone around you killed." Charles, always more quick-tempered than Medgar, had brought a gun with him and tried to use it. Medgar stopped him, telling him, "Charley, it ain't worth it." The brothers and their friends left, followed by a black Ford, whose passenger pointed a shotgun at them all the way home. Angry, they decided to arm themselves and return to the courthouse. But they did not really want a bloody confrontation with men, many of whom they knew since childhood, so they left their guns in the car. As they approached the polling place, they again faced a hostile crowd and left, this time for good. "I was born in Decatur, was raised there, but was never in my life permitted to vote there," Medgar Evers later said.[11]

What occurred next was extraordinary, a sign that a new generation was entering the fight for voting rights. Although Bilbo easily won the nomination, the NAACP and the newly formed Progressive Voters League complained that Bilbo's intimidating statements had kept thousands from the polls and urged the Senate to impeach him. The Senate's Committee on Campaign Expenditures agreed to hold hearings in Jackson, the state capital, in December. Few black activists were optimistic: The Committee was chaired by Louisiana Democrat Allen Ellender, Bilbo's close friend, and the other members were either southerners or Republicans who cared little about voting rights. Ellender refused to permit NAACP lawyers to act as counsel for witnesses who would appear voluntarily, so many feared that few if any would risk testifying against Bilbo. But to everyone's surprise, two hundred black Mississippians, mostly veterans, appeared at the segregated courthouse on December 2 seeking to testify. Vernando R. Collier, a veteran and NAACP official in Gulfport, testified that as he and his wife approached the polling booth in city hall, a group of white men stopped them, then began beating and dragging them from the building. Others described numerous violent incidents that occurred that day, and some testified about their unsuccessful efforts to register to vote.

The committee eventually found Bilbo innocent of any charges meriting censure, but the newly elected Republican Congress, sensing an opportunity for mischief, refused to seat him. The matter ended some months later when Bilbo succumbed to cancer.[12]

Medgar Evers became the NAACP's first field secretary in Mississippi in 1954, a post he held with distinction until his assassination in 1963. Following his death, Charles Evers assumed his position. In 1969, thanks to the Voting Rights Act, black voters in Fayette, Mississippi, elected him mayor, the first of his race to win the office since Reconstruction.

John Doar, the assistant attorney general for civil rights, was also seated in Statuary Hall that morning. Bored with his Wisconsin family law practice, he joined the Justice Department's Civil Rights Division in 1960, three years after the Civil Rights Act of 1957 authorized its creation. The Act also gave the attorney general new powers to prosecute those who obstructed voting in federal elections, but the legal route was filled with obstructions and almost inevitable failure. Doar, unwilling to trade one stuffy law office for another, soon went south to see personally what black Americans experienced when they tried to register to vote. On a trip to Haywood County, Tennessee, he visited a rural church and met sharecroppers, all of whom had been evicted from their land simply because they tried to register. Their courage affected him profoundly and convinced him that his original decision to leave Wisconsin had been correct. He was now on the front lines of a historic struggle against injustice, and there was no other place he would rather be.[13]

These and other trips to Mississippi, Alabama, and Louisiana showed Doar the inadequacy of the 1957 law and its similarly weak successor passed in 1960. Doar's efforts in Dallas County, Alabama, told the tale. In 1961 only 1 percent of eligible black citizens were registered to vote compared to their white counterparts, 64 percent of whom had encountered no difficulties and could vote. After finding reliable witnesses willing to risk testifying to alleged discrimination in open court before a hostile judge, Doar filed his first lawsuit on April 13, 1961. But the trial did not occur until May 1962—thirteen months later. It took an additional six months for the judge to issue his decision. Judge Daniel Thomas declared that the registrars had indeed been guilty of discrimination, but because they had resigned their posts and had been replaced by a new board, presumed innocent of wrongdoing, there was no need to issue an injunction prohibiting discrimination. Doar appealed Judge Thomas's decision to the US Court of Appeals for the Fifth Circuit, which ruled in September 1963 that discrimination had occurred but rejected the department's request that it order registrars to evaluate the suitability of black applicants as it did whites. Nearly three years of legal efforts had met with failure. And discrimination in Dallas County continued.[14]

Doar's experiences, along with those of other members of the Civil Rights Division who were also in Statuary Hall that day, had helped shape the Act. They hoped that this legislation, by giving the federal government the authority to intervene directly to guarantee black people the right to vote, would at last eliminate literacy tests and end the power of southern registrars.

John Lewis was there. At twenty-five he was already a veteran activist, leader of the Student Nonviolent Coordinating Committee (SNCC), and a man who had seen the inside of more jails than a career criminal. He had begun fighting for voting rights in Selma, Alabama, in 1963, two years before Martin Luther King Jr. chose that city to create a crisis that would force President Johnson to send a voting rights bill to Congress. In 1965 Lewis had almost died on Selma's Edmund Pettus Bridge in the assault that had paved the way for the event he was celebrating this day.[15]

And, of course, King himself was present for the signing of the Voting Rights Bill. Although trying to desegregate some of the South's most dangerous cities had occupied his time recently, winning the right to vote was always high on his agenda. On May 17, 1957, in an event at the Lincoln Memorial called to commemorate the third anniversary of the *Brown* decision, King told a crowd of twenty-five thousand that disenfranchisement was a form of slavery. "So long as I do not firmly and irrevocably have the right to vote I do not possess myself," he said. "I cannot make up my mind—it is made up for me. I cannot live as a democratic citizen, observing the laws I have helped to enact—I can only submit to the edict of others." Therefore, "our most urgent request to the president of the United States and every member of Congress is to give us the right to vote." That request was ignored then, but now, more than eight years later and at the cost of three lives, it had been answered.[16]

He was surprised that he had lived to see this moment, having told colleagues that he had expected to be assassinated during the voting rights campaign. Another threat had also haunted him: J. Edgar Hoover and the FBI had long wanted to destroy King and his movement, and in recent months they had very nearly succeeded.[17]

Parks, Doar, Lewis, and King shared one other similarity besides their presence in the Hall that day: they were all either Alabama-born or had spent time in the state in the course of their work, and their experiences there had profoundly affected their lives. As one of the most extremely segregated states in America, Alabama had become a decisive battleground in the struggle for civil rights, and it would be instrumental in the passage of the Voting Rights Act. "Mark it well: Alabama passed this law," the *Alabama Journal* would complain on August 9, three days after the signing ceremony in Washington. No other southern state played such an important role in the history of the civil rights movement—from the 1955 Montgomery Bus Boycott, to the Civil Rights Act of 1964 desegregating public accommodations, to the brutal events in Selma that resulted in the 1965 Voting Rights Act. Ironically, Alabama's intense racial divisions made these civil rights victories possible.[18]

Parks and Lewis both called Alabama home. In 1961, the same year Doar filed his first lawsuit against the registrars of Dallas County, Alabama, an angry mob in Montgomery beat Lewis badly while he was working as a Freedom Rider. Montgomery had also launched King's career as both pastor (at Dexter Avenue Baptist Church) and as leader, first of the city's famed bus boycott and, eventually, the civil rights movement itself. In many ways, then, the story of the Voting Rights Act and its defenders is also the story of Alabama and the depredations and struggles that took place there.

The date of the bill's signing, August 6, had been picked specifically for its historical significance. On that day in 1861 President Lincoln had signed the Confiscation Act, freeing all slaves who were being used to aid the Confederacy; that act was a precursor to the Emancipation Proclamation, which liberated the rebel states' remaining slaves. To assure that no one missed the connection between the sixteenth president and the thirty-sixth, President Johnson had ordered his lectern placed so that he would be flanked by Lincoln. When the president arrived in the Statuary Hall at noon, he took his place to the left of Gutzon Borglum's celebrated bust of Lincoln, a likeness that also adorned Mount Rushmore. To Johnson's right was Vinnie Ream's marble statue of the Great Emancipator, commissioned by Congress in 1866 when the talented female sculptor was just eighteen. To heighten the historic nature of the occasion, Johnson also evoked the spirit of George Washington: behind him was John Trumbull's immense portrait depicting the *Surrender of Cornwallis.*

The president's speech, televised nationally, also reflected a sense of history. Johnson reminded viewers and the assembled dignitaries that the bill he was about to sign into law was long overdue. "To seize the meaning of this day we must recall darker times," Johnson said. "Three and a half centuries ago the first Negroes arrived in Jamestown. . . . They came in darkness and they came in chains. . . . When the Liberty Bell rang out in Philadelphia it did not toll for the Negro. When Andrew Jackson threw open the doors of democracy they did not open for the Negro. It was only at Appomattox a century ago that an American victory was also a Negro victory. Yet for almost a century the promise of that day was not fulfilled."

Now, when the Voting Rights Bill became law, "that promise will be kept," the president declared. "Today, we strike away the last major shackle of those fierce and ancient bonds. . . . The vote is the most powerful instrument ever devised by man for breaking down injustice and destroying the terrible walls which imprison men because they are different from other men."[19]

Speaking to his southern brethren, Johnson asked them to accept the changes in "habit and custom" brought by recent civil rights laws—changes that would liberate white as well as black citizens. "Today I say simply this: It must come," Johnson said. "It is right that it should come and when it has you will find a burden that has been lifted from your shoulders, too." To the black members of his national audience, he offered a challenge: "you must register; you must vote. . . . Your future and your children's future depend upon it and I don't believe you're going to let them down."

His remarks finished, Johnson then invited his audience to watch the signing of the bill in the President's Room, located on the Senate side of the Capitol, where Lincoln had signed the Confiscation Act 104 years earlier. More than a hundred people followed Johnson into the small, richly furnished chamber. Johnson sat behind a mahogany desk, the very desk he had used when he was

Senate majority leader. It too was specially selected because the president wanted Americans later to have a physical object that reminded them that Lyndon Johnson was the one who brought about this historic achievement.[20]

The president methodically scratched "Lyndon B. Johnson" at the bottom of the last page of the document, after each stroke bestowing a pen on those who had helped make this day possible. At least fifty were passed out. Vice President Hubert Humphrey received the first pen, Senator Everett M. Dirksen, the Republican minority leader who had helped draft the bill, the second, and Senator Robert Kennedy, the third. Handing one to Dr. King, Johnson, who had always disliked King's public demonstrations, told him his work was now done, that the time for protest was over.[21]

Even at a moment of glory, Johnson couldn't resist a bit of revenge. He ignored CORE leader James Farmer, who had annoyed the president by refusing to call off demonstrations during the 1964 presidential campaign. Heretofore, Farmer had always had a good working relationship with Johnson, but after this incident he could no longer reach the president by phone and received only perfunctory notes written by an aide. Hoping to receive one of the pens, Farmer had intentionally seated himself near the president's desk, but as he later wrote, "It seemed everyone in the room got a pen . . . except me. The president passed pens to my right, to my left, over my shoulders, but not to me, all the while his eyes avoiding mine." Roy Wilkins tried to help by pointing at Farmer and yelling, "Jim Farmer, Mr. President, Jim Farmer. Give Jim a pen!" Nothing happened. Then, Whitney Young, Urban League director, called out, "Here's Jim, Mr. President. Jim Farmer. He hasn't got a pen yet." Finally, Farmer walked up to the president and took a pen from his hand while Johnson looked elsewhere.[22]

Following the signing ceremony, King and other civil rights leaders (but not Farmer) met privately with the president at the White House. All still felt the glow of the ceremony. "There was a religiosity about the meeting," a presidential aide recalled. "[It] was warm with emotion—a final celebration of an act so long desired and so long in achieving."[23]

Absent that day were other men and women whose names were less well known than the president and the preacher but whose actions were essential to the successful passage of the Act. Missing, for instance, was Amelia Boynton, who, with her husband, Sam, began their fight for voting rights in Alabama in the 1930s, when Martin Luther King was a child. Sam Boynton's efforts ruined his business and his health. Missing too were Bernard Lafayette and James Forman, two young members of SNCC who went to Selma in 1962 and 1963 and helped create the movement King relied on when he arrived in 1965. The voting rights movement needed enemies as well as friends, and those roles were played masterfully by Jim Clark, the sheriff of Dallas County, and Governor George C. Wallace. Their brutality aroused the conscience of the nation and intensified Johnson's desire to push for an immediate voting rights bill. Had Clark and Wallace been invited, it was unlikely that they would have come, but the fact remains that without their actions, there might have been nothing to celebrate that day.

The history of the Voting Rights Act is filled with similar ironies and accidents. Whereas Selma, Alabama, was ground zero in the struggle, it was the death of a young activist, Jimmie Lee Jackson, in nearby Marion that actually led to the march on "Bloody Sunday," which shocked the nation and probably assured the passage of a law to protect the rights of black voters. That event was almost canceled; when it occurred on Sunday, March 7, 1965, Martin Luther King, whose movement benefited the most from the ensuing police brutality, was not even there. During these and many of the other stages in the story of the Voting Rights Act, as Lyndon Johnson noted in the most famous speech of his presidency, "history and fate" came together "to shape a turning point in man's unending search for freedom."[24]

That search continues. First enacted in 1965, the Voting Rights Act has been reexamined by Congress and then extended four times — in 1970, 1975, 1982, and in 2006. Each time the Act has been amended to meet changing times and circumstances. It will undergo congressional scrutiny again in 2031. Few deny its importance; it ended a half-century of practices that prevented African Americans from exercising what Johnson called "the most basic right of all," and it transformed American politics by turning a once-solid Democratic South into a Republican stronghold. But the Act nevertheless has powerful critics who believe that it has served its purpose and that the election of America's first African American president proves that it is no longer needed. Among such detractors are Supreme Court Chief Justice John Roberts and Associate Justice Clarence Thomas, both of whom have expressed doubts about the Act's necessity, thereby raising the possibility that the Court might soon abolish it. To others, the Act is a fundamental part of American law and must be preserved without major change.[25]

It is impossible to understand fully the significance of the Voting Rights Act to people on both sides of this debate without first considering how the Act came about and why. The story of its creation and of the forgotten men and women who risked their lives to dramatize the need for such an act should form the foundation for any assessment of its ongoing importance. Marked by heroism and sacrifice, oppression and triumph, the origins of the Voting Rights Act reveal both its necessity and its promise.

Despite its empowerment of millions of black Americans, the future of the Act remains in doubt. Although it did succeed in eliminating many of the fundamental injustices that prevented black citizens from voting, some have endured, and should the Act be overthrown by the Supreme Court or significantly revised by a hostile Congress, the sacrifices of those who labored in its behalf will have been in vain. The circumstances that gave birth to the Act may not have an exact parallel today, but their echoes can be found across the country in more subtle and more insidious efforts to prevent black people from having a voice in the nation's future. Only by knowing its history, then, can we truly appreciate what the Voting Rights Act achieved and how it remains necessary to preserve American freedom.

Although he is only twenty-one years old, Bernard Lafayette is already a seasoned civil rights activist: a veteran of the Nashville sit-ins, the Freedom Rides, organizing in Mississippi, he now comes to Selma to take a job nobody wanted.

Preface for the Paperback Edition: "Rainstorm"

August 6, 2015, marks the fiftieth anniversary of the signing into law of the 1965 Voting Rights Act, arguably the most important law in modern American history. It will be a bittersweet anniversary, both a celebration of past achievements and, what some fear, a eulogy for a bygone age.

Honored will be the many African Americans who risked everything—their homes, their jobs, even their lives, to win the right to vote. As they do every year, thousands will gather in Selma, Alabama, in early March to remember the pivotal event that led to the passage of the Voting Rights Act. On March 7, 1965, a day later remembered as "Bloody Sunday," civil rights activists, demonstrating for voting rights, were savagely attacked by Alabama state troopers and vigilantes armed with bats, electric cattle prods, and tear gas as they tried to cross the Edmund Pettus Bridge. That night, ABC News interrupted its Sunday Night Movie to inform the nation of the tragedy. The raw footage shown had no narration and ran for fifteen minutes. Viewers, estimated at 48 million, were stunned by the sight of peaceful demonstrators being beaten and tear-gassed.

Others who later saw pictures of the event had similar reactions—horror, shame, and an overwhelming desire to do something. Thousands poured into Selma. Those who could not go south demonstrated in their own communities, from Maine to Hawaii.

Washington was besieged by demonstrators calling for a Voting Rights Act. President Lyndon B. Johnson was sympathetic to their demand but had been hesitating to act because he had signed the Civil Rights Act of 1964 the previous July and believed that Congress was not yet ready to pass another such law so soon. Bloody Sunday changed everything. LBJ later called it "a turning point in man's unending search for freedom" and submitted a tough voting rights bill, which the Congress enacted four months later.

Never before had the federal government played such an intrusive role in an activity—voting—once left totally to the states. The most controversial provisions were Sections 4 and 5. Section 4 contained the criteria—literacy tests, low voter turnout—that placed certain states, then mostly in the South, under federal coverage while Section 5 was designed to prevent future discrimination by requiring states to seek "preclearance," the permission of the Justice Department, or a Washington, DC, federal court before changing any voting practice.

On March 7, 1966, the first anniversary of Bloody Sunday, the US Supreme Court, in *South Carolina v. Katzenbach*, ruled that the Act was constitutional. Congress, it said, had responded correctly in redressing a historic grievance when it enforced the Fifteenth Amendment by passing the Voting Rights Act. "Hopefully, millions of non-white Americans will now be able to participate for the first time on an equal basis in the government under which they live," wrote Chief Justice Earl Warren on behalf of the Court. Over the following forty-eight years, the temporary provisions of the Act were renewed by Congress four times—in 1970, 1975, 1982, and, overwhelmingly, in 2006.

The Act was immediately transformative. It removed obstacles—such as literacy tests—that had prevented African Americans from voting for the last sixty years. Black candidates across America were eventually elected to state and federal offices in record numbers. And, in 2008, Senator Barack Obama, an African American, was elected president of the United States.

The Voting Rights Act also transformed American politics. The segregationist South was once thoroughly Democratic while the Republican Party was disparaged as the party of Abraham Lincoln and the abolitionists. Lyndon Johnson's civil rights acts caused white southerners to flee first to the party of Richard Nixon and then to his Republican successors. Bureaucrats in the Nixon, Ford, and Reagan Justice Departments (such as a young John Roberts Jr.) tried to weaken the Act but its popularity, even among some congressional Republicans, prevented them from dismantling it. In the end, that would be left to the Supreme Court.

On November 9, 2012, three days after the re-election of Barack Obama, the Supreme Court announced that it would hear the case of *Shelby County, Alabama v. Holder.* Its plaintiffs charged that Section 5 of the Voting Rights Act was unconstitutional and asked the Court to overturn it. Oral arguments began on February 27, 2013, and it was immediately clear that the Voting Rights Act was in trouble. Two issues were paramount. Was the Act still necessary in the Age of Obama? And what branch of government was constitutionally authorized to answer that question? Justice Antonin Scalia sarcastically dismissed the Act as "a racial entitlement," and accused the Congress of political cowardice when it easily renewed the Act in 2006 without updating its coverage formula. "Even the name of it is wonderful, the Voting Rights Act," Scalia said. "Who is going to vote against that?" Justice Anthony Kennedy, considered the court's swing vote because he sometimes sided with his liberal colleagues, doubted that the law was still necessary. "The Marshall Plan was very good, too," he asserted, "[and]—the [nineteenth century's] Northwest Ordinance, the Morrill Act—but times change."[1]

Burt Rein, the lawyer for Shelby County, went further than Kennedy, asserting that racial discrimination was no longer a problem in the South. "Who gets to make that judgment really?" Justice Elena Kagan asked Rein. "Is it you, or is it the Court, or is it Congress?" "It is up to the Court," Rein replied. Kagan was stunned: "Well, that's a big new power that you are giving us—that we have the power now to decide whether racial discrimination has been solved? I did not think that fell within our bailiwick." Summing up the day's heated discussion, Pete Williams, NBC News' legal correspondent, asserted that "it's safe to say there are five votes to strike down . . . parts of the Voting Rights Act."[2]

Williams was correct. On June 26, 2013, the Chief Justice and his four Republican colleagues declared that "our country has changed" and that the Voting Rights Act had completed its historic mission. Writing for the majority in *Shelby County, Alabama v. Holder,* Roberts noted that black voter turnout in five of the six covered states now surpassed white turnout and two southern cities, Philadelphia, Mississippi (where three civil rights workers were murdered in 1964) and Selma, Alabama, scene of Bloody Sunday, now had African American mayors. Such progress, he asserted, meant that the

Act's Section 4, which contained the formula that led to the coverage of the southern states, was outdated. And since those states were treated differently, Section 4 violated "the fundamental principle of equal sovereignty among the states," and was therefore unconstitutional. The covered states were now freed from Section 5, the provision requiring "preclearance" before changing voting practices. Abolishing Section 4 left Section 5 moribund. (In a concurring opinion, Associate Justice Clarence Thomas called for the elimination of Section 5.)[3]

Associate Justice Ruth Bader Ginsburg, representing the Court's Democratic minority, summarized her view from the bench, a rare occurrence, which one Court expert called "a sign of deep disagreement." She rejected Roberts's notion that America was free of blatant discrimination in voting, noting that when the Congress renewed the Act in 2006, it did so based on extensive evidence that "second generation barriers"—gerrymandering, for example—still obstructed African American voting. Black empowerment *had* occurred, she insisted, precisely because of the existence of the Voting Rights Act. "Throwing out preclearance when it has worked and is continuing to work to stop discriminatory changes is like throwing away your umbrella in a rainstorm because you are not getting wet," Ginsburg said.

She also accused her conservative colleagues of unwarranted judicial activism since the Voting Rights Act was explicitly created to enforce the Constitution's Fifteenth Amendment requiring that the Congress—not the Supreme Court—create "appropriate legislation" to guarantee that a US citizen's right to vote could not be "denied or abridged by the United States or by any state on account of race, color, or previous condition of servitude." "The court errs egregiously," she ended, "by overriding Congress's decision" to renew the Voting Rights Act in 2006.[4]

Another distinguished jurist joined the debate in August. Reviewing *Bending toward Justice* for the *New York Review of Books*, former Supreme Court Justice John Paul Stevens, a lifelong Republican appointed to the Court by President Gerald Ford, issued his own dissent from the Court's ruling. He thought Robert's opinion ahistorical and "questionable." His reliance on "the fundamental principle of equal sovereignty among the states" was also most curious since the Chief Justice accused the Voting Rights Act of violating it but ignored the fact that for almost a century the Constitution allowed southern slave states to count their slaves as three-fifths of a man—a "slave bonus" that increased the South's congressional and electoral college influence. Furthermore, Roberts treated that principle as constitutional doctrine when in fact, Stevens noted, it only applied to how states were admitted to the Union.

Finally, he called Justice Ginsburg's thirty-seven page dissent (which was longer than the majority opinion) concise, clear, and "eloquent," and shared the minority's view that Congress — not the Supreme Court — was "the branch of government designated by the Fifteenth Amendment to make decisions of this kind."[5]

The months that followed the Court's decision provided additional evidence of the need to restore the Voting Rights Act to its formal glory. Texas, South Carolina, Mississippi, North Carolina, Georgia, and other formerly covered states announced their intention to enact redistricting plans, limit voting time, and require voter IDs, which the Justice Department had earlier blocked under Section 5. Congressional efforts to enact a new Voting Rights Act were making little headway given the Republican-dominated House, and the party of Lincoln showed little interest in supporting new legislation. "The South continues to restrict voting rights more aggressively than anywhere else in the country," noted journalist Ari Berman. "What has changed in recent years isn't the South but the fact that states like Kansas and Ohio and Wisconsin and Pennsylvania have adopted southern-bred voter suppression tactics. Just when the VRA should've been expanded to cover the surprisingly wide scope of twenty-first-century voting discrimination, the Supreme Court instead gutted the law."

There have been a few victories for voting rights advocates. In January, March, and May 2014, judges in Pennsylvania, Wisconsin, and Arkansas blocked voter ID laws that discriminated against blacks, the elderly, the poor, and students. In North Carolina, a biracial group called the Moral Monday Movement fought the efforts of the Republican state legislature to curtail voting rights and pass legislation benefiting the wealthiest citizens.[6]

America is evolving into a more multiethnic nation much to the displeasure of Donald Trump, Bill O'Reilly, and Cliven Bundy, the Nevada rancher who famously remarked that African Americans were better off as slaves. America has not changed as much as Chief Justice Roberts and his colleagues believe. It is necessary to strengthen voter protections not dismantle them. "Race matters," Justice Sonia Sotomayor noted recently, "because of the slights, the snickers, the silent judgments that reinforce that most crippling: 'I do not belong here.' . . . While the enduring hope [is that] race should not matter, the reality is that too often it does. Racial discrimination . . . is not ancient history."[7]

While it is impossible to predict the future, what is past is prologue. It seems certain that the struggle for black equality in the polling booth and in many other places will go on. It is up to every citizen to join this struggle. "The right to vote is . . . the lifeblood of our democracy," says Attorney General Eric Holder. "The arc of American history has bent toward the inclusion, not the exclusion, of more of our fellow citizens in the electoral process. We must ensure that this continues."

NOTES

1. Ryan J. Reilly, "Voting Rights Act Supreme Court Case: Scalia Condemns the Perpetuation of Racial Entitlement," http://www.huffingtonpost.com/2013/02/27 /voting-rights-act-supreme-court_n_2768942.html.

2. Quoted in ibid.

3. *Shelby County, Alabama v. Holder, Attorney General, et al.*, No. 12–96. Argued February 27, 2013 — Decided June 25, 2013, 2, 10–12, 15–16, 25; for Thomas's opinion see *Shelby County*, Thomas, J., concurring, 1–3; Adam Liptak, "Supreme Court Invalidates Key Part of Voting Rights Act," *New York Times*, June 25, 2013.

4. Liptak, ibid.

5. John Paul Stevens, "The Court and the Right to Vote: A Dissent," *New York Review of Books*, August 15, 2013, 37–39.

6. Dale Ho, "2014: The Voting Rights Spring," *Huffington Post*, May 15, 2014, http:// www.huffingtonpost.com/dale-ho/2014-the-voting-rights-sp_b_5331509.html; Ari Berman, "Fifty Years After Freedom Summer, the Voting Rights Act Is Needed More Than Ever," *Nation*, June 24, 2015, http://www.thenation.com/blog/180389/fifty -years-after-freedom-summer-voting-rights-act-needed-more-ever.

7. Sotomayor is quoted in Jeffrey Toobin, "Chief Justice Roberts, Meet Bundy and Sterling," *New Yorker*, April 29, 2014, http://www.newyorker.com/online/blogs /comment/2014/04/chief-justice-roberts-meet-bundy-and-sterling.

ONE

PLANTING THE FIRST SEED

BY 1962 THE CIVIL RIGHTS MOVEMENT HAD ALL BUT GIVEN UP ON SELMA, Alabama. Bernard Lafayette, a twenty-one-year-old member of the recently created Student Nonviolent Coordinating Committee (SNCC), learned as much that summer when he visited the organization's headquarters in Atlanta. A city of some thirty thousand people, 57 percent of whom were black residents, Selma was the seat of Dallas County, an area encompassing roughly a thousand square miles in central Alabama. The racial inequality of this area was legendary; it was so entrenched and institutionalized that SNCC had practically no luck in its attempts to organize the city's black population so as to fight for their civil rights. The economic plight of blacks was even more serious: more than two-thirds lived below the poverty line, barely subsisting on what they earned by working the land as sharecroppers and farm hands or as the city's laborers, janitors, and maids. For SNCC Selma seemed like a hopeless case. But for Lafayette it represented a golden opportunity.[1]

A student at Nashville's Fisk University, Lafayette had just finished his final exams and longed to return to his more exciting life as a committed civil rights activist. He was a veteran of Nashville's sit-in movement and had spent the last several years honing his skills as a nonviolent protestor in some of the civil rights movement's most dangerous battlegrounds. Now, in the summer of 1962, he was again looking for a project he could call his own—and he was about to find it. Although he did not know it at the time, his performance in the coming voting rights campaign would make him one of the founding fathers of the Voting Rights Act.[2]

Born in Tampa, Florida, and reared in the local chapter of the Baptist Church that his grandmother founded, Lafayette's ancestry was an unusual mix of African, Cuban, Bahamian, and French. Sophisticated and smart, he was naturally drawn to religion, and after receiving his minister's license in 1958, he sought further instruction at Nashville's American Baptist Theological (ABT) Seminary, where he roomed with John Lewis, a shy, earnest young man from Alabama. Both were attracted first to the Reverend Kelly Miller Smith who, in 1957, joined Martin Luther King Jr. in organizing the Southern Christian Leadership Conference (SCLC) and later became head of its Nashville branch. Fusing Christianity with social activism, Smith risked his six-year-old daughter's life in the violent struggle to integrate the city's schools. For Lafayette and Lewis, the hefty, handsome preacher was a model of inspiration and emulation.

It was Smith who introduced Lafayette and Lewis to an even more influential figure, Reverend James Lawson Jr. Born into a family of Ohio Methodist ministers, Lawson received his own preacher's license when he graduated from high school in 1957. But he followed his faith in a different direction. Joining the Fellowship of Reconciliation (FOR), he became a committed Christian pacifist. It cost him his freedom when he was imprisoned for thirteen months in 1951 for refusing to fight in the Korean War. His interest in Gandhi's principles took him to the city of Nagpur in central India, where he was a teacher and campus minister at Hislop College from 1952 to 1955. He came to Nashville in 1957, studying at Vanderbilt's Divinity School and holding Tuesday night workshops, at which he taught his brand of nonviolent civil disobedience that was rooted in Christianity.

Lafayette and Lewis attended Lawson's Nashville workshops and were struck by the spiritual power of his appeal for nonviolence. "When you are a child of God . . . you try thereby to imitate Jesus, in the midst of evil," Lawson told his students. "If someone slaps you on the one cheek, you turn the other cheek, which is an act of resistance. It means that you . . . recognize that even the enemy has a spark of God in them . . . and therefore needs to be treated as you, yourself, want to be treated." Lafayette and Lewis—along with figures like James Bevel, Diane Nash, and C. T. Vivian—later became prominent civil rights activists in Selma and elsewhere. "We were just kids," Lewis later recalled, "totally mesmerized by the torrent of energy and ideas and inspiration washing over us ... in those Jim Lawson workshops."[3]

In the view of its acolytes Christian nonviolence was not just one tactic among many, a strategy that could be discarded for another if it failed to work; rather, it was a way of life. As a philosophy that required extreme commitment and self-sacrifice from those who practiced it, nonviolence deeply challenged many of Lawson's students. Lafayette, who had spent some time in Philadelphia's mean streets when his father took a job there, was more accustomed to fighting back when attacked. "When the time really came to turn the other cheek, I wanted to know if I could do that," he later recalled. "Could I actually feel love for somebody who was abusing me? Those were the questions I had to face."[4]

Lafayette's faith was bolstered in February 1960 during an event that occurred after more than a year of exposure to Lawson's teaching. The occasion was a desegregation campaign that had its origins in one of the weekly workshops. During a meeting a woman had spoken up, her voice tinged with anger. "You men don't really know what life is like in segregation," she said. "We are the ones who shop. When we go into downtown Nashville there is no place that we can stop with dignity and rest our feet. There are no restrooms that are not marked ... 'Colored.' ... There's no place that [you can] sit down and have a cup of coffee. So ... we're the ones who bear the brunt of the racism ... in Nashville." It was a challenge as much as a statement of fact. In that moment the Nashville Movement was born.

Soon Lafayette and hundreds of other students occupied stores in downtown Nashville, taking seats at segregated fountains as angry young whites cursed them, poured ketchup on their heads, then dragged them off their stools. The protestors remained true to nonviolence but were arrested while their attackers went free. That following Saturday, February 27, was going to mark the second wave of the sit-in, but as Lafayette and his colleagues were leaving Reverend Smith's First Baptist Church, "young toughs," all dressed in black pants, black leather jackets, and motorcycle boots, assaulted them. The men knocked to the ground and brutally kicked Lafayette's friend Solomon Gort. Instantly, Lafayette threw himself on top of Gort, protecting him from the blows and distracting the men in black, exactly as Lawson had instructed him to do. In response, the men began beating and cursing

Lafayette. Attempting to defuse the situation, Lawson approached the leader of the pack, but the man only spat on him.

Then, something extraordinary happened. Lawson quietly asked the tough if he had a handkerchief. Startled by the question, the man pulled one from his pocket and gave it to Lawson, who cleaned himself up.

That small touch of humanity gave Lawson the opening he was hoping for—a conversation ensued. Lawson asked him what he drove, a jalopy or a motorcycle? Motorcycle, the man said. How fast did it go? Lawson asked. What had he done to it? While they chatted, Lafayette and Gort ran off. Although Lawson did not convert the enemy into a friend, he had, however briefly, breached the wall of prejudice and established common ground on which both could peacefully stand. The incident had a powerful effect on Lawson's young protégés. The workshops had not been a waste of time, Lafayette concluded. Further, the incident had aroused his protective—not his aggressive—instincts. There was something to this philosophy after all.[5]

In the months that followed, Lafayette committed his life to nonviolence. In 1961, while attempting to desegregate interstate bus terminals as a Freedom Rider, he was almost killed when a crazed mob attacked his group in Alabama. During the campaign he was arrested at least ten times and survived Mississippi's dreaded Parchman Penitentiary. Not all of his experiences were so harrowing, however. In early 1962, while he worked with other young men and women desegregating the downtown businesses in Jackson, Mississippi, one of his fellow activists caught his eye. Her name was Colia Liddell, a brilliant young organizer and assistant to Medgar Evers, Mississippi's NAACP field secretary. Within a month they were engaged.

Lafayette and his fiancée were now members of a new organization, the Student Nonviolent Coordinating Committee (SNCC, pronounced "Snick"). Founded in April 1960 in the aftermath of the sit-in movement, its driving force was James Lawson's Nashville students, including Lafayette, Lewis, Nash, and Bevel, all of whom wanted a group separate from Martin Luther King's Southern Christian Leadership Conference, which funded the meeting at which SNCC was created, and the more conservative NAACP, which relied on the courts to win their victories. As in Nashville, SNCC would take to the streets to win their freedom, mounting desegregation campaigns and voter registration. They would become the shock troops of the civil rights movement, going wherever they were most needed. For instance, when the

Freedom Riders faltered under violence in Montgomery, Alabama, in May 1961, SNCC members Lafayette and Nash joined the group so that it could complete its mission.

Nonviolence had sustained and empowered Lafayette during each new crisis, and as the summer of 1962 approached, he began looking for his next assignment. Visiting SNCC's headquarters in Atlanta, Georgia, he considered his options. James Forman, SNCC's executive secretary, showed him a map of the South dotted with tacks, each of which indicated where the movement was active. One place, however, was marked with a giant X. Lafayette was immediately drawn to the spot.

That was Selma, Alabama, Forman told Lafayette. SNCC had abandoned the city because organizing voters there successfully "was too hard." As soon as SNCC workers arrived, they were arrested, then run out of town. During the past decade only seventy-five blacks—twenty-eight of them college graduates—had tried to register, and all had failed; this in a county where fifteen thousand were eligible to vote. That dismal record had aroused even the Justice Department to send lawyers to examine the situation. Attempting to steer his young colleague away from such a difficult assignment, Forman urged Lafayette to join Bob Moses, who was working in Mississippi, but Lafayette refused. "I want to . . . develop a community to the point where the community [is] willing to go to jail and take a stand. That's when you get change," he said. He would go to Selma.[6]

LAFAYETTE COULD NOT HAVE PICKED A MORE DESPERATE—OR MORE challenging—community in which to take a stand against racial injustice, as African Americans' oppression was practically the cornerstone of Selma's history. Founded in 1819, Selma had quickly become the center of the region's Black Belt, so called for its rich, fertile soil. The cotton grown in this area was the foundation of its economic success, but so too were the slaves who picked it. The slave trade's season began in September each year and ended in April, a lengthy window that gave Selma's slaveholding elites ample time to replenish their ranks of workers, many of whom often had perished during the growing season from starvation, accidents, or disease. Wealthy citizens would congregate in one of three large buildings built especially for their use when purchasing slaves. There black prisoners were exhibited and examined—men and women who would work as carpenters, blacksmiths, seamstresses, house slaves, or field hands. This combination of rich soil and plentiful slaves made Selma and Dallas County the dominant cotton-producing section in Alabama.[7]

Selma's economic success also brought woe upon the southern city. In the nineteenth century, thanks to the influx of German immigrants who began arriving in the late 1840s, Selma had also become famous for iron casting and gun making. Those industries along with the city's naval yard made Selma militarily important to the Confederacy during the Civil War and, therefore, a prime target for the Union Army, which struck on April 2, 1865. The city's guardian, General Nathan Bedford Forrest (later the first Grand Wizard of the Ku Klux Klan), fought bravely but was overwhelmed by General James Harrison Wilson's superior forces. According to Selma legend, the "devils from Hell" laid waste to the city, destroying homes and businesses, molesting women, and setting afire the bales of cotton that had long sustained the county's wealth. A week later Robert E. Lee surrendered.[8]

Federal troops occupied Dallas County during Radical Reconstruction and transformed its political environment. Four African Americans were appointed policemen in Selma. Among elected officials were two congressmen, five city councilmen, five county commissioners, and thirteen legislators—all black. Congressman Benjamin Turner, a former slave who transformed himself into a successful businessman, urged his colleagues to enact what he called "universal suffrage and universal amnesty"—universal voting and pardons for former Confederate leaders.[9]

However, the end of Radical Reconstruction brought an end to black progress in Selma and Dallas County. Whites quickly returned to the offices that black politicians recently held, and between 1882 and 1913 voting plummeted and nineteen lynchings occurred in the county, a record that startled even the most racist whites. "Why now," wondered a former Confederate officer, "when the negro is doing no harm, [do] people want to kill and wipe him off the face of the earth!"[10]

In the twentieth century a different kind of slavery existed for Selma's black residents. Jim Crow laws mandated strict racial segregation in the city, as they did elsewhere in the South, and the sharecropping system kept land ownership concentrated in the hands of wealthy whites and imposed crushing financial burdens on black farmers. These institutionalized barriers to full social and economic participation kept the vast majority of both urban and rural African Americans poor and isolated.

Selma's black population also saw their newfound political rights formally stripped away for good. In 1901 Alabama created a new state constitution designed to prevent black suffrage, and the state later amended it twice, in 1946 and 1951, giving significant power over the registration process to the board of registrars. Applicants were forced to fill out a questionnaire, and if they made even the most minor error, they were rejected. They were also tested orally on the state and federal constitutions as well as confronted with questions so abstruse that law professors would fail them. The registrars also sometimes required that applicants be accompanied by voters who would "vouch" for their honesty. Because whites refused to act as vouchers, the few black residents who could vote assumed the role until those who did it regularly were forbidden from helping their friends. The results of these tactics were not surprising. African Americans constituted 57 percent of Dallas County's population, but less than 1 percent of them were registered at the county courthouse in downtown Selma. It was even worse in Alabama's rural counties like Wilcox and Lowndes, which had black populations of 77.9 and 80.7 percent, respectively—but not a single person was registered.

Other forces, some more official than others, conspired to keep Selma's black residents voiceless and impoverished. Selma was the home of the first ultrasegregationist White Citizens' Council, established in 1954, whose businessmen controlled the economic life of the city. Perhaps Selma's most strident opponent of black equality was the city's sheriff, Jim Clark, who dressed like George S. Patton and, with a private posse at his beck and call, ruled with an iron fist. Clark, the voting registrars, and the city's longtime mayor, Chris Heinz, were the face of racial inequality in Selma. Their primary aim was to maintain the status quo that had elevated Selma's white residents over their black neighbors since the city's founding. "Selma," said Heinz, "does not intend to change its customs or way of life."[11]

Lafayette had heard about Selma and had read up on the city's history, but, in the fall of 1962, he wanted to see the situation there for himself. While his fiancée remained behind in Jackson, Mississippi, preparing for their wedding, Lafayette asked SNCC for a car to take him south. He wanted something new, large, and comfortable. Not a good idea, his colleague Julian Bond told him. A black man who arrived in Selma in a fancy car would stand out immediately. Bond recommended instead a 1948 black

Chevrolet—heavy, reliable, and ordinary. Nobody would notice the Chevy; in addition, its heavy doors and small windows would offer some protection from snipers. "It's hard for them to get a very good shot at you in this one," Bond said. Lafayette agreed; but despite these precautions, it would not be long before everyone in Selma knew the black man driving the black Chevrolet.[12]

In Selma, Lafayette was not without allies. There was a small group of veteran activists who had been risking their lives and careers for decades trying to improve the lives of the city's black residents. These activists were led by Amelia and S. W. (Samuel) Boynton, graduates of Tuskegee Institute, who in the 1930s had worked for the Department of Agriculture teaching black tenant farmers and sharecroppers how to survive—if not prosper—in Alabama. They quickly learned, however, that it was an almost impossible task. Black farmers were totally dependent on the owners of the land they cultivated. These landowners, overwhelmingly white, also sold the sharecroppers their equipment, animals, feed, seed, food, clothing, and medical care. When it was time to be paid, the owners subtracted what they were owed, leaving the farmers almost nothing. The Boyntons found it difficult to be a part of such a cruel system, so Mrs. Boynton resigned in 1936, the same year they joined the tiny and powerless local chapter of the NAACP led by a railroad worker named C. J. Adams. Together, the Boyntons and Adams reopened the Dallas County Voters League that same year, an organization dedicated to encouraging black Selmians to register, though it had accomplished nothing since its founding in 1926 and, as a result, shut down. The Boyntons also tried to secure funds to support farmers who wished to purchase their own land.[13]

For a long time Adams and the Boyntons *were* the civil rights movement in Selma—and their activism ruined them. Adams, a notary public, acted as a lawyer for the black community, although he never attended law school; he was later charged with falsifying birth certificates, leading to his incarceration in the state penitentiary. The black community believed that hostile segregationists had framed him, a likely possibility. After serving a difficult sentence, he left Selma for good in 1948. But before setting out for his new home in Detroit, he gave some advice to the man acting as his driver that day. "Don't give an inch," he told young J. L. Chestnut Jr., who would eventually become Selma's first black lawyer. "Never let them break your spirit."[14]

Sam Boynton took Adams's place as head of the NAACP and the Dallas County Voters League, and in the process he experienced just as much harassment as his predecessor did. After leaving his government job in 1953, he and Amelia started an insurance company, and Sam Boynton also took over Adams's position as notary public and counselor for the black community. He had barely settled into his new positions when he was drawn into an incident that would attract the attention of the entire nation.

In the summer of 1953 Sam Boynton came to the aid of William Earl Fikes, a mentally impaired gas station attendant who had been tried and found guilty of burglary and rape on the basis of a coerced confession and questionable eye-witness testimony. Fikes was sentenced to ninety-nine years because one member of the all-white jury was opposed to capital punishment—a sentence that bitterly disappointed the white community, which largely preferred the death penalty. When County Solicitor James Hare decided to try Fikes again, however (this time for the new crime of attempting to rape Mrs. Jean Heinz Rockwell, who happened to be the mayor's daughter), he and the other prosecutors faced new combatants—two brilliant black lawyers, Peter A. Hall and Orzell Billingsley Jr., who Sam Boynton and his NAACP colleague John Hunter had persuaded to take the case. Boynton also visited local churches seeking money for Fikes's defense fund.

For the first time in Selma's history, two black lawyers stood on equal legal footing with white prosecutors, police, and the judge. It created a sensation. "I don't know if Fikes is guilty," the handsome and elegant Hall said before the proceedings started, "but it is damn certain that the system is guilty. And I intend to try the system while the circuit solicitor tries Fikes." The judicial system was obviously biased against Fikes and violated his rights under the US Constitution's Fourteenth Amendment, which guaranteed equal protection and due process to all citizens: he was illegally denied a preliminary hearing, the police interrogation was twenty hours long and psychologically intense, he was isolated from his family and a lawyer, and neither the grand nor petit jury contained a single black juror, a fact to which Sam Boynton testified in court.

Hall fought tirelessly on Fikes's behalf but in the end won a Pyrrhic victory: the indictment was overturned, the jury was removed, and a pool that now included black candidates was created, though none of them ended up serving on Fikes's second jury. He was again found guilty but this time was sentenced to die. Hall appealed to the Supreme Court, which reversed the conviction in January 1957 on the basis of Fikes's mental condition—three psychiatrists had judged him schizophrenic—and what appeared to be a coerced confession.

But because the first conviction was not appealed, it stood, and Fikes entered prison to serve his earlier ninety-nine-year term. Twenty years later, in 1975, Chestnut was able to win his release, and Fikes left Selma forever.[15]

Although it had, for the moment, ended in defeat, the Fikes trial galvanized Selma's black community. "What a hell of a fight!" Chestnut later said. "Folks brought their children to the courtroom to see black men who weren't bowing or Uncle Tom-ing in the presence of important white people. Boynton got maybe a hundred new NAACP members." He also inherited a host of troubles. After the Fikes case Selma's white establishment turned on the Boyntons. The couple suddenly encountered problems: the bank called in loans, and insurance policies they had sold were suddenly canceled. Sam applied to sell mutual funds and passed the exam, but Alabama's attorney general rejected him because of his financial problems and his "advanced age," although he was only fifty-one. Most hurtful was the Dallas County registrar's decision to remove him as a voucher for voter applicants because his character, the registrar claimed, was obviously deficient. At long last, the stress began to tell: Sam Boynton had several minor strokes and was hospitalized.[16]

Despite their financial worries and Sam's poor health, the Boyntons continued to fight for voting rights. In December 1958 they asked a group of their fellow citizens to testify about their experiences in front of the US Commission on Civil Rights, which having received a number of complaints about Alabama voting practices, decided to hold public hearings in Montgomery. The Commission did not receive a warm reception. No hotel would accept Commissioner J. Ernest Wilkins, a former assistant secretary of labor, because he was black. The Commission was eventually forced to stay at Maxwell Air Force Base, located on federal property a few miles from the city.[17]

The Commission encountered obstruction in other areas as well. Their investigators had subpoenaed voting records in six counties, only to learn that half of them had been impounded by State Circuit Judge George C. Wallace, who threatened to jail anyone who sought them. When several registrars were called to testify before the Commission, they refused, claiming protection under the Fifth Amendment.[18]

But Judge Wallace could not gag the black witnesses whom the Boyntons had rallied for the occasion; they told their stories with a quiet but powerful eloquence. Seventy-seven-year-old Frank D. Gordon, a retired Selma schoolteacher, reported trying to register almost a dozen times without success.

Once, after being rejected, he asked the registrar "if she would please point out any errors in the application so I could straighten it up and get it right," but she refused. That was more than two years ago, but he still wanted to vote: "It is my constitutional right," he testified.

Aaron Sellers, a farmer from Bullock County, came close to being registered in 1954—or so he thought. He went to the county courthouse with six friends also seeking applications, and when they arrived the registrar said, "We're quite busy today . . . you all come back tomorrow with a voucher." They found one to accompany them the next day. They were told to wait their turn in the small anteroom used exclusively by "colored people." Then a man showed up and told them to go home. Instead, they waited, and after a half hour passed, the man returned. "I thought I told you all to get the hell out of here," he said. Frightened, they departed, unregistered.

Sellers and his companions returned two weeks later, again with a voucher. After waiting several hours they were told they couldn't apply because only one of the required three registrars was present. Again they left, but this time they decided to hire a lawyer and file a lawsuit against the Board—only to be informed that the registrars had resigned, so their lawsuit was moot. A year and a half passed before another Board was appointed. Sellers and a few friends visited the new registrars in 1956. The applicants were given a form to fill out, but again nothing happened. They filed applications a fifth time in September 1957, but there was no response from the Board. They went back in October, but the Board was gone; it had apparently moved, and nobody seemed to know its new location.

"Mr. Sellers, are you going to keep trying?" asked the Reverend Theodore Hesburgh, the president of Notre Dame and a commissioner.

"Oh, yes," said Aaron Sellers, "I'm determined."

"God bless you," said Hesburgh.

Black merchants from Lowndes County, where not a single black had registered in the twentieth century, testified that if they showed an interest in voting, the trucks that regularly delivered their goods stopped coming. When it was time to renew their mortgages, the banks canceled them or suddenly demanded the payment of loans not yet due.[19]

And then there were men who paid the ultimate price for wanting to vote. Everyone knew about the Reverend George Washington Lee of Belzoni, Mississippi, the first black resident of Humphreys County to register to vote since Reconstruction. From his pulpit he encouraged his parishioners to follow his example; however, knowing that Lee had received death threats and was almost bankrupt because local Klansmen had crippled his business, few did. Nevertheless, he established a local chapter of the NAACP, and with his friend Gus Courts printed proregistration literature and held rallies. Interest in registering intensified; it was reported that some ninety black citizens intended to visit the courthouse imminently. But on May 7, 1955, while driving his car, Lee was shot-gunned to death by a group of white men. The local sheriff refused to investigate, claiming that Lee had died in an automobile accident and that the lead pellets found in his face were "dental fillings." Although the FBI later identified the killers, they were never punished. Six months later Gus Courts was shot, and when he recovered he left Mississippi for good.

Reverend Lee's death did not deter Lamar Smith, a sixty-three-year-old Mississippi farmer and veteran. Like Lee, he was passionate about voting and even attempted to run for office, openly campaigning against white politicians. On Saturday, August 13, 1955, he visited the Lincoln County courthouse, where a group of angry white men who resented his activism approached him. An altercation ensued, and a white man pulled a gun and shot Smith to death. The killer, his shirt drenched with blood, coolly walked away. The shooter was later arrested, but no witnesses would testify against him. The grand jury returned no indictment.[20]

The black men and women fighting to vote in the Deep South harbored no illusions about the forces they were up against or the reasons for their troubles. When the Commission asked fifty-five-year-old farmer Hosea Guice why the Dallas County registrars had rejected him four times, he replied, "Well, I have never been arrested and always has been a law-abiding citizen, [with] no mental deficiency, . . . I was just a Negro. That's all."[21]

When Bernard Lafayette arrived in Selma in late October 1962, he headed straight for the one place he knew he would be welcomed: 1315 Lapsley Street, the modest white frame home of Amelia and Sam Boynton. Mrs. Boynton was happy to see Lafayette—she had been working privately to obtain funding to support a full-time organizer—but her husband was not there. He'd suffered a major stroke the year before and was now living at the Burwell Infirmary.

Lafayette visited Sam Boynton that same day. It was obvious that he was very ill and had little time left, but the fire inside him still burned. Anyone who visited him there was greeted with the same question: "Are you a registered voter? I want you to go down and register," he'd say. "A voteless people is a hopeless people." He insisted that his wife continue the struggle after he was gone. "I want you to see that all Negroes are ready to vote," he told her. Later Lafayette would recall the evenings he spent with Sam Boynton, the two men sitting quietly on the porch. Occasionally Lafayette would feel the older man softly take his hand and squeeze it. He thought it "an act of transference." Boynton was passing to the younger activist the burden he had carried for so long.[22]

Lafayette worked quickly to acquaint himself with Selma's other residents as well. Amelia Boynton introduced him to the members of the Dallas County Voters League, and lawyer J. L. Chestnut showed him around town, where Lafayette met a cross-section of the black community. The people were polite but not enthusiastic about his plan to organize potential voters. Even Chestnut's own mother was unhappy. "That boy ought to go home," she said of Lafayette. "He's gonna get the white people all stirred up, then he'll run back to Atlanta and we'll be picking up the pieces." Others expressed the same concern: "It's not gonna come to a damn thing," said one black merchant. "Somebody'll get their brains blown out." A black minister told him that his presence was not necessary—Selma had no racial problems. ("Not criticizing civil authority . . . was deeply ingrained in the black ministry," Chestnut later explained. "King once told me that everywhere he went, the first opposition came not from whites but from black preachers.") Most of the black people Lafayette spoke with were less satisfied than the minister, however. "This is the worst place in the world," they said. "Nothing is ever going to happen here."[23]

Lafayette was neither surprised nor discouraged. He had heard such pessimistic voices before, and he understood them. He appreciated the perspectives of the poor black people who couldn't believe that voting might improve their lives. Further, he could comprehend why the middle class who had made an uneasy peace with the white establishment—people such as the teachers, ministers, doctors, some of them members of the Dallas County Voters League—felt they had too much to lose in the quixotic crusades that they equated with SNCC's brand of direct action.

Not all of the naysayers, of course, were black, and not all were content merely to speak out against Lafayette. The white members of the segregationist opposition were certainly vocal in their denouncement of Lafayette's efforts in Selma, but he had much more to fear from the extremist fringe of that group—rabid segregationists who were willing to stop Lafayette by killing him. Most dangerous among these extremists were the members of the Ku Klux Klan, which maintained a public presence throughout the American South and counted among its ranks many police officers, sheriff's deputies, and posse members. Selma, as Lafayette was undoubtedly aware, was no exception to this grim rule.

Lafayette returned to Mississippi on Thanksgiving Day, married Colia Liddell five days later, and the couple returned to Selma on February 10, 1963. Their first home was a room at the Torch Motel ("For Colored Guests"), where visiting activists often stayed. Finding a permanent residence proved difficult. "The people didn't want us because they suspected that they might have a bomb in their front room some evening," Lafayette later recalled. Eventually, the couple found an apartment on Union Street. They set up their headquarters at the Boynton Insurance and Real Estate Agency.

After Lafayette's initial visit, Marie Foster, a dental hygienist with a passion for civil rights who had tried eight times to register before succeeding, had organized a voter's clinic to teach Selma's citizens how to run the registration gauntlet. At its first meeting only one person appeared—an elderly, illiterate man named Major Washington. Foster held class anyway, and Washington departed knowing how to write his name. And he returned the following week with a friend who, in turn, brought another. When Lafayette and his new bride settled in Selma, they took over the leadership of these meetings, which were held twice a week. Their purpose was not only to provide Selma's black aspiring voters with specific information—the Lafayettes and Foster distributed copies of the three-page voter's application and went over the possible questions the registrars might ask during the oral exam, like the name of every Alabama county judge (there were sixty-seven)—but also to give them the confidence to endure the abuse they would receive at the courthouse. By the end of February fifty-three people had attended the workshops.[24]

It was a beginning, but this citizen army was still too small to attack the barricades of prejudice. In order to fully mobilize Selma's black community, Lafayette would have to prove to them that the prize was worth the struggle.

"Our big problem was the Negro himself who wouldn't risk the possible loss of his job and other kinds of hardship just to vote," Lafayette later noted. "We had to convince him that he wouldn't ever get any place until he could vote." For the time being Lafayette turned to those who had not only less to lose but also more energy to fight for freedom. Recalling Isaiah 11:6, which read, in part, "and a little child shall lead them," he chose a strategy that Martin Luther King Jr. would adopt during his Birmingham campaign later that spring: recruiting an army of children—or, in this case, high school and college students—to serve as the movement's shock troops. And where the children went, Lafayette hoped, their parents would follow.

Lafayette embarked on a recruitment campaign, trying to enlist young volunteers for the upcoming struggle. Chestnut took him to Selma University, where Lafayette picked up several students who became his followers. The university president had given Lafayette a cool reception and warned students that they risked expulsion if their civil rights activities embarrassed the school, so Lafayette continued to recruit students in secret, avoiding the president's office. He also visited Selma's Hudson High School, adding to his growing army while also earning the wrath of Joseph Yelder, the principal, who threatened to have him arrested.[25]

Selma's black students loved Lafayette. He was young—only twenty-two—and he spoke their language and shared their culture. He was a veritable celebrity to them, their very own Freedom Rider. He loved them too, and he sought them out wherever they might be.

Lafayette found sixteen-year-old Charles Bonner and his friend Cleophas Hobbs on a Sunday morning as they pushed Bonner's broken-down '54 Ford along Church Street. Suddenly, they later remembered, there appeared a slender young man with a thin mustache wearing a bow tie and jacket, on which was pinned a strange button showing a black hand and a white hand clasped together above the letters SNCC. The man offered to help them and, without waiting for an answer, got behind their car and pushed. By the time they reached Bonner's home, they knew everything about Lafayette—the reverend down from Nashville, working for an organization called "Snick," trying to get people to register.

Lafayette asked Bonner and Hobbs to join his cause, and for the next hour they sat on Bonner's porch discussing how the youths could contribute. Lafayette explained that they could canvass the neighborhoods, pass out leaflets, encourage folks to attend the voters' clinics, and help adults pass the literacy test so as to become full-fledged citizens. Then direct action would follow: demonstrations and sit-ins at segregated lunch counters, libraries, and movie theaters until these establishments were open to black people as well as whites. There were risks, of course: arrests and beatings were likely, but Lafayette would show the teenagers "how to duck, how to dodge, how to lay on the ground and go limp," and, most important, he said, how to respond nonviolently.

Bonner, who had grown up in poverty on a cotton farm in nearby Orrville, was immediately receptive to Lafayette's pitch. "What Bernard was telling us was like opening a window to an entire new world. We were totally primed to take some action, against what my friend Cleo and I both saw as tremendous unfairness in the world," Bonner later recalled. "So that's what we did." The teenagers accepted Lafayette's challenge, and he urged them to tell their friends at Hudson High School about him and his movement. They did, and soon a new group was ready to follow Lafayette.[26]

What Lafayette's movement lacked so far was a mass rally. The speeches on the evils of segregation, the freedom songs, the sermons and the passionate audience response, the chance to promote and publicize—nothing energized and unified people more. But a rally required a site, which eluded him. Most of the city's black clergy were hostile, avoiding Lafayette as if he carried the plague. The Reverend Lewis Lloyd Anderson of the Tabernacle Baptist Church was sympathetic, but the deacons in his congregation were conservative, and Anderson himself had been personally tarnished in 1959 when an automobile he was driving collided with another and killed a pedestrian. He was indicted for murder and convicted of manslaughter; although an appeals court decision had kept him from prison, he expected to be tried again. Opening his church to Lafayette was just too risky.[27]

Then, on May 13, 1963, Sam Boynton suffered a fatal stroke, and Lafayette again turned to Anderson. Why not honor Mr. Boynton by holding a memorial service that also promoted voter registration, his life's work? Anderson agreed but had to confront angry church officials (one called Lafayette a "rabble rouser"), who he ultimately shamed into permitting—if not supporting—the event.

It was decided the rally would be held the next day, May 14, at 7:30 p.m. at the Tabernacle Baptist Church. News went out via leaflets ("We'll Never

Turn Back. God Is On Our Side," they read), telephone calls, and word of mouth in taverns, barbershops, and grocery stores. As word of the gathering reached members of Selma's black community, it also caught the attention of white officials and organizations, both local and federal. Among them was the FBI. Its director, J. Edgar Hoover, hated both the civil rights movement and the Ku Klux Klan, which were bound to clash as movement activities intensified. Because of this, he assigned his agents to shadow both groups. Those observing Lafayette's preparations informed their field office in Mobile and headquarters in Washington, DC, that Sheriff James Clark, his eight deputies, and possibly his two-hundred-man posse would watch the gathering. FBI agents had also notified the military authorities and were following events closely.[28]

Bernard Lafayette arrived at the Tabernacle Baptist Church at 6:30, an hour before the proceedings were set to start. The police presence outside the church seemed light. He went inside to greet people as they filed in. They seemed "serious" and "apprehensive," Chestnut later observed. The sanctuary filled quickly, with the crowd numbering about 425, many of them high school students. "There were black people as far as the eye could see," Colia Lafayette recalled. "It was as if you had never seen so many black people in your life."[29]

Shortly before 7:30 Lafayette returned to the street to find the authorities now out in full force. There were fifty or sixty cars and at least as many police officers and sheriff's men along with countless members of Jim Clark's infamous posse—private citizens he had deputized to protect Selma from a black uprising. Each carried the posse's signature weapon, a club formed from a table leg hollowed out to contain a heavy steel rod. Some were taking pictures of people entering the church.[30]

Lafayette returned inside and mounted the stage, joining the other men scheduled to speak that night. Everyone present could see the police cars' red and blue lights flashing through the stained-glass windows, intensifying their anxiety. Suddenly, the door burst open, and down the main aisle strode Sheriff Jim Clark, accompanied by two deputies and a police officer, all obviously armed. Physically, Clark was a formidable figure: six feet two inches tall, 220 pounds, resplendent in his tailored brown Eisenhower jacket and silver helmet, his .38-caliber pistol, cattle prod, and rope holstered at his side. When the church deacons approached him, he presented them with a court order giving him access to the building. Clark positioned his men at the back and sides of the room and joined them there for the entire evening. One communicated with outside authorities through a walkie-talkie, while the others took notes on everything that was said. Their purpose for being there, Clark later said, was "to see if they [the attendees] were going to start any demonstrations or riots in the church and come outside."[31]

The ceremony began with a prayer by the Reverend C. C. Hunter, one of the more conservative members of the Voters League, then hymns were sung and Sam Boynton memorialized. The evening's main speaker was James Forman, the executive secretary of the Student Nonviolent Coordinating Committee. Chicago-born and educated, Forman had spent his summers as a child with his grandparents in Mississippi, and he knew firsthand the humiliations black southerners had to endure. At the age of eight, while visiting a town store, Forman apparently forgot to say, "Yes, ma'am," to the female clerk, prompting a group of white men to threaten to lynch him. Years later, while Forman was attending the University of Southern California, Los Angeles policemen falsely accused him of robbery and beat him severely. By 1963 those experiences were turning him into "a full-fledged revolutionary," as he declared to his audience that night.[32]

Forman's sermon was titled "The High Cost of Freedom," and Lafayette recalled that it was "one hell of a speech." Despite the presence of Clark and his deputies, Forman said that Selma's black citizens were fed up with the way whites were treating them, and he urged them to honor Sam Boynton's memory by marching to the courthouse and registering to vote, even if it cost them their lives. "Before this is over some of us are going to be dead," he said. "Even though you slay me, others will come along to take our places. Kill one of us going down to vote and there will be 1,000 to take his place." The audience cried "Amen!" When Forman finished, Reverend Hunter delivered a closing prayer and apologized for Forman's remarks. "You shouldn't put all the blame on the white man," Hunter said. "We've got a lot to do in our own homes and own community before we talk about these other things." The assembly, which had cheered Forman, received Hunter's words with an icy silence.[33]

The sound of shattering glass broke the silence. Outside, Clark's men were breaking car windows and tail lights; tomorrow, the attendees would have to watch carefully for the police who would cite them for driving a damaged vehicle and, at the same time, add their names to their lists of local criminals. By now, the crowd was becoming very nervous, so Lafayette tried to restore calm by having them sing freedom songs and urging them to remain in their seats until they felt ready to leave. It was close to 1:00 a.m. when Lafayette and the last of the crowd left the building. Suddenly, a flatbed truck carrying white men armed with axe handles came roaring around the corner and stopped nearby. They leaped to the street and approached the blacks. Luckily, another white man appeared, a coach at the all-white Parish High School. He recognized the would-be thugs as his student athletes and ordered them to go home. His intervention was "the only thing that saved us," Lafayette believed.[34]

Lafayette's efforts, bolstered by Selma's first civil rights rally, began to generate results. His staff now numbered fifty, and more and more black citizens were trying to register to vote. During the year before Lafayette's arrival in February 1963, only about three residents of the city and its surrounding county applied each month—that is, until September and October. At that time the number dropped to zero, probably because a few months earlier the Dallas County Board of Education fired thirty-six black teachers who were working with Justice Department lawyers investigating the registrars' abusive tactics. In June of 1963, by contrast, after five months of canvassing and the confrontation with Clark at Tabernacle Baptist, the number of applicants had grown to forty-one. Even among those who were not yet eligible to vote, the change was obvious. For Selma's black youth, the rally "motivated everyone, particularly the students, to get involved in the Movement and to really try to get Black people registered to vote," Bonner later recalled.[35]

While Lafayette's public visibility increased, so did the dangers he and Colia faced. After the rally the *Selma Times-Journal* introduced Lafayette to the segregationist community in a front-page story that also included his home address. Obscene phone calls increased after the story appeared, and the couple discovered that local authorities were monitoring their telephone calls. When they called SNCC headquarters in Atlanta, they communicated in code until the telephone operator interrupted one night to say, "I know who you are—you're Colia Lafayette and I know *where* you are too."[36]

The couple took extra precautions. They drove slowly, careful not to exceed the speed limit so as to avoid giving local police a reason to stop them. They checked their rearview mirror to see if they were being followed. They watched for strange cars parked near their apartment on Union Street. The dangers were ever-present, forcing the Lafayettes to be constantly vigilant.

Late on the night of June 11, as he returned home from a meeting, Lafayette saw a strange car, an unknown '57 Chevrolet parked across the street from his apartment building. The car's hood was up, and a heavy-set white man was apparently fixing the motor while a second man sat behind the steering wheel.

For a moment Lafayette thought everything was all right. He parked in his driveway and was gathering his books and leaflets when he heard the sound of footsteps approaching. As a movement man, he'd been through it all and well knew those times when danger threatened. Now he felt that time had come.

"Buddy," a voice said, "how much do you charge . . . to give me a push?" *Thank God*, Lafayette thought, *that's all it was, a motorist in trouble*. With a mixture of excitement and relief, he immediately replied, "I won't charge you anything, gladly give you a push."

He pulled his car around closely behind the other Chevrolet. "Maybe you ought to come out and take a look . . . see if the bumpers match, so [they] won't get stuck," the man said. Lafayette left his car and looked down at the bumpers. Seeing nothing amiss, he looked up—just as the man struck him on the forehead with a gun.

Lafayette fell to the ground, but his movement training automatically took over, and he got back up to look death in the face. The man hit him again; again Lafayette fell, only to force himself back to his feet. The man struck him a third time, leaving "a deep gash" in Lafayette's forehead, but Lafayette pulled himself up once more to confront the stranger. Although bloodied and dazed, he remembered what Jim Lawson had said: "unexpected behavior" could touch the "conscience" of an attacker, who typically expected their victims to run or beg for their lives. So Lafayette just stood there staring at the man.

Apparently startled, his assailant began to back away, but Lafayette now feared that he was about to shoot. He called for help, and Mack Shannon, his neighbor, came running out with a shotgun. "Don't shoot, don't shoot," Lafayette yelled at Shannon, fearing that even the defensive killing of a white man would send both black men to an Alabama prison for life.

Thankfully, neither Shannon nor the stranger fired, and the men got in their car and drove away. The moment had come and gone, and Lafayette was still alive, although badly injured. Shannon cleaned him up. Then, before driving himself to the hospital, Lafayette called SNCC headquarters, the police, and the FBI, which was unwilling to investigate the attack because it was not a federal crime. The men were never apprehended.[37]

Lafayette spent the night in the hospital, where he received eleven stitches and was told repeatedly that he was a very lucky man. Just how lucky became clear later. That same night, in Jackson, Mississippi, Byron De La Beckwith, a Klansman, assassinated Medgar Evers, the NAACP's most celebrated and beloved field secretary as well as Colia Lafayette's former boss. In Louisiana, meanwhile, the Klan had gone after Ben Cox, a CORE activist, but failed to find him. The FBI suspected that Lafayette's assault was linked to the others and that his assailants had planned to knock him out and drive him to some remote spot and kill him. Shaken as he was, the news of Evers's death hit Lafayette especially hard: not only had Colia worked closely with Evers, but she was also in Jackson at the time with her family, recovering from wounds sustained while demonstrating with King's troops in Birmingham. No one had the heart to tell her about husband's close call until several days had passed.[38]

When the doctors examined Lafayette the next morning, he asked to leave—there was work to be done. They released him, but despite his sorry condition, he didn't go home to change his clothes. Instead, he immediately went into the downtown streets, a walking advertisement that showed the city's racists that they could not run him out of town. Chestnut found Lafayette on Washington Street and was shocked by his appearance: "eyes all swollen, face bruised, blood all over his shirt." He urged Lafayette to go home, but Lafayette refused. "No way," he said. "This is the symbol we need." He continued to wear the blood-stained shirt for almost a month.

Lafayette's example had an indelible effect on many of those who had previously been reluctant to endorse direct action in the city. Chestnut thought the incident was "a turning point in terms of public sympathy in black Selma. Even the blacks who were most apprehensive about him couldn't help but respect his commitment and courage." Although Lafayette had narrowly survived the encounter, it lent untold credibility to his movement—proving yet again the power and effectiveness of nonviolence in organizing and inspiring black activism.[39]

Lafayette's courage, however, did not stop the white authorities from harassing him and his staff. On June 17 Lafayette sent two aides—Alexander

Brown, sixteen, and Bosie Reese, nineteen—to the courthouse to verify a rumor that voting applicants were being roughed up. A few minutes later an
excited Brown returned to report that Sheriff Clark had attacked Reese, arrested him, and thrown him in jail; Brown himself had fled when an alarm
went off in the courthouse. Lafayette rushed to the sheriff's office. There,
Clark told him that Reese had been charged with resisting arrest and failing
to obey a police officer, but he refused to provide Lafayette any information
about bail.

Later that afternoon Lafayette and Mrs. Boynton went to the county jail
hoping to see Reese, but they were turned away. Two days passed before Lafayette saw Reese again. When he did, it would be under circumstances neither
man expected.[40]

The next day, June 18, began as a typical day for Lafayette. He rose early
and went into the streets to see how people had reacted to the rally held the
previous night at the First Baptist Church. "You could see the new hope and
smiles as [people] talked about the Mass Meeting," he later reported to
SNCC headquarters. "They felt proud of themselves and . . . proud of the
people helping them." That night, after attending meetings and a clinic at
Mrs. Boynton's, Lafayette left for home at about 10:30. A few minutes later
he saw the unmistakable red light of a sheriff's patrol car flashing in his
rearview mirror and pulled over.[41]

The charge was a new one even for a veteran civil rights activist experiencing his tenth arrest: vagrancy. His car impounded, Lafayette was driven to
the county jail on Alabama Avenue, where he was searched. Inside his wallet
the deputy found twenty-seven dollars and seventy-five cents; Lafayette
pointed out that the money indicated that the charge was groundless and
asked to read the warrant. Officer Weber refused, saying that he was just following Sheriff Clark's orders. According to Clark's later testimony, he had received telephone calls and official reports that Lafayette had been seen
"begging," so he issued the warrant. Lafayette was booked, told he would be
photographed and fingerprinted later, and placed in a dark cell. "No strange
place for me," he later wrote, "so I made myself at home and relaxed for the
rest of the night."

News of Lafayette's arrest reached the black community quickly. Chestnut arrived home at midnight, less than an hour and a half after Lafayette
was arrested, to find forty angry young blacks staging a sit-in and demanding that he free their leader immediately.[42]

That was accomplished the next morning, June 20, when Marie Foster and Henry Shannon put up the $1,500 bond necessary for Lafayette's release. Lafayette reported that when the cell doors were opened the first prisoner he saw walking to breakfast was Bosie Reese, who was stunned to see that his boss was in jail too. Lafayette reassured the young man that they were working on his case and that his arrest had been reported to the Justice Department.

Lafayette was tried on June 21, and his defense attorneys, Chestnut and Solomon Seay Jr., quickly established that he was gainfully employed by the Student Nonviolent Coordinating Committee, had no outstanding debts, and had money in his wallet when arrested. Judge Hugh Mallory, who detested all black lawyers, treated Chestnut rudely but nevertheless dropped the charges against his client. Reese, however, was found guilty of resisting arrest, and it took SNCC lawyers additional time to win his release.[43]

Despite the false arrest, the beating, and the other forms of intimidation, Lafayette spent the early summer canvassing, speaking, and organizing rallies. The mass meetings were now becoming a weekly occurrence. Attendance grew from five hundred in June to eight hundred in September, although the FBI agents who observed the meetings were quick to point out that about half of the audiences were teenagers—too young to vote. But although the youths may not have been eligible yet to go to the polls, they had a perceptible effect on the atmosphere in Selma, speaking out against racial injustice and, thereby, encouraging other, older black men and women—their parents, grandparents, teachers, and ministers—to consider doing the same.

By early summer Lafayette began to feel that he had done all he could to advance the cause in Selma. His organizational efforts and advocacy on behalf of the city's black residents had generated an outpouring of sympathy from the black community, some of whom were now open to the idea of going on the offensive to secure their voting rights. The city's black middle class remained the most resistant, however, but Lafayette's achievements, Chestnut later noted, made it "more difficult for them to speak flatly against civil rights activities." Divisions also opened within the Voters League between those Chestnut called the "Young Turks" and the "older heads." Chestnut, Amelia Boynton, Marie Foster, Frederick Reese, Henry Shannon, and young veterans of World War II called for more direct action, including inviting Martin Luther King Jr. to campaign in Selma. Their opponents fought against that suggestion—some thought King was "a rabble rouser"—and recommended that they reach out to moderates in the white community. These tensions would continue in the months ahead, but unexpectedly violent events both outside and within Selma would lead to an increased militancy and a continuing role for SNCC.[44]

Lafayette had created an army of young activists ready for action and had laid the groundwork for the next stage of the campaign: the mobilization of the city's black men and women to register to vote. For the moment, however, with Colia pregnant with their first child and still recovering from the injuries she had sustained in Birmingham, the time had come for Lafayette to return to school. In early August he left Selma, bound first for Jackson, where he was reunited with Colia, and the pair then returned to Nashville and Fisk University.

SNCC's leadership was both surprised and very pleased with what Lafayette had accomplished in Selma. It was no longer the city marked by an X on their organization's map; now a tack indicated that it was an active center of resistance. Jim Forman would later praise him "for quietly laying the foundations for events that would rock the world in the near future." Although other activists would soon shed blood in Selma to defend African Americans' voting rights, Lafayette could take pride in "laying the first stone, breaking the first earth, planting the first seed."[45]

TWO

AN IDEAL PLACE

WHEN BERNARD LAFAYETTE DEPARTED SELMA IN AUGUST 1963, HE LEFT behind a group of impatient teenagers eager to carry on the struggle against racial injustice. They had become charged with the same restless energy that had inspired Lafayette himself to join SNCC and had provoked their elders in Selma—men and women like C. J. Adams, J. L. Chestnut Jr., and Amelia Boynton—to stand up against the forces of segregation in their own community. They eagerly awaited their next adventure, which came in the aftermath of the most tragic event in the history of the civil rights movement.

On Sunday, September 15, 1963, Charles Bonner and Cleophas Hobbs, Lafayette's recruits, learned that Birmingham's Sixteenth Street Baptist Church had been bombed. Killed instantly were three fourteen-year-old girls, Carole Robertson, Cynthia Wesley, and Addie Mae Collins, along with a fourth, Denise McNair, who, at eleven, was the youngest of the victims. The children had been dressing for the Sunday service. Addie Mae's sister, thirteen-year-old Sarah who was blinded and bleeding from the twenty-one pieces of glass in her face, eyes, chest, and legs, somehow managed to find her way out of the wreckage. The doctors saved her life but had to remove her right eye. Sixteen others—parishioners and people just walking past the church—were injured. "In church! My, God, we're not even safe in church," said one anguished woman.[1]

An angry crowd quickly gathered outside the damaged building. They threw rocks and pieces of glass at the police and sheriff's deputies who had responded to the bombing. The police and deputies, facing the unruly group, fired shotguns over the people's heads, forcing them into nearby streets and alleys. Miraculously, no widespread rioting occurred, but senseless violence did claim two other lives that day. Birmingham police shot a black teenager in the back, claiming that he ran after throwing rocks at them. In a Birmingham suburb a sixteen-year-old Eagle Scout shot at two black boys on a bike, killing one, Virgil Ware. In all, the bombing and its aftermath caused six fatalities, none older than sixteen.[2]

The bombing was the work of Klansmen seeking revenge for Martin Luther King Jr.'s recent campaign in Birmingham. In the spring of 1963 King had launched "Project C—for Confrontation," aimed at the city's businesses. King's hope was that boycotts, sit-ins, and marches would cripple Birmingham's economic life and force the city's merchants to allow blacks to patronize their stores. His strategy had worked brilliantly, much to the chagrin of the city's many segregationists.

Although terrorist groups like the Klan would later retaliate against King, his chief enemy at first was Birmingham's Commissioner of Public Safety, Eugene "Bull" Connor. King hoped that Connor, a fiery racist, would give in to his worst instincts and commit a public atrocity that would capture the nation's attention—and he did. Under Connor's direction, the city police roughly arrested demonstrators, and the jails were soon filled to capacity. Running out of troops, King accepted a plan from his aide Jim Bevel to turn to the city's high school and even grammar school students for help, just as Bernard Lafayette was then doing in Selma.

The students had responded with enthusiasm, and their efforts fanned the flames just as King intended. On May 3, as more than a thousand young protestors poured out of the Sixteenth Street Baptist Church, which had become the movement's second home, Connor let loose his police. They beat black youths with their nightsticks and allowed their vicious attack dogs to leap and bite the demonstrators, tearing their clothes and flesh. Then came the city's fire hoses that, when turned on, swept people away under streams of pressurized water. The protestors rolled and tumbled like rag dolls; among them was Colia Lafayette, whose injuries would incapacitate her for several months. After the assaults came more arrests. By the end of the day over nine hundred children were in jail.

Television brought these images into American homes, sickening many people far removed from the atrocities. Among them was President John F.

Kennedy, who determined to rein in the violence in Birmingham before it spiraled out of control. On his orders, Justice Department officials flew to Birmingham to meet with local businessmen, and on May 10 they reached a settlement. The merchants, whose businesses were badly hurt by the boycott, agreed to desegregate drinking fountains, restrooms, lunch counters, and dressing rooms within the next ninety days. They also promised to employ blacks in jobs that served the public; within sixty days a black clerk could help a black patron.

The Justice Department's efforts in Birmingham were just part of a broader federal intervention in the South. On June 11 two qualified black students—James Hood and Vivian Malone—were admitted to the University of Alabama at Tuscaloosa over the protests of Governor George C. Wallace, who literally stood in the schoolhouse door. President Kennedy federalized the Alabama National Guard, and Wallace stepped away. That same night the president also announced that he would soon send Congress a strong civil rights bill designed to give blacks access to public accommodations, from restaurants and hotels to theaters, parks, and swimming pools. Segregation in public spaces was the most visible manifestation of racial inequality in the United States, and under his administration, Kennedy hoped to end it. In a televised address to the nation Kennedy called civil rights a "moral issue . . . as old as the Scriptures . . . and as clear as the American Constitution." America "for all its hopes and all its boasts," the president concluded, "will not be fully free until all its citizens are free."[3]

The summer of 1963 had ended with an event that echoed and amplified President Kennedy's promise for racial justice. On August 28 a massive civil rights rally was held in the nation's capital. The March on Washington for Jobs and Freedom had originally been planned during World War II, but its architect, the legendary civil rights leader and labor organizer A. Philip Randolph, had agreed to call off the march in exchange for President Roosevelt's promise to end discriminatory hiring practices in defense-related industries. In 1963, however, the march finally became a reality. Organized by leaders from CORE, SNCC, SCLC, NAACP, and the National Urban League, it was scheduled for the one hundredth anniversary of Abraham Lincoln's signing of the Emancipation Proclamation. The march was a historic event in and of itself, composed of some two hundred thousand to three hundred thousand people, both white and black, who gathered on the Washington Mall to hear songs by Joan Baez, Bob Dylan, and Peter, Paul and Mary as well as speeches by the assembled civil rights luminaries. Its crescendo was without a doubt Martin Luther King Jr.'s famous "I Have a Dream" speech, which—together with the remarkable turnout and favorable response throughout much of the nation—seemed to represent a stunning groundswell of support for the men and women fighting for their rights on the ground in the Deep South.

King's was not the only address heard that day. John Lewis, Bernard Lafayette's old friend from the Nashville movement and the Freedom Rides, who was representing SNCC, wanted to send a message to President Kennedy: "that," as he later wrote, "the President was being too cautious, doing far too little when it came to meeting the needs of black Americans." Among his complaints was a voting rights section of Kennedy's proposed Civil Rights Bill requiring that black applicants show evidence of having had a sixth-grade education before being permitted to register. Lewis and his colleagues were furious. Southern states had prevented them from receiving an education equal to that of whites, and now they were being "punished" for that denial at the ballot box. Randolph and other leaders of the march forced Lewis to revise his remarks so as not to insult the president, but he nonetheless managed to anticipate King's later campaign in Selma by saying, "The Voting section of this bill will not help the thousands of black people who want to vote. It will not help the citizens of Mississippi, of Alabama and Georgia who are qualified to vote but lack a sixth-grade education. 'One Man, one vote' is the African cry. It is ours, too. It must be ours." The day's events overshadowed Lewis's words, but his remarks were a sign that the movement's unity was more apparent than real.[4]

THE BIRMINGHAM BOMBING WAS RETRIBUTION FOR THE PROGRESS THAT King had made in the South as well as the triumphant March on Washington, but rather than deterring protestors in Selma, it galvanized them. The violence in other parts of the South renewed homegrown activists' determination not to suffer such terrorization silently. The nature of the struggle in Selma was changing. Previously much of the official resistance to the activists' efforts had been manifested in intimidation, harassment, and bureaucratic obstacles; private citizens perpetrated what violence the activists had endured, and they had done so surreptitiously, out of the public eye. But as the movement there gained new momentum in the wake of the Birmingham tragedy, Selma would also witness a surge in reactionary violence, and that change would mark an important, if lamentable, new chapter in the struggle for voting rights.

Saddened and angry by the Sixteenth Street Baptist Church bombing, teenage activists Chuck Bonner and Cleo Hobbs searched for a way to honor the memory of the four girls. The pair called SNCC headquarters for instructions because they'd never participated in a demonstration, and without Lafayette to guide them, they didn't know what to do. But nobody in Atlanta could help, so they decided to act alone. On September 16 Bonner and Hobbs gathered a few friends and marched to Carter's Drugstore, which refused to serve blacks at its lunch counter. When Willie Robinson, nineteen, and Lulu Brown, fifteen, took stools, Harmon Carter, the owner, ordered them to leave. They refused, so he called Sheriff Clark, who sent his posse to eject them. Carter himself struck Robinson in the head with an axe handle, and another officer shocked Brown with a cattle prod. An ambulance took them away while deputies arrested the other demonstrators. Carter was not arrested or charged for assaulting Robinson. After the Civil Rights Act became law in July 1964, he removed his counter so he would not have to serve blacks.

On the same day as the demonstration at Carter's Drugstore, young activists also sat in at Kress's Drugs, local libraries, and the Thirsty Boy, a whites-only drive-in restaurant. In the next few days almost one thousand students refused to attend school; those found by police in the streets were arrested for violating truancy laws. Between September 16 and October 3, 250 youngsters between the ages of six and twenty-one were arrested and charged with unlawful assembly, parading without a permit, picketing, and trespass. Most spent a day to a week behind bars. "The Movement was on," Bonner said later.[5]

Also seeking their own revenge for the bombings were King's aides Diane Nash and James Bevel, a married couple and veteran civil rights activists who, like Lafayette, had been part of Reverend James Lawson Jr.'s nonviolence workshops, the resulting Nashville movement, and the Freedom Rides. They had also been intimately involved in the recent struggle in Birmingham. Bevel had played an especially important role in bringing children into Birmingham's streets, so he felt almost personally responsible for the bombing and loss of life. "We felt like our own children had been killed," Nash later said. Both were so angry that they considered rejecting nonviolence to pursue the bombers and kill them.

There was something of the odd couple about this pair. Nash, brilliant and beautiful, was a Chicago-born, middle-class Catholic and a runner-up in the Miss Illinois pageant. Bevel came from Itta Bena, Mississippi, was the thirteenth of seventeen children, had been dishonorably discharged from the Navy for insubordination, worked as a bricklayer, and sang in a doo-wop group before God called him to the ministry. He was "like no one I'd ever met before," John Lewis later recalled when the two encountered one another at American Baptist. "Wild. Crazy. . . . A man who . . . worshipped the Scriptures so much that he [wore] a skullcap to honor the prophets of the Old Testament." Despite their different backgrounds and personalities, Nash and Bevel shared a passionate dedication to the movement—a commitment that inevitably brought them together.[6]

That commitment led them to reject their inclination to murder the bombers. Instead, they recommended a militant version of the peaceful March on Washington, one that targeted Governor Wallace. In it, thousands would march on Montgomery to isolate George Wallace in his own capital. Their plan included cutting Montgomery off from the rest of the state with an army of students and sympathizers who would disrupt rail, bus, and even plane travel to and from the capital. They would register every Alabama resident of voting age, launch a general strike, and ask President Kennedy to withhold federal funding from Alabama and withdraw recognition of Wallace's government. Such measures would, they hoped, draw even more national attention to their cause and put immediate political pressure on Wallace, forcing him to take decisive steps to end the injustices in Alabama. Nash took their proposal to Birmingham, where King was officiating at the funerals of the young girls.[7]

King listened politely but rejected their plan. He thought it was just too impractical and so radical that it would damage the movement. Although disappointed, both Nash and Bevel remained committed to what they called GROW—Get Rid of Wallace—and over the next year Bevel often went to Selma to assist the organizers working there. "If it took twenty years," Nash later said, "we were going to get the right to vote in Alabama."[8]

Jim Forman, along with John Lewis, Lafayette's former roommate at the American Baptist Theological Seminary and SNCC's current executive secretary, came to Selma eight days after the church bombing. Both saw immediately that Lafayette had succeeded: Selma, which Forman had once urged

Lafayette to avoid because the situation there seemed so hopeless, had become "an important center of resistance," Forman thought. To Lewis, the city "looked like a different place. Tensions were incredibly high. Armed troopers and police were everywhere." That night Lewis spoke to an immense audience at the First Baptist Church while fifty Alabama state troopers, armed with machine guns and commanded by their leader, Colonel Al Lingo, stood guard.[9]

The next day, September 24, Lewis, holding a sign reading "One Man, One Vote," was arrested for unlawful assembly while picketing the courthouse. Herded into a waiting bus by posse men with cattle prods, he and the others were driven to the Selma Prison Farm, a facility that reminded Lewis of Mississippi's infamous Parchman Penitentiary. His cell, filled to capacity with other demonstrators, contained only soiled mattresses and a single sink and toilet. The floor was so dirty that he ate standing up. It took several weeks for him to win his freedom.[10]

Meanwhile, Jim Forman continued the struggle for voting rights, hoping that Jim Clark's brutality against the demonstrators would force the federal government to intervene. Forman also conceived of a new initiative, under which massive numbers of Selma's black citizens would gather peacefully at the courthouse to register. He designated the effort, set for October 7, as Freedom Day. To energize his troops, Forman invited comedian Dick Gregory, whose caustic wit had won him national fame, to address a rally just before the event. Gregory didn't hesitate—he had participated in movement activities in Greenwood, Mississippi, had come to Birmingham when King called him, and had attended the March on Washington in August. His wife, Lillian, was equally passionate about civil rights. Although pregnant, she also came to Selma to join in the Freedom Day march.[11]

On Sunday night, October 6, Gregory entered African Methodist Episcopal Zion Church flanked by Clark's posse. There were police inside as well as out, waiting to record his every word. Gregory didn't disappoint his fans or his enemies. He attacked Clark and his men, calling them "peons, the idiots who do all the dirty work, the dogs who do all the biting." The audience cheered; never had a black man dared to talk to a white man that way, let alone a cop or state trooper.

"You tell 'em, brother," someone called out, and the rest laughed.

Go out and support the kids, Gregory urged. Register! Vote! If his audience would do that, he said, then "freedom will run all over this town."

Thunderous applause followed, and when it subsided Jim Forman took the stage. "Call . . . people," he instructed, "and tell them to come down to the courthouse tomorrow, that it's freedom day. You take a baloney sandwich and a glass of cool water and go down there and stay all day." The message was clear: the marchers would need both numbers and stamina on Freedom Day if they were to have any chance at success.[12]

Forman awoke early the next morning tired and worried about what the day would bring. Before leaving he pocketed a bottle of Maalox tablets to sooth the ulcer he had developed during his work in the movement. Among other things, Forman was still concerned about the turnout for Freedom Day, knowing that a large presence at the courthouse was crucial to the marchers' success. About that, at least, Forman needn't have worried.

A short time later Forman, accompanied by the writer James Baldwin, discovered that there were already about 125 people lined up at the courthouse. They were older men and women, dressed neatly. By 10 a.m. there were 175, the line beginning to snake around the corner. Forman happily greeted them: "Now you just [wait] here . . . and get some sunshine," he said. Present too was Sheriff Clark, with a gold star pinned prominently to his chest and wearing a green helmet emblazoned with the Confederate flag. He was supported by 50 state troopers and 40 posse men, all armed with guns, cattle prods, and nightsticks; they walked along the sidewalk close to the waiting people.[13]

By noon there were three hundred people waiting to enter the courthouse, but only twelve had actually gone in and applied. Clark's men took pictures of those inside, another deterrent to registering. Those outside knew they would probably not be among the lucky ones that day, and they were growing hungry and thirsty; still, they waited. Other activists attempted to encourage them. Across the street, on the steps of the Federal Building, stood two SNCC workers holding signs that read "Register to Vote" and "Register Now for Freedom Now." When Sheriff Clark saw them, he and three deputies hurried over. They grabbed their signs while Clark bellowed, "You're under arrest for unlawful assembly." A couple of white observers cheered him on, yelling, "Get 'em, Big Jim! Get 'em!" As two FBI agents and two Justice Department lawyers stood silently by, SNCC workers were taken to a waiting police car and driven away.[14]

Forman's next challenge was to feed those in line, which had now grown to 350 people. Clark's men had told them that if they left to eat, drink, or use the

Freedom Day, 1963. Sheriff Clark and his deputies arrest two demonstrators for "unlawful assembly." © Danny Lyon/Magnum Photos

bathroom, they might as well not return. Forman, chewing Maalox tablets, joined Amelia Boynton to discuss this problem with Sheriff Clark. Historian Howard Zinn, a scholar-participant of the civil rights movement, was also there and came along to record their conversation. "We'd like to bring food to these people on line. They've been waiting all day," Forman told Clark.

"They will not be molested in any way," an angry Clark replied.

"Does giving them food mean molesting them?" Amelia Boynton asked.

If the applicants were touched, Clark warned, he would arrest Forman and Boynton.

Forman tried another approach: "They're standing on line to register to vote, and we'd like to explain registration procedure to them." It was his right, he said.

Clark was unreachable. "Your civil rights be damned. They will not be molested in any way, and that includes talking to them."[15]

Howard Zinn conferred with Dick Wasserstrom, a Justice Department lawyer. It was now two o'clock, Zinn said, and people were hungry and especially thirsty from standing under a hot sun; surely the federal government would rescue the folks now surrounded by Clark's posse. "Is there any reason why a representative of the Justice Department can't go over and talk to the state troopers and say these people are entitled to food and water?" asked Zinn. The question clearly bothered the lawyer, and he took a moment to reply. "I won't do it," Wasserstrom finally said. "I believe they do have the right to receive food and water. But I won't do it."[16]

After two o'clock Forman, out of options, decided to defy Clark and bring food to the line, despite knowing what that would cause. His aides Carver Neblett and Avery Williams were the sacrificial lambs for that day, and Forman invited reporters and photographers to join them and witness the response to their charity. In doing so, he reflected an understanding—shared by other leaders of the nonviolent movement—that the media could serve as a crucial tool for publicizing the abuses black southerners suffered and for rallying public sentiment against racial injustices. Provoking outbursts of violence from segregationist authorities had become a cornerstone of the civil rights movement, as was having reporters and cameramen on hand to capture the atrocities.

As they approached the line with sandwiches and drinks, Major Joe Smelley, leading the state troopers, yelled, "Move on!" When they didn't, Smelley shouted to his troopers, "Get 'em out of here, they are just trying to cause trouble." A trooper pushed Neblett, and he dropped to the ground to protect himself. Williams joined him. "Let me at 'em," cried several deputies, and twelve state troopers quickly surrounded Neblett and Williams, kicking them and striking them with billy clubs. At least one jabbed Neblett with a cattle prod—Zinn saw his body convulse.[17]

The photographers moved in, and the sound of their flashbulbs popping covered the men's cries. "Get in front of those cameramen," Smelley yelled, and the troopers first blocked them, then attacked them. One trooper tried to strike CBS News's Wendell Hoffman in the groin, but Hoffman used his camera to deflect the blow. A reporter from the *Montgomery Reporter* wasn't as lucky: a posse man punched him in the mouth. Meanwhile, officers dragged Neblett and Williams away and threw them on a bus. When they arrived at the jail, the beatings resumed—this time out of sight of the cameras.[18]

Forman feared that the police assault would cause the voters' line to break; instead, it held and even grew longer as the afternoon waned. The registrar's office closed at 4:30, and only then did the people, some of whom had waited more than seven hours, disperse.[19]

The day ended with a jubilant rally at the Baptist Tabernacle Church. Six hundred people attended, and although three city patrol cars were stationed outside and one sheriff's car drove around the back from time to time, not a single policeman or state trooper entered the sanctuary. "We ought to be happy today," Jim Forman said, "because we did something great. Jim Clark never saw that many niggers down there!"

The crowd laughed and applauded.

"Yeah, there was Jim Clark, rubbin' his head and his big, fat belly; he was shufflin' today like we used to. He never thought we could get that many people to the courthouse to register. Well, the white man has had us shuffling for 300 years," Forman concluded. "We're going to catch up with him and he knows it."[20]

Reflecting on the day's events twenty-two years later, Jim Forman wrote, "There would be other events called Freedom Day in various parts of the South. But there would never be one like the first Freedom Day: the day when a century of southern fear and terror—of night riding Klansmen, of the smooth talking but equally murderous White Citizens' Council, of the vicious George Wallaces—when all these forces had not been able to stop the forward thrust of a people determined by any means to be free." Of course, a century's fear could not disappear in a single day, nor did the terror cease with Freedom Day—there would be more trials to come. But something had indeed changed within Selma's black community. Rather than being cowed by the white establishment, the city's black adults—those who knew the stakes better than the young activists and who also had more to lose—took a stand. They had done so despite the risks involved, and they withstood the intimidation and abuse of white officials who had been determined to stop them. John Lewis realized this, later calling Freedom Day "the turning point in the right to vote."[21]

The optimism Freedom Day created endured over the next few months but eventually ended in disappointment. At first the signals from Washington had been encouraging. On October 3, 1963, the US Court of Appeals for the Fifth Circuit, which had jurisdiction over Alabama and five other southern states, ordered the Board of Registrars there to ease the way applicants were questioned both orally and in writing. Moreover, if they were rejected on grounds of character, they were now entitled to a hearing to defend themselves. Black citizens of Selma again flocked to the courthouse. In October 215 were able to apply, the greatest number in recent history, and interest remained high until February 1964. At that time the Board introduced a more difficult test, created by the Alabama Supreme Court. Those who had managed to apply for their voter registration test found themselves being ultimately rejected in as great a number as before. The federal government would need to be doing much more if it truly wanted to safeguard the voting rights of black Alabamians.[22]

Although the civil rights movement was working through these setbacks, it was also reeling from a different sort of tragedy. On November 22, 1963, President Kennedy, the man who in June had promised black Americans a bill guaranteeing their access to public accommodations, was gunned down in Dallas. Now Lyndon B. Johnson of Texas was president, and his weak record on civil rights as a representative and senator was not reassuring. In his first speech to Congress as president, Johnson had pledged to continue Kennedy's policies and urged swift passage of Kennedy's Civil Rights Bill, which was tied up on Capitol Hill; whether this was just soothing rhetoric or a real commitment to civil rights remained to be seen. Many civil rights leaders had been critical of Kennedy's reluctance to help them until 1963, when Bull Connor's atrocities had pushed him to make a greater effort. Compared to the new president, however, Kennedy's death seemed a dark portent for the future.[23]

For Selma's activists the year 1963 had also ended on a depressing note. On December 30 Sheriff Clark had exacted his revenge for Freedom Day. Accompanied by County Solicitor Blanchard McLeod and four deputies, Clark broke into SNCC headquarters, assaulted twenty-one-year-old organizer James Austin, and arrested him and six colleagues. "We've been after you for a long time," Clark told the injured Austin. The charge was "illegal circulation of literature promoting a boycott." Still angry after beating Austin, Clark tore the telephone out of the wall and scooped up affidavits, leaflets, and other records. Next, his group entered Freedom House, a three-room apartment where some SNCC workers lived, and destroyed it.[24]

Seven months later, however, spirits within the movement lifted. On July 2, 1964, President Johnson signed the Civil Rights Act into law. Kennedy's successor had proven himself to be a stronger supporter of civil rights than activists had anticipated, and he had taken up the cause of Kennedy's initiative with unexpected zeal. With the passage of the act, black residents of Selma were free, theoretically, to eat at Carter's Drug Store or at the Thirsty Boy Drive-In, and they legally could sit anywhere they wanted at the Walton or

Wilby movie theaters or even rent a room at the exclusive Hotel Albert. But integration did not come as quickly as a stroke of the president's pen.

On the afternoon of July 4 four black college students visited the Thirsty Boy, but the owner turned them away and immediately called Sheriff Clark. Clark quickly arrived with his deputies and arrested the students, shocking one with a cattle prod in the process. One young woman was charged with carrying a concealed weapon when a search of her purse turned up a bicycle chain and lock. Later that day a group of black teenagers were admitted to the Wilby Theater without resistance and sat in the formerly forbidden white section. But when others appeared at 5:30, white citizens cried, "There's niggers in the Wilby!" and tried to prevent their entrance. The sheriff and his posse soon arrived, attacking the black moviegoers, then scattering both them and their white challengers. Some of the white men ran into the theater looking for the original group of black patrons. The vigilantes ran the teenagers out of the theater with the help of Clark's men, and the sheriff closed the theater to all patrons.[25]

And for the first time a Voters League mass meeting ended in violence. On the night of July 5, as the crowd of attendees left their meeting place, they ran into fifty to sixty posse men and deputies. A riot ensued. Deputies later claimed that rocks thrown from a nearby alley struck them and that, after hearing a gunshot, they fired tear gas at their alleged assailants. Jerry DeMuth, a writer working with SNCC, recalled the incident differently. As people were leaving, the posse men attacked them without provocation. DeMuth was struck in the head while his colleague, a photographer, was beaten and his camera destroyed. Solicitor McLeod ordered them to leave Selma immediately, regardless of their wounds. The violence rippled out from the hall. The deputies attacked two black residents living a few blocks away and shattered the windows of other African Americans' homes. By the time Sheriff Clark arrived fifteen minutes later, the excitement was over. But the incident could leave activists with no doubt that they were hitting a nerve; segregationist violence could only mean that their efforts in Selma were working.[26]

The holiday violence did not deter the Voters League; indeed, it intensified their desire to again try to register. Monday, July 6, was the first of five special registration days, and black applicants began to line up early in the morning for the event. Jim Clark's troops were there too. Deputies and posse men patrolled the entire neighborhood surrounding the courthouse as well as the building itself. Applicants could enter through only one doorway under the watchful eyes of Clark's men.

John Lewis had come out for the registration day and quickly found himself confronting Sheriff Clark. "I know you," a furious Jim Clark said. "You are here to cause trouble." Clark began slapping his nightstick in the palm of his hand. "You don't live here. You are an agitator and that's the lowest form of humanity," he said.

Lewis disagreed. "Sheriff, I may be an agitator," he said, "but I'm not an outside agitator. I grew up only ninety miles from here. These people invited us to come and we're going to stay until they are registered to vote."

Clark wasted no time in arresting Lewis, but this time the sheriff cast his net even wider, seizing any black bystanders watching from the courthouse steps or even those who happened to be in the area engaged in other business. A United Press International (UPI) journalist using a public phone to report the story of the mass arrest was forcibly yanked from the phone booth. In all, fifty-three people were jailed, twelve of them adolescents or younger. Posse men prodded them with billy clubs and burned them with cattle prods as they force-marched them five blocks to the county jail. None of the fifty-three were formally charged then; the next day each received a predated warrant signed with a rubber stamp by an officer who had no knowledge of how the warrant would be used. They were charged with "interfering with a court in session"—a grand jury had been meeting, unbeknownst to the activists. Later there were additional charges for the adults, such as contributing to the delinquency of a minor, as some of those arrested were underage.[27]

More arrests followed over the next several days. Reverend Frederick Reese, a teacher at Hudson High School and member of the Voters League, was charged with contributing to the delinquency of a minor for driving two youngsters to a courthouse demonstration on July 8. The next day the number of activists in jail rose to seventy when more demonstrators were picked up. The return on their efforts was negligible: of the ninety men and women who tried to register that week, only six succeeded.

Because it seemed that almost nothing could deter the applicants, Sheriff Clark and Solicitor McLeod chose another, more far-reaching legal tactic. Seeking a judicial order that would undercut the powers of the civil rights "agitators," they turned to Circuit Court Judge James A. Hare, the aristocratic leader of Selma's segregationists. The short, slight, fifty-seven-year-old Hare could conceivably have become governor of Alabama—he certainly had the connections to make a strong bid for the position—but seemed content being a prosperous cattle rancher and, since 1956, a circuit court judge, albeit a very powerful one.[28]

Hare was also a passionate racist who believed he could identify a black's African roots simply by looking at him. Selma's "blue-gummed Nigras," he argued, descended from "Ebos" and "Angols," the "riff raff and river rats" of their race. "You will not be able to domesticate them any more than you can get a zebra to pull a plow, or an apache to pick cotton," he once said. According to Hare, the Justice Department and Martin Luther King Jr., who had "selected Selma for assassination back in the fall of 1963," had stirred up the city's African Americans. The city had been "subjected to something fantastic and terroristic," yet Selma's whites had "shown unbelievable restraint," Hare claimed. Earlier that very month he had told J. L. Chestnut that "If these unsanitary, unbathed ruffians think we are going to lie down and give Selma over to them, they have another thought coming. I am not going to sit idly by while they destroy this city."[29]

Hare kept his promise. On July 9, 1964, he issued an injunction that almost destroyed Alabama's civil rights movement. Hare's judicial order was directed against all civil rights leaders and organizations, including SNCC, King's Southern Christian Leadership Conference, the NAACP (which Alabama had banned in 1956), and the Dallas County Voters League. (He threw in the Klan and the Nazi Party for good measure.) His list covered almost everyone: Martin Luther King Jr., John Lewis, Amelia Boynton, James Bevel, Marie Foster, Frederick Reese, Reverend L. L. Anderson, J. L. Chestnut, and thirty-three other activists. Hare's judicial order stipulated that if three or more of the named people or other members of the named organizations gathered together, they could be arrested and jailed. Civil rights attorneys quickly asked federal judge Daniel Thomas (a racial moderate but no friend of the movement) to dismiss Hare's injunction as a gross violation of the First Amendment, but he agreed only to consider the lawyers' request and rule on it at some future time. Nor would Thomas issue a temporary stay prohibiting the injunction until he made a decision about its constitutionality. (His ruling did not come until April 1965, at which point events had rendered it irrelevant.)[30]

Hare's injunction was ruinous. Mass meetings and rallies disappeared in Alabama, and voter applications declined to their lowest number in years. Only one small ray of hope existed: a new mayor had recently come to power, bringing an end to the long, reactionary regime of Chris Heinz. Joe T. Smitherman could not have differed more from the wealthy, well-connected Heinz. Orphaned young, the skinny, "jug-eared" Smitherman had clawed his way up the economic ladder, becoming a successful appliance salesman before turning to politics and winning a seat on the city council. A segregationist less rabid than Heinz, he, like other young, moderate bankers, lawyers, and merchants in Selma, feared that the city's racial problems would ruin its reputation and prevent northern businessmen from investing in municipal businesses.

Inaugurated in October, Smitherman's earliest actions encouraged Selma's black community that the future might be somewhat better than the past. The city council, at the mayor's request, established a new agency, the office of public safety. The agency's director, Wilson Baker, a professional police officer and an enemy of Sheriff Clark, promised to treat all of Selma's citizens courteously and fairly. Previously Mayor Heinz had given Clark the authority to handle all civil rights disturbances, and the results had been disastrous. Now Baker was in charge of city law enforcement, and he commanded Selma's police officers as well as Clark and his deputies. Clark's domain was relegated to the area around the courthouse and beyond the city limits.

Baker, like Smitherman, gave black residents of Selma some reason to hope. Speaking to the exclusive Selma Exchange Club, whose members included Judge Hare and ex-Mayor Heinz, Baker announced that, given recent court and congressional actions, segregation was ending and that he would "lead Selma in dignity" to a more integrated society. Most importantly, Baker later announced that he would not enforce Judge Hare's infamous injunction because it was now being challenged by the Justice Department and evaluated by federal judge Thomas. For a black community that had long been abused by reactionary public officials, Baker's decisions, compared to Clark's, must have seemed almost unbelievably progressive.[31]

There were other encouraging signs of change as well. Reverend Ralph Smeltzer of Pennsylvania's Church of the Brethren had been working quietly in Selma for more than a year, reaching out to moderates in both the white and black communities in order to broaden the base of support for further desegregation within the city. His efforts were beginning to bear fruit. A public housing project for Craig Air Force Base servicemen was integrated in May 1964, as were extension classes at the University of Alabama in Tuscaloosa, a ninety-minute drive away. Restaurant owners were seriously considering serving blacks, as now required by law. Public libraries again had furniture so black citizens could sit and read there.[32]

For Amelia Boynton and others in the Dallas County Voters League, these changes, though encouraging, were too modest to be satisfying. Yes, the racial signs that marked the water fountains in the courthouse and city hall had been removed, but the bathrooms were still segregated. Chief Baker was certainly preferable to Sheriff Clark, but Clark was still a threatening presence in Selma, and the new mayor had also chosen McLean Pitts, an ardent segregationist, as city attorney. Moreover, the White Citizens' Council, three thousand strong, remained a powerful force, willing to destroy the businesses of moderates, regardless of race. "We are not going to give in," said one Selma official. "If we let them have one inch, they would want to go all the way." The idea of black citizens using water fountains and restaurants was one thing; the idea of them enjoying political parity with white Americans was quite another. But Amelia Boynton was not deterred—she had been fighting for voting rights for more than thirty years, and she was not about to stop now. So she decided to enlist Martin Luther King Jr. in her cause.[33]

On November 11, as she drove to Birmingham for a meeting with King, SCLC's leaders were discussing their next moves. At first King thought of moving into the North to attack segregation and poverty there, but his aides recommended a voting rights campaign somewhere in the Deep South. Jim Bevel had been urging a return to Alabama to fight for voting rights since the church bombing fourteen months earlier, and he did so again that day. C. T. Vivian, Bernard Lafayette's friend from the Nashville days, agreed. Selma could be "a rallying point," he said, one that could be used to "stir the whole nation." King realized that shifting the focus to Selma would mean confronting Sheriff Clark, but if he was as bad as Bull Connor, then a public, bloody confrontation would actually be advantageous. Bull Connor's violence had forced Kennedy to act, and the result was the 1964 Civil Rights Act. Clark was cut from the same cloth, King suspected, and his brutality might help create a voting rights act.[34]

King knew that only the federal government could guarantee the voting rights of black southerners, as it had recently done for their right to use public accommodations. Although the Civil Rights Act contained a minor voting provision that prohibited the unequal application of voter registration requirements, it did not provide for federal registrars to go south to help black citizens actually vote. What was needed was either a constitutional amendment or more desirable, national legislation that eliminated literacy tests and other obstacles preventing black Americans from voting. King knew that until they could speak their voice at the polls and hold politicians accountable for their actions, African Americans would never see any true change in their communities. And until the federal government was willing to back up its rhetoric about voting with enforcement, states and their white-led districts would continue to deprive black residents of this fundamental right.

Now, as the result of President Johnson's great electoral victory a week earlier, the federal government might be willing to match words with deeds. Not since the early New Deal had a Democratic president had such overwhelming liberal majorities in both houses of the next Congress, and Johnson had already expressed his desire to eliminate poverty and injustice, to create what he called the Great Society. Surely there would be room for a voting rights act on Johnson's legislative agenda.[35]

The November 11 meeting ended without a final decision as to the location and tactics for the SCLC's next move. That decision came the next day, when Amelia Boynton met with King and described to him life in Selma under the Hare injunction: the paralyzed movement, the decline in voter applications, the despairing activists. King should, she hoped, make Selma his next priority. Ralph Abernathy, King's closest friend, also pushed strongly for Selma as the "site to fight our next battle." Any doubts that King had whether Selma was the best site for this new campaign now vanished. Assignments were made: Bevel would be in charge of direct action, and Vivian would meet with the Dallas County Voters League to win their approval and, thus, avoid a turf war.[36]

Boynton had not exaggerated the problems or the divisions inside the movement, as Vivian learned during his meeting with the Voters League leaders in Selma. Some were still wary of King, fearful that his star quality would "destroy" their organization, as one critic put it. Others remained loyal to SNCC; after all, Lafayette and Forman had come when no one else would. Even King had gone to Birmingham rather than Selma. But they understood that SNCC had "just about run its course," as Reverend Reese put it, and that the movement "needed some rejuvenation." Moreover, there were signs that the moment was right to step up its efforts in Selma. The changes in Selma's government, however minimal, suggested that the segregationists were not as unified as they had once been. Vivian convinced the Selma activists that SCLC was committed to the struggle, which went far beyond Selma. "We wanted to raise the issue of voting . . . as a way to shake Alabama," he later remembered telling them, "so that it would no longer be a Selma issue or even an Alabama issue but a national issue." Their city was "an ideal place to do it." Reassured, the League authorized Boynton to formally invite Dr. King to come to Selma. Vivian told them that a tentative date for King's arrival had been set: January 2, 1965.[37]

JUST AS SAM BOYNTON HAD PASSED THE TORCH OF LEADERSHIP IN THE Selma movement to Bernard Lafayette and he, in turn, had passed it to Jim Forman, now that responsibility fell to Martin Luther King Jr. And he was worried that he might not be strong enough to bear it.

King wasn't worried about his health, although it was not good. Two months before he met with Amelia Boynton in Birmingham, his doctors had forced him to check into Atlanta Hospital for treatment of exhaustion, high blood pressure, and a viral infection. But those troubles were not uppermost in King's mind. Nor did he fear the personal threats that increased every day. He was long accustomed to the midnight phone calls ("Listen, nigger . . . if you aren't out of this town in three days, we gonna blow your brains out.") and the crosses burned on his front lawn. His home had been bombed during the Montgomery Bus Boycott in 1956. In 1958 a lunatic stabbed him in the chest, and although the deadly seven-inch blade came close to piercing his heart, he survived. Then, in 1964 an airplane he boarded was ordered back to the terminal due to a bomb threat, but he had lived through that too.[38]

In the early days of King's career as the foremost spokesman for the civil rights movement, the possibility—indeed the likelihood—that he might be killed did frighten him. The apostle of nonviolence carried a gun and surrounded himself with bodyguards. But in a moment of emotional agony, he prayed, "Lord, I'm losing my courage"; he then heard what he believed was "the voice of Jesus" urging him to persevere and "stand up for truth [and] righteousness." Suddenly, his fear diminished and all doubt vanished. The next morning he told his parishioners, "I am not afraid of anybody."[39]

Nor was he especially anxious about the coming Selma campaign, although he knew it would be dangerous. "Somebody was going to get killed," he told his colleagues. But the cause was too important to turn back now.[40]

What King feared most was a personal scandal that threatened to destroy him along with the civil rights movement just at the moment that the movement hoped to win its most important victory: securing a guarantee of black Americans' voting rights.[41]

Movements like King's that challenged the existing social order especially worried the one Washington official who considered himself the guardian of domestic harmony: FBI director J. Edgar Hoover. For a time the fear of domestic Communism occupied his time, but now, in 1964, he became obsessed with the changes in racial relationships that the civil rights movement brought about. As early as the 1920s Hoover, then a young Justice Department official, had fought Black Nationalism; during World War II he had called Negroes a "seditious minded group." As King rose to prominence, so did the director's fears. When FBI surveillance of the movement in the late 1950s revealed that King's adviser Stanley Levison had once had Communist Party connections, Hoover's two great passions—anti-Communism and fighting black activism—combined to lead him into what eventually became a full-scale assault on King.[42]

By 1964 Hoover had become less concerned about King's political affiliations than about the shocking news his agents had discovered while tracking the reverend's recent travels: King apparently had a voracious sexual appetite that no number of women could satisfy. The Bureau's surveillance was all-encompassing: King's mail was opened, he was followed by agents equipped with cameras when he vacationed abroad, and listening devices were installed in his home, offices, and, if the FBI could gain admission first, in every hotel room in which he stayed. This most recent—and, to Hoover, most important—information had come from the bugs planted in King's room at Washington's Willard Hotel on January 7, 1964. They recorded what sounded like "a lively, drunken party involving King, several colleagues, and two women from Philadelphia."

To Hoover, the recordings offered solid evidence that King was depraved. The reality, of course, was more complicated. King often attracted women parishioners who were drawn to him like fans to an adored celebrity. King's career, with its constant travel as well as attendant dangers, strained his marriage and gave him the opportunity to indulge his desires, which he considered "a form of anxiety reduction."

Whatever pleasure King's philandering brought him, he also suffered greatly from the profound and tormenting guilt he felt about his betrayals.

He knew he was violating creeds he strongly believed in: morality and fidelity, to both his wife and the movement he cherished. "Each of us is two selves," he once sermonized. "And the great burden of life is to always try to keep that higher self in command. Don't let the lower self take over." But sometimes it did. "I make mistakes morally," he admitted, "and . . . ask God to forgive me. . . . There is a Mr. Hyde and Dr. Jekyll in us." King's struggle between his private and public lives may well explain the risks he took in the movement, for only in suffering was there redemption; saving the soul of America would, King may have hoped, win this sinner a place in the Kingdom of Heaven.[43]

The announcement on October 15, 1964, that King had won the Nobel Peace Prize did not lift his spirits. He thanked the Swedish officials and said that he would accept the honor at the ceremony in Oslo in December on behalf of the movement he led. "History has thrust me in this position," he said. "It would be both immoral and a sign of ingratitude if I did not face up to my moral responsibility to do what I can in this struggle."[44]

Hoover's reaction to King's award was incendiary. On a news clipping that carried the story, Hoover scrawled, "King could well qualify for the 'top alley cat prize.'" He also sent reports of King's philandering to the president, the attorney general, and other officials. On November 18 Hoover attacked King publicly for the first time, calling him "a notorious liar"; in private he told reporters that King was "one of the lowest characters in the country." Hoover's remarks stunned King. In response, he issued a sympathetic statement asserting that the director had "apparently faltered under the awesome . . . responsibilities of his office." Privately, FBI taps revealed King's true sentiments: Hoover, he told an aide, was "old and getting senile," and President Johnson should force him to retire.[45]

Hoping to repair their relationship, King met with Hoover on December 1, when the SCLC's plans for Selma were taking shape. Both men spoke past one another and never discussed what divided them. Further, while they talked, FBI officials offered derogatory information about King to a reporter who was waiting outside hoping for an interview. King also later learned that agents were even then visiting important journalists, offering them copies of King's FBI files for their use, so long as no one cited the Bureau as their source. "We're not a peephole journal," the *Atlanta Constitution*'s Eugene Patterson told the agent who approached him with the classified material. "What *you're* doing is the story . . . the federal police force . . . doing this to an individual citizen." Surprisingly, there were no takers, and King's activities remained secret.[46]

Just as serious as its ongoing efforts to malign King in the media was the malicious plan the Bureau hatched even before King's meeting with Hoover. FBI assistant director William Sullivan decided that the FBI could use King's own voice to destroy him. Officials prepared a tape recording of his various assignations accompanied by an anonymous letter urging King to kill himself. The FBI called it "the suicide package." They gave it to a veteran FBI agent, who flew to Miami, where he mailed the box to King at SCLC headquarters in Atlanta. With any luck it would arrive in time for Thanksgiving, hopefully spoiling what the Bureau anticipated would be the last holiday King would ever celebrate.[47]

But the FBI had miscalculated. The package, which appeared to contain a reel of tape, joined the many other cards and letters that normally piled up at the SCLC office every month. Eventually an aide delivered it and the other mail to the King home, where it lay unopened—for the time being.

What should have been a glorious occasion—the December 1964 trip to Europe to receive the Nobel Prize—was, for King, an agonizing time. "Only Martin's family and close staff members knew how depressed he was during the entire Nobel Trip," Coretta Scott King later recalled. "He was worried that the rumors might hurt the movement and he was concerned about what black people would think. . . . We had to work with him and help him out of his depression. Somehow he managed all the official functions, the speeches, the whole trip and the public never knew what he was going through." In Oslo he accepted the Nobel Peace Prize on behalf of the movement's foot soldiers, who he described as the "humble children of God [who] were willing to suffer for righteousness' sake."[48]

King's private sufferings notwithstanding, his selection for the Nobel Prize marked an outpouring of support for him and the civil rights movement both abroad and in the United States. At thirty-five King was the youngest man to win the prize and only the second African American. Many of his countrymen—white and black—took pride in his achievement. New York celebrated King's return to America with fire boats in the East River, dinner at the Waldorf-Astoria Hotel with Governor Nelson Rockefeller and Vice President-elect Hubert Humphrey, and a "Martin Luther King Night" at the Harlem Armory.[49]

King's visit to Washington at President Johnson's invitation on December 18 was less extravagant, a reflection of the president's ambivalent feelings for the preacher. Given Johnson's Texas-size ego and insecurities, there was little room for others on the national stage. He resented the international attention King was receiving and complained to aides that his own efforts, like winning congressional passage of Kennedy's Civil Rights Bill, went unappreciated. He disliked demonstrations and resented being pressured by the young black activists who had the nerve to picket his White House. He also feared that developing a close relationship with King—in light of Hoover's discoveries— might tarnish him in the eyes of the American people, although he permitted the FBI director to disseminate his vicious reports on King throughout the government.

The president would have preferred working with other, more conservative civil rights leaders like Roy Wilkins and Whitney Young, who Johnson called "team players." Still fresh in his mind were those activists who had caused him trouble during the recent presidential campaign, like CORE's James Farmer, who had refused his request to call off demonstrations that Johnson thought would only help the Republicans. And black Mississippians had created a more serious threat to party unity when they organized the Mississippi Freedom Democratic Party and hoped to unseat the regular segregationist delegation at the 1964 Democratic National Convention. Johnson had feared that if the all-white delegation was ousted, Texas and Georgia delegates would walk out, creating a backlash that would cost him other southern states in the fall. "The only thing that can really screw us good is to seat that group of challengers from Mississippi," Johnson told Walter Reuther, president of the United Auto Workers. "Now there's not a damn vote we can get by seating these folks." Johnson had ordered Senator Hubert Humphrey, beloved by the civil rights community, to forge a compromise that, in the end, pleased neither side but nonetheless avoided the disunity that an always-anxious Johnson believed might cost him the election. For the domineering Johnson, loyalty came first, and Farmer and the Mississippians had made it clear that the movement had other priorities besides fealty to the White House.[50]

Although King had never been as openly rebellious as those detested groups, Johnson remained suspicious of the reverend. Because of this, their visit was a hurried affair, with Johnson doing most of the talking. After showing

King some cherished Johnson family heirlooms, the president launched into a monologue about how much he was doing for black America. His War on Poverty would go a long way to relieve black suffering. "Now what's Georgia doing?" Johnson asked. "You ought to get back down there and get them to work." His next destination was Selma, Alabama, King replied, where the movement would fight for voting rights. He hoped that the president would support his efforts by immediately sending a voting rights bill to Congress.

"Martin . . . I'm going to do it eventually, but I can't get voting rights through in this session of Congress," Johnson said. He explained that Congress and the country needed time to adjust to the recent passage of the 1964 Act. Acting precipitously on voting rights would alienate southern legislators, whose votes Johnson needed to pass his Great Society initiatives. The president hoped that programs like Medicare, aid to education, and antipoverty measures would win him a place in history as the greatest president, greater even than his beloved Franklin Delano Roosevelt. He was quick to remind King that these programs would aid blacks too—and would be more difficult to get through Congress if the more controversial and divisive voting rights bill came first.

Voting rights was as important as anything else on the president's agenda, King asserted, but Johnson continued to disagree. "I can't get it through," he insisted. "It's just not the wise and the politically expedient thing to do."

"We'll just have to do the best we can," replied a disappointed King, who then departed the White House for a flight to Atlanta.[51]

Actually, things were not as bleak as Johnson suggested. He had been considering a voting rights bill as early as July 1964, following the passage of Kennedy's Civil Rights Act. Johnson's team was not pleased, however. Exhausted by the long struggle, they looked forward to a rest from such contentious issues. But Johnson was just getting started. After signing the bill on July 2 he told a shocked Acting Attorney General Nicholas Katzenbach, "I want you to write me the goddamndest, toughest voting rights act that you can devise." It must also be constitutional and effective. "I could have shot him," Katzenbach later said. "I was so tired of being down in the halls of Congress on the '64 act." But the president had no intention of resting on his laurels after the Civil Rights Act passed. Johnson was "hell bent to get every piece of civil rights legislation he could get," remembered Larry O'Brien, Johnson's chief legislative strategist.[52]

In part, Johnson's personal history can explain his zeal for civil rights. Early in Johnson's career, as a Texas representative and senator, he consistently voted with the southerners who opposed antilynching legislation, a Fair Employment Practices Commission, and other civil rights programs. But as his presidential ambitions grew, he knew he had to carefully separate himself from his old friends. He did not sign the Southern Manifesto attacking the Supreme Court's *Brown* decision, and as majority leader, he worked to pass the 1957 Civil Rights Act, the first since Reconstruction. That act created a Civil Rights Division in the Justice Department and a Civil Rights Commission to investigate national voting practices. Further, it empowered the attorney general to punish anyone who interfered or prohibited any citizen from exercising the franchise. The 1957 Civil Rights Act seemed like a step forward, but Johnson, while steering it through the Senate, had weakened its provisions so as not to alienate southerners completely. His attitude toward civil rights seemed to grow more sympathetic in the next few years, however. As Kennedy's vice president he often privately criticized the president's reluctance to commit himself to the black cause. Johnson was always torn between his compassion for the underdog and his political ambitions. As president, in 1964 these two inclinations fused when he moved actively to pass Kennedy's Civil Rights Act, which was lodged in Congress. And a voting rights bill was always on his mind as well. "I initiated . . . the voting rights [bill] myself, nobody else did," he later claimed.[53]

Johnson's landslide victory over Republican senator Barry Goldwater on November 3, 1964, also intensified his desire to push for reform. Democrats now dominated the House of Representatives, 295 to 140, as well as the Senate, 68 to 32—the largest majorities since FDR was president. Following the election Johnson excitedly told an aide that "We can pass it all now." Everything liberal Democrats had wanted for decades—medical care for the elderly, federal aid to education, help for the crumbling cities, and more—now seemed possible, even inevitable.

But the 1964 election brought bad as well as good news. The South, once the most reliably Democratic section of the country, was beginning to drift away from the party. Goldwater had narrowly won more white votes than Johnson had in ten former Confederate states, except Johnson's home state of Texas. And in states where civil rights workers were the most active—Alabama and Mississippi—Johnson won only 13 percent and 31 percent of the popular vote, respectively. Alabama, Mississippi, and Georgia elected Republicans to Congress for the first time in sixty-five years.

How could such Democratic losses in the South be offset? The election results were clear here too. It had been black votes that brought victory for Johnson in Arkansas, Florida, Tennessee, Virginia, and perhaps North Carolina. Without those black votes the South could go Republican in future presidential elections. If, however, more black voters were registered and they continued to vote Democratic, then Larry O'Brien believed that the GOP's success could be limited to Alabama and Mississippi, which were probably lost to the Democrats forever because of the party's support for civil rights.[54]

Johnson was again thinking about voting rights on December 14, just four days before his secret meeting with King. That was when he told a surprised Katzenbach to begin to draft a bill secretly. There must be "a simple, effective way of getting 'em registered," Johnson insisted. Katzenbach disagreed; he thought it would take a constitutional amendment to do the job, as the Constitution gave the states the authority to define voting qualifications, a stipulation ostensibly protecting the states that were systematically disenfranchising black voters. "Let's find some way," the president said, urging his acting attorney general to think big. "Get me some things you'd be proud of, to show your boy, and say, 'Here is what your daddy put through in nineteen sixty-four-five-six-seven.'"

Katzenbach sent the president a list of options on December 28. Johnson was surely dismayed to see that the creation of a new law was at the bottom of the list, indicating that it was the least desirable choice. Katzenbach, a cautious, conservative lawyer, still felt that a constitutional amendment would be necessary to alter the time-honored tradition of allowing states to determine their own voting requirements. Such an amendment, he proposed, would require that registrants be twenty-one years of age, be residents of their state for a short time, and have no record of incarceration or confinement in a mental institution. Literacy tests and poll taxes would be eliminated. Although amending the Constitution might be the most "drastic choice," wrote Katzenbach, he thought it the most "effective"—although opposition was a certainty. Furthermore, its passage would take at least two years, and it needed only thirteen state legislatures to vote no to defeat it.[55]

The second option Katzenbach put forward would create a new government agency to supervise registration only in federal elections, whereas the last, the one Katzenbach called "least desirable," would permit an existing agency to control registration in *all* elections—local, state, and federal. The final option, a new law, Katzenbach noted, "would quickly provide political power to Negroes." Its constitutionality, however, was doubtful, and Republicans had opposed such an approach when the Kennedy administration considered it in 1963. Even if Johnson could get it through Congress, it would not likely survive a legal challenge.[56]

Other aides were also urging the president to be cautious. White House counsel Lee White believed that, given the recent passage of the 1964 Act after a long southern filibuster, it would be wise to wait before becoming embroiled in another controversial congressional struggle. Also, because the 1964 Act prohibited the unequal application of voting requirements and extended the investigative power of the Civil Rights Commission, that act should serve to alleviate the voting injustices in the South for the time being. Pending lawsuits in several southern states might also lessen the need for immediate action. If new legislation was required, it could be submitted in 1966, when the majority of the president's Great Society measures would have passed, and a safe amount of time would have elapsed since the passage of the Civil Rights Act.[57]

Torn between his desires and constitutional and political realities, Johnson wavered. He had ordered his staff to prepare a voting rights bill, and the possibility of seeking a constitutional amendment remained an option, albeit one Johnson preferred to avoid. For now, while Justice Department lawyers worked their way through this tangled thicket, voting rights would take a backseat to Johnson's other objectives. Above all, he was intent on doing things his way. If there was to be a voting rights bill, it would be Lyndon Johnson's, and it would come at a time and place of his choosing.[58]

THREE

"GIVE US THE BALLOT!"

ONCE AGAIN, MARTIN LUTHER KING JR. WAS THINKING OF DEATH. IT WAS January 2, 1965, and King, driving from Atlanta to Selma with his close friend Ralph Abernathy, reflected on his past brushes with mortality and those that lay ahead. "You know, I had the feeling I was going to be killed in Mississippi," Abernathy later recalled King saying. "I was certain of it. Fortunately, it didn't happen. But I'm sure it will be in Selma. This is the time and place."

King told Abernathy, SCLC's vice president, that he wanted Abernathy to assume the presidency of the organization if he died. Abernathy, who was accustomed to King's morbidity, shrugged off the request as impractical. Because they were almost inseparable, he too would likely lose his life along with King. But King insisted, and Abernathy, hoping to change the subject, agreed.[1]

It was snowing lightly when they arrived at their first stop in Selma, the home of Sullivan Jackson, the city's only African American dentist, who always provided King with a place to stay, food to eat, and even clothes to wear during his trips to Selma. There, the two men met with old acquaintances and rested briefly until leaving for King's sole event that day, a celebration of the 102nd anniversary of the Emancipation Proclamation at Brown Chapel A.M.E. Church and the opening of King's campaign for voting rights in Alabama.[2]

As King and Abernathy neared their destination, the headquarters of the voting rights movement in Selma, they saw police cars parked at both ends of Sylvan Street, flanking the church. They wondered if the police were there to arrest them for violating Judge James Hare's blacklist that prohibited them from gathering together in a group. But nobody bothered them. As they entered the building, they could hear singing, clapping, and loud, boisterous music. The crowd, later estimated at seven hundred, had filled the chapel to see King. He was greeted with a burst of applause and received a standing ovation as he took the pulpit.

He had come to Selma, King told his audience, because American democracy was in peril: it did not exist for America's "22 million black children," many of them mature adults who, despite their rights as citizens, could not vote. His listeners were familiar with the obstacles Alabama placed in their way: the Board of Registrars, located in the Dallas County Courthouse, opened only twice a month, and its staff usually arrived late, took long lunches, left early, and almost always ignored black visitors. Their oral and written tests were so complicated that not even the most brilliant teachers at Tuskegee Institute could pass them. And if that failed to dissuade black applicants, intimidation and violence were used against those who showed up to apply.

King told his audience that he had come to join their fight against the injustices in their city. "Today marks the beginning of a determined, organized, mobilized campaign to get the right to vote everywhere in Alabama," he said, and the people cheered with an intensity that shook the building. "If we are refused, we will appeal to Governor George Wallace. If he refuses to listen, we will appeal to the legislature. If they don't listen, we will appeal to the conscience of the Congress in another dramatic march on Washington." His voice rose as he challenged them to march and "be willing to go to jail by the thousands." Drawing on the speech that he delivered at the Lincoln Memorial on May 17, 1957, he said, "Our cry to the state of Alabama is a simple one, 'Give us the ballot!'"

"That's right!" they yelled back, everyone now on their feet.

"When we get the right to vote we will send to the statehouse not men who will stand in the doorways of universities to keep Negroes out, but men who will uphold the cause of justice: Give us the ballot!"

They were all with him now as he repeated the phrase again and again, crying out, "Speak! Speak!"

"We are not on our knees begging for the ballot," he concluded. "We are demanding the ballot! . . . We will bring a voting bill into being on the streets of Selma!"

Martin Luther King Jr. addressing a Selma audience on January 2, 1965. King's re-peated admonition "Give Us the Ballot!" marked the official beginning of the voting rights crusade. © HORACE CORTY/AP/AP/CORBIS

"It's time," the people agreed. "Yes! Yes!" Then everyone linked arms and sang, "We Shall Overcome," providing the opportunity for three white observers, a state trooper and two deputy sheriffs, to slip out of the room unseen.[3]

King had shown that he was ready to join the voting rights struggle in Selma, just as Bernard Lafayette and James Forman had done before him. King's day was not over, however—he still had work to do. Before leaving Selma he met with reporters and later held a long strategy session with Amelia Boynton and other colleagues. John Lewis, representing SNCC, was there. This pleased King, as he was hoping to avoid the internal antagonisms that threatened to tear the movement apart. King's old aide, Jim Bevel, was present as well. He and Hosea Williams, a decorated World War II veteran and another member of King's inner circle, would be responsible for finding people willing to participate in the first march on Freedom Day, another voter-registration event like the one Jim Forman had organized in Selma in the fall of 1963. The date for the demonstration was set for just over two weeks away, on January 18, when the Board of Registrars would reopen for business.

Having helped to lay the groundwork for Freedom Day, King and his colleagues departed Selma. They were now part of a motorcade. Following them were FBI agents and Alabama law enforcement officers. If one were white, their presence might have been reassuring. In King's case, however, it was not.[4]

PUBLICIZING FREEDOM DAY WAS DIFFICULT. BECAUSE THE CITY HAD NO newspapers, radio stations, or television stations targeted at the black community, Jim Bevel and his staff took to the streets. Workers were assigned to each of the city's five election wards, where, in pairs, they passed out leaflets and encouraged folks to attend meetings on January 7. Mustering voters in each ward would be essential to effecting political change in Selma—once, of course, enough of its black voters succeeded in registering. "If we can get out and work," Bevel told them, "Jim Clark will be out picking cotton with my father."[5]

As usual, they found that older citizens were unwilling to join them. One elderly woman confessed that she had never heard of voting, and when they described its benefits—electing men who would see that their streets were paved and the garbage collected—she said it was just too dangerous for her to become involved. Others took the leaflets quickly and said, "Yeah," obviously hoping to get rid of the civil rights workers before the police arrived.[6]

But Bevel and Williams were eloquent and persuasive speakers, and on occasion they shocked their listeners into action. At a youth rally that attracted two hundred students, Williams said, "If you can't vote, then you're not free. And if you ain't free, children, then you're a slave." And when Sheriff Jim Clark's deputies showed up at a meeting at Brown Chapel, Bevel wasn't intimidated; instead, he commanded them to leave immediately and even yelled at one who tried to take his picture, both acts riveting an audience unaccustomed to seeing Clark's troops follow a black man's orders. "Things are starting to move here," a volunteer from California wrote his parents. Bevel, Williams, and the other SCLC and SNCC workers were becoming cautiously optimistic that Freedom Day would be a success.[7]

King's troops were unaware, however, that the greatest danger to Freedom Day—and to the civil rights movement itself—came not from black apathy or from Sheriff Clark's brutality but rather from the FBI's war against King. On January 5, while going through the mail that had accumulated over the Christmas holidays, Coretta Scott King opened a box containing a spool of tape and a letter. Believing that the tape was a recording of one of Martin's speeches, she played it. She heard men laughing and sounds that seemed unmistakably sexual. Shocked and confused, she turned to the letter, which read,

> KING,
>
> In view of your low grade . . . I will not dignify your name with either a Mr. or a Reverend or a Dr. And, your last name calls to mind only the type of King such as King Henry the VIII. . . .
>
> King, look into your own heart. You know you are a complete fraud. And a great liability to all of us Negroes. . . . You are no clergyman and you know it. . . . You could not believe in God. . . . Clearly you don't believe in any moral principles.
>
> King, like all frauds your end is approaching. You could have been our greatest leader. You, even at an early age have turned out to be not a leader but a dissolute, abnormal moral imbecile. We will now have to depend on our older leaders like Wilkins a man of character and thank God we have others like him. But you are done. . . . Satan could not do more. What an incredible evilness. . . .
>
> The American public, the church organizations, that have been helping—Protestant, Catholic and Jews will know you for what you are—an evil, abnormal beast. So will others who have backed you. . . .
>
> King, there is only one thing left for you to do. You know what this is. . . . You better take it before your filthy, abnormal fraudulent self is bared to the nation.[8]

Mrs. King was aware of her husband's philandering, but she seemed to accept it gracefully: "If I ever had any suspicions . . . I never would have mentioned them to Martin," she later noted. "I just wouldn't have burdened him with anything so trivial." She was less concerned about the tape than the threatening letter. She immediately called her husband, who summoned his friends Ralph Abernathy, Andrew Young, Joseph Lowery, and his father, the Reverend Martin Luther King Sr. They listened to the tape and heard King teasing Abernathy along with "big, deep belly laughs"—so that part of the tape was authentic. As for the erotic noises, Young did not think it sounded like King. "Martin had a distinctive voice," Young later wrote, "and it certainly wasn't his."[9]

King was stunned but knew immediately the source of this cruelty. The box was postmarked Miami, but of course it had originated in Washington, DC. He realized that the Bureau had him under close surveillance and possessed material that could destroy him. "They are out to get me, harass me, break my spirit," he told friends in telephone conversations the FBI recorded, but he admitted that he was the author of his own misery. Whether he recognized the recording from his night at Washington's Willard Hotel roughly a year before or he simply accepted that his infidelity had opened him up to this sort of attack, the reverend appeared resigned to his fate.

Confronting the FBI about the recordings did no good. Andrew Young and Ralph Abernathy agreed to meet with Hoover; however, the director passed them on to his assistant, Cartha "Deke" DeLoach, who flatly denied that the FBI had King under surveillance, claiming that his personal life was of no concern to the agency. The trip, Abernathy later wrote, was "a waste of time and money."[10]

Those closest to King feared that he was on the brink of a nervous breakdown. He believed that the spool of tape was "a warning from God," a sign that the Almighty Himself knew that King wasn't "living up to his responsibilities." He became an insomniac, and the Bureau did all it could to exacerbate his suffering. When King tried to steal a few hours of sleep at a safe house, the FBI learned its location and called the local fire department, which sent engines, their sirens screaming, to disturb his rest.[11]

The FBI's latest outrage probably made King more determined than ever to launch the Selma campaign. He returned briefly to the city on Thursday, January 14, to announce new plans for Freedom Day. The events scheduled for that Monday, January 18, would now include not only a march on the courthouse in Selma but also similar actions in ten rural counties as well as an investigation of local restaurants and hotels to determine if they were now open to blacks as the 1964 Civil Rights Act required. King himself planned to request a room at the Hotel Albert, an Italian-like palace built by slaves. And black workers would apply for city jobs reserved for only whites to see if the city's government still used discriminatory hiring practices.[12]

The day after King announced the expanded agenda for Freedom Day was the reverend's thirty-sixth birthday, and he was happily surprised when Lyndon Johnson telephoned to congratulate him and express enthusiasm for voting rights. "[It] will answer [most] of your problems," he told King. "There's not going to be anything . . . as effective as all of them voting."

"That's right," King replied.

Johnson ran through some possible options for how the federal government could help to reform voting registration in the South. "No tests on what Chaucer said or Browning's poetry or constitutions. . . . We may have to put [voter registration] in the post office. Let the postmaster [do it]. That's a federal employee that I can control. . . . If he doesn't register everybody, I can put a new one in. . . . They can all just go to the post office like they buy a stamp. . . . I just don't see how anybody can say that a man can fight in Vietnam but he can't vote in the post office." No politician, wherever he lived, could ignore the interest and desires of people who could vote.

Johnson also offered some specific suggestions about how King and his fellow activists could get the American people on their side. The president suggested that the best way to build public support was to find the worst example of "voter discrimination where a man got to memorize Longfellow or . . . quote the first ten amendments . . . and if you just take that one illustration and get it on the radio, and get it on the television, and get it in the pulpits . . . pretty soon, [ordinary Southerners] will say, 'That's not right. That's not fair.'"

For his part, King reminded Johnson of the political advantages the president stood to gain from helping black southerners to cast their votes freely. "The only states you didn't carry in the South [in 1964] . . . have less than 40 percent of the Negroes registered to vote," King told the president. "It's so important to get Negroes registered to vote in large numbers in the South. It would be this coalition of the Negro vote and the moderate white vote that will really make the new South." King's message was unmistakable: if Johnson could ensure that black southerners were able to register and vote, their resulting support at the polls would give him tremendous political power.

"That's exactly right," Johnson said. But then, having raised King's hopes that he would move swiftly to shore up African Americans' voting rights, he dashed them. His first priorities, he said, remained aid to education, the war on poverty, and Medicare. "We've got to get them passed," Johnson told King, "before the evil forces concentrate and ... block them." Once these goals were accomplished, he could turn to voting rights. For the already-harried King, who had been intending for the upcoming Freedom Day demonstrations to inspire action in Washington, the president's remarks could not have been more poorly timed.[13]

WHILE KING WAS PLANNING FOR FREEDOM DAY, HIS ADVERSARIES HAD been making preparations of their own. Wilson Baker, the newly appointed public safety director for Selma, had been carefully considering his options about how to direct the official response to Freedom Day. Baker knew that King would be powerless without a violent—and well-publicized—confrontation with segregationist forces that would capture the public's attention and pressure Congress and President Johnson to act. Baker hoped to emulate Laurie Pritchett, the affable police chief of Albany, Georgia, who, after studying the reverend's tactics, had decided to respond nonviolently when King came to Albany in December 1961. The chief treated demonstrators with civility, and when King himself was jailed for parading without a permit and similar charges, he ordered the cell cleaned and supplied his prisoner with a radio and plenty of reading material. "We killed them with kindness," said an Albany official after King's campaign there had failed and he had left the city. Baker hoped to achieve the same result in Selma. For his plan to work, however, he would need Sheriff Jim Clark to cooperate. So Baker and Mayor Joseph Smitherman met with Clark and managed to persuade him to control himself and his posse during the Freedom Day demonstrations.[14]

As it turned out, Freedom Day was more of a success for Baker than it was for King. The public safety director met King and four hundred volunteers as they walked to the courthouse on the cold Monday morning and warned them that if they didn't rearrange their ranks he would arrest them for parading without a permit. King complied. At the courthouse, where Clark claimed jurisdiction, they found the sheriff awaiting them, billy club at the ready. But Clark only led the group to an alley where they were told to wait for the registrar to summon them. They had waited for several hours "feeling like caged rats," Abernathy recalled, when King decided to visit the Hotel Albert to see if he could become the first Negro to rent a room. Aber-

nathy, John Lewis, and Wilson Baker also went along to observe this potentially historic event.

He was received cordially at the luxurious hotel, but then a muscular
white youth suddenly pushed Abernathy aside and punched King in the
head. When King fell to the floor, the youth kicked him in the thigh. John
Lewis grappled with the man, and Baker quickly subdued and arrested him.
He was Jimmy George Robinson, a member of the fanatical National State
Rights Party, which had come to Selma to harass King.

Abernathy and Dorothy Cotton, King's secretary, helped him to his feet.
He appeared unharmed but stunned, so aides hurried him to his room. "He
packs a pretty good wallop," King said, mopping the sweat off his face and
sipping a can of beer. Mrs. King later said that her husband complained of "a
terrible headache" that lasted several days.[15]

That night King told his advisers to increase the pressure. On Tuesday,
January 19, fifty volunteers would refuse to stand in the alley, hoping that
would produce the violent incident that would arouse the conscience of the
nation. If not, they might have to try a new approach, such as moving to
other nearby cities like Marion or Camden, where not a single black was registered. The fight for Selma, it appeared, was faltering.

WILSON BAKER MUST HAVE FELT GOOD AS HE PREPARED FOR BED ON
Monday night. His strategy was working. Any satisfaction, however, surely
evaporated when he received a call from Mayor Smitherman. Come to the
county jail now, the mayor told Baker. There was trouble.[16]

It was Clark. The sheriff had become unhinged, telling Baker that he was
"giving the city away to the niggers" and that his posse was about to mutiny.
Tomorrow he would arrest "every goddamned" demonstrator who came to
the courthouse, Baker remembered him saying. Baker and Smitherman
pleaded with him to remain cool for just a few more days, but the angry sheriff would not listen.[17]

On Tuesday morning Clark got his revenge. When sixty-seven marchers
arrived at the courthouse, he ordered them to take their places in the alley,
and when they refused, he arrested them all on charges of unlawful assembly. Amelia Boynton, long a thorn in his side, received harsher treatment
than did her comrades. While Clark's men corralled the other demonstrators, the sheriff dragged Boynton down the street to a waiting police car. The

other demonstrators called out to her, "Go on, Mrs. Boynton, you don't have to be in jail by yourself, we'll be there." Pointing to reporters and cameramen, she told Clark, "I hope the newspapers see you acting this role." Clark replied, "Damnit, I hope they do." And they did. The following day, in their coverage of the day's events, the *New York Times* and the *Washington Post* featured a front-page photograph of Clark manhandling Boynton.[18]

At the police station Boynton was charged with criminal provocation. Clark later claimed that she had ordered the marchers "to take over the offices and to . . . urinate on top of the desks and throw the books on the floor." She was fingerprinted, photographed, and thrown into a cell, where she sat alone, feeling like a common criminal. Then she heard the demonstrators arriving in the jail: the old walking with difficulty up the stairs, the young skipping, everyone singing loudly. As they passed her cell, one said, "I told you we would be here with you," and Boynton immediately felt better.[19]

By the end of the day the demonstrators were freed thanks to the efforts of SCLC lawyers, who came to Selma to arrange for their release. Boynton and the others were honored that night at a rally at Brown Chapel, where Reverend Abernathy recommended that the Voters League make Sheriff Clark an honorary member of their group in recognition of everything he was doing to publicize their struggle to vote. The audience agreed enthusiastically.[20]

The demonstrations and arrests continued on Wednesday and Thursday, but Friday, January 22, was an unforgettable day for Selma's black community. It began first as a rumor, then by late afternoon rumor became fact as the news spread like wildfire: "The teachers are marching! The teachers are marching!" They were indeed: 105 black men and women—nearly every teacher in Selma—dressed impeccably, with the women wearing "flowery hats and gloves" and the men in "somber colored suits and hats," the journalist Charles Fager later recalled. Many were happily waving toothbrushes, signaling their commitment to spend the night in jail if necessary. Their students and parents cheered and wept as the teachers strode confidently down Sylvan Street to the courthouse. "This is bigger than Lyndon Johnson coming to town!" exclaimed one black reporter.[21]

Leading the teachers were the Reverend Frederick Reese, a science teacher and president of the Dallas County Voters League, and Andrew J. Durgan, the new president of the Selma Teachers' Association. Earlier that week Reese had written the Board of Registrars, asking them to open their office, usually closed on Friday, but the Board refused: to do so would violate Alabama law, they claimed. Reese was himself registered, but many of his colleagues, including some with advanced degrees, had been repeatedly rejected without cause. He had asked them over and over, "How can you teach citizenship [when] you're not a first-class citizen yourself?"

Never in the history of the movement in Alabama had teachers participated in such numbers. Economically, they had the most to lose from speaking out, much less joining a demonstration; the members of the local school boards that employed them and the superintendents who supervised them were white men capable of firing them for the slightest infraction. And sure enough, as Reese and the others approached the courthouse steps, there stood Joseph Pickard, the superintendent of schools, and Edgar Stewart, chairman of the Selma School Board. Stewart warned them that entering the courthouse was illegal. "You are in danger of losing all of the gains you have made," he said. Reese thought this ridiculous. After all, people entered the courthouse every day to pay their taxes, and the building belonged to the teachers as much as it did to Jim Clark and the chairman of the school board. "We want to see for ourselves if the Board is open," Reese said, and by twos, the teachers climbed the steps to the courthouse door.

As the teachers approached it, the glass door swung open, and Clark and five deputies appeared. "You can't make a playhouse out of the corridors of this courthouse," the sheriff yelled. He gave the teachers one minute to leave. Suddenly the door opened again, and Blanchard McLeod, the circuit solicitor, pulled Clark back inside, leaving his men behind. A moment later Clark returned and again ordered them to move back. A deputy began counting off the seconds. Then the sheriff and his deputies moved forward, their billy clubs forcing the teachers back down the stairs. Clark and his men returned to the courthouse door, but turning around, again found themselves facing Reese and his colleagues. Stewart warned them off. "The sheriff is custodian of this courthouse," said the school board chairman, "and he has been most forbearing." Stewart urged them to retreat. They did not, and again Clark and his men pushed them down the steps.

At that moment Reese realized that Solicitor McLeod must have told Clark not to jail Selma's teachers and that Clark, perhaps fearing that the teachers' incarceration would have left young black children free to run wild in the streets, was obeying. Without the possibility of arrest and without being able to enter the courthouse peacefully, the demonstrators were stymied. So Reese and his colleagues turned around and marched to Brown Chapel, where they received a hero's welcome. "The place erupted into a tumultuous cacophony of cheers and applause," said one observer, "an ovation that continued until the last of the [teachers] had assembled around the pulpit. Behind them veteran civil rights workers wept at the spectacle and teachers and students both joined them, the teachers overcome by a wave of self-respect and unrestrained admiration from their students that they had never experienced before." Andrew Young called the day "the most significant thing that has happened in the racial movement since Birmingham."[22]

Although the teachers' march and the demonstrations preceding it were emotionally satisfying, they had accomplished little in the way of advancing the movement's goals. More than two thousand protestors had been arrested, but not a single person had been registered to vote. Nor had Clark's brutality moved the president to announce that he would soon be submitting a new voting rights bill to Congress. In order to appease King and alleviate some of the pressure he was feeling from civil rights activists, the president had already mentioned such an initiative in his State of the Union message on January 4, but he buried it under an avalanche of other proposals. Adding to the sense of stagnation was federal judge Daniel Thomas's temporary order, released on January 23, the day after the teachers' march. Thomas's order restrained Dallas County officials like Jim Clark from interfering with voter registration. This was not, however, the victory for the movement that it seemed. Although his order was aimed at Clark, Judge Thomas also blamed civil rights workers for the disruptions that had occurred. Frustrations were intensifying on both sides.[23]

Annie Lee Cooper, for one, was losing patience. The fifty-three-year-old Alabamian had no trouble voting when she lived in Kentucky, Pennsylvania, and Ohio, but when she returned to Selma in 1962 to care for her ailing mother, she became a second-class citizen. She tried to register several times, including one fateful day in 1964. While waiting in a long line at the courthouse, she was spotted by Dr. Dunn, owner of the nursing home where Cooper worked and a diehard segregationist. Dunn was jotting down the names of would-be registrants in a notebook, and he glared at Cooper when he saw her. The next day he fired her. Eventually she got another job as night manager at Selma's Torch Motel—and continued her efforts to register.[24]

On Monday, January 25, Cooper joined the protestors in line at the courthouse, again hoping to register. As she waited, she heard a noise behind her—a policeman was beating an activist. Cooper moved for a better look, then cried out, "He's kicking him!" A woman nearby told her to be quiet. "We're not in slavery time here," Annie Lee Cooper replied. "Nobody's afraid of them."

Suddenly Sheriff Clark appeared and pushed Cooper with a force that almost knocked her down. "Don't jerk me like that," she snapped. Clark backhanded her. She reared up and punched Clark in the eye, then punched him again. Stunned, Clark fell back and yelled to his deputies nearby, "You see this nigger woman! Do something!" One grabbed her from behind, but she continued to resist until she was free. She again lunged at Clark, hitting him a third time.

At 220 pounds, Cooper's blows nearly had the sheriff on the ground. It took three deputies to subdue and handcuff her. But she had enough strength left for one final taunt: "I wish you would hit me, you scum," she yelled at Clark. The sheriff, now disheveled, his cap, tie, and badge torn away during the struggle, whacked her on the head with his club, the impact making a drumlike sound that reverberated down the street.

Clark himself drove Cooper to jail, on the way repeatedly asking, "How much is that damned Martin Luther King paying you?" She spent eleven hours in a cell, nursing her wounds and singing spirituals while Clark drank himself into a stupor. Near midnight the jailer, fearful that the drunken sheriff might actually kill her, let her go.

Clark's brutality had given the movement the opening it had been waiting for. The next morning the *New York Times* ran a photograph on its front page showing Mrs. Cooper being held on the ground by two deputies while she and Sheriff Clark grappled for his billy club. Yet the incident prompted no national outcry, and signals from Washington were discouraging. King had heard nothing from Johnson after his birthday phone call, and there had been no mention of a voting rights bill in the president's inaugural address on January 20. There were only vague press reports that the Justice Department was preparing a constitutional amendment prohibiting literacy tests, but its passage was far off and uncertain. Worse still, the *New York Times* was reporting that the movement in Selma had reached a dead end.[25]

King's top aides decided that it was time to up the ante. The reverend himself must go to jail. If that didn't produce the crisis King needed, the movement would go to Perry and Wilcox Counties, where blacks lived under conditions that approximated slavery and white officials were even more brutal than Clark. "It was midnight in Selma," King told his followers on January 31. They would do whatever was necessary to secure the right to vote. "If Negroes could vote," he told his audience, "there would be no Jim Clarks, there would be no oppressive poverty directed against Negroes, our children would not be crippled by segregated schools, and the whole community might live together in harmony." In order to make that vision a reality, he would march with them in the morning.[26]

It was bitterly cold on the morning of February 1, 1965, so King and more than 260 of his followers donned coats, hats, and muffs for the march from Brown Chapel to the courthouse. They walked together down the center of Sylvan Street, and Wilson Baker quickly arrested them for parading without a permit. Most were released on bond later that day, but King and Ralph Abernathy declined and remained imprisoned in an eight-foot cell. In addition to fasting, praying, and reading the Bible, King also drafted orders for SCLC executive director Andrew Young, designed "to keep national attention focused on Selma." Baker visited the reverend in jail to express concern about the children who had just joined the demonstrations and were being arrested. Because the jail was overflowing, the children were being sent to state prison farms. King told him that they deserved to "make witness" too.[27]

King's arrest produced front-page headlines in the nation's most prominent papers, and the three television networks covered it. More journalists hurried to Selma. Fifteen congressmen from New York, Michigan, and California, sympathetic to the cause, also announced that they would soon meet with King. Governors sent messages of support. Even President Johnson, who had lately been so reticent about the voting rights struggle, told a press conference, "All of us should be concerned with the efforts of our fellow Americans to register to vote in Alabama. I intend to see that the right [to vote] is secured for all our Americans." But, Johnson added, he would use the authority he already possessed under existing laws; he said nothing about the possibility of new legislation to guarantee black voters' rights.[28]

The movement seemed to have won another victory on February 1, when Judge Daniel Thomas issued a judicial order that appeared to solve the Selma problem. Henceforth, city and state officials must stop harassing those who wished to register, the judge commanded. The complicated test of an applicant's knowledge of government would also be eliminated. Registrars must process at least one hundred applicants on the days they were open, and everything must be completed by July 1. Failure to do so would result in a federal registrar being brought to Selma.[29]

Judge Thomas's order created confusion in King's camp. Although the order eliminated many of the obstacles to black voters in Selma, it still left the registration process in the hands of local officials at the courthouse run by Clark, who was sure to thwart any black applicants' attempts to register. Andrew Young was disappointed and said that demonstrations would continue. By way of explanation, he added, "We are so emotionally caught up in the moment that it is hard for us to be objective. We feel that we can have very little faith in this unless something is done about Jim Clark." Asked for King's response, Young said, "He would like to think about it overnight." But as a sign of good faith, Young canceled the demonstrations scheduled for that day.[30]

King was angry and criticized Young's decision to halt the demonstrations. "Nothing has been done to get Judge Hare's injunction dissolved," he wrote Young. "Nothing has been done to clear those who were arrested. . . . Also please don't be too soft. We have the offensive. . . . In a crisis we must have a sense of drama. . . . We may accept [Thomas's] order as a partial victory, but can't stop." The marches resumed.[31]

On Friday, February 5, four days after King's arrest, the *New York Times* ran "A Letter from MARTIN LUTHER KING from a Selma, Alabama, Jail." It read, in part,

> By jailing hundreds of Negroes, the city of Selma, Alabama, has
> revealed the persisting ugliness of segregation to the nation and the
> world. When the Civil Rights Act of 1964 was passed many decent
> Americans were lulled into complacency because they thought the
> days of difficult struggle were over.
>
> Why are we in jail? Have you ever been required to answer 100
> questions on government . . . merely to vote? Have you ever stood in
> line with over a hundred others and after waiting an entire day seen
> less than ten given the qualifying test?

THIS IS SELMA, ALABAMA. THERE ARE MORE NEGROES
IN JAIL WITH ME THAN THERE ARE ON THE VOTING ROLLS.
[*sic*]

 . . . [M]erely to be a person in Selma is not easy. When reporters
asked Sheriff Clark if a woman defendant was married, he replied,
"She's a nigger woman and she hasn't got a Miss or a Mrs. in front of
her name."

"This is the U.S.A. in 1965," King concluded. He asked for the nation's
support, which, he said, not even "the thickest jail walls can muffle."[32]

The power of King's statement, modeled after his more celebrated "Letter
from a Birmingham Jail," was weakened when reporters noticed that, in fact,
King was out of jail by the time the letter was published. His advisers urged
him to hold a press conference to address the timing of the letter and the circumstances of his release, but he had nothing new to say. Someone suggested that King could explain that he had left jail to prepare for a meeting
with President Johnson to discuss a new voting rights law. After that alibi
was approved, King's lawyer Harry Wachtel hurriedly contacted the White
House, only to find that officials there were not receptive to a King visit.
Johnson, erratic as ever, flew into a rage at the request. "Where the hell does
King get off inviting himself to the White House?" he asked an aide. Also annoyed was Acting Attorney General Nicholas Katzenbach, who had hoped
that Thomas's order would end the demonstrations and silence the calls for
a voting rights bill; indeed, Katzenbach had urged Thomas to issue his order
and now was exasperated that it hadn't had the intended effect. "They've
gotten about everything they wanted," he told Johnson. "But they're still
demonstrating. . . . And they've got these kids whipped up there."

Rather than meeting with King, Johnson preferred the idea of a cooling-
off period to see if Thomas's order would solve the problems. Johnson realized that Clark's actions had the potential of creating sympathy for the
movement, thereby making it easier for Johnson to justify his defense of voting rights. However, he also feared that if Clark went too far, it might provoke a black riot, creating a white backlash that would doom King's efforts.
In short, Johnson wanted King to give Thomas's order a chance and stop
pressuring him to submit a voting rights bill immediately. "I was determined
not to be shoved into hasty action," Johnson later observed.[33]

Johnson hated to be shoved, but he also knew that he needed King as much as the preacher needed him. Although the president feared the political repercussions of supporting a voting rights bill, he also took pride in his recent achievements in civil rights and knew that the reverend would be a crucial ally in helping to push through another historic piece of legislation similar to the 1964 Civil Rights Act. But Johnson had a more immediate, pressing need for King's help as well. King was the only brake on a civil rights movement that often seemed on the verge of anarchy, and if King failed to keep the movement unified, a possible successor was waiting in the wings.

While King had been in jail, Malcolm X had made a surprise visit to Selma and, at SNCC's invitation, addressed a rally at Brown Church. Even though the radical Muslim minister and activist had once called King "a little black mouse," a recent pilgrimage to Mecca had opened his eyes to the possibility of interracial brotherhood. He was beginning to temper his philosophy of black supremacy; however, the message he delivered in Selma was still much more menacing than King's. "I think the people in this part of the world would do well to listen to Dr. Martin Luther King," Malcolm X said, "and give him what he's asking for and give it to him fast before some other factions come along and try to do it another way." Privately he told Coretta Scott King that he hadn't come to Selma to make King's life harder; in fact, the opposite was true. He thought his very presence on February 4 would scare white people into King's arms. Within a few hours of their conversation Malcolm X was gone. Two weeks later he would be assassinated while preparing for a speaking engagement in Manhattan.

Malcolm X's brief appearance in Selma may have had the effect he intended, for two days later Johnson reversed himself. On Saturday, February 6, a slow news day, Press Secretary George Reedy announced that the president planned to urge Congress to enact a voting rights bill during that session and that Vice President Hubert Humphrey and Acting Attorney General Nicholas Katzenbach would meet with King on Tuesday, February 9. Privately, King was informed that he might be able to see the president as well if the chance arose, but for now, that possibility must be kept secret. If the news leaked, there would be no meeting with Johnson.[34]

On Tuesday, while President Johnson was secluded with his national security team discussing whether to commit American ground troops to defend South Vietnam, King sat anxiously in Vice President Humphrey's office, hoping for a few minutes with Johnson. He had made it clear to Humphrey, Katzenbach, and other Justice Department lawyers assembled that a new voting rights bill should mandate an end to literacy tests and the creation of federal registrars appointed by the president to guarantee that the federal voting laws laid out in the Fifteenth Amendment, the Civil Rights Act, and elsewhere would be applied fairly in all elections—local, state, and national. The vice president expressed doubt that such a bill could pass at present, and neither he nor Katzenbach endorsed King's recommendations.

Finally, after ninety minutes passed, Humphrey's phone rang, which was the signal to sneak King into the Oval Office. King and Johnson met for only fifteen minutes, but the president seemed more receptive than Humphrey did to a bill that eliminated literacy tests, applied to all elections, and was backed up by federal registrars. Leaving the White House, King told reporters that the meetings had been "very successful." Privately, King was less confident. Given Johnson's volatile temperament—one day warm and supportive, the next cold and distant—it was impossible for King to know precisely where the president stood. An even greater effort would be required to get the administration to transform its statements into action.[35]

King returned that night to a sea of troubles in Selma. The movement there was exhausted, its leaders divided over how next to proceed. Judge Thomas's order had called for the creation of an "appearance book" that those seeking registration could sign when the Board was in recess. The applicants who signed the book would then receive a number that allowed them to be served first when the Board met again. Local leaders like Reverend Reese, who had led the schoolteachers' march, supported the move, whereas the fiery Jim Bevel denounced it as "a white man's trick," a ploy designed to obstruct registration. Their conflict reflected deeper tensions among the movement's various groups: the Selma activists who for decades had been fighting for voting rights and saw Thomas's order and the appearance book as positive signs; the young men and women of SNCC who often accused King of being a celebrity who went briefly to jail, settled for symbolic settlements of deep-rooted grievances, and then moved on while local activists repaired the wreckage left in his wake; and the ministers and other organizers of SCLC who saw the voting rights issue as part of a larger struggle for black emancipation that could be achieved only with federal assistance. Ironically, the more that the registration process improved, the more it threatened

King's movement by placating local activists and sapping their energy for the broader fight for civil rights.[36]

While King had been busy with Johnson, Bevel had led sixty demonstrators to the courthouse, where they refused to sign the appearance book. "You're making a mockery of justice!" screamed Sheriff Clark. Out came the billy club, and Clark jabbed Bevel down the courthouse steps, then arrested him. The jabbing turned into a beating that continued even as five deputies dragged Bevel to jail. Bevel fainted and drifted in and out of consciousness. When he awoke he was wet and freezing: Clark's men had turned a fire hose on him and left the windows of his cell open on this cold February day. When Bevel's colleagues eventually located him, he was under armed guard and chained to his bed. They called a doctor, who examined Bevel, diagnosed viral pneumonia, and immediately ordered him moved to a hospital.[37]

Bevel's fellow protestors continued to be brutalized. On Wednesday, February 10, the day after King's meeting with Johnson, 161 students picketed the courthouse with signs that read, "Let Our Parents Vote" and "Jim Clark Is A Cracker." By the afternoon Clark had had enough: if the kids wanted to march, he would oblige them. Charging them with truancy, he and his posse forced them to run three miles along a road that took them out of town. Those not fast enough received shocks from the posse's cattle prods. Those who fell back were beaten with billy clubs. Some vomited and collapsed in a nearby gravel pit. When one of those students, Letha Mae Stover, looked up from where she had fallen, she faced an officer who forced her to rise by continually jabbing her in the back. If she wanted to march, he said, he would show her how. Exhausted and unable to take another step, she told him that he might as well kill her, because she couldn't get up. The officer turned away to pursue others trying to escape.[38]

Wilson Baker was furious. For weeks he had warned the mayor that Clark was "out of control," playing into the hands of the civil rights activists. If Clark attacked any other children, Baker said, he would arrest him. Clark ignored such threats. Returning to town, he happily told reporters—who had been blocked from observing his latest atrocity—that because the jail was filled, he was just escorting the young folks to a comfortable lodge owned by the Fraternal Order of Police. A journalist asked Clark whether he had used cattle prods on the children, to which Clark replied, "Cattle prods? I didn't see any." It was a bald-faced lie. In addition to the word of the many students who had endured the abuse, an FBI agent who observed the event (but did nothing to stop it) later testified to seeing "four or five or six instances" of Clark's men shocking the students with cattle prods.[39]

That night King held a strategy session with his top aides. King himself thought that the demonstrations in Selma had run their course and that SCLC should now move on to more fertile territory, like Lowndes County, or as it was better known to civil rights veterans, "Bloody Lowndes." Of the almost six thousand blacks who were eligible to vote there, not a single one had ever tried to register. "You should not only know how to start a good movement," King said, "[you] should also know when to stop." SCLC should "make a dramatic appeal" in Lowndes or some other equally embattled county.

King's colleagues agreed. Ironically, Selma had proven to be less hostile than they had expected, a fact typified by the clashes between Clark and Baker. Further, some considered Judge Thomas's rulings to be a good-faith effort to accelerate the registration process. King and SCLC were after bigger game than what they thought could be found in Selma: they wanted a change that would affect not simply Alabama but the entire South.[40]

Selma's white elites were indeed divided over Sheriff Clark's outrageous behavior. Selma's political and business establishment felt that Clark's actions reflected poorly on their community and jeopardized the northern investments on which the city's economy depended. Because of this, they had begun to criticize him openly. Roughing up an outside agitator like Jim Bevel was one thing; attacking children, even if black, was quite another, they contended. The editor of the *Selma Times Journal*, a prominent member of the White Citizen's Council, weighed in, attacking Clark's viciousness and demanding that it cease.

The sheriff read everything written about him, and the criticism deeply hurt him—so much so that his angst began to manifest itself physically. Early on the morning of February 12 a sleepless Clark complained to his wife of chest pain and was quickly admitted to Vaughn Memorial Hospital. "The niggers are givin' me a heart attack," he cried, although medical tests later found no such condition. When young activists—many of them casualties of Clark's march—learned of his illness, they hurried to the hospital where, as a gentle rain fell, they knelt in prayer, beseeching God to heal their nemesis. Some carried signs that read, "We Wish Jim Clark A *Speedy Recovery*." "It just wasn't the same without Jim Clark fussing and fuming," one of the demonstrators later told a reporter. "We honestly miss him."[41]

Clark recovered quickly and was on duty when the Reverend C. T. Vivian led a group of aspiring voters to the courthouse on February 16. Vivian, one of King's key lieutenants, personified the modern civil rights movement: he had desegregated a cafeteria when he was twenty-three; learned nonviolence from Jim Lawson like his fellow seminary students, John Lewis and Bernard Lafayette; and joined the Nashville sit-in movement and the Freedom Rides. Tough and determined, Vivian wasn't afraid of Jim Clark, and his boldness would soon rejuvenate the movement in Selma.

Arriving at the courthouse with his group, Vivian found about one hundred would-be voters already waiting in line. Soon it began to rain, and he sought shelter for them inside the courthouse. The door was locked: Clark had seen them coming and made sure they couldn't get in. They stood under an overhang and sang freedom songs. Apparently the singing annoyed the sheriff, because his deputies opened the door wide enough for him to yell at Vivian. Network TV cameramen moved in to capture the confrontation.

"Turn that light out," Clark screamed at the cameramen. "You're blinding me and I can't enforce the law with a light in my face."

Vivian seized the moment. "We have come to register," he said. Then, as the cameras rolled, Vivian launched into a philosophical discussion of evil that ranged from Hitler's Germany to Clark's Alabama. To the deputies, Vivian said, "There were those who followed Hitler like you blindly follow this Sheriff Clark, who didn't think their day would come, but they were pulled into a courtroom one day and were given death sentences. You're not that bad a racist but you're a racist in the same way Hitler was a racist. . . . You can't keep anyone in the United States from voting without hurting the rights of all other citizens. Democracy is built on this."

Clark was near the breaking point. His deputies told him to return to his office, assuring him that they would handle the situation. Clark turned away, but Vivian didn't stop: "You can turn your back on me but you can't turn your back on justice." Suddenly Clark whirled and punched Vivian in the mouth with such force that he fractured a finger. The minister fell back down the steps but got up shakily, his face bloody. "What kind of people are you?" he asked Clark and the others. "What do you tell your children at night? What do you tell your wives at night? . . . We're willing to be beaten for democracy, and you misuse democracy in this street. You beat people bloody [so] they will not have the privilege to vote. . . . We have come to register to vote."

Sheriff Jim Clark seizes C. T. Vivian, King's aide, during a demonstration on February 16, 1965. After Clark punches him in the mouth, Vivian asks Clark and his deputies, "What kind of people are you?" © BETTMAN/CORBIS

"Arrest him now!" Clark ordered, and Vivian was taken away. That evening the confrontation aired on national television. "Every time it appears that the movement is dying out," said a King aide, "Sheriff Clark comes to our rescue."[42]

Vivian's lip had been split in the assault, but he was undeterred. After his release from jail he quickly answered Albert Turner's call to come to rural Marion, an outpost of activism, to preach at Zion's Chapel Methodist Church. Turner, a bricklayer and local civil rights leader, had been born in a shack in Perry County, of which Marion was the seat. His father had been a sharecropper, but Turner himself had escaped poverty, attending Alabama A&M. When he returned home after college he was depressed to find so many black residents of Marion, himself included, unable to vote. "I always thought I was a pretty good student," he later said, "and it . . . was an affront to me that these dummies who were the registrars were saying to me that I couldn't pass [their] test and they couldn't hardly write their names. . . . [T]hat built up and built up . . . and people became angry and I did myself." Just 150 of Marion's black residents were registered out of an eligible population of over 5,000—a fact that Turner was determined to change.

In 1962 Turner organized the Perry County Voters League, an organization dedicated to helping people register and pass the extraordinarily complicated registrar's test. But most applicants still failed, including a twenty-six-year-old Army veteran named Jimmie Lee Jackson and his grandfather, Cager Lee. Both had tried to register five times but were consistently rejected. "I been here a long time and I ain't never voted," Lee once told Turner. "You say it's time I did; I say I'm ready."

Turner had welcomed King's coming to Selma, and was soon joined in Marion by SCLC's James Orange. They created voter workshops and organized demonstrations. When Vivian arrived in the city on the night of Thursday, February 18, a black boycott had crippled local business, and Orange was in jail, charged with multiple counts of contributing to the delinquency of a minor after he led 700 students on a protest march around the county courthouse. At the conclusion of his address at Zion's Chapel Methodist Church that night, Vivian departed through a rear exit and left Marion, a move that may have saved his life. The congregation, numbering about 450, planned to march on the jail to serenade Orange with freedom songs.[43]

Night marches were always potentially dangerous for demonstrators because darkness gave their enemies a better chance to waylay them and flee, but Turner and the others were surprised to see what awaited them when they left Zion's Chapel Methodist Church. Arrayed before them were more than two hundred angry law enforcers—including Marion police, Perry County deputy sheriffs, and one hundred state troopers dressed in riot gear—as well as townspeople brandishing clubs. State officials believed that the activists planned to break into the jail to free Orange.[44]

Nearby the horde was Sheriff Jim Clark, tonight casually dressed and without his usual helmet but nevertheless armed with a nightstick. "Don't you have enough trouble of your own in Selma?" asked a reporter.

"Things got a little too quiet for me . . . tonight, and it made me nervous," he replied. Some wondered if Vivian's presence explained Clark's appearance in Marion. Indeed, both Turner and Vivian later concluded that state troopers planned to kill Vivian in retribution for his earlier confrontation with the sheriff.[45]

Television reporters and photographers, who had been capturing the images of Clark's brutality and broadcasting them on the networks' evening news programs, were another target of the law enforcers' wrath. When NBC News's Richard Valeriani and his crew arrived in Marion, they received a very unpleasant welcome. Townspeople cursed them, and some sprayed their cameras with paint. Local police quarantined Valeriani and other journalists and photographers near city hall to prevent them from observing events. The cameramen turned their lights on anyway, hoping to photograph the march, but then an officer yelled, "Turn those goddamned lights off!" They did.[46]

When Turner and the other marchers appeared outside Zion's Chapel Methodist Church, Marion police chief T. O. Harris stepped forward and told them to return to their church or face arrest for unlawful assembly. Turner's colleague, the Reverend James Dobynes, asked Harris, "May we pray before we go back?" and he knelt. However, the only answer he received were blows from state troopers. He cried, "Jesus! Oh Jesus! Have mercy." The troopers ignored his pleas, grabbed his arms and legs, and dragged him away. That seemed to be a signal to the other officers and townspeople, because suddenly the streetlights went out and the mob attacked demonstrators and reporters alike. From his vantage point John Herbers of the *New York Times* observed "state troopers shouting and jabbing and swinging their nightsticks. The Negroes began screaming and falling back around the entrance of the church." Their proximity to a place of worship didn't prevent the troopers and other officers from kicking and beating them. Others fled to the nearby Tubbs Funeral Home, but the troopers followed and beat whomever they could get their hands on. Screams and the sound of clubs hitting bodies echoed through the town square.[47]

When United Press International photographer Pete Fisher snapped a picture of the mayhem, someone behind him hit him on the head with a nightstick. Fisher ran toward city hall but never made it. A group of men surrounded him, slapped him, and destroyed his camera. His assailants left Fisher, but a few minutes later another man, Woodfin Nichols, accosted him. Nichols, a grocer, punched Fisher in the face repeatedly until the chief of police stopped Nichols and sent him on his way. A deputy sheriff attacked Reggie Smith, another UPI photographer, and jabbed him in the ribs and smashed his camera. Local police stood by silently while Fisher and Smith were attacked and other reporters called for help.[48]

One of Pete Fisher's attackers approached NBC's Richard Valeriani and asked, "Who invited you here?" Valeriani moved away but then felt a severe blow to the back of his head. To the *Times*'s John Herbers, the impact sounded "like a gourd being hit with a baseball bat." A state trooper took a blue axe handle out of the hands of Sam Dozier, a lumber salesman. Tossing the club away, the trooper told Dozier, "I guess you've done enough damage with that tonight." Dozier fled, and the trooper walked away without offering help to the injured journalist.

Dazed and held upright by his cameraman, Valeriani touched the back of his head and found his hand covered with blood. Another man approached him and asked, "Are you hurt, do you need a doctor?"

"Yeah, I think I do," Valeriani replied, appreciating the man's concern. "I'm bleeding."

The man looked Valeriani in the eye and said, "Well, we don't have doctors for people like you." Only when someone from city hall offered to take Valeriani to the hospital did he receive treatment for his head wound.[49]

Eighty-year-old Cager Lee, who wanted to vote at least once before he died, was one of the last to leave the church through its rear exit. Walking around to the side he saw a crowd of white townspeople milling about. One approached him and said, "Go home, Nigger. Damn you, go home." Lee said nothing, and, at five feet and 120 pounds, posed no threat, but the man struck him on the head anyway. Lee fell to the ground. When he tried to get up the vigilante kicked him twice in the back. "It was hard to take for an old man whose bones are dry like cane," Lee later told a reporter. One of his assailants recognized Lee, which may have saved him from a worse beating. "God damn, this is old Cager. Don't hit him anymore," he said, then helped him up.[50]

Lee paused to catch his breath, then went to Mack's Cafe, where he found the rest of his family: his grandson Jimmie Lee Jackson, Jackson's mother, Viola, and sister, Emma Jean. Jackson, seeing the bloody cut on Lee's head, exclaimed, "Grand-daddy, they hit you! Come on out of here and let me carry you to the hospital."

As they started to leave, state troopers burst into the café, overturning tables, smashing lamps, and hitting black patrons. Norma Shaw, the manager of the café, yelled at them, "Y'all ought to be ashamed of yourselves. These folks not doing anything [*sic*]." The troopers hit Shaw with their billy clubs, searched through her purse and, finding a gun, arrested her, and dragged her away to jail without shoes or a coat.

What happened next is unclear. Some eyewitnesses later claimed that a trooper clubbed Viola Jackson and threw her to the floor. Her son rushed the trooper but received a punch in the face while another threw him against a cigarette machine. A third trooper, James Bonard Fowler, drew his service revolver and calmly shot Jimmie in the stomach. Fowler later claimed that Jackson attacked him with a beer bottle and tried to seize his gun, causing him to fire in self-defense.

Although seriously hurt, Jimmie staggered outside, running a gauntlet of troopers who yelled, "Get that nigger." A deputy sheriff ran after him, hitting him on the head until he collapsed. Jackson lay on the ground for half an hour until an ambulance picked him up and took him to Perry County Hospital for treatment. "I have been shot, don't let me die," Jackson mumbled as he lay on a stretcher waiting for a doctor to appear. Eventually he was treated for a scalp laceration and a gunshot wound, but because he needed surgery and the facility lacked a blood bank, physicians decided to move him to Good Samaritan Hospital in Selma. Robert B. Tubbs, the owner of Tubbs Funeral Home, drove Jackson the thirty miles to Selma; he later told FBI agents that Jackson repeatedly said, "Lord, save me." It was almost midnight when Jackson was admitted to Good Samaritan, more than two hours since the shooting, and he was now in critical condition. Grimacing with pain, Jackson told a doctor that an Alabama state trooper shot him while he was trying to defend his mother, who was being beaten. One nurse who examined him did not expect him to survive, saying later that "his insides are torn up and his body is infected."[51]

Martin Luther King was in Atlanta suffering from a bad cold when he received news of the Marion tragedy later that night. He immediately wired the Justice Department asking for help, but Katzenbach, who the president had finally elevated to Justice's top job the week before, did not reply until the next morning. He said only that the FBI was on the case—a not very encouraging response, given the agency's history of hostility toward the civil rights movement. Indeed, J. Edgar Hoover had informed Attorney General Katzenbach that the Marion riot was "grossly exaggerated," that there was "no truth to the statements that Negroes have been brutally assaulted." The White House reaction was equally tepid: the president was being kept abreast of developments, said a spokesman the following day. Apparently, the administration believed Hoover's report that there had been "no police brutality but only the use of force necessary to handle an unruly mob." The evening news programs showed no film, and America's most influential newspapers published no photographs to prove Hoover wrong.[52]

King's illness prevented him from returning to Selma until Monday afternoon, February 22. He saw immediately that the Marion incident had increased tensions in the city. Colonel Lingo's state troopers, fresh from their Thursday night victory, were now present on the streets of Selma, backing up Clark's posse. Later that night Katzenbach telephoned King with the news that the FBI had learned of a plot to assassinate the reverend during his visit. King asked for the FBI's protection, but Hoover refused.

Nonetheless, death threats did not stop King from leading two hundred senior citizens to the courthouse the next morning. There they waited patiently in line to sign the appearance book. There were no incidents, but the group noticed many more sullen white men on street corners observing them than had been present at earlier marches. Afterward King briefly visited Jimmie Lee Jackson at Good Samaritan Hospital. "He seems to be in good spirits," King later told reporters. He also visited Marion that afternoon, where he found the Zion's Chapel Methodist Church filled to overflowing with the crowd waiting to hear him speak. "There is no price too great to pay for freedom," he told them. "We have now reached the point of no return. We must let George Wallace know that the violence of state troopers will not stop us." One possible response was to organize a motorcade from Selma to Montgomery, but King didn't say much more about it. He left Selma that night for a fund-raising trip to California.[53]

During the next few days Jackson improved slightly, so hopes rose that he might recover. His legal prospects were grimmer. Following the shooting Colonel Al Lingo formally arrested him, charging him with "assault and battery with intent to murder a peace officer." On February 23 he was interviewed by FBI agents and allowed photographers to take pictures of his wound, where the bullet had entered his stomach and exited through his left side.

Then Jackson took a turn for the worse. Late on the night of February 25 he had difficulty breathing. Doctors rushed him to surgery, where they opened his stomach to find a massive infection. He slipped into a coma and died at 8:10 the following morning. The official cause of death was listed as "Peritonitis due to gunshot wound of abdomen." His killer would not be brought to justice until November 2010, when retired trooper James B. Fowler pled guilty to a charge of "misdemeanor manslaughter" in the Jackson shooting and was sentenced to six months in prison. Even then, Fowler insisted that he shot Jackson in self-defense.[54]

Jim Bevel, recovering from pneumonia, blamed himself for Jackson's death and the injuries Marion's demonstrators sustained. After all, Bevel and his wife, Diane Nash, were the ones who for two years had worked on Martin Luther King until they finally persuaded him to go to Selma to campaign for voting rights. So they demanded action. Bevel met with James Orange and other activists and discussed the King motorcade. Lucy Foster, a Marion resident, suggested instead that they march from Selma to Montgomery, and Bevel was immediately taken with the idea. Others were thinking along similar but more brutal lines. Albert Turner was so angry that he "wanted to carry Jimmy's body to George Wallace and dump it on the steps of the capitol." That anger had to be diffused, Bevel thought, and a five-day march would help to do so as it would also focus the nation's attention on Alabama's politically sanctioned brutality and the cause that had led to Jackson's murder: the need for a voting rights bill.[55]

The time was right "to do something dramatic," Bevel told Bernard Lafayette on February 26 as they drove to Marion to express their condolences to Jackson's family. Lafayette was shocked at the appearance of the Jackson home. He was used to seeing the impoverished conditions in which most blacks in the South lived, but Jackson's farm and tiny shack, which housed four people and had neither electricity nor running water, was especially stark and depressing.

Cager Lee and his daughter Viola were bandaged and still in pain, but they were willing to talk about Jimmie Lee and the future of the civil rights movement. "I wish they had taken me instead of the boy," Lee told them over and over. Bevel asked him if he thought they should march again or end the demonstrations. Lee replied quickly: "Voting is what this is about"—they must continue. Bevel invited Lee to join him at the head of the march, and the old man agreed. "I'll walk with you," he said. "I've got nothing to lose now, . . . they've taken all I have. We've got to keep going now." Leaving the Jackson family to their grief, Bevel burst into tears.[56]

That night, at a mass meeting in Selma's Brown Chapel, Bevel talked about Jackson's death and how the community should respond. "I tell you, the death of that man is pushing me kind of hard," he told his audience of more than six hundred people. "The blood of Jackson will be on our hands if we don't march." They must take their message directly to George Wallace in the Alabama capital, he said. "Be prepared to walk to Montgomery. Be prepared to sleep on the highways," Bevel urged the crowd, and the people cheered.[57]

Bevel had committed King's organization to an action his boss had not yet approved, but his actions had left King little choice. Caught between the agony of his supporters—who needed desperately to respond to Jackson's death—and his awareness of the dangers that he and his fellow activists would face, they went forward with their plans, and King reluctantly chose to march. Privately, however, he looked for ways to limit his participation in an honorable way.

On March 3 King spoke at Jackson's funeral at Zion's Chapel Methodist Church, telling the crowd of four hundred that "Jimmie Lee . . . is speaking to us from the casket and he is saying to us that we must substitute courage for caution. . . . We must not be bitter, and we must not harbor ideas of retaliating with violence. We must not lose faith in our white brothers." As he led a crowd that now numbered one thousand to the gravesite, he again expressed worry about his own future, as death threats multiplied. To the Reverend Joseph Lowery, an SCLC board member, he said, "Come on . . . this may be my last walk." Later that day Bevel, with King's approval, announced that King would lead a march from Selma to Montgomery, a fifty-four-mile trek, on Sunday, March 7.[58]

News of the march created consternation on both sides of the struggle. SNCC saw it as another publicity stunt, a staged theatrical event that starred King at the expense of local leaders who had long struggled in the shadows. While they rode the Freedom Rider buses and were beaten in Birmingham and Montgomery and risked their lives in Mississippi during Freedom Summer, King—who they derisively called "de Lawd"—remained above the battle, hiding in the pulpit. Nonviolence didn't help the victims of Marion, SNCC

activists pointed out. Their leaders met twice in long and bitter meetings, finally deciding to give the march only "token support." Individual members
could participate if they wished. John Lewis, who helped found SNCC and
was a battle-scarred veteran, broke with his friends and associates. "If these
people want to march," he said, "I'm going to march with them."[59]

In Montgomery, Governor Wallace and his advisers sought a way to
handle this crisis. Bill Jones, an influential aide to the governor, surprised
everyone by recommending that they do nothing. He felt that King's forces
expected to be arrested and were not seriously planning for such a long and
difficult trek. Informants planted inside the movement revealed that the
marchers thought Selma's jail was their likely destination, not the state capitol. Just ignoring the marchers would, Jones hoped, "make them the laugh-
ingstock of the nation and win for us a propaganda battle." At first Wallace
accepted this strategy. However, he changed his mind when he encountered
opposition from state legislators, especially those from Lowndes, the most
dangerous county in south-central Alabama and the area through which the
marchers would pass. "I'm not going to have a bunch of niggers walking
along a highway in this state as long as I am Governor," he proclaimed. Later
he announced that nobody would be allowed to march and that Colonel Al
Lingo was instructed to "take whatever steps necessary" to stop it.[60]

King met again with the president on the evening of March 5. And again
there was good news and bad. The president now seemed committed to a
voting rights law, not a constitutional amendment, and he urged King to
meet with Katzenbach to work out the details. But he provided no specific
information about the substance of the bill and promised nothing. Then suddenly Johnson switched course: his top priority for the moment was his education bill, and he asked King to contact legislators to push for its passage. It
was lack of education that hurt blacks most, Johnson claimed, stating, "Now,
by God, they can't work in a filling station and put water in a radiator unless
they can read and write. . . . Now that's what you damn fellows better be
working on." The two spent little time discussing the coming march on
Selma, now just two days away. A disappointed King returned to Atlanta.[61]

The march from Selma to Montgomery would be a historical event that
President Johnson would later compare to Lexington and Concord, as it
would transfix the nation and help smooth the passage of the Voting Rights
Act. But this momentous episode in the history of the civil rights movement
began as a comedy of errors. Learning of Wallace's plans to stop the marchers

and fearful of violence and the possibility of his own assassination, King met with his top aides on the night of March 6. Perhaps it might be wise to postpone the march, he told them, although he had not decided what to do. Everyone except Jim Bevel and Hosea Williams agreed that a postponement might be the best course.[62]

Early the next morning King made up his mind. Hurriedly he called Andy Young and asked him to go immediately to Selma to cancel the march. Young took an 8 a.m. flight to Montgomery, rented a car, and raced to Selma. When he drove over the Edmund Pettus Bridge, which the marchers would have to cross when leaving downtown Selma on their way to Montgomery, he saw an ominous site: hundreds of state troopers, city police, and Clark's posse already in place atop their horses. At Brown Chapel he received another shock: six hundred would-be marchers—men, women, teenagers, and even children—all preparing for the journey ahead. Among them were heartbroken but determined people from Perry County who wanted to honor Jimmie Lee Jackson.

Young cornered Williams, asking why he had not followed King's order to postpone the march. Williams claimed that King had "reauthorized the march." Find Bevel, Williams said, he had talked recently to King and would back up Williams's story. Bevel did, stating that King had changed his mind and had said that the march should go forward. Young must have felt like a character in *Through the Looking-Glass*.

The only way to resolve the conflicting information was to ask King himself, a difficult task, as King was preaching at his father's church in Atlanta. With Ralph Abernathy's help, Young and the march's organizers were able to confer with King. By this time Young was in favor of the march going forward. "All these people are here ready to go now," Young told King. "The press is gathering expecting us to go, and we think we've just got to march, even if you aren't here. There'll probably be arrests when we hit the bridge."

King reluctantly gave his assent. But he did issue one command: two of his top assistants should stay behind to be ready for any unexpected emergencies. Because Lewis was technically a SNCC man, Williams, Bevel, and Young flipped a coin to see who would join him. Williams won.[63]

And so at 2:18 p.m., after a prayer led by Andy Young, the singing of "God Will Take Care of You," and a command from Wilson Baker that the marchers re-form themselves into proper parade order, the six hundred set out, with Williams and Lewis in the lead. Lewis didn't know what the day

Rev. Andrew Young leads a prayer before the marchers set out for the Edmund Pettus Bridge on March 7, 1965. Kneeling, to Young's right, are Hosea Williams and John Lewis (tan raincoat); to Young's left are Albert Turner and Amelia Boynton. © 1965 SPIDER MARTIN

would bring. Nobody was really ready for a five-day, fifty-mile hike. He was "playing it by ear." In his backpack were an apple, an orange, a toothbrush, toothpaste, and something to read—everything he needed to pass the time in one of Selma's rancid jail cells.

A few days before, King had said, "We will write the voting rights law in the streets of Selma." He was wrong. The Voting Rights Act would be written—in blood—on the Edmund Pettus Bridge.[64]

FOUR

NOTHING CAN STOP US

SUNDAY, MARCH 7, WAS A PLEASANT DAY FOR THEIR JOURNEY: BALMY WITH a brisk wind and no sign of the snow and rain that had pelted demonstrators earlier. Jonquils and forsythia were starting to bloom—a sign, perhaps, that winter might finally be over. Selma seemed quiet, almost deserted except for a few unhappy-looking people standing on street corners watching the throng pass by. "Black bitch. Got a white boy to play with, huh?" yelled one man at a young female marcher whose companion, Jim Bentson, was white. At Broad Street a white woman driving a pickup truck veered toward Bentson, but he jumped away before she hit him.[1]

At about 4:00 p.m. the marchers came to the Edmund Pettus Bridge, named for a Confederate general. They saw what John Lewis called "a vast sea of blue": state troopers wearing blue uniforms and dark blue helmets bearing Confederate emblems, stretched shoulder to shoulder across the four-lane highway. Some sat atop horses that moved restlessly in place. Clark's personal army, bearing nightsticks, whips, and electric cattle prods, were there too. They were wearing tattered khaki shirts, mismatched pants, and helmets better suited for football games or motorcycle rides than police action. Some were also on horseback, carrying clubs as big as baseball bats. One special deputy had wrapped barbed wire around a rubber hose.[2]

The marchers could either turn around or, if need be, leap off the bridge and drop one hundred feet into the Alabama River. "Can you swim?" Hosea Williams asked John Lewis.

"No," Lewis replied.

"Bloody Sunday," March 7, 1965. John Lewis, Hosea Williams, and their fellow marchers confront Major John Cloud and Alabama state troopers on the Edmund Pettus Bridge. "You have two minutes to turn around and go back to your church," commands Major Cloud. Before that time elapsed, the troopers attacked. © 1965 SPIDER MARTIN.

"Neither can I," Williams said. "But we might have to."

Instead, Lewis, Williams, and the others walked forward until they were about fifty feet from the troopers. They halted at the voice of the commanding officer coming through a bullhorn: "I am Major Cloud," he said. "This is an unlawful assembly. This demonstration will not continue. You have been banned by the Governor. Your march is not conducive to the public safety. You are ordered to disperse and go back to your church or to your homes." While he spoke, the troopers donned gas masks.

"Mr. Major, I would like to have a word," said Hosea Williams, winner of the lucky coin toss.

"There is no word to be had," replied Major Cloud.

Williams again asked politely if they could talk, and again Cloud said no, adding, "You have two minutes to turn around and go back to your church."

There was a momentary silence. Lewis instructed the group to kneel and pray, but only a few got the message. Then, before the time ran out, Cloud yelled, "Troopers, advance." Turning their nightsticks horizontally, they rushed into the crowd, knocking people over like bowling pins. People fell "to the ground screaming, arms and legs flying . . . packs and bags skittering," noted Roy Reed of the *New York Times*. Whoops and cheers came from a crowd of white onlookers, who yelled, "Give it to the niggers." John Lewis was one of the first to be hit. As he crouched on the ground, praying, a trooper struck him in the head, and he fell over. When he tried to rise he was hit again. "I'm going to die here," was his last thought before falling back to the ground. Marie Foster and Amelia Boynton were also struck in the head. Foster fell, but Boynton only staggered, so the trooper hit her again and she collapsed. The trooper continued to beat her unconscious body, screaming, "Get up, nigger! Get up and run." Albert Turner, standing behind Lewis, also fell as bodies knocked him down. When someone called for an ambulance, Jim Clark said, "Let the buzzards eat them."[3]

Then came the men on horseback, troopers and posse men alike, swinging their clubs and ropes like cowboys driving cattle to market. Reporters heard

John Lewis is beaten by troopers. "I'm going to die here," he thought. © 1965 SPIDER MARTIN.

rebel yells and Sheriff Clark screaming, "Get those God-damned niggers! And get those God-damned white niggers!" Suddenly there were sounds like gunshots. Troopers were firing and throwing canisters of highly noxious C-4 tear gas—"gas so thick you could almost reach up and grab it," remembered one of the blinded and sickened victims. Forty canisters were used that day, causing gray clouds of tear gas to spew over the scene, thus preventing Reed and other newsmen and photographers from seeing clearly what was happening. When the haze parted momentarily, Reed saw troopers' nightsticks raining down on the heads of the marchers. Standing nearby were two young FBI agents taking notes and filming the event. They never tried to stop it.[4]

Amelia Boynton, badly injured, is carried away by fellow marchers.
© 1965 SPIDER MARTIN.

And so, coughing, choking, and vomiting, the marchers ran from the bridge back into the streets of Selma, hoping to find safety there. But there was none. Troopers and the posse on horses followed, clubbing them until they fell, then laughing with pure pleasure as they tried to get their horses to rear up and crush the fallen. "Bite the niggers," one posse man told his horse. Clark's men also followed in cars, and when they found their targets, they leaped out and whipped them. Still the marchers ran, knapsacks pulled over their heads for protection, trying to get to the First Baptist Church or Brown Chapel. Posse men, now led by Sheriff Clark himself, fired tear gas into First Baptist. Some entered the church, throwing one young man who was inside through a stained-glass window. Wilson Baker, who had jurisdiction over most of downtown Selma, tried to block Clark and his men. But Clark refused to leave. "I've already waited a month too damn long about moving in," he yelled, pushing Baker aside.[5]

The rampage continued. Troopers patrolled the streets, attacking any black citizens they could find. "Get the hell out of town!" they commanded. "We want all the niggers off the streets." They entered the Carver housing project, chasing people and throwing tear gas canisters into buildings. More than 150 officers gathered near Brown Chapel, where a few were pelted with bricks and bottles. Charles Bonner, Lafayette's young recruit, picked up a brick and was about to throw it at a posse man when Jim Bevel stopped him: "Look at this kid's head bleeding," he said. "Is that what you really want to do to that trooper?" Bonner dropped the brick and entered the church.[6]

The Brown Chapel parsonage had become a sort of MASH unit staffed by volunteer members of the Medical Committee for Human Rights, an extraordinary group of doctors and nurses committed to treating those who had been injured while fighting for social justice. They cared for nearly one hundred marchers that day: people with cuts, bruises, lacerations, tear gas–related injuries, and fractured and broken arms and legs. Those who had more severe wounds were taken by ambulance to the black-run Good Samaritan Hospital, but that outflow of bodies did little to stem the tide of suffering at Brown Chapel. Somehow John Lewis got back to the church, where he found people on the floor or in pews, moaning and crying. Marie Foster and Amelia Boynton were there unconscious, barely breathing. Lewis had a terrible headache but refused to go to the hospital.[7]

But it was the marchers' anger as well as their pain that threatened to destroy the nonviolent movement. Running from the posse men or even throwing a few bricks simply wasn't enough, many of the wounded believed. If Clark really wanted war, they should get guns and bring it to him. Andy Young was able to calm them down—not with King's lofty claims about suffering and redemption, words now stained with the marchers' blood, but rather by making them think about violence. "What kind of gun you got, .32, .38?" Young asked them. "How's that going to hold up against the automatic rifles and their shotguns.... You ever see what buckshot does to a deer?" Forcing the marchers to consider "the specifics of violence," Young thought, led them to conclude that a war against Clark's overwhelming forces was madness.[8]

WORD OF THE TRAGEDY ON THE EDMUND PETTUS BRIDGE REACHED KING in Atlanta later on Sunday afternoon. He was grief stricken, feeling that he should have been with the marchers. Given recent events in Marion, he had thought Clark and Lingo would not dare repeat such an atrocity so soon. Their outbursts of violence, after all, severely damaged their cause while creating sympathy for King's. And as long as they ignored that fact, King and the marchers had an advantage.

Consulting with his top advisers, King decided that there must be another march as soon as possible, perhaps on Tuesday, March 9, so as to give the marchers a day to recuperate and regroup. He also asked movement lawyers to seek an injunction from federal judge Frank M. Johnson, a fair, objective jurist, allowing them to march to Montgomery and prohibiting the Alabamians from violently interfering again.

Always respectful of the Selma activists who had fought alone for decades, King telephoned Frederick Reese, president of the Dallas County Voters League. "I understand you are having trouble over there," said King with a touch of facetiousness that was meant to comfort the stricken Reese.

"Yeah, we do," Reese replied, too exhausted to banter.

"Well," King said, all traces of humor gone, "I'm gonna put out a call for help."[9]

Ignoring his injuries, Lewis called for a mass meeting that night at Brown Chapel to rally and reunite their forces. Hosea Williams, who had escaped injury by outrunning the troopers and hiding in the home of a friendly bystander, spoke first. "I fought in World War II and I once was captured by the German army and I want to tell you that the Germans never were as inhuman as the state troopers of Alabama."

Lewis, still wearing his blood- and mud-stained raincoat, electrified the crowd with his unprepared remarks. "I don't see how President Johnson can send troops to Vietnam . . . and he can't send troops to Selma, Alabama," he said.

"Tell it," the church roared.

"Next time we march, we may have to keep going when we get to Montgomery. We may have to go on to Washington."

"Amen!" and "Yes !" cried his audience. Their show of resiliency seemed to settle something for Lewis. When he finished speaking he finally agreed to go to the hospital.[10]

AMERICANS WERE NOT IMMEDIATELY AWARE OF WHAT OCCURRED ON THE Edmund Pettus Bridge that Sunday. In 1965 the age of instant communication was still a long way off. Newsmen from ABC, NBC, and CBS who were on the scene that day were uncertain whether their cameras had captured anything, as the film would have to be processed before being shown. Nelson Benton, CBS's correspondent, felt lucky that he had one of the best cameramen in the business, Laurens Pierce, a fearless Alabamian who loved to cover the most dangerous events, his half glasses pushed up on his head, eye pressed firmly against the lens. But Pierce had the defects of his virtues. His cameras were often held together with tape and chewing gum, and he worried constantly about the quality of his product, often saying, "I think I got it. I mean I hope I got it. I feel like I got it." That day, he did. And his footage would prove indispensable to Martin Luther King at a critical moment.[11]

Hoping that their cameras had recorded the most dramatic incident in the history of the civil rights movement, Benton and his competitors drove hurriedly to Montgomery, where technicians at the local affiliates gave the stock a chemical bath to develop the film. Then the correspondents put their bagged film canisters aboard a plane bound for Atlanta, where they would be switched to a flight to New York. There, film editors and producers who had been hastily summoned to the networks' headquarters would decide what could be shown and when.[12]

King did not yet know that television would soon transform a local event in Selma into a national crisis, but he was well aware of the fundamental power of the media. For years King and his top aides had understood that television, which fed on drama, was the only vehicle that could bring the

plight of black Americans into every home in the country. The SCLC's leaders even timed demonstrations so that they could be shown on the evening
news. Young, who had once worked in media, became King's chief television
adviser, urging him to prepare simple messages that would fulfill television's
insatiable need for sound bites. King's media savviness even affected how he
chose cities for new campaigns. Each location had to have the personalities
necessary to create a morality play. Bull Connor in Birmingham and Jim
Clark in Selma were the perfect antagonists, villains the audience would love
to hate. Arouse the conscience of the nation, King believed, and the government would be forced to act. Images rather than words were becoming critical in shaping public opinion.[13]

King's strategy was confirmed that Sunday evening. CBS and NBC aired
short segments on their West Coast six o'clock evening news shows, but
ironically the network that reached the largest audience was ABC News, the
third broadcaster to air the fifteen-minute footage from Selma. An estimated
forty-eight million people watched ABC's coverage, although many had not
planned to do so. ABC executives, after studying the raw film, had decided
to interrupt its Sunday night movie, Stanley Kramer's critically acclaimed
1961 film, *Judgment at Nuremberg,* at a little after 9:00 p.m. (EST) to run its
footage. Viewers were suddenly transported from the Nuremberg Trials of
1948 to the Edmund Pettus Bridge in 1965. Introduced by Frank Reynolds,
the segment had no narration and ran for fifteen minutes. "Unhuman," the
journalist George B. Leonard later called what he saw on television. "The
bleeding, broken and unconscious passed across the screen, some of them
limping alone, others supported on either side, still others carried in arms or
on stretchers. It was at this point that my wife, sobbing, turned and walked
away, saying, 'I can't look any more.'"[14]

Some who saw the horrific scenes in the midst of watching a film about
Nazi atrocities now wondered if America suffered from its own native fas-
cism. Father James Carroll had been a student in Germany in the 1930s, and
the sound of Jim Clark's voice saying, "Get those God-damned Niggers,"
took him back to that earlier time. "I remembered my apartment in Berlin,
the Jewish family with whom I lived, the steel that was to be used to bar the
front door when 'they' came; the bottle of cyanide in the medicine cabinet—
everybody knew why it was there," he later told Leonard. "Could this be happening here?"[15]

Others who saw the pictures on the front page of the *New York Times,* the *Washington Post,* or the *Los Angeles Times* the next day had similar reactions: horror, shame, and an overwhelming desire to do something about the atrocities taking place in the Deep South. Leonard spoke for many when he wrote, "I was not aware that at the same moment people . . . were feeling what my wife and I felt . . . [and] that [they] would drop whatever they were doing . . . leave home without changing clothes, borrow money, over-draw their checking accounts, board planes, buses, trains, cars, travel thousands of miles with no luggage . . . to place themselves alongside the Negroes they had watched on television." They may not have known how widely their concern was shared, but many Americans did indeed drop everything and rush southward to help.

Over the next several days thousands poured into Selma. Some came in response to telegrams King sent to America's religious leaders, asking them to join him in "a ministers' march to Montgomery" on Tuesday, March 9. "No American is without responsibility," King wrote. "All are involved in the sorrow that rises from Selma to contaminate every crevice of our national life. The people of Selma will struggle on for the soul of the nation, but it is fitting that all Americans help to bear the burden." Many religious leaders responded. By Tuesday, March 9, more than 450 clergy, both black and white, had come to Selma—ministers, priests, nuns, and rabbis. For the first time in the history of the movement Catholics were well represented. Heretofore their bishops had prohibited them from participating in civil rights marches. Now, however, that ban was lifted in many places. Later more volunteers would come from everywhere and from all walks of life: teachers, lawyers, labor leaders, college professors, homemakers, entertainers, laborers, civil rights activists bloodied in other southern states, and wives and children of Washington officialdom.[16]

Those who could not go south demonstrated in their own communities, from Maine to Hawaii. "Rarely has public opinion reacted so spontaneously and with such fury," *Time* magazine observed. In Detroit, Mayor Jerome Cavenaugh and Governor George Romney led ten thousand people in a march demanding federal intervention to protect civil rights workers. Among them was a thirty-nine-year-old homemaker, mother of five, and part-time college student named Viola Liuzzo. The events of Bloody Sunday caused her to break down and cry. A few weeks later she left her family and classes at Wayne State University to go to Selma.

There were also demonstrations in eighty other cities, including Boston, Joliet, Ann Arbor, Kansas City, and San Diego. Four hundred people blocked the entrance and exits at the Los Angeles Federal Building and were arrested for obstructing justice. In Philadelphia college students mounted a sit-in at the Liberty Bell, while in Texas black ministers marched on the Alamo. Statements of support came from state legislatures, labor unions, universities, and chambers of commerce. "The mournful, determined tones of 'We Shall Overcome' rang out from Miami to Seattle," noted the *New York Times*.[17]

Washington, DC, in particular became a center of protest. A dozen black activists led by Reverend Jefferson Rogers confronted Attorney General Nicholas Katzenbach in his office, demanding that US marshals be sent to Selma immediately. But Katzenbach refused. Rogers and his colleagues left, but a short time later three others arrived to sit in at Katzenbach's office. Guards dragged them away as one shouted, "Freedom, buddy, Freedom!" Then twenty more appeared, sitting down outside the office door and refusing to leave. Katzenbach told them that their tactics would not affect him. At 10 p.m., after a struggle, US marshals finally picked up the demonstrators and removed them from the building. The president was outraged: "I think it's absolutely disgraceful that they would get in the Justice Department building and have to be hauled out of there," he told Bill Moyers. As long as he was president such people "were going to respect the law." But still they kept coming.[18]

Demonstrators also picketed the White House day and night, marching, praying, and singing. Their presence annoyed the president, who complained about the noise: "Those god damned niggers have kept my daughters awake every night with their screaming and hollering," Johnson later remarked privately. Telegrams poured into the White House, asking about his promised voting rights act. It would be coming "soon," the president's spokesmen said. This tepid response angered journalists across the political spectrum. *Life* magazine, whose publisher was a longtime Republican, thought the president's statement "had almost no impact." Two liberal journalists, who had covered the Selma crisis for *Ramparts* magazine, commented that "People were horrified. They were grieved. They were angry. They sought a catharsis. They looked to the White House—but they found nothing. No call for a day of contrition and mourning, no statement of outrage, no personal presence in Selma, no symbolic arrest of Sheriff Clark or Colonel Lingo. Nothing but an announcement that there would be a new voting rights act as soon as the lawyers could finish drafting it. Wait calmly, please." The president seemed frustrated and sometimes downright odd. Roger Wilkins, a young black member of the Community Relations Service, visited the White House one day and unexpectedly ran into the president. Johnson knew him well—Roger was the nephew of the NAACP's Roy Wilkins—but now the president barely recognized him. "It was really frightening," Wilkins later recalled. "I said, 'Hello, Mr. President.' And he looked at me and he said, 'These demonstrations, what are they all about?' And I said, 'People really want to vote, Mr. President. We really need a voting rights act.'" The president growled at him. "No words came out, just Rrrr."[19]

While Johnson struggled to navigate the fallout from Selma, his staff continued to draft a voting rights bill. Justice Department lawyers, well aware of the imperfections in the earlier bills affecting voting rights, had concluded by March 1 that only a new law enforced by the federal government would suffice. The president agreed. Initially, there was little enthusiasm for it among Johnson's top advisers, who feared that the bill was, as aide Horace Busby noted, "a return to Reconstruction . . . a most radical intervention Federally in this long inviolable domain of the states." Katzenbach also shared Busby's reservations. But the continuing violence in Selma, climaxing with Bloody Sunday, left Johnson and his advisers little choice. A draft of the bill had been completed on March 1, six days before the incident on Edmund Pettus Bridge, but they would continue to tinker with it for several weeks.

Johnson was hopeful that he had the votes in both the House and the Senate, but he feared that a southern filibuster might dilute or even defeat the bill. To prevent a filibuster, two-thirds of the Senate would have to approve cloture, a measure that would cut short debate on the bill and force a vote, and getting two-thirds of the Senate behind cloture would require Republican votes. So Johnson turned to his old colleague and sometime antagonist, Illinois senator Everett McKinley Dirksen, the Republican minority leader, for help.[20]

At first glance they seemed polar opposites. Dirksen, sixty-nine, was a Midwest conservative in love with his own voice, a throwback to the Senate's golden age, when the eloquence of a statesman like Daniel Webster could unify the nation. To preserve his voice, Dirksen daily gargled and swallowed a mixture of Ponds Cold Cream and warm water. His melodious baritone led colleagues to call him "the Wizard of Ooze." His image and political style stood in stark contrast to that of Johnson, the southern populist who preferred working behind the scenes to bend men to his will. But at heart each was a pragmatist, "two brother artisans in government," Lady Bird Johnson once called them. "I feel a kinship for him," Johnson said of Dirksen. "We've had lots of battles, mostly on opposite sides of the aisle, but he always comes to the top."[21]

Dirksen had come to the top in 1964 when he eventually supported the Civil Rights Bill and corralled enough Republicans to invoke cloture, thereby ending the long southern filibuster. In order to bring Dirksen over to his side, Johnson had instructed Senator Hubert Humphrey, the bill's manager, to court Dirksen intensely. "You talk to Dirksen! You listen to Dirksen," Johnson had ordered. "And don't forget that Dirksen loves to bend at the elbow. . . . [D]rink with him till he agrees to vote for cloture and delivers me two Republicans from the mountain states." Johnson had also wooed the Illinois senator himself during the debate over the Civil Rights Bill. "Dirksen, you come with me on this bill," Johnson told him, "and two hundred years from now school children will know only two names: Abraham Lincoln and Everett Dirksen." Dirksen had eventually agreed, but in addition to winning a place in history, he extracted from Johnson public works programs for his state and the appointments of his favorite candidates to administration posts. But despite its cost, his support had been invaluable. Now in 1965, Johnson hoped the Wizard would be with him again.[22]

Initially, the senator was reluctant to support a Voting Rights Bill, coming as it did so soon after the earlier Act. But Bloody Sunday enraged him. Now, he told associates, he was willing to accept "revolutionary" legislation. He even began to work privately with administration officials to fine-tune the bill, and the final version was written in S-230, Dirksen's ornate conference room dominated by a magnificent chandelier that once belonged to Thomas Jefferson. Circulating air caused its pendants to strike one another, providing a musical accompaniment to the men's labors. Dirksen always sat at the head of the room's large mahogany table next to Attorney General Katzenbach, leaving no doubt as to who was in charge and annoying Majority Leader Mike Mansfield, who complained that he was being ignored. Later some would call the legislation the "Dirksenbach bill."[23]

At the president's insistence, the draft under consideration reflected King's demands as well as many of the other reforms civil rights groups had long recommended. It was radically different from earlier congressional efforts. The 1957 Civil Rights Act, besides creating the Justice Department's Civil Rights Division and a Civil Rights Commission with the power to investigate abuses, had authorized the attorney general to prosecute those, particularly in the South, who violated a citizen's right to register or vote in a federal election. But those charged in criminal cases could rely on local white juries to find them innocent. Hardly any progress was made; only four lawsuits were filed in the two years following the Act's passage. The 1960 Act had scarcely done better. Ultimate control over elections still remained in the hands of local judges. In theory these judges could help to enforce the spirit of the law; they could register voters themselves or appoint referees to examine voter applications and approve them if applicants were found to be as qualified as white voters. But with so many racially biased judges in the South, neither was likely to happen. Accordingly, southern senators had called the bill "a victory for the South," while the NAACP's Thurgood Marshall complained that "it would take two or three years for a good lawyer to get someone registered under this bill." And like the Civil Rights Acts of 1957 and 1960, the historic 1964 Act— though a breakthrough in terms of securing black Americans' access to public accommodations—did little to provide access to the ballot box. A sixth-grade education could now be offered as proof of literacy, and registrars were prohibited from disqualifying applicants who made minor mistakes on their registration forms, but other forms of discrimination persisted.[24]

The 1965 bill gave the government new and extraordinary power over voting procedures, shifting responsibility from the courts to the executive branch. Justice Department lawyers, bruised from their battles in the South, adopted a "triggering" formula whereby literacy and other tests that prevented registration would be eliminated in those states where less than 50 percent of the voting-age population had registered or voted in the 1964 presidential election. If the attorney general received at least twenty complaints from disenfranchised citizens or if he determined in some other manner that voting had been obstructed, he was authorized to dispatch federal registrars to solve the problems. And all elections—local, state, and federal— would be covered. To prevent southern states from adopting voting procedures to circumvent the new law, a "preclearance" provision prevented them from making changes without first submitting them to the Justice Department or a Washington, DC, court. States immediately affected were Alabama, Georgia, Louisiana, Mississippi, South Carolina, Virginia, and parts of North Carolina.

But the version of the bill the Justice Department had drafted still had significant flaws. Not covered were Arkansas, Florida, Tennessee, and Texas, all of which had no literacy tests but exhibited discrimination, whereas the bill would also target four states with low African American populations and correspondingly low rates of black registration—Alaska, Arizona, Idaho, and Maine—despite having little or no demonstrable discrimination toward black voters. Along with the solicitor general, who still feared that the bill was unconstitutional, Justice Department lawyers continued to work on other versions up until the moment Dirksen and the committee in room S-230 became involved.[25]

Although Dirksen had agreed to cooperate with Johnson to pass a voting rights bill, this did not mean that he would automatically approve the administration's draft. He thought it was too long and complicated; one estimate put it at forty pages. "We went laboriously through every line," recalled Assistant Attorney General Stephen Pollak, who took part in the proceedings. Dirksen and his chief aide, Neil Kennedy, closely reviewed each provision but accepted them if Pollak and his colleagues could make a case for them, as invariably they did. Pollak did find it annoying that "Dirksen's bombers," as the Democrats called the senator's lawyers, sought mostly cosmetic changes that delayed final agreement. Katzenbach thought Dirksen enjoyed "demonstrating his power. . . . It was something of an ego trip."[26]

But Dirksen *was* genuinely concerned that the federal government would play too great a role in administering the new voting program. He preferred that federal judges appoint the registrars and enforce registration and voting while leaving enforcement of the law to judges within each state. Mansfield and Katzenbach disagreed. For them, southern senators, nearly all of them segregationists, played the central role in selecting those who became judges, so the latter could not be trusted to administer the law fairly. Dirksen was also troubled that the new law would primarily affect seven southern states, a fact that itself could be construed as a form of discrimination. Katzenbach, however, disagreed, and for good reason. "Because of [those states'] past history, we have the right to put this restriction on them," he insisted. But he did appreciate that the title "Registrar" might be inflammatory and instead agreed to call them "Examiners." A more important concession allowed a federal court in Washington, DC, to exempt a state from the bill if the court found that it had not discriminated against blacks during the past ten years. That addition to the bill would prevent the law from unfairly targeting states like Alaska or Maine, where voting rights were not such a problem as to have warranted federal intervention.[27]

The workday usually ended around five o'clock, but Katzenbach and his aides were not allowed to escape until they had spent some time in the "Twilight Lodge," that part of Dirksen's office that contained a fully stocked bar. Dirksen did not consider this frivolous; for him it was an important part of the legislative process. "It generates a fellowship you can't generate in any other way," he stated. Occasionally even Lyndon Johnson dropped in asking for a root beer but was happy to accept a scotch and soda. Johnson probably enjoyed the drink and comradeship, but the Wizard of Ooze was working his magic too slowly to please him. As Johnson had told Katzenbach months before, he needed a bill that was constitutional and effective, and he needed it soon.[28]

MARTIN LUTHER KING RETURNED TO SELMA ON MARCH 8, THE DAY AFTER Bloody Sunday, to find that he faced a new crisis. His lawyers informed him that Judge Frank Mims Johnson Jr., the federal district judge for the Middle District of Alabama, wanted him to postpone the forthcoming march. Johnson planned to hold hearings later that week before deciding whether to grant King's request to issue an injunction that would prohibit Alabama authorities from interfering with another march to Montgomery. The federal courts (outside the South) had been good to the civil rights movement, certainly better than Congress or the presidents, regardless of party. King had never defied a federal court and was agonized at the thought of doing so now. Such an act would also alienate the Johnson administration, which was hard at work preparing a voting rights bill. But King had called for a march, and the people responded. Could he now call it off and still retain leadership of the movement? He had not been present on Bloody Sunday; was he to hide again? How could he restrain his own people who wanted an immediate march—SNCC activists, the Marion veterans who were beaten on Sunday, and the hundreds of new allies who were still arriving in Selma? They could easily march without him and again face the wrath of Jim Clark and the state troopers.

Later, at the home of the dentist Sullivan Jackson (a place Jim Bevel called the "Crisis Center"), King's lieutenants provided no help in resolving his conflicts. Hosea Williams, who had led Sunday's march, wanted to go forward. They owed it, he said, to those whose limbs had been broken and throats burned the day before. CORE's James Farmer sympathized but recommended that they wait. SNCC's James Forman wanted to march. King had learned from Democratic Party chairman Louis Martin that Lyndon Johnson wanted him to postpone the march. King was willing, he told Martin, if the president sent a prominent official to act as a mediator, a step that might buy him some time. King's lawyers recommended caution: give the judge time to decide, they counseled. As King hurried to a midnight rally, he agreed.[29]

Perhaps it was the size of the crowd that filled Brown Chapel—more than one thousand, the veterans of the day before now augmented by distinguished clergymen and other volunteers who had just arrived from thirty states—that led King to change his mind. "We've gone too far to turn back now," he told them. "We must let them know that nothing can stop us—not even death itself. We must be ready for a season of suffering. The only way we can achieve freedom is to conquer the fear of death," King concluded. "Man dies when he refuses to stand up for what is right, for what is just, for what is true." Although King did not explicitly say it, his audience thought his decision was irrevocable. They would march again tomorrow, and this time he would lead them.[30]

In fact, King was uncertain about leading the march, and later that night the Crisis Center again rang out with angry voices debating King's options. He went to bed at 4:00 a.m., but the attorney general woke him at 5:00 to persuade King not to march. When Katzenbach complained that it was just a matter of time before Judge Johnson issued an order that, in all likelihood, would protect the marchers, King reminded him that he knew all about promises. "Mr. Attorney General," he said, "you have not been a black man in America for three hundred years." There was nothing Katzenbach could say to that.

Developments in Selma were also driving a wedge between King and the White House. Johnson felt another march would be disastrous, and he was furious that King was even considering violating Judge Johnson's order. "Listen," he told Bill Moyers, late on the night of March 8, "[King] better go to behaving himself, or all of them are going to get put in jail. I think that we really ought to be firm on it. . . . I just think it's outrageous what's on TV. I've been watching it here, and it looks like that man's in charge of the country and taking it over. I just don't think we can afford to have that kind of character running [around]. I'd . . . take a very firm line with him." Stopping what Johnson called that "goddamn march" became the president's top priority, as King would soon learn.[31]

Early the next morning, on the day of the planned march, two visitors arrived to see King: John Doar, assistant attorney general for civil rights, and LeRoy Collins, a former governor of Florida and now the director of the new Community Relations Service tasked with mediating such crises. President Johnson personally sent Collins to persuade King to call off the march. King hurried from his bedroom still wearing the burgundy pajamas he borrowed from Sullivan Jackson. He was followed by his staff, who had slept everywhere in the house, including the family bathtub. Doar was upset that King had reversed himself; the attorney general, the president, and, most importantly, Judge Johnson believed that he'd agreed not to march. King replied that a nonviolent march to request a redress of grievances was a thoroughly American act, absolutely constitutional. Collins and Doar feared a repetition of Bloody Sunday. In response, the Reverend Fred Shuttlesworth, leader of the movement in Birmingham, told the federal men that they should confer with those who had ordered the attack on Bloody Sunday, Sheriff Clark and Wallace's director of public safety, Al Lingo. King would not be moved. Even if he called off the march, he felt his angry supporters would go ahead anyway.

Finally Collins suggested a compromise: King and his company would march until they reached the spot of the recent assault, acknowledge Bloody Sunday through prayer, then turn around and return to the church. Clark and Lingo were not known for restraint, King countered. Collins asked whether, if he could get such an assurance from the Alabamians, King would accept his proposal. "I cannot agree to do anything because I don't know what I can get my people to do," King replied, "but if you will get Sheriff Clark and Lingo to agree to something like that, I will try." As Collins and Doar departed, King received final confirmation of the news he feared the most: Judge Johnson had issued an injunction prohibiting the march and ordered King to appear Thursday at a hearing to consider his petition to block state interference. That led to another round of conference calls with New York lawyers, all of which settled nothing.[32]

The day began hopefully after King's uplifting remarks at the midnight rally, but it would end disastrously, especially for King himself. Many thought it was his worst moment as a leader. He arrived at Brown Chapel at 2:30 p.m. to find a crowd of about fifteen hundred assembling in the playground adjacent to the chapel. "The doctor's arrived! The doctor's arrived!" one excited woman yelled as he entered the church. The marchers waited impatiently, some relishing another confrontation with Clark and Lingo's forces. Many sang, "Ain't gonna let nobody turn me 'round, I'm gonna keep on walkin', keep on talkin', marching up to freedom land." Black construction workers wore hard hats. "I ain't going to get bopped this time!" one said. "We were waiting for the shit to get on," another young man later recalled. "We were ready for the rumble." Jim Bevel, dressed as usual in blue overalls and skullcap, tried to calm them down. "Any man who has the urge to hit a posse man or a state trooper with a pop bottle is a fool," he told them. "That is just what they want you to do. Then they can call you a mob and beat you to death."[33]

At around 3 p.m. King addressed the crowd. "We have the right to walk the highways, and we have the right to walk to Montgomery if our feet will get us there," he said. "I have no alternative but to lead a march from this spot to carry our grievances to the seat of government. I have to march." Cheers and applause rang out. "I do not know what lies ahead of us. There may be beatings, jailing, tear gas. But I would rather die on the highways of Alabama than make a butchery of my conscience! There is nothing more tragic in all this world than to know right and not to do it." As the nearly thousand people—almost four times greater than Sunday's group—began to ready themselves, LeRoy Collins forced his way through the crowd and handed King a map. "If you follow this," Collins said, "I think everything will be all right." Although Clark and Lingo were receptive to Collins's plan, King was skeptical. He asked whether Collins thought that Clark and Lingo would really abide by such an arrangement. Collins promised to personally seize the first trooper who advanced.[34]

And so they set out. King was in the lead, flanked by John Wesley Lord, Methodist bishop of Washington, DC, and Dr. Harold Schoemer of the Chicago Theological Seminary along with King's colleagues Reverend Fred Shuttlesworth, CORE's James Farmer, and SNCC's James Forman. The line behind them stretched for a mile—rich young women wearing polo coats followed by bearded poets, senators' wives and widows, and ordinary folks, both black and white. Walking through the white business district, one angry young man yelled at King, "You son of a bitch—you want to vote, why don't you act like a human being?" King ignored him. Suddenly a car approached and its door flew open, but it was only Governor Collins with some good news. He thought they definitely had a deal: Clark and Lingo would not attack if King followed the map's route precisely. "I'll do my best,"

King told him, fearful that he might not be able to control his own followers and they might refuse to turn around. Collins departed.[35]

Nearing the bridge they were halted by Stanley Fountain, chief deputy marshal of the Southern District of Alabama, who read Judge Johnson's long legal order without missing a beat. "I am aware of the order," King replied, then he led the crowd onward, perhaps wondering if he was now in contempt of court and thinking too about Collins's last hurried remarks. There was no way that King could be sure whether he could rely on a promise made by Clark or Lingo's boss, George Wallace. This could easily be a trick, and another bloodbath might be awaiting them at the bridge. King would know shortly.

Just ahead was what John Lewis and Hosea Williams first saw two days earlier: state troopers backed up by Jim Clark's posse men. (In fact, it was now an even stronger force. One hundred fifty carloads of troopers, five hundred in all, had been added to the existing force. Nearly every member of Al Lingo's corps was on the bridge.) Then Major John Cloud and his bullhorn appeared, and veterans of Bloody Sunday momentarily relived the event. "You are ordered to stop and stand where you are," he said, his voice echoing over the crowd. "This march will not continue."

"We have a right to march," King countered.

"This march will not continue," Cloud repeated. "It is not conducive to the safety of this group or to the motoring public." Behind Cloud stood the troopers, grim faced, with their nightsticks at the ready.

King asked for a moment to pray. "You can have your prayer," Cloud said, "and then you must return to your church." As King and his followers knelt, Ralph Abernathy spoke. "We come to present our bodies as a living sacrifice. We don't have much to offer, but we do have our bodies, and we lay them on the altar today." While they prayed, a trooper raised his nightstick and, pointing it at a minister near King, said, "He's mine."

But the attack never came. As King and the others rose, Major Cloud suddenly called out, "Troopers, withdraw. Clear the road completely—move out." The blue wall opened, leaving King in an excruciating position. They could now cross the bridge and proceed to Montgomery fifty miles ahead. Or they could turn around, an act that would (as Wallace wished) embarrass and perhaps destroy King's leadership of the movement but would hopefully not violate Judge Johnson's order while also giving the marchers more time to prepare for the long trek to the capital.

Without hesitating, King whirled around and announced, "We will go back to the church now." And the great mass began to turn around, some happy but many more confused, disappointed, and furious at King.[36]

The *Times*'s Gay Talese interviewed the contented ones. "They had found the experience moving and inspiring and unforgettable," he wrote. "It was a perfect day"—but not for everyone. Many demonstrators wondered if King had made a secret deal with Wallace and if their whole effort had been a charade. "We were mad, we were all ready to get our ass kicked that afternoon," said Hardy Frye, a veteran of the Mississippi campaigns. "There were ministers, some Catholic priests, they were mad because they thought they were going to be martyrs for the cause that morning." Unitarian minister Orloff Miller was confused, then upset: "What is going on?" he later recalled. "Are we not going to go through with this confrontation? . . . I felt just awful. . . . I had come to lay myself on the line just as much as people in Selma had . . . on Sunday." But it was SNCC's James Forman who spoke most harshly. "Turn-Around Tuesday," as the event became known, was "a classic example of trickery against the people," he said.[37]

Back at Brown Chapel King faced his critics, who thought his behavior shameful. "We did march and we did reach the point of the brutality and we had a prayer service and a freedom rally," King explained. "And we will go to Montgomery next week in numbers that no man can number." Few were convinced. Willie Ricks, an early advocate of "Black Power," questioned King's courage, producing a rare public outburst. "I'm in charge here and I intend to remain in charge," King yelled. "You are not Martin Luther King! I'm Martin Luther King. No matter what you do, you'll never be Martin Luther King." As soon as he could, King left for Montgomery, where he found a temporary refuge from his enemies.[38]

One of the great ironies of Martin Luther King's career was that when he found himself in crisis, acts of violence would rescue him. When the movement stalled in Birmingham in 1963, Bull Connor's police dogs revived it. When the press began losing interest in voter registration in Selma, Jim Clark beat Annie Cooper, and the story was again front-page news. Now, when King seemed about to lose control of his people, another tragedy occurred to draw attention away from his troubles. Among those who came to Selma after Bloody Sunday were James Reeb, Clark Olsen, and Orloff Miller, all Unitarian ministers. After listening to King's apologia Tuesday night, they decided to go to dinner, and having been warned that white restaurants would not be hospitable, they dined at Walker's, not far from SCLC headquarters and Amelia Boynton's insurance office. They found the café crowded with other ministers, journalists, and black workers dining on pigs' feet, sausage, collard greens, and fried chicken while the jukebox blared Sam Cooke's "A Change Is Gonna Come."

After an enjoyable meal, the three ministers set out for Mrs. Boynton's office two blocks away, taking a shortcut that accidentally took them into hostile territory. Suddenly, four white men dressed in casual clothes ran toward them, yelling, "Hey you niggers, hey you niggers!" "Oh, oh, here's trouble," Olsen remarked, and the three hurried away. But the men were faster, and Olsen, looking over his shoulder, saw one, his face twisted in hate, swing a long club that caught Jim Reeb on the left side of his head. "Here's how it feels to be a nigger down here," Reeb's attacker screamed. The men kicked and punched Olsen and Miller and then fled, leaving the three ministers lying in the street.[39]

Miller yelled for help but nobody came. He and Olsen were able to get Reeb to his feet, but his injury was serious; he was incoherent and complaining of terrible pain. They were able to get him to Mrs. Boynton's office, where Diane Nash quickly arranged for an ambulance to take Reeb and the others to the Burwell Infirmary, a small hospital that treated blacks and their white allies. Dr. William Dinkins, who had cared for Jimmie Lee Jackson a few weeks earlier, examined Reeb, who was becoming agitated, and decided that he needed to go to Birmingham Hospital. Calls were made to obtain another ambulance, and the ministers learned that the hospital required a $150 deposit before they would admit Reeb, so Miller rushed back to the Boynton office, where Nash gave him a check to cover that expense. The ambulance arrived, picked up the unconscious Reeb and his two fellow ministers, and set out for Birmingham, one hundred miles away.

Ten minutes into their trip the ambulance blew a tire. The driver, afraid to stop, drove on, the ambulance bouncing on three tires and a metal rim. Eventually they stopped at a radio station and called for another ambulance. Just as Reeb was transferred to the new ambulance, however, Dallas County deputies pulled up, blocking the vehicle's exit. Precious time was lost as the officers interrogated the ministers and refused their request to escort them to Birmingham. After they departed, the ambulance took off, reaching speeds at more than eighty miles an hour. But it did not arrive at the Birmingham Hospital until 11:00 p.m., nearly four hours after the assault. The doctors found that Reeb had sustained multiple skull fractures, and they rushed him into surgery for a seventy-minute operation. The prognosis was grave.[40]

Coming less than a week after Bloody Sunday, the attack on a thirty-eight-year-old Boston minister and father of four brought even more Americans to Selma for what King promised would be the final—and successful—march to Montgomery. Rallies in Washington and around the country continued, and more people denounced the president's inaction. Johnson sent Mrs. Reeb a bouquet of yellow roses, prompting one activist to remark, "Flowers instead of marshals, that's what they give us. That's really big of him."[41]

King's seclusion ended on Thursday, March 11, when he appeared in Judge Johnson's Montgomery courtroom for the injunction hearings that King hoped would pave the way for a march to Montgomery. At forty-seven, the judge was already a southern legend, hated by segregationists (George Wallace called him "a low-down, carpetbaggin', scalawaggin', race-mixin' liar") and admired by civil rights workers—not because he was their advocate, for he was not, but rather because they knew they would receive a fair hearing in his courtroom. King had the utmost respect for Johnson, and although visibly nervous, he hoped for a positive outcome from the hearings.

W. McLean Pitts, Jim Clark's lawyer, attacked immediately, asking Judge Johnson to find King in contempt for violating his ban against marching. Johnson sharply rejected his motion. When Pitts insulted King and other black witnesses on cross-examination, Johnson proclaimed that everyone in his court would be treated courteously. "I'm trying very hard," Pitts stuttered. "Try a little harder," the judge shot back.

But Johnson also examined King closely about his decision to turn the march around on Tuesday. This forced King to admit that Governor Collins had brokered a deal between him and the Alabamians and that he never intended to begin a march to Montgomery that day. "I was disturbed," King testified. "Thousands of people who had come to Selma to march were deeply aroused by the brutality of Sunday. I felt if I had not done it, pent-up emotions could have developed into an uncontrollable situation. I did it to give them an outlet." He had made a difficult choice but one that was consistent with his belief in nonviolence. Although King's lawyers hoped that would be enough to save King from a contempt citation, it was also sure to enlarge the growing gulf between him and SNCC's young followers. Indeed, some of them told reporters privately that they felt King had betrayed the movement. Further, SNCC leader Jim Forman, demonstrating what the *New York Times* called "open contempt" for King, on Wednesday had moved his followers into Montgomery, where demonstrations led to violent confrontations with police and state troopers. And more days of hearings lay ahead before the judge made a final decision.[42]

That Thursday was also a hard day for President Johnson. In the president's quarters he could hear the sounds of picketers—hundreds of them, he later learned, marching along Pennsylvania Avenue, some chanting, "Freedom Now," others singing, "We Shall Overcome," and many bearing signs that read, "Go All The Way, LBJ." A few hours later they blocked traffic by lying down in the street.[43]

More trouble followed later that day. A group of twelve young people (ten females, two males) joined a White House tour at 11:00 a.m., and as they strolled along the main first floor corridor they suddenly stopped and sat down. They declared their intentions by singing, "We Shall Not Be Moved." Professor Eric Goldman, Johnson's presidential historian, thought them a disorderly, disheveled bunch. "They sprawled across the floor, shouted songs interspersed with crude insults directed at the President, demanded that he speak to them, and that he speak 'right,'" Goldman later wrote. As Goldman passed them, one young woman yelled, "Where you going, fink bastard—going to get him his bullwhip?"[44]

The sit-in came at the worst possible time. That evening Johnson planned to brief eighty congressmen and senators on civil rights and Vietnam, then join them and their wives at a reception in the State Dining Room. So the young demonstrators had to be removed as quickly as possible. When his aide Lee White suggested that the group be arrested and forcibly removed, Johnson chose a more clever approach. "Let them eat and drink, but don't let them go to the bathroom," he ordered. So with Mrs. Johnson's help, the group received cup after cup of coffee, and sure enough, after a few minutes two left hurriedly, never to return. Ten remained. The president ordered that the group be totally isolated in their nest in the East Wing's corridor. White House police placed screens around them, passersby avoided them, and reporters were not allowed to interview them. At 3:30 Johnson sent Lee White, Clifford Alexander, and Press Secretary Bill Moyers to meet with them to see if it was safe for Johnson to talk with them. "We want to see the President!" cried one stocky young man, but his colleagues, fearing the president's well-known temper, shouted him down. Moyers asked, "How would you like it if someone came into your house and refused to move?" and the dialogue quickly deteriorated. When the president learned of the exchange, he became "snappish," according to one aide: "I send three of the supposed smartest guys in the world on a simple assignment," Johnson barked, "and they can't even get some kids to talk to me."[45]

Finally tiring of this annoyance, Johnson developed the plan that brought an end to the six-hour-long sit-in. While he attended the dedication of a new gymnasium on Capitol Hill at 6:00, two plain-clothes police officers, one white, one black, dragged off just two demonstrators, placing them in an unmarked car and driving them away. A few minutes later a second team of officers removed two more and so on until the hall was cleared. All the demonstrators ended up at different police stations throughout the city where, eventually, they were freed without an arraignment or posting bond.[46]

The protestors were gone, but the attacks on Johnson continued. Now, however, they came from the senators and representatives who, like his earlier visitors, showed little respect for the president. "Where is your bill? . . ." asked an angry New Hampshire Republican. "Why has it taken four months?" The president immediately jumped to his feet, "obviously stung," recalled one who was present. With equal heat, Johnson replied that there were complicated obstacles to overcome. They had labored long to create a bill with nearly impossible features: it must be constitutional, able to pass quickly through Congress, and emerge in a form strong enough to register all eligible voters—not an easy task. Mississippi congressman John Bell Williams and his colleague Glenn Andrews, whose district included Selma, blamed the president for not controlling King who, Andrews said, was responsible for the violence that had wracked his city. Johnson asked them to consider the causes that produced the crisis—denying blacks the right to vote. Then, presidential aide Marvin Watson entered the room and handed the president a note. It contained the grim news he had expected: Reverend James Reeb had died. Johnson excused himself, and he and Mrs. Johnson telephoned their condolences to Mrs. Reeb and the minister's father. It was "a helpless and painful talk," Lady Bird Johnson thought, one that lasted fifteen minutes. Later the president dispatched an Air Force C-140 jet to Birmingham to fly Mrs. Reeb and her father-in-law home to Boston.

Before retiring for the night the First Lady tape-recorded her thoughts on that evening's events: "When we went upstairs we could hear the Congressional guests and the music still playing below; and out in front the chanting of the civil rights marchers. What a house. What a life."[47]

With Reeb's death, the fires of protest in Selma and around the country flamed anew. "Reverend Reeb now joins the ranks of those martyred heroes who have died in the struggle for freedom and human dignity," Dr. King said. He was "murdered by an atmosphere of inhumanity in Alabama that tolerated the vicious murder of Jimmie Lee Jackson . . . and the brutal beating of Sunday in Selma." To undermine King's eulogy, Sheriff Clark issued his own statement, in which he described Jackson as having "died under very mysterious circumstances," whereas Reeb's mortal injuries were the result of a barroom fight. Police Chief Wilson Baker announced the arrest of four suspects, but despite the seriousness of the alleged crime, all were quickly freed after posting an unusually modest bail. Demonstrations increased, and those who were holding an around-the-clock prayer vigil in a chilly rain were pelted with rocks and bottles by angry whites. Snipers, perched further away, fired their rifles at the group, slightly injuring four, including a teenage girl who suffered a split lip and the loss of a tooth.[48]

In Washington, DC, three thousand clergymen from throughout the United States—priests, ministers, and rabbis—gathered to attend an interfaith rally called by the National Council of Churches' Commission on Religion and Race. On Friday morning, March 12, they filled a church on East Capitol Street to overflowing, where they listened to their colleagues report on the violence they had observed in Selma, violence that had now claimed the life of a fellow cleric. The speakers called on President Johnson to send a voting rights bill to Congress and provide protection for civil rights workers in Alabama. "I know that President Johnson is a deeply concerned and troubled man," said Methodist bishop John Wesley Lord, who had marched with King on Turn-Around Tuesday. "But I also believe, that due to the inability of the President to act . . . many Negroes and whites have become disenchanted and are in deep despair." Lord called on the president to visit Selma, an act that "would do much to restore lost confidence and increase hope in the future." When the session ended around noon, hundreds marched to the capitol to confer with their representatives and senators.[49]

Johnson faced his critics head-on that morning. They came first from a local civil rights group, led by the Reverend Walter Fauntroy, the Washington, DC, director of the Southern Christian Leadership Conference, which met with the president for two hours in the Cabinet Room. Besides clergymen, members of SNCC, CORE, and the Mississippi Freedom Democratic Party—veteran activists who had seen their colleagues beaten and killed throughout the South—were also in attendance. They were in no mood for presidential bromides. "Why has it taken so long for you to send a voting rights bill to the Congress?" asked an angry Paul Moore Jr., the liberal Episcopal bishop of Washington, DC. "Two reasons," Johnson replied. "First, it's got to pass. We can't risk defeat or dilution by filibuster on this one. This bill has to go up there clean, simple, and powerful. Second, we don't want this bill declared unconstitutional. This can't be just a two-line bill. . . . The wherefores and the therefores are insurance against that."

Others wanted to know why he refused to send troops or even US Marshals to protect the beleaguered activists in Selma. Johnson explained the difficulties involved but did admit that he had placed seven hundred federal troops on alert and would have moved them quickly to the Edmund Pettus Bridge if Tuesday's agreement had broken down. Johnson was reluctant to use force, believing that it would drive southern moderates into George Wallace's camp. He informed the activists that the Justice Department had filed an amicus brief supporting King's request that Judge Johnson prohibit Alabama forces from attacking another march, and the president stressed the importance of waiting for the judge's decision. If Wallace failed to protect the marchers and violence again erupted, Johnson would then send in troops.

Never one to respond well to threats or pressure, Johnson attacked the demonstrators outside who, he said, had disturbed his family's sleep. Such acts would not affect him, he insisted. He would not be "blackjacked" into hasty action, whether it was sending troops to Selma or sending a voting rights bill to Congress.

"I don't think anyone is interested in whether your daughters could sleep or not," said a brazen young SNCC activist named Hubert Brown. "We are interested in the lives of our people. Which side is the federal government on?" This would not be the last time that Brown, who his friends called "Rap," made statements designed to enflame those in power. Within two years he would become one of the foremost advocates of Black Power, proclaiming, "If America doesn't come around, then black people are going to burn it down."

Brown's remarks on this day must have shocked the president, because suddenly a different Lyndon Johnson appeared, one whose powerful soliloquy about the importance of the black struggle held his listeners spellbound for an hour. Speaker of the House John McCormack, also present, remarked, "Good Lord, Mr. President, why don't you say that to the people? I think you should come up to the Congress and say it there."

"At the right time, I will, Mr. Speaker," he said. "At the right time."

The group departed at 12:10 p.m., no doubt confused by the president's erratic behavior.[50]

Johnson skipped lunch, and five minutes later he met the delegation from the National Council of Churches. Sensing tension, he tried to diffuse it by joking that the demonstrators outside were so noisy that they were "violatin' *my* civil rights." Nobody found this amusing, so Johnson tried to win them over by recounting his achievements in civil rights. When that failed to win them over, Johnson likened himself to a tormented Abraham Lincoln, whose ghost, he said, was "moving up and down the corridors of the [White House]," adding for good measure, "I am a greatly anguished man." He promised that the bill would be forthcoming in a matter of days. But he had said that so often that the group departed unconvinced of his sincerity. One participant later called Johnson's remarks "a snow job."[51]

When Johnson returned to his office later that afternoon he learned that telegrams had been pouring in to the White House, each demanding a voting rights bill. Fifty people telephoned Johnson, expressing their anger about what had happened to Reverend Reeb. (No one called him when Jimmie Lee Jackson died.) New reports noted that student protestors had been especially active that day: in Berkeley, California, they had dived into a pool that reflected the towering federal building behind it, while students from Harvard, Brandeis, Radcliffe, and MIT had staged a sit-in at Boston's federal building and forced police to drag them away.[52]

Those who observed the president most closely thought the continuing crisis was physically and emotionally exhausting him. Mrs. Johnson worried most of all: "There is this heavy load of tension and this fog of depression," she noted in her diary at the time. What the president needed was "exercise, diet, and a break—to get off to sunshine and rest for a couple of days. . . . But Lyndon feels chained right here, and it's having a corrosive effect on his personality." There was no escaping that fog or the frustrations and uncertainties he was experiencing. Just four months earlier he had won the presidency with 60 percent of the popular vote, the greatest landslide in history. Now he seemed to be at odds with everyone: civil rights workers and religious leaders attacked him to his face, southerners hated him, and, most seriously, he felt he was losing control of Congress. "Is Dirksen planning to pull out on us?" Johnson had asked Katzenbach earlier that week. The attorney general assured the president that the Illinois senator was still on board. But Johnson remained nervous: Forty-three members of the House and seven senators—Republicans and Democrats alike—had urged him to submit a bill immediately. Powerful members of the Senate and the House disliked the Justice Department's draft and privately threatened to submit their own versions of the bill. Although Katzenbach and the others were still working on the bill—tightening words here, providing more detail there—by that Friday afternoon he had decided to submit the bill within the next few days, however imperfect it still might be.[53]

Then came a telegram from Governor Wallace requesting a meeting with the president to discuss the Alabama crisis. Johnson was not surprised: Wallace had leaked news of his request to the press before Johnson actually received the message. And the president had been trying for several days to reach the governor to see if they could talk about avoiding another catastrophe. But his southern contacts were discouraging. Buford Ellington, a former Tennessee governor now serving as director of the Office of Emergency Planning, warned Johnson that "you can't trust [Wallace]. I can talk to him anytime, but there's an element of danger there." Alabama senator Lister Hill agreed with Ellington's assessment of the governor: "That damned little Wallace," he told Johnson. "The trouble is he just wants people to say, 'Oh, God, he died for the cause—he stayed back for the bitter end.'" But Johnson did receive the impression, as he told Hill, that the governor "wants a way out because this is getting pretty bad from their standpoint." With this in mind, Johnson quickly responded to the telegram and invited Wallace to come to the White House on Saturday, March 13.[54]

What ensued was "the most amazing conversation I've ever been present at," Nicholas Katzenbach later recalled, and at three hours and seventeen minutes, it was surely one of the longest. Johnson invited Wallace and Seymore Trammel, Wallace's closest aide, into the Oval Office, directing the bantam-weight governor to take a seat on a spongy couch into which he sank, reducing his already tiny stature by a foot. Pulling his rocking chair close by, the six-foot-four Johnson, though seated, still towered over the helpless Wallace. For a few minutes there was just pleasant banter. Johnson proudly introduced the governor to his dogs, Him, a tan beagle, and Blanco, a white collie who sniffed at the governor with canine curiosity. It might have been the high point of Wallace's reception in the Oval Office.

"Well, Governor," Johnson finally asked, "you wanted to see me?"

Wallace told the president that "malcontents, many of them trained in Moscow and New York," were disrupting Alabama. It was Johnson's responsibility to stop them.

The governor was wrong, Johnson replied. All the protestors sought was the right to vote. "You can't stop a fever by putting an icepack on your head," he said. "You've got to use antibiotics and get to the cause of the fever."

"You cannot deal with street revolutionaries," Wallace countered. "You can never satisfy them. First it is a front seat on the bus; next it's a takeover of the parks; then it's public schools; then it's voting rights; then it's jobs; then it's distribution of wealth without work."

Johnson looked at Wallace with a mixture of scorn and pity. "George, why are you doing this?" he asked. "You came into office a liberal—you spent all your life wanting to do things for the poor. . . . Why are you off on this black thing? You ought to be down there calling for help for Aunt Susie in the nursing home."

Trammel tried to interrupt the president, to shift the conversation back to what he and his boss thought was the central issue—the Communist protestors who were tearing up Alabama—but Johnson refused to yield the floor.

"George," Johnson said, "do you see all of those demonstrators out in front of the White House?"

"Oh, yes, Mr. President, I saw them," Wallace replied.

"Wouldn't it be just wonderful if we could put an end to all those demonstrations?"

"Oh, yes, Mr. President, that would be wonderful."

"Well, why don't you and I go out there, George . . . and let's announce that you've decided to [let the blacks vote] . . . in Alabama. . . . Why don't you let the niggers vote? You agree they got the right to vote, don't you?"

"Oh, yes, there's no quarrel with that," Wallace said.

"Well, then, why don't you let them vote?" Johnson asked.

"I don't have that power. That belongs to the country registrars in the state of Alabama."

"George," he said, "don't you shit me as to who runs Alabama."

Wallace continued to claim that he had no legal power over state registrars.

"Why don't you persuade them, George?"

"I don't think I could do that."

"Now, don't shit me . . . George Wallace."

Looking Wallace straight in the eye, Johnson said, "George, you're fucking over your president. Why are you fucking over your president?

"George, you and I shouldn't be thinking about 1964," Johnson continued. "We should be thinking about 1984. We'll both be dead and gone then. Now, you've got a lot of poor people down there in Alabama, a lot of ignorant people. A lot of people need jobs. A lot of people need a future. You could do a lot for them." Appealing to Wallace's better nature, he said, "Now, in 1984, George, what do you want left behind? You want a great big marble monument that says, 'George Wallace: He Built', or do you want a little piece of scrawny pine laying there along that hot Caliches soil that says, 'George Wallace: He Hated'?"[55]

The long conversation with Wallace had energized the president as it also reduced the governor to what one observer called "a mass of quivering flesh." Before leaving the White House Wallace met with reporters, one of whom thought that he "looked considerably sobered and shorn of his accustomed cockiness." Ignoring the questions they fired at him, he thanked the president, who he called "a great gentleman, as always," for his hospitality. Then he departed, surrounded by Secret Service agents and police. Later Wallace confessed to an aide that Johnson had simply overwhelmed him. "Hell," he said, "if I'd stayed in there much longer, he'd have had me coming out for civil rights."[56]

Later that afternoon Johnson met with more than one hundred reporters who had gathered in the Rose Garden for a special Saturday press conference. He was no longer the indecisive, hesitant leader who had met with the clergymen just a few days prior. Now Johnson was "forceful and in full command," the New York Times's Tom Wicker later wrote. Typically the president's opening remarks at a news conference were brief and unremarkable. Not today. "This March week has brought a very deep and painful challenge to the unending search for American freedom," the president said. "That challenge is not yet over but before it is ended every resource of this Government will be directed to insuring justice for all men of all races in Alabama and everywhere in this land."

Those who had demonstrated peacefully in Selma on Sunday, March 7, were protesting "against a deep and very unjust flaw in American democracy itself," the president insisted—the denial of the right to vote because of the color of their skin. They were then attacked in an event Johnson called an "American tragedy:" "The blows that were received, the blood that was shed . . . must strengthen the determination of each of us to bring full and equal and exact justice to all of our people." Toward that end he surprised reporters by announcing that a new voting rights bill would be sent to Congress on Monday, March 15—just two days away. The new law "would strike down all restrictions used to deny the people the right to vote. . . . This is not just the policy of your Government, or your President," Johnson said. "It is in the heart and the purpose and the meaning of America itself." Never before had the president been so publicly supportive of the civil rights movement and the fight for voting rights.[57]

That evening the president and Mrs. Johnson attended a dinner party celebrating the appointment of a new American ambassador to Spain. Gone was the morose, anguished Johnson. "He was more in control of himself than I've ever seen," said one guest. "It was as if he had climbed a high place and could see things better than anyone else and fit them together." He had heard the painful pleas from the blacks of Selma and Marion but had waited. He withstood the attacks brought on by Reverend Reeb's death and listened to angry clergymen and congressmen. But still he waited, allowing the pressure to build until public opinion polls indicated overwhelming support for a voting rights act. Now he could move forward, although the future remained far from clear. Not even Lyndon Johnson, master of Congress, could predict how the legislature would react on a subject so controversial as the place of black citizens in American life. But doing nothing was no longer a reasonable option. For Lyndon Johnson action was always the best medicine, better than exercise or sunshine. The chains that had bound him were broken, and the fog of depression that had plagued him had lifted. So he partied late into the night, not retiring until 4:25 a.m.[58]

Sunday, however, was no day of rest. Late in the afternoon Johnson called congressional leaders together for a meeting in the Cabinet Room to discuss the next steps. He described the provisions of the bill the Justice Department had now completed and asked if he should submit the bill to Congress along with a written statement, as was usually done, or if he should personally present the bill to a joint session of Congress that would also be televised to the nation. Not since 1946 had a sitting president appeared before Congress to ask them to consider a piece of legislation. Mike Mansfield and Everett Dirksen, the Senate's leaders and protectors of that body's prerogatives, preferred the traditional way. Dirksen feared that Johnson would look like he had been forced into submitting the legislation, and Congress would no doubt resent such public pressure.

John McCormack, Speaker of the House, disagreed. At seventy-three, he was the oldest man in the room, and his colleagues respected him greatly. The president should present the bill in person, he insisted. House Majority Leader Carl Albert agreed: "I don't think your coming before the Congress would be a sign of panic. I think it would help." This was Johnson's view too. By 6:30 p.m. a consensus had formed: Johnson would speak to a joint session of Congress and the nation from the House chamber at 9:00 p.m. the following night.[59]

Little time remained to produce the most important speech of Lyndon Johnson's career. A Justice Department lawyer had been working on a draft for weeks, but "it just doesn't sing yet," Katzenbach had told the president on March 10. Johnson's aide Horace Busby, a Texan and a longtime friend of the president's, was given the assignment of revising the lawyer's draft rather than Johnson's favorite speechwriter, thirty-three-year-old Richard Goodwin. When Johnson heard the news he was enraged. "Don't you know a liberal Jew has his hands on the pulse beat of America, and you asked a Texas public relations man?" he asked his aide Jack Valenti. "Get Dick to do it. And now!"[60]

Valenti hurried to Goodwin's office early on the morning of March 15, only to learn that the young speechwriter rarely showed up for work before 9:30 a.m. He waited there nervously until Goodwin arrived, startling him with the news that he was to write that evening's speech on voting rights. "Get to work," Valenti said, then left Goodwin to his task, which had to be completed by mid-afternoon so that aides could load it into the presidential teleprompter. Goodwin relished the job. "It was great working for Johnson," he later reflected. "I had come to know . . . his pattern of expression, patterns of reasoning, the natural cadences of his speech." Goodwin also knew that Johnson preferred "forceful, eloquent straightforward" speeches, and that's what Goodwin would deliver.[61]

Goodwin's past was not very different from Johnson's. As boys both had experienced near poverty—Johnson in the Texas hill country, Goodwin in

Boston and then in rural Maryland, where his father landed a war-time job. Johnson's modest education and southern roots had left him with a sense of inferiority that no political achievement could wipe away, whereas Goodwin had experienced the taunts and blows of young anti-Semites. Those shared experiences were in the minds of both men as Goodwin worked on the speech. As he stared at the blank page in his typewriter, he could see "images tumbling through my mind—black bodies on the Pettus Bridge . . . the fear of my youth and the horrified terror of . . . men whose faces were contorted by bigotry—'kike,' 'nigger.' By the purest chance, an accident of time and place, I had been given an opportunity to strike back. . . . I could, that is, if my craft was equal to my passion."

Goodwin worked tirelessly all morning and into the early afternoon. As he finished a page, it was immediately taken to the president, who left Goodwin alone except for one afternoon call. "You remember, Dick, that one of my first jobs after college was teaching young Mexican-Americans down in Cotulla," Johnson said after Goodwin had picked up the phone. "I thought you might want to put in a reference to that."

"Yes, Mr. President," Goodwin said. He knew the story; it was one of Johnson's favorites.

"I just wanted to remind you," the president said, then hung up.[62]

The silence of Goodwin at work, the only sound the tap-tap-tap of the typewriter keys, contrasted sharply with the noise in Lyndon Johnson's office as he and his aides went over Goodwin's draft. Long after the point when the speech should have been loaded into the teleprompter, they were still revising it. "As the afternoon wore on, the tension began to mount for everybody," Lady Bird Johnson later wrote in her diary. "[Lyndon] was going over it . . . a page at a time . . . scratching out lines, giving directions to Jack [Valenti], who looked pale, harassed . . . almost at the breaking point. I could very nearly hear him groan whenever Lyndon marked out a line and wrote in something else. This was still going on at 7 o'clock, and he had to be on the stand delivering it at 9." Johnson barked at a secretary who typed, he said, "with fourteen goddamn wooden fingers." Bill Moyers and Harry McPherson offered editorial changes he disliked, causing him to fume, "Every goddamn body around here thinks he's smarter than I am! I told them what I wanted to say, but this shit has no resemblance to what I want to say."

Finally, around 7:00, the president announced, "Let's close it up." The speech was done. Mrs. Johnson usually saw to the president's clothes, but this night she had already left for the capitol with daughter Linda Bird, so Paul Glynn, a White House military aide who often doubled as valet, dressed the president in a dark blue suit and light blue shirt, which would come through well on Americans' black-and-white television screens.[63]

Johnson invited Goodwin to ride with him to the capitol, allowing the speechwriter to observe the president closely at this historic moment. He was silent, absorbed in the text he was reading by the light of a special lamp installed in his limousine. Occasionally he would underline words or phrases he wished to emphasize. He never looked at his aides or said a word. Not even the chants of the protestors across the street disturbed his reverie, although, as Horace Busby later recalled, "he heard [them]." Only half the speech had been installed in the teleprompter, so Johnson would have to read much of the address from the black loose-leaf notebook in which it rested. Jack Valenti would have the unenviable task of slipping into the well of the House chamber and inserting the rest of the address in the machine. "If you can't get it on the TelePrompTer," Johnson warned Valenti, "then I can't speak."[64]

At first, ritual suggested Johnson's appearance was just an ordinary event, not unlike the president's State of the Union Address delivered just three months earlier. Tonight, as on January 4, it began with the bellowing voice of the doorkeeper, William "Fishbait" Miller, who informed Congress that they had a visitor: "Mistah Speak-ah! The President of the United States!" A burst of applause greeted a sober-faced Johnson as he made his way to the rostrum, not pausing, as in the past, to shake hands, say a word to old friends, or touch their shoulders. As the new vice president, Hubert H. Humphrey, looked on, Speaker of the House John McCormack introduced the president. There was more applause. Johnson nodded and looked out at his audience. No doubt he was aware that some of his former colleagues were missing; the Virginia and Mississippi delegations as well as other southerners had decided to boycott the president's speech. With the crack of McCormack's gavel, people sat, and there was a moment's silence as Johnson looked down at his notebook, tweaked his nose, and looked up. "What followed," noted *Time* magazine's correspondent, "was a departure from . . . routine, so startling, so moving, that few who saw it or heard it will ever forget it."

Slowly, deliberately, he began: "Mr. Speaker, Mr. President, I speak tonight for the dignity of man and the destiny of Democracy. I urge every member of both parties, Americans of all religions and of all colors, from every section of this country, to join me in that cause.

"At times, history and fate meet at a single time in a single place to shape a turning point in man's unending search for freedom. So it was at Lexington and Concord. So it was a century ago at Appomattox. So it was last week in Selma, Alabama. There, long suffering men and women peacefully protested the denial of their rights as Americans. Many of them were brutally assaulted. One good man—a man of God—was killed."

There wasn't a sound in the crowded chamber—not a cough, not a whisper, not a stir. The usually raucous House was as silent as a church.

"There is no cause for pride in what has happened in Selma. There is no cause for self-satisfaction in the long denial of equal rights of millions of Americans. But there is cause for hope and for faith in our Democracy. . . . Our mission is at once the oldest and the most basic of this country—to right wrong, to do justice, to serve man. . . . Rarely in any time does an issue lay bare the secret heart of America itself. Rarely are we met with a challenge, not to our growth or abundance, or our welfare or our security, but rather to the values and the purposes and the meaning of our beloved nation. The issue of equal rights for American Negroes is such an issue. And should we defeat every enemy, and should we double our wealth and conquer the stars, and still be unequal to this issue, then we will have failed as a people and as a nation. For, with a country as with a person, 'what is a man profited if he shall gain the whole world, and lose his own soul?'"

The biblical quotation produced the first applause. "You can always count on the Bible to get them going," Goodwin later reflected. But Johnson did not smile or recognize the response in any way. When it was quiet again, he continued.

"There is no Negro problem. There is no Southern problem. There is no Northern problem. There is only an American problem." That produced the second sustained applause of the evening.

"And we are met here tonight as Americans—not as Democrats or Republicans . . . to solve that problem."

He reminded Congress and the country of America's founding principles, ideas that were beloved by all its citizens. "To deny a man his hopes because of his color or race or his religion or the place of his birth is not only to do injustice, it is to deny Americans and to dishonor the dead who gave their lives for American freedom," he said. "Many of the issues of civil rights are very complex and most difficult. But about this there can and should be no argument: every American citizen must have an equal right to vote.

There is no reason which can excuse the denial of that right. . . . Yet the harsh fact is that in many places in this country men and women are kept from voting simply because they are Negroes."

Then the president became what he had once been—a teacher, explaining to his countrymen what happens when a southern black man or woman tries to register to vote. "Every device of which human ingenuity is capable, has been used to deny this right. The Negro citizen may go to register only to be told that the day is wrong, or the hour is late, or the official in charge is absent. And if he persists and, if he manages to present himself to the registrar, he may be disqualified because he did not spell out his middle name, or because he abbreviated a word on the application. And if he manages to fill out an application, he is given a test. The registrar is the sole judge of whether he passes this test. He may be asked to recite the entire Constitution, or explain the most complex provisions of state law.

"And even a college degree cannot be used to prove that he can read and write. For the fact is that the only way to pass these barriers is to show a white skin. . . . No law that we now have on the books can insure the right to vote when local officials are determined to deny it. In such a case, our duty must be clear to all of us. The Constitution says that no person shall be kept from voting because of his race or his color."

Now the applause came in continual waves, sometimes after every sentence. Valenti, the official speech statistician, counted thirty-six interruptions, whereas *Newsweek*'s Samuel Shaffer put it at thirty-nine.[65]

To correct this denial of the fundamental right to vote, the president proposed a remedy. "Wednesday, I will send to Congress a law designed to eliminate illegal barriers to the right to vote. . . . This bill will strike down restrictions to voting in all elections, federal, state and local, which have been used to deny Negroes the right to vote.

"This bill will establish a simple, uniform standard which cannot be used, however ingenious the effort, to flout our Constitution. It will provide for citizens to be registered by officials of the United States Government, if the state officials refuse to register them. It will eliminate tedious, unnecessary lawsuits which delay the right to vote. Finally, this legislation will insure that properly registered individuals are not prohibited from voting. . . . The command of the Constitution is plain. . . . It is wrong—deadly wrong—to deny any of your fellow Americans the right to vote in this country.

"On this issue, there must be no delay, or no hesitation, or no compromise with our purpose. We cannot, we must not, refuse to protect the right of every American to vote in every election that he may desire to participate in.

"And we ought not, and we cannot, and we must not wait . . . before we get a bill. We have already waited 100 years and more and the time for waiting is gone. So I ask you to join me in working long hours and nights and weekends, if necessary, to pass this bill. And I don't make that request lightly, for, from the window where I sit, with the problems of our country, I recognize that from outside this chamber is the outraged conscience of a nation, the grave concern of many nations and the harsh judgment of history on our acts."

The chairman of the House Judiciary Committee, Brooklyn Democrat Emanuel Celler, leapt to his feet to lead what became a standing ovation that lasted thirty seconds. Senate Majority Leader Mike Mansfield, usually shy and retiring, was "shaking with emotion" and had tears in his eyes, noted Shaffer. The excitement in the chamber gave Valenti the opportunity to slip into the well of the House to insert the rest of the president's speech into the teleprompter. ("I almost died a thousand deaths getting it here in time," Valenti said later.)[66]

Only the speechwriters knew what was coming next, the words that would forever mark that moment as perhaps the greatest in Johnson's presidency. "What happened in Selma is part of a far larger movement which reaches into every section and state of America. It is the effort of American Negroes to secure for themselves the full blessings of American life. Their cause must be our cause too. Because it's not just Negroes, but really it's all of us, who must overcome the crippling legacy of bigotry and injustice." He paused, and then, slowly and distinctly, the president uttered the words never before said by an American president: "And—we—shall—overcome." For a moment there was only stunned silence, as it dawned on all who listened that President Lyndon Johnson, a son of the South, had just evoked the anthem of the civil rights movement. Then the room erupted in applause. Almost everyone rose—save the southerners ("Goddamn," one cursed) and Senator Dirksen. Johnson glared at Dirksen and paused until the television cameras focused on the senator, who then rose, joining the others who were giving Johnson a standing ovation. "In the galleries, Negroes and whites . . . wept unabashedly," noted a presidential aide.[67]

In Selma the movement's leaders had gathered at the home of Sullivan Jackson to watch Johnson's speech. When he uttered those three incredible words, "We shall overcome," King's lieutenants were shocked, then cried out, "Can you believe he said that?" John Lewis looked over at King and saw him wipe tears from his cheek.[68]

In private, during the days before the speech, Johnson had often complained about the demonstrators' impatience and their failure, as he saw it, to appreciate all that he had done for black Americans. Tonight, however, he had only empathy and praise for these men and women. "A century has passed—more than 100 years—since the Negro was freed," Johnson said after the applause had died down. "And he is not fully free tonight. It was more than 100 years ago that Abraham Lincoln . . . signed the Emancipation Proclamation. But emancipation is a proclamation and not a fact. . . . The time of justice has now come, and I tell you that I believe sincerely that no force can hold it back. It is right in the eyes of man and God that it should come, and when it does, I think that day will brighten the lives of every American.

"The real hero of this struggle," Johnson continued, "is the American Negro. His actions and protests, his courage to risk safety, and even to risk his life, have awakened the conscience of this nation. His demonstrations have been designed to call attention to injustice, designed to provoke change, designed to stir reform. He has been called upon to make good the promise of America. And who among us can say that we would have made the same progress were it not for his persistent bravery and his faith in American democracy? For at the real heart of the battle for equality is a deep-seated belief in the democratic process. Equality depends, not on the force of arms or tear gas, but depends upon the force of moral right."

His speech had already gone past the half-hour mark, and for all its drama, his audience was growing restless. But he had more to say. In the last few minutes of his speech Johnson took Congress and the country back into his own past for another lesson on the evil of prejudice. He was just twenty years old, he told his audience, when his first job took him to the small, impoverished town of Cotulla, Texas, where he taught young Mexican Americans. He smiled at the memory of it but then grew serious again. "Few of them could speak English and I couldn't speak much Spanish. My students were poor and they often came to class without breakfast and hungry. And they knew even in their youth the pain of prejudice. They never seemed to know why people disliked them, but they knew it was so because I saw it in their eyes.

"I often walked home late in the afternoon after the classes were finished wishing there was more that I could do. But all I knew was to teach them the little that I knew, hoping that I might help them against the hardships that lay ahead. And somehow you never forget what poverty and hatred can do when you see its scars on the hopeful face of a young child.

"I never thought then, in 1928, that I would be standing here in 1965. It never even occurred to me in my fondest dreams that I might have the chance to help the sons and daughters of those students, and to help people like them all over this country. But now I do have that chance."

His eyes narrowed and his voice grew more determined: "I'll let you in on a secret—I mean to use it. And I hope that you will use it with me." He was almost finished, but he wanted all to know what kind of president he wished to be—one who educated the young, fed the hungry, helped the poor, ended hatred, "and protected the right of every citizen to vote in every election." He asked Congress to join him in this historic task.[69]

He departed the House chamber "a changed man," *Time* later observed, "certain that he had launched the U.S. itself inexorably toward a new purpose." But although Johnson had stirred the nation's soul, the true impact of his words had yet to be gauged. He would now need the members of Congress to do more than just applaud. If his words were to be turned into deeds, Congress would have to turn his bill into law.[70]

TO THE PROMISED LAND

THE PRESIDENT HAD SPOKEN. A VOTING RIGHTS BILL WOULD SOON BE SENT to Congress. Martin Luther King greeted the news with relief, but he could not afford to celebrate for long.

The civil rights coalition was as fragile as ever, and there was no guarantee that lobbying for the Voting Rights Bill would hold it together. Lawyer J. L. Chestnut, reflecting the views of many Selma activists, feared that Lyndon Johnson—not King—had become "the number-one civil rights leader in America," that the president had "outfoxed" and "co-opted" King and his allies. "If [Johnson] became recognized as the man responsible for our civil rights victories and allowed to set our agenda," Chestnut later wrote, "did this mean the end of the movement?" Marches and demonstrations should continue, Chestnut believed, so that the president understood that they still controlled the movement.[1]

SNCC's Jim Forman and his followers agreed. They were not impressed by Johnson's speech—which King had publicly called "one of the most eloquent . . . and passionate pleas for human rights ever made by a President of the United States." SNCC's official photographer, after listening to Johnson, said he "wanted to puke," whereas Forman thought that by invoking "We Shall Overcome," Johnson had simply "spoiled a good song." If the movement splintered, violence might result, thereby affecting Judge Johnson's pending decision to allow another march to Montgomery and also play into the hands of the bill's congressional opponents. That was Martin Luther King's fear following Johnson's address, and events quickly proved that his concern was well founded.[2]

Forman had already moved his troops into Montgomery, and although King publicly endorsed continued demonstrations in the city as a way to keep pressure on the Johnson administration, SNCC activities were becoming more violent. Less than twenty-four hours after Johnson spoke a SNCC-led march on the capitol caused state troopers to go berserk again, riding their horses into the marchers and hitting them with ropes and billy clubs. This group, which included students from nearby Alabama State University and a large contingent of white students from northern schools, turned on the troopers. "Kill them!" one yelled, and some threw bricks as others screamed "Pigs!" and "Fascists!" Although such confrontations were exactly what organizers wanted, the demonstrators also knew that responding with force could hurt their own cause. Jim Bevel, a King lieutenant but one whose relationship with SNCC was good, urged the demonstrators not to battle with the police, stating, "Wallace would love for you to knock a policeman's eye out. Then he could go on television and talk about a one-eyed policeman for two months."[3]

In Selma the protests also took a new turn when a group of thirty-six whites, many of them ministers dressed in clerical garb, attempted to picket the home of Mayor Smitherman, located in a more affluent part of the city that civil rights workers had not yet targeted. They accused Smitherman of doing nothing about the unpaved streets and uncollected garbage in the city's black section, and they carried signs that read, "When Will You Hire Negroes For Decent City Jobs" and "We Demand Integrated Education For All." Wilson Baker protected the mayor's home, and when some of the neighborhood's white residents attacked two of the protestors, the usually unflappable police chief lost his temper. "We [warned] them there would be trouble out here," he told reporters, adding that he believed that the ministers "want people killed. They really want people killed."

Baker turned on the protestors in much the same way that Jim Clark had in past confrontations. With his cigar clamped firmly between his teeth, Baker grabbed the Reverend Boniface Prater of Chicago and roughly turned him around. When Prater's colleagues tried to restrain Baker, he yelled, "Don't put your damned hands on me, you non-violent fools." To Prater, Baker said, "I'm going to take you to a mental institution. You're sick." They were all "mentally sick," he told the protestors. He arrested all thirty-six of them for picketing in a residential area. While they waited to be loaded onto school buses, they sang, "We Shall Overcome" in a rather off-key fashion. "This has ceased to be a Negro movement," Baker told the *Times*'s Roy Reed. "It's become a misfit white movement. At least we had good music when the Negroes were demonstrating."[4]

While Wilson Baker was cursing ministers in Selma, Judge Frank M. Johnson in Montgomery was having a similarly harsh conversation with Attorney General Nicholas Katzenbach. The attorney general had called Johnson on March 17 asking when a decision to allow or prohibit King's march might be forthcoming. Johnson had already decided to allow the march to proceed, but he wanted some guarantees: "I want the assurance that when I issue this order—and they rightly deserve this order—that it will be backed by the government of the United States."

Katzenbach was confused. "Backed? Well, I think we can back it."

"I don't care what you think," Johnson bluntly told the attorney general. "I don't intend to go out on a limb with an order that will not be backed up by this government. If Wallace pulls some grandstand play . . . I want to know that this government will be prepared to meet it. It won't be fair to this court and to the people to have an order that does not have support."

"All right. You've got my assurance," Katzenbach said.

That was not good enough for Johnson, a judge whose withering stare was known to cause lawyers to faint in his courtroom. "I don't want your assurance, Mr. Katzenbach. I want it from the President. I want to know before I issue this order."

"OK," the attorney general sighed. "I'll get back with you, Judge."[5]

Judge Johnson made up his mind largely in response to the testimony from those who were assaulted on Bloody Sunday, the violence of which he wanted to avoid at the next march. On Monday, March 15, the last day of the proceedings, he permitted the showing of CBS's footage of what occurred on the Edmund Pettus Bridge. Luck was with the movement, because the CBS film, just three minutes long, was the footage taken by Laurens Pierce, whose camerawork had captured the most shocking aspects of the attack on the marchers. John Lewis, in court that day, studied the judge closely. Johnson seemed transfixed by the scenes, and when the film ended, he looked "obviously disgusted. . . . From his demeanor, I just knew he was going to rule for us," Lewis later wrote.[6]

He did. On the evening of March 15, while President Johnson was addressing the nation, Judge Johnson contacted King's lawyers and asked them to draft a plan detailing how they would march from Selma to Montgomery: How many people would be involved? How would they be fed and sheltered during the fifty-mile trek? What route would they take? The judge wanted answers and fast. The lawyers worked all evening and gave the document to Judge Johnson the following morning. That day and the next, Johnson worked on his order. On Wednesday the telephone interrupted him with the call from Katzenbach, who gave him the assurances he had demanded.

"You got it," the attorney general told him.

Johnson wanted to make sure there would be no mistakes. "From the President?"

"Yes, sir. From the President."

"Good enough," Johnson said. Later that afternoon he publicly issued his order.[7]

Frank Johnson didn't care much for Martin Luther King or sit-ins, boycotts, and marches because in his view the courts were available to redress black grievances. But he did believe strongly that all Americans had a constitutional right to assemble peacefully, and that was the issue now before him. The evidence the plaintiffs presented was clear, the judge proclaimed. Since January 2, 1965, Sheriff Clark, his deputies, and posse men had been guilty of "harassment, intimidation, coercion, threatening conduct, and sometimes, brutal mistreatment" of black Americans in Dallas County, violating rights guaranteed by the First Amendment to the Constitution as well as the Fourteenth and Fifteenth. Such misconduct had climaxed on Bloody Sunday.

The judge admitted that a future march might affect the right of Alabamians to travel along the prescribed route, so he rested his decision on what some thought was an unusual principle, which he called "proportionality." An American's right to protest, Johnson said, "should be commensurate with the enormity of the wrongs that are being protested and petitioned against. In this case," he concluded, "the wrongs are enormous . . . and the right to demonstrate against these wrongs should be determined accordingly."

Johnson ruled that a new march could proceed between March 19 and March 22, protected by Alabama law enforcement. However, if the state found it too difficult to provide such protection, the US government would handle it at the governor's request. There would be no further violence. The court specifically prohibited Sheriff Clark and Wallace's Al Lingo from "arresting, harassing, thwarting or in any way interfering with the effort to march from Selma to Montgomery."[8]

For King, Johnson's decision could not have come at a better time. On that Wednesday he was in Montgomery to show his support for SNCC, although privately their violent actions distressed him. At a rally at the Baptist Beulah Church the previous night he had listened uncomfortably as Forman whipped the crowd into a frenzy. "There's only one man in the country that can stop George Wallace and those posses," Forman said. "These problems will not be solved until the man in that shaggedy old place called the White House begins to shake and gets on the phone and says, 'Now listen, George, we're coming down there and throw you in jail if you don't stop that mess.'" Then Forman had shocked his audience of clergy and black families, including women and children, by saying, "If we can't sit at the table of democracy, we'll knock the fucking legs off!" His followers erupted in cheers, drowning out his quick apology for the expletive. King's own speech attempted to restore order, but it was Forman who won the night and the next day too— until Judge Johnson came to King's rescue.[9]

Before news of Johnson's order came through, Forman and SNCC had seemed to be ascending in Montgomery. City officials, also worried by the violent turn of events, had apologized for the assault on SNCC protestors and invited King and Forman to discuss how to handle future protests in the city. At the conclusion of their meeting King told a crowd that had waited for him in the rain that Montgomery's leaders had agreed to prohibit Clark's posse from enforcing the law, a decision that seemed to vindicate Forman's more radical approach—until Andy Young excitedly informed him of Judge Johnson's decision. "I think this will come as a source of joy to all of us," a smiling King proclaimed: "Judge Johnson has just ruled that we have a legal and Constitutional right to march from Selma to Montgomery!" The people cheered, encouraging King's hope that nonviolence had carried the day. But once again Forman and other SNCC officials refused to endorse the march, although they would allow individual members to participate. Nobody would prevent an excited John Lewis from crossing the Edmund Pettus Bridge, and in the end, Forman would join the marchers too.[10]

Only one issue remained. Who would protect the marchers—Alabama troopers or federal forces? Governor Wallace quickly made it clear that he

opposed the march and that the state could not afford to police such an ambitious endeavor. On March 18 he called the president: "These people are
pouring in from all over the country," he complained. "It infuriates people. . . .
They're going to bankrupt the state." Wallace did not want to ask for federal
help, and an angry Johnson, knowing that the governor commanded ten
thousand National Guardsmen, urged him to call them up, but the governor
refused. "You're dealing with a very treacherous guy," Johnson told an aide
after getting off the phone with Wallace. "He's a no good son of a bitch."[11]

In Alabama, however, Wallace was a hero. His fellow citizens saw themselves as victims of "Communist trained anarchists" and thought of Wallace
as their savior. His refusal to protect the marchers only added to his popularity. Addressing a special joint session of the state legislature, Wallace
called Frank Johnson "a hypocritical judge" who believed in "mob rule." He
claimed that the march would bring to Alabama "every left wing, pro-
Communist . . . and Communist in the country . . . along with the usual
number of dupes and poor misguided individuals." Women wept, and legislators applauded wildly.[12]

Johnson had only one option. To enforce Judge Johnson's order, he federalized the state's National Guard, just as Presidents Eisenhower and
Kennedy had done in earlier racial crises in Arkansas, Mississippi, and, in
1963, in Alabama itself. The president also directed the secretary of defense
to employ the armed forces of the United States, if necessary. He sent one
hundred FBI agents and US marshals, one thousand military policemen,
and two thousand US Army troops to Selma, eventually bringing Washington's protective presence there to more than three thousand. Deputy US attorney general Ramsay Clark supervised the federal effort, and Assistant
Attorney General John Doar would also accompany the marchers.[13]

King announced that the march would begin on Sunday, March 21, and
end in Montgomery four days later. He invited "all of our friends of goodwill
across the nation to join with us in this gigantic witness to the fulfillment of
democracy." On March 25 he would speak on the steps of the state capitol,
and a delegation would give Governor Wallace a petition describing black
grievances.

During the days that followed, King's staff hurried to complete the
arrangements for the trip. Campsites were located, plans to feed the marchers
were finalized, and medical support was arranged. Anyone who became ill or
was injured would be cared for by the Medical Committee for Human Rights,

which had provided heroic service on Bloody Sunday. Almost one hundred physicians and nurses soon descended on Selma to assist them. Black morticians turned their hearses into ambulances, and the International Ladies Garment Workers Union donated a mobile hospital capable of responding to almost any medical crisis that developed.[14]

The size of the crowd was greater than King had hoped. There were thirty-six hundred would-be marchers waiting to follow him: rabbis, ministers, nuns, and prominent religious leaders as well as civil rights icons like Rosa Parks and A. Philip Randolph, the seventy-six-year-old president of the Brotherhood of Sleeping Car Porters, whose threat to lead a black march on Washington in 1941 forced FDR to ban discrimination in war-time industry. Dr. Ralph Bunche, UN official and winner of the Nobel Peace Prize, would participate, as would teachers and college professors, alongside their students, who were dressed casually in denim and sweaters; labor leaders and New York politicians; actors and musicians; and ordinary men and women like Detroit mother and part-time student Viola Liuzzo, who had loaned her car to the movement and greeted newcomers at the movement's hospitality suite. She wanted to do more than just march, and later she would get her chance. Physical problems wouldn't stop Joe Young, a poor Georgian who was blind, or Michigan's Jim Letherer, whose disability forced him to walk on crutches. "My handicap is not that I have one leg," he told a reporter. "It is that I cannot do more to help these people vote." The movement's leaders and victims of the Marion riot were also represented: John Lewis and Hosea Williams, who were bloodied on the bridge; Amelia Boynton and Annie Cooper, who were beaten by Sheriff Clark; and Cager Lee, Jimmie Lee Jackson's eighty-two-year-old grandfather, who remarked that if Jimmie Lee "had to die for something, thank God it was for this," the right to vote.[15]

Perhaps no one was more excited about the coming journey than eight-year-old Sheyann Webb and her best friend, nine-year-old Rachel West. They had first met Dr. King during his visit to Brown Chapel in February and formed an affectionate bond between them. He often invited the girls to join him at the pulpit to sing one of his favorite freedom songs, "Ain't Gonna Let Nobody Turn Me 'Round." But they also defied their parents by attending rallies and marches on the courthouse, where Sheyann had seen Sheriff Clark drag Amelia Boynton off to jail. On Sunday, March 7, the two girls had even joined those headed for the Edmund Pettus Bridge, but when they arrived there Rachel was too afraid to go forward. Sheyann went on alone and was there when the attack occurred. Coughing and choking, she had turned away from the troopers when suddenly a man, Hosea Williams, picked her up and carried her through the clouds of tear gas, which blinded them both. But Williams wasn't moving fast enough to suit Sheyann, so she yelled, "Put me down!" He refused until they were safely off the bridge, then put her down. She left him far behind, running faster than she thought possible through the streets of Selma, dodging cars and men on horseback until she reached her home. As her stunned parents tried to comfort the shaking child, she was ashamed rather than frightened, feeling, she later confessed, like a slave who had been beaten by her master.[16]

On Sunday, March 21, before sneaking out of the house to join Rachel and the others at Brown Chapel, Sheyann left her parents a note. It was her own obituary, so that they would know where to look for her body. It read, "Sheyann Webb, 8 years, was killed today. She was one of Dr. King's freedom fighters. She was a student at Clark School, Selma. Sheyann want [sic] all the people to be free and happy."[17]

At 12:30 Dr. King addressed the marchers who had assembled at Brown Chapel, telling them to maintain their resolve during the coming march. "You will be the people that will light a new chapter in the history of our nation," he said. "Walk together, children, and don't you get weary, and it will lead us to the promised land. And Alabama will be a new Alabama. And America will be a new America."

Suddenly, a group of Alabama National Guard jeeps appeared and began driving through the crowd, which parted to avoid being run down. "Didn't realize we were interrupting," laughed one driver, his uniform emblazoned with the letters D.D.—Dixie Division—his southern accent unmistakable. The jeeps withdrew, leaving no casualties behind. It was never determined whether the incident was an accident or a deliberate provocation. King, fearing that the marchers' confidence had been undermined, quickly finished his remarks and asked Sheyann and Rachel to sing "Woke Up This Morning with My Mind Stayed on Freedom." There was a final rendition of "We Shall Overcome" before the leaders organized the group into columns and the marchers moved into the street.[18]

It was an inauspicious beginning that left some participants in a nervous frame of mind. The marchers, however, weren't the only ones who were apprehensive. Mayor Smitherman expressed his unhappiness to a reporter: "I will be glad to get these people out of town—but I am afraid that some of them will come back." Sheriff Clark thought the whole thing was unnecessary: "We were very happy before and I say 90 percent of our colored people was happy [*sic*]." But these were only words; no Selma official tried to block the marchers, so the protestors' fears passed quickly, especially when they saw US Army helicopters circling above them and a truck leading the procession, providing some protection from a frontal assault. It carried network television cameramen photographing them as well as the National Guardsmen, who were thus forced by the cameras to be on their best behavior as they accompanied the marchers through the city streets.

If no one tried to assault the marchers, it wasn't because Selma's white population had suddenly grown more accommodating. Perhaps Sheyann and Rachel were too young to appreciate the meaning of the song a local radio station played, blasted through loud speakers someone had set up in the crowd of onlookers. The refrain repeated again and again,

> *Pack up all my care and woe,*
> *Here I go,*
> *Singing low,*
> *Bye bye blackbird*

But the girls were long accustomed to seeing the signs unhappy white men held: "I Hate Niggers," "Too Bad Reeb," and "Walk Coon."[19]

The marchers stopped on the Edmund Pettus Bridge where, two weeks before, Major Cloud had yelled, "troopers advance," and the assault had commenced. Hosea Williams had particularly bad memories of the bridge. "This is the place where State Troopers whipped us," he told King. "The savage beasts beat us on this spot." There was silence. Some of the younger marchers lay down on the ground, then there were cheers as many sang out another movement anthem:

> *Paul and Silas bound in jail*
> *Had no money for da go de bail*
> *Keep your eyes on the prize, hold on*
> *Hold on, hold on,*
> *Keep your eyes on the prize, hold on.*[20]

Leaving the bridge, they marched down four-lane Jefferson Davis High-way, where they encountered more hecklers. One driver yelled, "Go to hell," while one of his children cried out, "Look at them niggers." A heavy-set woman shouted at several nuns, "You're going to burn in hell with the rest of them." The marchers, however, seemed unaffected by their taunts: "The people just seemed like something had been lifted from their shoulders," Sheyann later recalled. "They were so proud, but it was a pride that was dig-nified. We had always maintained that dignity."[21]

They covered a little over seven miles by sundown. At that time the marchers turned off Jefferson Davis Highway and proceeded to David and Rosa Bell Hall's eighty-acre farm, where they would spend the night. The Halls, neither of whom was registered to vote ("it just never seemed worth-while to try," said Mrs. Hall), lived with their eight children in a three-room shack without indoor plumbing. Fearing retaliation, they had first hesitated when asked if King's people could bed down in their field. "David didn't know what to do," Mrs. Hall told the *Times*'s Paul A. Montgomery. "But fi-nally we decided we just had to do it."[22]

At the Hall Farm most of the first day's group prepared to return to Selma. Only three hundred marchers would be allowed to proceed past the point where the highway became a two-lane country road—one of the conditions of Judge Johnson's order—so the rest boarded cars and buses that took them back into town. Sheyann and Rachel were exhilarated and wanted to keep marching. "It seem like we marchin' to Heaven today," Sheyann told Rachel, who replied, "Ain't we?" It was then that Dr. King discovered the two youngest marchers. "Aren't you tired?" King asked, delighted to see them. The girls laughed and Sheyann said, "My feets and legs be tired, but my soul still feels like marchin'." But when Sheyann admitted that she was there without her mother's permission, King made sure they were put on a bus for home.[23]

The lucky 300 who remained—280 black Alabamians and 20 white volun-teers from across America—ate a buffet dinner of spaghetti and meat sauce, served on paper plates from new, immaculately clean trash cans. Men and women slept in separate tents to squelch the accusations of hostile southern-ers like Alabama's Congressman William Dickinson, whose words were broadcast over the transistor radios many of the marchers carried. "Free love among this group is not only condoned, it is encouraged," the congressman proclaimed. "Only by the ultimate sex act with one of another color can they demonstrate that they have no prejudice." This produced laughter from the exhausted marchers: "These white folks must think we're supermen to be able to march all day . . . make whoopee all night and . . . then march all day again," said one black man. But the scurrilous charges persisted. A Montgomery radio personality informed his listeners that white women marchers would be returning to their homes in Boston and San Francisco "as expectant unwed mothers." The remark didn't surprise John Lewis: "These white segregationists always think about fornication," he remarked. "That's why you see so many shades of brown on this march."[24]

King spent the night uncomfortably nestled inside a sleeping bag at the command headquarters, a mobile van. That day's walk had left him with a painful blister on his left foot, and he told Ralph Abernathy that he doubted whether he would be able to complete the long journey. The younger marchers, meanwhile, were too excited to sleep. They gathered around campfires singing freedom songs, disturbing the sleep of older folks, who had a restless night. There was a shortage of blankets, and the temperature dipped below freezing. To one reporter, the encampment, its perimeter guarded by US Army troops, "resembled a cross between a 'Grapes of Wrath' migrant labor camp and the Continental Army bivouac at Valley Forge."[25]

The next morning the marchers ate toast and oatmeal without milk, which caused one man to complain that the cereal tasted like "unfermented library paste." An angry Andy Young told them, "You're not better than two-thirds of the Negroes in Alabama. The average Negro here makes less than $2,000 a year and you can't put cream on your oatmeal with that." After breakfast the weary travelers set out slowly on a sixteen-mile journey to their next campsite. "You are going too slow," Young called out. "You're holding up the civil rights movement."

The day began uneventfully, but there were ominous signs on the horizon. Lowndes County lay ahead, infamous for the number of black citizens who had been lynched or had died mysteriously. Rumors put the marchers on edge: someone had heard that bombs and land mines had been hidden along the route and that Klansmen were planning to set loose deadly snakes when the marchers stopped for lunch or left the road to relieve themselves. The county's landscape intensified their fears: They walked by moss-covered trees that might hide snipers and saw swamps filled with man-eating alligators. Troops and guardsmen combed the nearby woods but found nothing dangerous. This was "a full blown military operation," said one officer. "It's no different from the way we would screen a route in Vietnam."[26]

Protected by the federalized Alabama National Guard and US Army troops, marchers enter Lowndes County on their way to Montgomery. © 1965 SPIDER MARTIN

When they crossed the county line and entered Lowndes County at 12:13 p.m., King called out, "Pick it up, now. Everybody join in," and he began singing, "We Shall Overcome." His followers joined him. Abernathy, the official cheerleader, turned to the marchers and loudly asked, "What do you want?"

"Freedom!" they answered back with equal enthusiasm.

"What are we going to get?" Abernathy asked.

"Freedom!" they yelled.

Danger seemed to rear its head when a small plane swooped down over the marchers. Its payload turned out to be leaflets, announcing that the black activists could expect to lose their jobs. The plane was later identified as belonging to the Confederate Air Force. A reporter asked Jack Rosenthal, a Justice Department official, if they could do anything about the plane, as it might be capable of bombing them. "What do you want us to do?" asked an exasperated Rosenthal. "Use anti-aircraft guns?"[27]

Later word reached King that down the road men were erecting signs accusing him of being a Communist. When the marchers came upon one, it was a billboard depicting King in a meeting with a group said to be "national Communist leaders." The picture did not surprise King. It had been taken in 1957, when he spoke at the twenty-fifth anniversary of the founding of Highlander Folk School in Monteagle, Tennessee, a controversial center of economic and political activism in the South. During a break in the march King told reporters that he had visited the school eight years earlier, as had many veterans of the civil rights movement. The school's enemies had considered it a center of Bolshevism since its creation in 1932. The photograph had been a staple of southern segregationists because it was taken by a spy for the Georgia White Citizen's Council. "There are about as many Communists in the Civil Rights movement as there are Eskimos in Florida," King joked. He called the accusation "absurd."[28]

Soon the marchers began to see Negro bystanders along the road, staring at them in silence as if they couldn't quite believe what they were seeing: a rag-tag army, some wearing berets, cowboy hats, or head scarves—anything to protect them from sunburn or sunstroke—led by a black man wearing a green cap and ear muffs. At Trickem Fork, an especially impoverished black community, Young called the marchers' attention to a run-down church on the verge of collapse. "Look at that! That's why we're marching!" Hopefully, such dwellings would disappear when black voters elected representatives who cared how they lived and died. Nearby was a structure in even worse condition—its windows covered by cardboard, its walls pocked by holes, its roof almost open to the sky. It was Trickem's only school.

They stopped briefly so King could talk to some older citizens, who treated him as if he were a movie star. After embracing him a woman cried, "I done kissed the Martin Luther King!"

"Are you people gonna register to vote?" Young asked them. "We're not just marchin' here for fun."

"Yes sir," they told King and Young, and they kept their promise. Later these elderly men and women walked to the registrar's office in Hayneville, the county seat, and were among the first blacks in a century to demand the right to vote.[29]

The marchers spent a quiet, uneventful night at Rosa Steele's farm near Big Swamp Creek. Mrs. Steele, seventy-eight years old and widowed, owned a small grocery store on Highway 80 and had shared the Halls' reluctance to work with King. "At first I didn't think [the movement] amounted to much," she told a reporter. "I guess I've lived too long and just didn't think things would change—until I heard the president's speech. . . . If the president can take a stand, I guess I can too." Later local segregationists tried to destroy her business by threatening the vendors who stocked her shelves, but another black merchant helped drive them off.[30]

After a journey of more than twenty-three miles, some of the marchers required medical attention, and all were thoroughly worn out. Like King, many had blistered feet and sunburned faces. Most went to bed early. King left the party briefly to go to Cleveland to fulfill a speaking commitment arranged earlier. "De Lawd departs," said one member of SNCC contemptuously. Williams quickly defended King. "It isn't the President's job to be in the sun and the mud all the time," Williams insisted. "His job was to lead us out of Selma—that was the most dangerous part. Then he's gone, trying to raise our budget around the country. He is telling our story."[31]

On Tuesday, the third day, nature turned against the marchers. It rained all day—a cold, heavy storm that lashed them unmercifully. They quickly improvised, turning cereal boxes into hats and sheets of plastic into ponchos. Everyone was drenched, from the poorest seamstress to Assistant Attorney General John Doar, who was "soaked to the skin, his hair hanging across his forehead in weeping ringlets," according to the *New York Times*'s Roy Reed. But the downpour did not dampen the marchers' spirits. "Somebody started to sing," one of the marchers later recalled. "Everybody's head snapped up and people had fire in their eyes, and suddenly it was a march again. It was incredible."[32]

The rain was unrelenting, and their campsite that night, a pasture owned by black millionaire A. G. Gaston, was a mud-filled morass. King's staff put down hay, but it was sucked into the ooze. Tempers flared: two photographers got into a fistfight, an Alabama guardsman spat on a priest, and Alabama troopers insulted black passersby. Wet, dirty, and bedraggled though they were, all took comfort in the fact that half their journey was over: Montgomery was just twenty miles away.[33]

They were up very early the next morning. By seven o'clock they were again on the road, with Andy Young in front, the group's leader for at least a few hours. A mile later the marchers crossed the Montgomery County line, leaving Lowndes County behind. The road again became a four-lane highway, and hundreds of new marchers joined the throng. King arrived with his wife, Coretta, and Abernathy at eleven o'clock. "We have a new song to sing," he said. "We *have* overcome."[34]

John Doar, assistant attorney general for civil rights, accompanied the marchers on their fifty-four-mile journey from Selma to Montgomery and protected Dr. King from a would-be assassin. © 1976 MATT HERRON/TAKE STOCK/THE IMAGE WORKS

As they entered the city of Montgomery, their numbers had grown from the original three hundred to about five thousand. They had walked sixteen miles that day mostly in sunshine, but just as they reached the city, torrential rainfall briefly doused them. It didn't dampen their spirits, however. "The marchers were ecstatic," noted one reporter. "[They] pushed down the street joyfully, singing 'We Shall Overcome' at the top of their lungs." Decades later Bruce Hartford, a white Californian, remembered one incident that, for him, personified the meaning of the march. They were in the business district, passing a motel, and saw standing outside its cleaning staff with their carts of fresh linen and towels. "The maids were excited to see the marchers, they wanted to cheer, they wanted to join the march," Hartford thought, but to do so would undoubtedly cost them their jobs. Behind them was their boss, "glowering at them" and at the marchers too. "Suddenly one of them started to cheer, and they all started to cheer, and several of them . . . ran out and joined the march under the eyes of their supervisors." Joining the marchers had allowed these workers, however briefly, to break the shackles of an in-formal peonage, ignoring the likely consequences in order to achieve a very personal fulfillment. Such moments of individual liberation would be the march's greatest achievement.[35]

No one would forget the last night of the march, when the participants camped in a muddy ballpark on the grounds of the City of St. Jude, a Catholic medical, religious, and educational complex outside Montgomery that also served as a movement headquarters. Answering the call of Harry Belafonte, musicians, actors, and comedians from Broadway to Hollywood had arrived in Montgomery to entertain the marchers, whose numbers had now swelled to approximately ten thousand. The celebrities performed on a stage built from coffin crates, surrounded by a crowd so densely packed that fifty-seven people fainted. Sammy Davis Jr. serenaded the marchers. Peter, Paul and Mary sang "Blowin' in the Wind," a movement anthem. Mike Nichols and Elaine May, the brilliant satirists, added their own unique brand of humor: Alabama could not afford to protect the marchers, they said, because jailing protestors was so expensive, "to say nothing of the upkeep on cattle prods and bull whips." Nina Simone probably stole the show with her angry rendition of "Mississippi Goddam." Also there were Dick Gregory, Alan King, and actors Anthony Perkins and Shelly Winters, among many more.

Dr. King spoke as well, urging "every self-respecting Negro here" to march with them on the capitol. "Yea, Yea," screamed the crowd, an overwhelming assurance that they would be with him tomorrow.[36]

So far the trek had been peaceful. The only casualties were those people with blistered feet and sunburned faces. King's fears about an assassination attempt had also proved unfounded—until, that is, terrible news reached him early on the final day, March 25.

Andy Young was the first of King's inner circle to learn of the newly discovered threat to their leader's life. "Andy, we have reports that there's a sniper in the outskirts of Montgomery waiting to shoot Dr. King," Assistant Attorney General John Doar told Young. The FBI was busy checking out the buildings that overlooked their route, but there wasn't enough time to examine every spot. King should leave the march and drive to the capitol, Doar strongly urged. But, as Young expected, King refused to leave his supporters behind. "I don't care what happens," King said. "I have to march and I have to be in the front line." When Young told Doar of King's response to the news, Doar shrugged fatalistically and said, "In that case there is nothing we can do."

But Young would not let King march unprotected, so he developed a scheme he hoped would work. He was of course familiar with the old racist adage that "all blacks look alike," so he invited black ministers who resembled King in physique and dress to join their leader at the head of the march. Fifteen happy ministers, each wearing a blue suit like King's, quickly came to his side. "They never did find out why they were there," Young later wrote.[37]

Doar didn't abandon King to his fate, either. Accompanied by US marshal James McShane, the assistant attorney general walked casually up Dexter Avenue, almost a block ahead of King and the thirty thousand marchers. Doar looked like he was just enjoying an afternoon stroll—he was eating an apple as he walked—but he and McShane were surreptitiously scanning open windows along the route, looking for places where an assassin might lurk. There were eight hundred soldiers stationed along the parade route, and helicopters hovered above, but Doar and McShane were taking no chances.

At several fearful moments it seemed like violence was indeed going to mar the last day of the march. Despite the overwhelming presence of troops and FBI agents, violent encounters still occurred, as when a fistfight erupted between marchers and angry whites. And at one point McShane stopped suddenly, removed his sunglasses, and pointed to what looked like a rifle protruding from a window. He moved toward it cautiously. A closer look revealed that it was only a television camera, much to McShane's relief.[38]

When the marchers reached the white-colored State House, they noticed that its dome flew the Alabama and Confederate flags, whereas off to the side the American flag fluttered slightly in the breeze. Someone began singing the "Star Spangled Banner," and everyone joined in, then adding, for good measure, "The Battle Hymn of the Republic." That popular anthem of the northern cause must have annoyed Governor Wallace and the city's citizens, many of whom stood by waving tiny Confederate flags. For many white southerners Montgomery was historically sacred, as the place where Jefferson Davis was inaugurated president of the Confederate States of America.

For Wallace, however, the city had a more contemporary meaning. It was here in 1963 that he had officially become governor of Alabama, proclaiming, "Segregation now, segregation tomorrow and segregation forever." And Wallace was not going to renege on that promise with anything resembling grace or good humor. He had placed uniformed members of the Alabama Game and Fish Service at the capitol steps "to keep that s.o.b. King from desecrating the Cradle of the Confederacy," said the governor's aide. Wallace occasionally peeked through his office blinds, watching the demonstrators—now numbering close to thirty thousand—through a pair of binoculars. He too was awed by the size of the crowd. "My God, it looks like an army," he told reporter Bob Ingram. And someone added, "Those are the next voters in Alabama."[39]

The march's final mass meeting began around three o'clock, as speakers and entertainers climbed atop a specially built platform that acted as a stage. Young was the first to speak: "This is a revolution," he cried, "a revolution that won't fire a shot. We come to love the hell out of the State of Alabama." Albert Turner, leader of the Marion group and friend of the fallen Jimmie Lee Jackson, expressed embarrassment: "I look worse than anybody else on this stage," he told the crowd. That's because I marched fifty miles." Amelia Boynton read the petition they hoped to present to the governor at the conclusion of the day's events and received warm applause. Dr. Bunche spoke, as did A. Philip Randolph and Rosa Parks, who was treated like the real star of the festivities. But soon the crowd grew restless, as most waited for the man they thought had made this triumph possible: Martin Luther King Jr.[40]

King's address, which began close to four o'clock, was so powerful and eloquent that it rivaled his "I Have a Dream" speech, although it is not as well

"The arc of the moral universe is long but it bends toward justice," Dr. King tells a crowd of twenty-five thousand at the end of the march. © 1965 SPIDER MARTIN

remembered. "They told us we wouldn't get here," he told the crowd, which the *New York Times* later called, "the greatest demonstration in the history of the civil rights movement." "And there were those who said that we would get here only over their dead bodies," he continued, "but all the world today knows that we *are* here and we are standing before the forces of power in the state of Alabama, saying 'We ain't gonna let nobody turn us around.' We are on the move now and no wave of racism can stop us."

King then discussed the specific issues that had brought so many people to Montgomery that day. "Let us march on segregated schools," he admonished, "until every vestige of segregation and inferior education becomes a thing of the past and Negroes and whites study side by side in the socially healing context of the classroom. Let us march on ballot boxes until race baiters disappear from the political arena."

The past two months had seen incredible progress, King assured his audience. "Selma, Alabama, has become a shining moment in the conscience of man. If the worst in American life lurked in the dark streets, the best of American instincts arose passionately from across the nation to overcome it."

The crowd remained quiet at first, reflecting the split within the movement. Although many of the older veterans saw the day as the culmination of a long struggle (which, indeed, had begun a decade earlier in these very streets with the Montgomery Bus Boycott), many of the young activists in the crowd were disgusted by what they saw as King's opportunism and by the media attention King had received. The three major television networks covered both the march and the speech. But it was hard to be unaffected for long by King's enthusiasm, and the divisions disappeared as everyone responded with cries of "Speak! Speak!" Among them were Sheyann Webb and Rachel West, brought to Montgomery by their equally excited parents. Viola Liuzzo applauded with tears in her eyes, while Annie Cooper, who had lost her job because she'd tried to register to vote, thought she'd never see King more passionate: "His eyes were just a'twinklin," she told the journalist Frye Gaillard many years later.[41]

"Our aim must never be to defeat or humiliate the white man," King continued, "but to win his friendship and understanding. The end we seek is a society at peace with itself, a society that can live with its conscience. That will be a day not of the white man, not of the black man. That will be the day of man as man.

"How long must justice be crucified and truth buried?" he asked then quickly answered. "How long? Not long because no lie can live forever. How long? Not long, because you still reap what you sow. How long? Not long because the arc of the moral universe is long, but it bends toward justice. How long? Not long, 'cause mine eyes have seen the coming of the Lord." Then the crowd repeated after him, "He is trampling out the vintage where the grapes of wrath are stored. He has loosed the fateful lightning of his terrible swift sword. His truth is marching on. . . . Glory, glory hallelujah." At those words the crowd rose together, cheering and clapping so loud that the sound echoed through the capitol. Then they sang "We Shall Overcome," bringing to a close this joyous—and hard-won—event.[42]

But the day was not over for Amelia Boynton and the delegation appointed to present Governor Wallace with their list of grievances. When they marched to the capitol steps, however, state troopers blocked them, informing them that the governor was no longer in his office. A few minutes later they tried again, and this time managed to meet with Wallace's secretary. But he would not commit the governor to any future meeting. In one sense, at least, the marchers had failed.[43]

PRESIDENT JOHNSON AND NICHOLAS KATZENBACH WERE GREATLY RELIEVED that nothing had occurred to mar the Selma-to-Montgomery march. So was Andrew Young. After returning to the church on Dexter Avenue where King had once pastored a decade earlier, Young "just let the tears flow," he later recalled. "Tears of relief that we had completed the march without any bloodshed, that we had actually pulled it off, this virtual strolling city of five days' duration across the lonely Alabama terrain, a feat we could not possibly have foreseen when we were beginning our campaign."[44]

John Doar also felt pleased but was still vigilant as the National Guard and federal troops withdrew from the capitol and the marchers boarded trains and planes for home. Although the marchers had been instructed to leave immediately, violent confrontations with local citizens were still possible, perhaps even inevitable. SCLC volunteers were driving people to the airport or back to Selma, but James Orange, King's aide in charge of transportation, urged them to use the movement's vehicles and travel in a caravan rather than driving their own cars, whose out-of-state license plates were sure to arouse the ire of the more violent townspeople. And above all, white volunteers should avoid being alone with black colleagues.

As the hours passed without problems, Doar's anxiety diminished enough for him finally to have dinner. An apple he'd eaten earlier was the only food he'd consumed that day. As he and a colleague were dining at Montgomery's Elite Café later that night, however, he received a disturbing telephone call. "It was the FBI," Doar later told his associate when he returned to their table. "A Mrs. Liuzzo has been killed on the road back to Selma."[45]

During her stay in Selma, Liuzzo had lived with a black family in public housing, feeding and caring for her hosts' grandchildren, and most recently had assisted the medical team at St. Jude. But she had wanted to do more. She had offered to be a volunteer driver, even though Orange had told her specifically that her services were not needed: "Vi, don't go out there," Orange later recalled telling her. "We've got trucks, we've got busses; there's no reason for you to use your car on that highway." But Liuzzo ignored these warnings and joined Leroy Moton, a young member of SCLC, as they ferried marchers back and forth between Selma and Montgomery.[46]

According to the FBI and local police, Liuzzo and Moton had been driving in Lowndes County when they were ambushed. A car filled with unknown suspects had pulled alongside Liuzzo's vehicle, spraying it with bullets. Liuzzo had been killed instantly, but Moton was miraculously unscathed, and he managed to return to Selma where state police and the FBI interrogated him. But he was a poor eyewitness. He could not identify the shooters or even recall the make or color of the car. It appeared that Liuzzo's killers would go unpunished.

Then suddenly, at 12:42 p.m. the following afternoon, President Johnson appeared on national television to announce that Liuzzo's killers had been identified and were in custody. The four suspects were members of the Alabama Ku Klux Klan. "Mrs. Liuzzo went to Alabama to serve the struggle for justice," Johnson said, before continuing with obvious revulsion. "She was murdered by the enemies of justice who, for decades, have used the rope and the gun, the tar and the feathers, to terrorize their neighbors. They struck by night, as they generally do. For their purposes cannot stand the light of day."

Flanked by J. Edgar Hoover and Nicholas Katzenbach, the president also told the nation that he had ordered the attorney general to create new legislation to combat the Klan and that he also encouraged Congress to investigate it and other violent organizations. Johnson's interest in the case was remarkable; he had first learned of the shooting not long after it had occurred on Thursday night and called the FBI several times before going to sleep at 1:00 a.m. and rising at six the next morning. It was not customary for the president to act as

America's top cop, but the tragedy of Liuzzo's death and the general fears about violence during the march—as well as, perhaps, the fact that Liuzzo was a white woman—help to explain Johnson's interest in the case.[47]

Johnson's statement was not completely true. One of the accused, thirty-five-year-old Gary Thomas Rowe Jr., was not in jail. He was helping the FBI build a case against the Klansmen, for Rowe had been the FBI's top informant inside the Alabama Klan for the past five years. According to Rowe, it was fellow Klansman Collie Leroy Wilkins, a mechanic, who had fired the shots that killed Liuzzo. Rowe himself claimed that he had stuck his gun out the window and had only pretended to shoot. The FBI believed Rowe's explanation and decided not to test his gun or bullet casings for fingerprints that might have cast doubt on his story.

It later emerged that the FBI had made a Faustian pact in order to get inside the KKK. Thanks to Rowe, the FBI arrested the suspects. In exchange for Rowe's pledge to testify against them, the Justice Department gave him immunity from prosecution and promised him a new life in the Federal Witness Protection Program. Rowe's activities in the Klan had been bloody and illegal: he had organized and participated in the attack on the Freedom Riders in Birmingham in 1961 and may have been involved in the bombing of the Sixteenth Street Baptist Church in 1963. But the FBI was willing to overlook Rowe's violent life in the hope that he would provide them with information necessary to destroy the Klan.[48]

To divert attention away from his informant—the press was starting to ask why Rowe had done nothing to prevent the shooting—Hoover created a more alluring subject for media attention. He and his men worked quickly to transform Viola Liuzzo, mother of five and part-time college student, into a blond seductress who came south not to fight for civil rights but instead to sleep with black men. Hoover told Johnson that Liuzzo's body had exhibited "numerous needle points indicating that she may have been taking dope." The Klansmen went after her, Hoover said, because they saw "this colored man . . . snuggling up pretty close to the white woman . . . it had all the appearances of a necking party."[49]

None of this was true, but Hoover's files eventually wound up in Klan literature. The killers' attorneys distributed the hate-filled pamphlets to reporters and made Liuzzo's character a major issue when their clients came to trial. Matthew Hobson Murphy, the Klan's Imperial Klonsul, called Liuzzo a "fat slob with crud that looked like rust all over her body [and] she was braless." She was not "the mother of five lovely children and a community worker," Hobson railed, but rather a "nigger lover" lusting after "black meat." It was perhaps no surprise when the four men were each acquitted by all-white Alabama juries. But in a federal courtroom in December 1965, with Judge Frank M. Johnson presiding and Assistant Attorney General John Doar prosecuting, they were convicted of violating Mrs. Liuzzo's civil rights, and each was sentenced to ten years in prison. Rowe was the prosecution's star witness, and in recognition of his services, the FBI gave him a $10,000 reward, a new identity, and an appointment as a deputy US marshal in San Diego, California.[50]

All this lay in the future. For now, however, the civil rights movement had another martyr whose sacrifice—though spat upon by many white southerners—weakened congressional opposition to the voting rights bill. Michigan governor George Romney declared March 29 and 30, 1965, to be days of statewide mourning for Viola Liuzzo, and Vice President Hubert Humphrey and Martin Luther King visited the Liuzzo family to pay their respects. Ministers throughout Detroit—both black and white—spoke of Liuzzo's sacrifice in their Sunday sermons, and the NAACP held a memorial service that thousands attended.

On Tuesday, March 30, as a gentle snow fell, Viola Liuzzo was laid to rest at the Holy Sepulcher Cemetery. King's great march, which had its origins in the death of Jimmie Lee Jackson, had ended as it began: with the spilling of blood.[51]

THE SELMA-TO-MONTGOMERY MARCH HAD ITS CRITICS, HOWEVER, AND NOT all were irate southerners. Former president Harry S. Truman, who had urged Congress to adopt a civil rights program seventeen years earlier, called the march "silly." Responding to a reporter's question, Truman went further: "They can't accomplish a darned thing. All they want is to attract attention." Renata Adler, a perceptive journalist who covered the march for the *New Yorker*, wondered what the march's purpose was. Judge Johnson's order, she argued, "had made the march itself ceremonial—almost redundant. The immediate aims of the abortive earlier marches had been realized: the national conscience had been aroused and federal intervention had been secured. It was unclear what such a demonstration could hope to achieve. Few segregationists could be converted by it, the national commitment to civil rights would hardly be increased by it, there was certainly an element of danger in it."[52]

King himself was forced to defend the event. When the reverend appeared on *Meet the Press,* moderator Lawrence E. Spivak asked King to comment on Truman's remark. "The march was not silly at all," King replied. If not silly, Spivak pressed, then perhaps it was unnecessary, at least in terms of obtaining a voting rights act. "Wouldn't you have gotten it whether or not you marched?" King dissembled: he did not want to antagonize Congress by suggesting that his efforts alone were responsible for the creation of the Act. Although the march had grown out of the voting rights campaign, he argued, it had also been intended to educate the country about Alabama's untold bombings of homes and churches. "We are marching to protest . . . these murders . . . as much as the right to vote." The other reporters on the panel that day showed little sympathy for King and his movement. They believed that King's work was finished and that his primary goals had been achieved; they thought there was no need for further demonstrations.

King could not have disagreed more. There was still so much to do, not the least of which was promoting the passage of the Voting Rights Bill. JFK's Civil Rights Bill, adopted by Johnson, had languished for a year, as it was derailed by the longest filibuster in American history, before Congress finally approved it in the summer of 1964. The same fate, King feared, might await the Voting Rights Bill.[53]

SIX

THE DIE IS CAST

ALTHOUGH THE PASSAGE OF THE VOTING RIGHTS BILL WAS BY NO MEANS guaranteed, Martin Luther King was in a stronger position than he knew. His strategy had worked brilliantly. By provoking Sheriff Clark into committing mayhem, which culminated in Bloody Sunday, King had aroused the nation and Congress to action.

Nevertheless, there were still doubts about the bill's eventual substance: Would it be as tough as Johnson wanted, or would the legislative process, with its usual compromises, weaken it? Would southerners mount another filibuster and delay its passage? Or would there be another unanticipated event that might change everything?

On Wednesday, March 17, two days after the president's speech and the same day that Judge Frank Johnson announced that the march to Montgomery could proceed as planned, reporters received word that there might be news about the Voting Rights Bill. They gathered outside Dirksen's office. Shortly before noon the senator appeared and announced dramatically, "We have resolved our labors and put the finishing touches on the bill." An exhausted Nicholas Katzenbach, grasping a marked-up copy of the bill, rushed to the White House, where the president studied it intently. After Johnson approved it, a clean copy was prepared and delivered to Congressman Emanuel Celler, the Judiciary Committee chairman, who slipped it into the hopper, the brown wooden box on the Speaker's rostrum that held all pending legislation until it was assigned to an appropriate committee. In this case the bill would go first to Subcommittee Number 5 of the House Judiciary

Committee chaired by Celler himself. If its members approved it, the bill would go to the full committee, whose approval was needed before it could be presented to the House membership for debate.[1]

The bill's sponsors in the Senate, Mike Mansfield and Everett Dirksen, the Democratic and Republican leaders, presented it to that body the next day. Mansfield had hoped for at least fifty cosponsors, so he was pleased when sixty-four senators joined them, an indication that the bill had bipartisan support. Further, the number of backers was almost enough to invoke cloture, which would shut down a southerner filibuster if it came.

The first legislative steps would be more difficult. The bill would go to the Judiciary Committee, traditionally the graveyard of civil rights legislation. Its chairman was Mississippi's James Eastland, a twenty-year veteran of the Senate and owner of one of the largest plantations in Sunflower County, where only 161 blacks out of a population of 13,524 were registered to vote. The sixty-year-old Democrat was another throwback to the Senate's earlier days, when southerners like John C. Calhoun fervently defended slavery. Eastland, a virulent racist, had urged Americans to defy the Supreme Court's decision in *Brown v. Board of Education* and gloried in his ability to block all civil rights legislation that came to his committee. Of the 1965 bill, Eastland said, "Let me make myself clear. I am opposed to every word and every line in [it]."[2]

Other southern senators were just as strongly opposed as Eastland was. Georgia's Senator Herman E. Talmadge thought the bill "grossly unjust and vindictive in nature," and South Carolina's Strom Thurmond predicted that if it passed, America would become "a totalitarian state." Louisiana's Allen J. Ellender planned "to talk against it as long as God gives me breath."[3]

Hoping to prevent the bill from dying in Eastland's committee, Majority Leader Mansfield proposed a motion requiring the committee to complete its work and report back to the Senate by April 9. That strict schedule angered both Eastland and his colleague John Stennis, and they urged their fellow senators to reject Mansfield's motion. Four other southerners joined them in opposition, but the motion carried overwhelmingly, a resounding defeat for the southerners.[4]

The southern senators' failure to defeat Mansfield's motion was a telling sign that the die-hard segregationists were no longer the powerful force they had been less than a year before. Then, through obstruction and delay, they had blocked the Kennedy-Johnson Civil Rights Bill for seventy-five days. That struggle, which ended with their filibuster broken, left them dispirited and exhausted. The "fight . . . really took the heart out of most of them," a Senate staffer told the *Wall Street Journal.* "They're tired. Many of them have been sick." Some, like Virginia's Harry Byrd and A. Willis Roberston, were in their late seventies and had no energy left for another battle. Olin Johnston, a veteran of many a civil rights fight dating back to the Truman years, was dying of cancer.

Also now on the sidelines was the leader of the Senate's southern wing, Democrat Richard Brevard Russell Jr. of Georgia. Scion of a distinguished Georgia family whose fortunes were destroyed by the Civil War, Russell had fought throughout his political life to restore the mythic South to its former glory. Since coming to the Senate in 1933, he had opposed every effort designed to help black Americans, from antilynching bills (they would, he argued, create a "Negro Soviet Republic") to the 1957 Civil Rights Act (its passage, according to him, would cause "unspeakable confusion, bitterness, and bloodshed") to the Civil Rights Act of 1964 (a "vicious assault on property rights and the Constitution").

But now, in March 1965, Russell's usually strong and eloquent voice was weak. Emphysema and a pulmonary edema had put him in the hospital for a month, and his convalescence in Puerto Rico, Florida, and at home in Winder, Georgia, did little to restore his health or his spirits. He seemed resigned to the bill's inevitable passage. "If there is anything I could do, I would do it," he told a friend, "but I assume the die is cast." In Russell's absence Louisiana's Ellender, who once proudly boasted, "I have always voted for white supremacy," would lead the fight against the bill.[5]

Not everyone in the southern bloc, however, was able to justify combating the bill. Other members, like Arkansas's J. William Fulbright and George Smathers, found it difficult to oppose such a fundamental American right as voting. Russell Long, son of Louisiana's famed Huey Long, had become the majority whip in January and was privately courting his state's NAACP chapter. "The Southern Senators will not be able to defeat a voting rights bill by taking the attitude that nothing is wrong and that no action is needed," he noted. Some reluctantly agreed with Byrd, who said, "We can't deny the negroes a basic constitutional right to vote." It would be left to the handful of die-hards to mount a final attack.[6]

Furthermore, just as the southern segregationists were growing weaker, moderate and liberal integrationists were growing stronger. Johnson's landslide in 1964 had reduced the number of southern Democratic senators by

8 percent, from thirty-one to twenty-three, putting the reins of the Democratic Party even more fully in the hands of northern liberals. Eastland's Judiciary Committee was a case in point: liberals were now in the majority, weakening Eastland's ability to destroy the bill. Among its members were Massachusetts's Edward M. Kennedy, Maryland's Joseph Tydings, and Indiana's Birch Bayh, all in their thirties. They were supported by more experienced veterans: Philip A. Hart of Michigan (who had been part of the original drafting team and would be the bill's floor manager) and New York's liberal Republican Jacob Javits. There were also thirty-five new representatives in the House who supported civil rights legislation, and the national popularity of voting rights led an additional twenty-five congressmen (ten of them southern) to espouse pro–civil rights positions.[7]

Given the liberal dominance of Congress, it is perhaps not surprising that the progressive senators on the Judiciary Committee—the purported "graveyard" of legislation—were actually the first to attempt to improve the bill. Their leader was Ted Kennedy, who had returned to the Senate in January after a near-fatal airplane crash in the summer of 1964. Still on crutches and wearing a back brace, he hoped to show his legislative abilities by amending the bill so as to allow it to eliminate the poll tax that civil rights activists had long opposed. Katzenbach and Dirksen had earlier been reluctant to confront the issue because of constitutional impediments. Just the year before, the country had ratified the Twenty-Fourth Amendment, which abolished poll taxes in federal elections, but the issue was still a contentious one. Earlier Supreme Court decisions in 1937 and 1951 had found that poll taxes did not necessarily discriminate against blacks and thus was not in violation of the Fifteenth Amendment. Vermont imposed such a tax, and few of its citizens were black. Eliminating the tax in state and local elections by statute, Katzenbach and Dirksen believed, might lead the Supreme Court to declare the Voting Rights Bill unconstitutional, so Dirksenbach did not include such a provision.

Nevertheless, Kennedy plunged ahead, ignoring pressures from Johnson and Dirksen, who felt the amendment threatened the very survival of the bill. Kennedy worked furiously to gain support for his effort, and the amendment won by a vote of nine to four. The bill now eliminated the poll tax—a major gain for civil rights activists, if only it could hold up under judicial scrutiny.[8]

Liberal Republican Jacob Javits also recommended broadening the bill's jurisdiction to cover those states that did not have literacy tests but where discrimination nonetheless prevented blacks from registering. Again, the liberals carried the day. They inserted a new trigger that would send federal registrars to those areas where only 25 percent of eligible black citizens were registered. Such low registration figures, the liberal senators reasoned, was a likely sign that discriminatory voting practices—even subtle ones—were preventing African Americans from going to the polls.[9]

The liberals' activism annoyed Dirksen. "In my judgment, their actions jeopardize this bill," he told a reporter. "I think the eager beavers are reaching a little bit too far." In retaliation the wily Dirksen added his own amendment early on the morning of April 8, when three of the committee's liberal members were absent. It allowed states that used literacy tests and the like to escape the bill's requirements if during the most recent presidential election a state's vote exceeded the national average or 60 percent of all its eligible citizens were registered. This weakened the bill significantly because Georgia, Louisiana, and perhaps South Carolina met the 60 percent requirement, whereas Alabama was close behind at 56 percent. That left only Mississippi under the jurisdiction of the proposed law. Liberals opposed the move but lacked their full contingent; they were unable to prevent the committee from adopting the amendment by a vote of six to five.[10]

The next day, April 9, marked the expiration of the time limit that Mansfield had imposed on the Judiciary Committee. If the committee did not vote, they could be held in contempt. For a while this seemed possible, as the committee had become deeply divided over the acceptability of the bill. The liberals were furious. They accused Dirksen of "gutting" the bill, whereas the senator claimed that the problem was their poll tax amendment. He reminded them that the attorney general had called it "unconstitutional."

The committee members argued for most of the day. Dirksen finally offered a deal: he would drop his amendment if the liberals would drop both of theirs. "When you make a trade, you've got to get a little something," he told them. "Don't you know that you can bargain and swap a hat for a monkey wrench?" The liberals didn't want a hat *or* a monkey wrench; they wanted to kill the poll tax. Vice President Hubert Humphrey, once the darling of the liberal bloc, urged them to compromise, but they rejected his pleas too. Finally Dirksen presented the liberals with an ultimatum: if the poll tax amendment remained, he would not join them in forcing a vote on the bill through cloture, causing the bill to "go down the drain." At eight o'clock that night the Judiciary Committee voted twelve to four to send the bill to the full Senate but without a recommendation. The liberals promised to continue their fight. A month before, the passage of the Voting Rights Bill had seemed practically inevitable. Now, suddenly, its fate was unknown.[11]

Fighting the liberals left Dirksen exhausted as well as angry. "I'm bushed," he had told the president on April 5. "This goddamned voting rights bill!" Johnson was worried about Dirksen's health. He had been hospitalized for stomach problems in February and March; Johnson worried that Dirksen might have a malignancy that would rob the president of his most reliable Republican ally. Dirksen's habitual smoking and his drinking—everything from coffee to bourbon—had caused a host of problems: emphysema, bleeding ulcers, and an enlarged heart. But he couldn't stay away from the Senate for long. The president had showered him with get-well cards, gifts, and mementos. When Dirksen finally returned to the voting rights wars, Johnson was thrilled that he was "up and at 'em again."[12]

The Senate took up the Voting Rights Bill on April 22, after pausing in memory of Senator Olin Johnston, who had died a few days earlier. Dirksen was the first to speak in support of the bill. He had worked hard preparing his remarks, which he typed in capital letters so he could read it easily. How could there be "government by the people," he asked, "if some of the people cannot speak? . . . Men are taxed but not permitted to pass upon those who impose such taxes. Can this be consent of the governed? Men are compelled to render military service but not permitted to pass upon those who decree such service. Is that the consent of the governed? . . . Now, one hundred years to the month after the [C]ivil [War] came to an end, we seek a solution which overrides emotion and sentimentality, prejudice and politics and which will provide a fair and equitable solution." Although three civil rights bills had been passed since 1957, he noted, because of discrimination, black Americans were still unable to vote. "Additional legislation is needed if the unequivocal mandate of the [Constitution's] 15th Amendment . . . is to be enforced and made effective, and," he concluded with words he had scrawled below the typed remarks, "if the Declaration of Independence is to be made truly meaningful."[13]

Dirksen's eloquence had no impact on the Senate's tiny band of southern die-hards. They insisted that the bill, in Senator Strom Thurmond's words, would lead to "despotism and tyranny." Senator Eastland spoke in similarly apocalyptic terms. "This bill is . . . designed to destroy the culture and civilization of a great people. . . . Some people say this bill furthers democracy.

The cold facts are that we are watching the sun set on human liberty and individual freedom in this country."[14]

The South's self-professed constitutional expert, Sam Ervin Jr. of North Carolina, was less hysterical, however. He liked to call himself "an old country lawyer" and was perhaps the Senate's most talented storyteller, lacing his tales with biblical quotes and Shakespearian sonnets. With his courtly manner, dancing eyebrows, and fleshy jowls, he looked like the stereotypical southern senator. But in his case looks were deceiving: he was a World War I veteran with a Silver Star, a graduate of Harvard Law School, and a former state supreme court justice. Ervin's affable, reasonable demeanor made him a formidable opponent. Lyndon Johnson's Voting Rights Bill, he said, "would make the constitutional angels weep." His opposition to the bill, unlike those of his peers, however, was based on a strict interpretation of the Constitution. Congress could not take away, Ervin argued, what the founding fathers had given specifically to the states in Article 1, Section 2—the right to set standards for voting eligibility—despite the existence of the Fifteenth Amendment. Moreover, the Voting Rights Act was illegal because it punished registrars selectively, in six southern states as well as thirty-four counties in North Carolina, simply on a presumption that literacy tests were being used to prevent blacks from registering. Where was the proof? It was "ex post facto to seek to correct violations of law and the Constitution that [had] existed for nearly a century," Ervin insisted. In response, Mike Mansfield leapt to his feet, arguing that Ervin's assertion had "a hollow and barren sound when measured against decades of abuse and contravention of the Constitution." Further, the idea that Congress was powerless to correct past abuses was "remarkable," he added. Indeed, that was the very purpose of the Voting Rights Act, noted Senator Javits: "The bill would attempt to do something about accumulated wrongs and the continuance of the wrongs."[15]

Ervin also argued that the bill gave too much power to the federal government and especially the attorney general, but to this Dirksen responded quickly. "People shout about the powers of the Attorney General," he objected. "I wish someone would tell me who in our form of government is to enforce the Constitution and the law if it is not the Attorney General."[16]

The southerners had seemed to have gained some ground at the beginning of the Senate debate. However, their power was first tested on May 6, when Senator Ervin offered an amendment that, if accepted, would have severely weakened the bill. Instead of the automatic trigger that would send federal registrars into the South, Ervin proposed that the decision be left to southern judges; if they decided that a violation of the Fifteenth Amendment had occurred, then the federal officials would be summoned. This marked a return to the discredited judicial approach, which left disenfranchised black voters at the mercy of local jurists who had consistently ruled against them.

The debate over Ervin's amendment lasted two hours and was generally sedate except for an argument that erupted between Frank Lausche, a conservative Ohio Democrat who supported the amendment, and New York's Jacob Javits, who was opposed to it. "You have got to stand by the Constitution, come hell or high water," Lausche yelled.

"I took the same oath," Javits angrily replied, "and I am not going to abandon the 15th Amendment."

The senators may have had varying impressions of how their opponents' proposals would affect the Constitution, but it was nonetheless clear that more senators supported robust legislation than opposed it. When the final votes were tallied, the Ervin Amendment was soundly defeated by more than two to one. Forty-two Democrats (including five southerners) voted no, and Dirksen was able to deliver twenty-two Republicans to join them. The minority included seventeen Democrats (five from the Deep South) along with seven Republicans and one Democrat, Frank Lausche, all politically conservative. That such a large majority supported the most important part of the bill showed how weak the southern forces were, and Ervin knew it. "I have nothing on my side but the right," he told Senator Mansfield.[17]

But the southerners still held out hope, however slight. Before the session ended it was announced that next on the agenda was Senator Edward Kennedy's poll tax amendment, which now had thirty-eight cosponsors. If it passed, it would shatter the bipartisan coalition that Mansfield and Dirksen had carefully constructed and perhaps give the southerners their only chance to block the bill. Worse still, if it passed with the provision intact, the entire bill might be judged unconstitutional.[18]

But the liberals would not be moved. Vice President Humphrey met with them again on the afternoon of April 27, but the meeting accomplished nothing. "I believe some people are in for a surprise," said Senator Javits, who strongly supported Kennedy's amendment. "I think the poll tax proposal will stay in the bill." Later, when asked if he and his progressive colleagues would accept a deal, Javits said no.[19]

On April 29 the creators of the original "Dirksenbach" version of the bill made one last attempt to draft a bill acceptable to the warring liberals. The result was a substitute that Dirksen felt would "cut the mustard." The poll tax ban would be eliminated, but the attorney general would be authorized to file lawsuits immediately in those states that required it; this, they believed, would eventually lead to a Supreme Court decision eliminating the tax. Dirksen's escape clause was weakened, and a new provision permitted the courts to appoint poll watchers if they felt it was necessary.[20]

Although Dirksen felt that the revisions strengthened the bill, thereby satisfying the liberals' priorities without unduly compromising the legislation itself, his draft still did not satisfy Kennedy and his allies. They felt it was Congress's responsibility, which Dirksen's provision avoided, to explicitly state that the poll tax was discriminatory and violated both the Fourteenth and Fifteenth Amendments. Such a statement of national policy would almost certainly affect the Supreme Court's eventual decision, as the Court usually did not overturn legislation that supposedly expressed the will of the people. Therefore, the liberals felt that including such a statement was essential. Meeting on the morning of May 3 in Jacob Javits's office, they endorsed the idea of a legal challenge but wanted the tax outlawed before the courts acted. And poll watchers, they insisted, should be appointed not by a local court but rather by the Federal Registrars.[21]

Both principle and politics motivated the bipartisan liberal bloc. Its members believed strongly that poll taxes harmed potential black voters, especially in the rural South, where poverty was rampant. Furthermore, the liberals also wanted the support of black voters in the East and Midwest—"I'm staring down the gun barrel of a sizable percentage of negro voters in two of our largest metropolitan areas," Indiana's Birch Bayh observed. Furthermore, these liberals felt that they had been excluded from the select group that had gathered in Dirksen's office to draft the original bill. One prominent liberal, Joseph L. Rauh Jr., counsel to the Leadership Conference on Civil Rights, spoke for some in the group when he said that it had been unnecessary to give Dirksen, a Republican senator, such power now that the Democrats were firmly in control of Congress.[22]

Having been left out of the original drafting process, the liberal bloc seized upon the debate over the bill as their only chance to influence its final outcome, and each side of the debate lobbied strenuously against the other. Kennedy, armed with advice from Harvard and Howard University Law

School professors as well as the Civil Rights Commission, spoke with every member of the Senate, including the most intransigent southerners. He and Jacob Javits spent hours plotting strategy, trying to find ways to convince their fellow senators to support the elimination of the poll tax. These hard-line liberals' opponents, meanwhile, tried to counteract their efforts by insisting that such an amendment might derail the bill. The president worked the phones—begging, cajoling, threatening. Dirksen also pressured Republicans to follow his lead.

As the debate over Kennedy's amendment opened, many observers felt the vote would be close, although Mansfield felt he had the votes to defeat Kennedy. After a quick count of his own, Kennedy sensed that Mansfield was right. At the last moment he asked the majority leader if it was still possible to forge a compromise. Mansfield felt there was not enough time to consult all the parties involved. They would have to proceed with the vote.[23]

The Senate gallery was packed on May 12 to watch Kennedy's attempt to revise the administration's bill. Kennedys were everywhere. Among the observers were the senator's wife, Joan, his sister Eunice Kennedy Shriver, and his sister-in-law Ethel Kennedy. By chance, Ted Kennedy's brother Bobby presided from the vice president's chair. Dirksen led off for those opposed to the Kennedy amendment. "If Congress can tell the states by statute this afternoon that they cannot impose a poll tax," he said, "why not tell them they cannot impose a cigarette tax or any other tax?" Mansfield chose a more practical approach: "The choice is between the course of risk and the course of sureness," he said.[24]

Ted Kennedy leaned on a silver-headed cane as he addressed his colleagues. He emphasized the cost the poll tax imposed on southern blacks as well as poor whites; paying a $3 tax amounted to almost a day's salary for many impoverished Mississippians. Clearly that was more than unfair—it was unconstitutional. "The question," he said, "is whether the Senate, in 1965, will say to the people of the country that the poll tax is being used to discriminate on the basis of the Fourteenth and Fifteenth Amendments. Why are we asking the Supreme Court to make this declaration if we are unwilling to make it ourselves? . . . It is settled constitutional doctrine that where Congress finds an evil to exist . . . it can apply a remedy."[25]

The final voting was more disorganized than usual. Democrats who wanted to vote for the amendment but hoped not to embarrass the president left the chamber but stayed close to see if their votes were needed. If not, they returned to oppose the measure. Meanwhile, Vice President Hubert Humphrey, who had always fought against the poll tax, was now lobbying to defeat Kennedy's effort to eliminate it. Such was the price of being Lyndon Johnson's vice president. Dirksen's troops stayed at their desks, ready to support their leader.

In the end the vote was forty-nine to forty-five in favor of the president's position; just four votes defeated the Kennedy amendment. The majority consisted of fourteen southern and ten border-state Democrats as well as nearly every Republican but six. Mike Mansfield was magnanimous in victory. "He almost—but not quite—persuaded me," he conceded.[26]

Although the liberals lost this fight, they could point with pride to several achievements. Their struggle had forced Mansfield and Dirksen to add to the bill the requirement that the attorney general immediately test the constitutionality of the poll tax. What's more, on May 19, with the liberals' support, the Senate (by a vote of sixty-nine to twenty) agreed to declare officially that in some places the poll tax was being used to prevent voting, thus violating the Constitution.

Robert Kennedy had voted for his brother's amendment but had not spoken for it, fearing to arouse the wrath of the president, who continued to worry that the Kennedys were determined to destroy his presidency. Instead, Robert Kennedy worked quietly, preparing his own amendment. This one would be aimed at New York's Puerto Rican citizens or other ethnic populations who had received an eighth-grade education in a non-English-speaking school but were illiterate, and it would give them the right to vote. With his wife, Ethel, watching from the gallery, Kennedy battled Senator Ervin, who argued that New York State, not Congress, should alter its voting requirements. Kennedy admitted that this was preferable, but in light of Albany's inaction, his constituents, "citizens of the United States," needed the federal government's assistance. His colleague Jacob Javits was more eloquent: just as the Voting Rights Act would encourage black citizens to participate in American politics, this amendment would "make a great difference in the feeling of . . . belonging . . . of 300,000 potential voters." Southern Democrats and some conservative Republicans were opposed, but the amendment passed by a vote of forty-eight to nineteen.[27]

The southern bloc was down but not out. Day after day they offered amendments that would weaken if not destroy the bill. And day after day they were soundly defeated, often by margins of two or three to one. "The way things are," said Senator Ervin, "I don't think I could even get a denunciation of the Crucifixion in the bill."[28]

There was no telling how long Ervin and company could delay a final vote or whether they would launch a formal filibuster. Three times Majority Leader Mansfield asked for unanimous consent to limit debate, but each time Louisiana's Allen Ellender, leading the southern forces, objected. "The Senate cannot be stalemated," Dirksen told him. Ellender reminded the minority leader that it was the liberals who had consumed so much time debating the poll tax ban. Johnson, however, was reluctant to shut off debate. "Let 'em talk for a while," he told reporters. "This is their job." With seventy-one southern amendments left to be considered, Dirksen told his colleagues to "start buying Christmas presents."[29]

There was only one way to stop the endless bickering: two-thirds of the Senate had to vote for cloture, thereby limiting further debate and forcing a vote on the bill. Only once before in its history, in 1964, had the Senate succeeded in ending debate on a civil rights bill, and that historic moment had come after seventy-five days of partisan and regional bickering. Although the Senate had been debating the bill for only six weeks, without cloture it was no longer so likely that the Voting Rights Bill would become law.

In 1964, President Johnson had depended on Everett Dirksen to produce enough Republicans to provide the winning margin, and Dirksen had delivered the necessary votes. But now, in the spring of 1965, the president was uncertain whether he could rely on Dirksen. He was again hospitalized in May and there were rumors of a rebellion against his leadership led by Iowa's Bourke Hickenlooper. The Iowan, chairman of the Republican Policy Committee, envied the influence and the national attention Dirksen had won as minority leader. Hickenlooper controlled critical midwestern votes, and although he had voted for cloture in 1964, he now opposed it and urged his colleagues to follow him. Suddenly, Dirksen's authority and his ability to secure the votes Johnson needed were in jeopardy.[30]

Dirksen worked tirelessly to keep the Republican Party unified. It was not easy. In the last presidential election the party had stood for states' rights against the expansion of federal authority. Although its standard-bearer, Barry Goldwater, was soundly defeated, most Republicans still believed in that creed. Yet historically Republicans prided themselves on being the party of Abraham Lincoln, as Dirksen constantly reminded them. "This involves more than you," he told wavering senators. "It's the party. Don't drop me in the mud." There were weeks of phone calls and meetings, with cigarettes and bourbon to cut the tension.[31]

Finally Dirksen thought he had the votes. So on May 22 the Senate leadership, backed by thirty-six others, filed a cloture petition to bring an end to debate. The vote would take place three days later. If cloture was imposed, a final vote on the bill itself would soon follow.

All one hundred senators were present in the chamber as the voting began at 1:00 p.m. on Tuesday afternoon, May 25. The final tally found seventy in favor of cloture—forty-seven Democrats and twenty-three Republicans. Thirty were opposed: twenty-one Democrats and nine Republicans. The margin of victory was only three votes more than the two-thirds required, which was narrow but sufficient. Cloture gave each senator the right to speak for only one hour, and although the southerners continued their attempts to weaken the bill, they failed. A final vote was scheduled for the following day.[32]

Now there were no more doubts. Ten weeks after President Johnson submitted the bill and following twenty-five days of debate, it was all over with the exception of the shouting. That was provided by Senator Allen Ellender who, before the vote was cast on May 26, called the bill a violation of every sacred American document ever created: the Declaration of Independence, the Constitution and the Bill of Rights. "It has taken us 100 years to catch up with this problem," Dirksen replied. "I am confident that this is constitutional." Seventy-seven of his colleagues agreed—forty-seven Democrats and thirty Republicans (including three who had opposed the 1964 Act: New Hampshire's Norris Cotton, Wyoming's Millard Simpson, and Dirksen's foe, Bourke Hickenlooper). Opposed were seventeen Democrats—all from the South—and two Republicans, South Carolina's Strom Thurmond and Texas's John Tower. Among the Democratic majority were five southerners—Texas's Ralph Yarborough, Tennessee's Ross Bass and his colleague Albert Gore, who had voted against the 1964 Civil Rights Act, as well as Oklahoma's Senators Mike Monroney and Fred Harris. The Voting Rights Bill had forced many politicians to rethink their principles and allegiances—and would have the same effect on many more before its final passage.

JOHNSON HAD WON THE FIRST MAJOR BATTLE IN THE FIGHT FOR THE VOTING Rights Bill, which was now headed to the House of Representatives, but he still had cause to be frustrated with the senators who had passed the bill. The president was especially disappointed by two party officials who had earlier encouraged him to believe that he would have their votes: Louisiana's Russell Long, the party whip, and Florida's George Smathers, former whip and secretary of the Party Conference. Also irritating was the opposition of Arkansas's erudite Senator J. William Fulbright, chairman of the Senate Foreign Relations Committee. Nonetheless, later that day the president expressed his thanks to those who led the fight in the Senate and supported the bill's passage. Their action, Johnson said, was "triumphant evidence of this nation's resolve that every citizen must and shall be able to march to a polling place and vote without fear or prejudice or obstruction."[33]

There were still tough times ahead, however. The great Democratic majority in the House—295 to 140—did not mean that the Voting Rights Bill was assured of quick and easy passage there. As in the Senate, the president faced angry southerners, determined liberal Democrats, and ambitious Republicans who wanted to put their own stamp on the measure to attract black voters. The House Judiciary Subcommittee considered the bill for twelve days and heard fifty-six witnesses before sending the bill to the full Judiciary Committee, whose approval would be needed before the bill would be sent to the House for open debate. Among the witnesses were twenty congressmen, including those who had introduced their own bills, opponents spewing bile, and civil rights veterans like NAACP head Roger Wilkins, who recommended eliminating the poll tax.[34]

Wilkins's testimony persuaded members of the subcommittee, so they added a provision banning all poll taxes. Other amendments provided new protections for civil rights workers. The administration's bill had penalized *officials* but not private citizens who interfered in the electoral process (the fine was $5,000 or five years in prison or both). Celler and his colleagues changed that to cover *anyone* who threatened or injured those encouraging blacks to vote. The subcommittee's amended bill was passed by a vote of ten to one and sent to the full Judiciary Committee.[35]

The full committee approved the bill by voice vote on May 12 but did not file its report until June 1. The report revealed divisions within the House committee, especially among Republicans. Eight had opposed the administration's version of the bill, believing it "hastily contrived, vague, inconsistent, and discriminatory." Their leader was Ohio's William McCulloch, the ranking Republican on the Judiciary Committee and a longtime supporter of civil rights. A modest man from a small conservative district with few African Americans, McCulloch hailed from a family of midwestern abolitionists and had risked his political career when he supported the 1957, 1960, and 1964 Civil Rights Acts. There was no question whether he would support a voting rights bill, but he wanted to eliminate both the poll tax ban as well as the automatic trigger that suspended literacy tests in those places that required them and where less than 50 percent of the citizenry had voted in the last presidential election. His objections were embodied in a new bill, HR 7896, cosponsored by House Minority Leader Gerald Ford, and would be debated by the full House.[36]

For now the bill was sent to the Rules Committee, controlled by archsegregationist Howard W. Smith of Virginia, famous for delaying civil rights bills until they expired. The Voting Rights Bill would be no exception. Smith thought it "venomous" and "abominable." The bill was expected to languish in Smith's fiefdom until he released it—or the administration could extricate it.[37]

But it was the poll tax ban—not Judge Smith—that caused Johnson the most worry. On May 13, 1965, House Speaker John W. McCormack endorsed the ban, making it likely that the House would approve the provision. Johnson was both angry and depressed. "McCormack was afraid that somebody would be stronger for the Negro than he was," he later complained, "so he came out red hot for complete repeal." Any change in the Senate's bill would require a conference committee in which representatives and senators would have to resolve their differences. This would result in a long delay in enacting the legislation. Worse still, any changed bill had to start all over again in either the Senate, where a southern filibuster loomed, or in the House, where Smith's committee would block it until a discharge petition was filed, which would take another three weeks—all while a restive Congress yearned to recess for the summer. Surely, Johnson thought, his enemies would take advantage of the delays and the bill would die. "They been doin' that for thirty-five years that I been here," Johnson moaned, "and I been watchin' 'em do it."[38]

As expected, Judge Smith dallied, refusing to hold hearings until criticism forced him to start on June 24. Another week dragged by before he released the bill. Like many southerners, the Ford-McCulloch measure encouraged him, and he urged his countrymen to vote for it. Associating themselves with Congressman McCulloch removed the racist stigma that had tainted southern politicians in the past as it also offered the only real chance to defeat the Senate version, which was much more severe. For Republicans, Ford-McCulloch offered both respectability and a bill that was truly their own, one that would still attract black voters, especially in the East. The Republicans hurried to support it. Even Johnson's special assistant, historian Eric Goldman, would later call the substitute "superior to the Administration legislation both in being less arbitrary and more comprehensive."[39]

The House's debate of the administration's version of the bill began on July 6. Immediately, it faced a challenge from the Ford-McCulloch contingent. Congressman McCulloch explained how his new bill differed from Johnson's: it removed both the poll tax ban and the automatic trigger that punished southern states primarily. In the new bill, once the attorney general received twenty-five serious complaints he could send registrars to look into the problem. Further, potential voters did not have to take a literacy test if they produced evidence of a sixth-grade education. If not, they had to demonstrate literacy to the federal registrar. In short, literacy tests were not eliminated in states with poor voter turnout nor were southern states with the worst records required to submit new voting laws to Washington. Administration spokesmen, supported by Dr. King and other civil rights groups, retorted that the trigger was essential because depending on local initiative was hopeless. Only federal power could truly guarantee black suffrage.[40]

For several days the administration was worried that the new southern Democratic-Republican coalition might derail the bill. The vote was expected to be close; those Republicans who supported voting rights but preferred a bill crafted by their own party leaders would determine its fate. Congressman John V. Lindsay, a Republican who supported the administration's version, worked hard to prevent defections; he thought he might have convinced as many as twenty to vote for Johnson's bill. But Congressman Ford disagreed. He predicted victory for the bill that bore his name.[41]

Then there occurred a historic accident that changed everything. Virginia congressman William Tuck, a former governor, banker, and tobacco grower, couldn't resist sharing a moment of candor with his colleagues. For all the world to hear, Tuck said that voting for the administration's bill would "foist upon your constituents this unconstitutional monstrosity" that would ensure that blacks would vote. The McCulloch version was less threatening to white southern interests. This, he said, was "the plain unvarnished truth." He was unaware that he had just alienated most of the substitute's backers. Minority Leader Gerald Ford appeared stricken and tried to repair the damage, but many Republicans, even the most conservative, fled the field. On July 9 the House rejected HR 7896 by a vote of 248 to 171; joining the 227 Democrats were 21 Republicans.[42]

The real triumph occurred later on the night of July 9, when two Louisiana congressmen unexpectedly found themselves at odds. Joe D. Waggoner, a conservative Democrat, rose to speak against the bill prior to the final vote. There were no problems in his home state, he asserted. Blacks could vote just like anyone else.

Hale Boggs, Waggoner's colleague and friend, was dumbstruck. He was the majority whip and, prior to hearing Waggoner's claim, had planned to vote for the bill but not speak in its favor. He felt that would be enough. He was a rising star in the party—many thought he would eventually become Speaker—and had signed the Southern Manifesto and opposed the 1964 Civil Rights Act.

But the pressure on Boggs to speak had become personal. Almost his entire family—his mother, his wife, her mother—wanted him to take a public stand. Just the previous evening at dinner his daughter Cokie, a twenty-one-year-old Wellesley student, and her fiancé, Steven Roberts, a young journalist, had joined the others. "We were just driving him completely nuts telling him that he had to speak," Cokie Roberts later recalled.

"Enough's enough," cried her father. "I am voting for it but I won't speak on it." The matter was settled. Nobody from the family planned to visit the House tomorrow to watch the ceremony.

But as Boggs listened to Waggoner's oration on the night of July 9 something "inside him snap[ped]," his wife, Lindy, later recalled. A brilliant speaker, Boggs rose and held the chamber spellbound: "I wish I could stand here as a man who loves his state, born and reared in the South . . . and say there has not been discrimination . . . but unfortunately it is not so." In his own district, he said, there lived more than three thousand blacks, but less than one hundred were registered. "Can we say there has been no discrimination? Can we honestly say that from our hearts?" he asked. "I shall support this bill because I believe the fundamental right to vote must be a part of this great experiment in human progress under freedom which America is." There was a momentary silence, then a burst of applause and a standing ovation.[43]

A short time later the House of Representatives passed the Voting Rights Bill decisively, 333 to 85. Among the majority were 112 Republicans (3 from the South) and 33 southern Democrats, including Majority Whip Hale Boggs. These southerners—from Florida, Georgia, Louisiana, and Texas—now understood the changing political environment. Henceforth, they would have to energetically seek black votes for the first time in their political careers. In this sense they were far ahead of many of their colleagues, who were still in denial about the prospect of black citizens in their states casting ballots.[44]

Johnson thanked the House for their action. But he had also unnecessarily enraged Republicans by attacking McCulloch's bill, now a dead letter. An angry McCulloch and Ford replied quickly, reminding everyone that Johnson, when he had been a representative and a senator, had opposed civil rights and was, therefore, a "Lyndon-come-lately" to the fight for equality. As the bill moved to the final stage of the legislative process, the remarks on both sides poisoned the political atmosphere.[45]

Because the House bill contained the poll tax ban, which the Senate had rejected, the measure would go to a joint House-Senate Conference Committee, whose members would hopefully resolve the differences. If they failed, there might be a stalemate that could threaten the bill's passage. The conferees included both passionate supporters of the bill as well as equally determined critics—not a perfect recipe for quick agreement.[46]

The poll tax ban proved to be the sticking point. The conferees accomplished nothing at their first meeting in late July. Katzenbach drafted a new provision, which was a somewhat stronger policy statement on the tax and the Fifteenth Amendment. He thought this might be acceptable to House liberals. It was like "walking on eggs all the way," Katzenbach told the president. Manny Celler and Everett Dirksen found Katzenbach's provision acceptable and recommended it to their colleagues. However, Democrats Peter Rodino and Harold Donohue felt it did not go far enough, while Republicans William McCulloch and William Cramer, seeing a chance to kill the bill, joined them in opposition.[47]

Johnson and his attorney general were on the brink of despair. Katzenbach called the president's handiwork that "damned bill." Johnson feared that the Republicans, the Kennedys, or the liberals would use the poll tax as an excuse to continue their public debate, which would destroy the Voting Rights Act and his entire liberal agenda. Something had to be done.

To break the stalemate Johnson and Katzenbach turned to Martin Luther King. On the night of July 28 Katzenbach and King spoke at length about the bill's problems in the Conference Committee. King detested the poll tax and had been disappointed when the Senate rejected the Kennedy amendment on May 12. Nonetheless, he certainly did not want the House ban to threaten the bill from becoming law. Katzenbach promised a more explicit statement, formally asserting that the tax deprived blacks of the right to vote, and would order the Justice Department to sue those four states that still required it. This was acceptable to King, who then dictated a statement that could be used to assuage the liberal opposition to the compromise the bill represented. "While I would have preferred that the bill eliminate the poll tax . . . once and for all," King's statement read, "it does contain an express declaration by Congress that the poll tax abridges and denies the right to vote. . . . I am confident that the poll tax provision of the bill—with vigorous action by the Attorney General—will operate finally to bury this iniquitous device." Katzenbach would also make public King's wish that the bill be quickly enacted.[48]

King's declaration broke the logjam. On July 29 the liberals on the House-Senate Conference Committee agreed to eliminate the ban, and in response, conservatives dropped their demands. Four days later the House, by a vote of 328 to 74, approved the Conference Committee's report and, with it, the Voting Rights Bill. The Senate voted on August 4, passing the bill by a vote of 79 to 18.[49]

The final version of the Voting Rights Act was remarkably similar to that originally submitted to Congress on March 17, 1965. Section 2 breathed new life into the Fifteenth Amendment by prohibiting acts that denied or interfered with a citizen's right to vote because of race or color. Section 4 contained the long-debated trigger, which immediately eliminated the voting or character tests in those places (mostly in the South) where less than 50 percent of eligible citizens had voted in 1964. A state or district could remove itself from federal supervision if it could demonstrate to the attorney general that it had not used any test or device that interfered with voting during the past five years. To prevent the delinquent states from creating new obstacles to voting, Section 5 required them to submit for "preclearance" any new voting practices to the attorney general or US District Court in Washington. Sections 6 through 8 permitted the attorney general to send federal examiners and poll watchers to the South to register and supervise elections if necessary. And in Section 10 Congress stipulated that poll taxes interfered with the right to vote and ordered the Justice Department immediately to bring suit against the four states where they still existed. Not since Reconstruction had

Senate supporters of the Voting Rights Bill examine the final vote tally. Left to right: Sen. Thomas H. Kuchel (R-CA), Sen. Philip A. Hart (D-MI), Sen. Edward M. Kennedy (D-MA), Sen. Mike Mansfield (D-MT), Sen. Everett M. Dirksen (R-IL), and Sen. Jacob K. Javits (R-NY). © BETTMANN/CORBIS

the federal government gone so far to provide black citizens with the opportunity to vote and participate fully in American political life.

These were the Act's achievements. But the Act also planted seeds for further disputes. Sections 4 and 5 expired after only five years, and therefore, future Congresses would have to reconsider them. Whether anyone sensed it at the time or not, these provisions of the Act, and especially Section 5 requiring "preclearance," would lead to new, impassioned debates about its limitations and its future.

On Friday, August 6, President Johnson signed the bill into law. The ceremony included many of the luminaries of the civil rights struggle, though most of the soldiers in the long Selma struggle—Bernard Lafayette, Amelia Boynton, Marie Foster, and others—were not invited. The White House staff preferred the more famous figures like Rosa Parks, whom presidential assis-

August 6, 1965. President Lyndon B. Johnson signs the Voting Rights Bill into law.
COURTESY LYNDON B. JOHNSON LIBRARY

tant Joseph Califano called "the woman who started it all." John Lewis was the
only veteran of Bloody Sunday to be present.[50]

Nevertheless, for those who had dedicated their lives to the civil rights
movement, it was a glorious occasion: with this victory, African Americans
had, at long last, achieved the political freedom that had been promised to
them in the Fifteenth Amendment a hundred years earlier. Although harassment and violence would continue, they had, after decades of suppression,
reclaimed their political voice—and more. "So long as I do not firmly and irrevocably possess the right to vote," King had said in 1957, "I do not possess
myself. I cannot make up my own mind—it is made up for me. I cannot live
as a democratic citizen, observing the laws I helped enact—I can only submit to the edict of others."[51]

Still, for John Lewis it was a bittersweet moment. Their success had been
achieved at great cost. In March 1965 alone three had died, and many, including Lewis, still bore scars, both physical and emotional, from the blows
they had received in Marion and Selma. Although King still insisted that
they avoid hatred and forgive their white enemies, Lewis wondered if nonviolence was the best strategy to fulfill the movement's unfinished agenda:

ending segregation in education and housing and, most important, eradicating economic inequality. He feared that the voting rights march had been the movement's last great unified event, a moment when blacks and whites traveled together toward the same destination. Asked to reflect on recent events, Lewis told a reporter for the *New York Times*: "We're only flesh. . . . The body gets tired. . . . Black capacity to believe white will really open his heart [and] his life to nonviolent appeal, [*sic*] is running out." Later, with the benefit of hindsight, Lewis concluded that "it had been Selma that held us together as long as we did. After that, we just came apart."[52]

SEVEN

BREAKING DOWN INJUSTICE

While Lyndon Johnson celebrated his greatest triumph at Camp David that weekend, the men of the Justice Department were at their desks. Their job was to transform that legislative Act into what Johnson called "the most powerful instrument ever devised by man for breaking down injustice."

They wasted no time. On Saturday the attorney general filed a lawsuit in Jackson, Mississippi, to abolish that state's poll tax. Katzenbach's staff was preparing similar suits against Alabama, Texas, and Virginia. The bill's automatic trigger eliminated literacy tests, and if the attorney general thought it was necessary, federal examiners could be sent to the covered states—Alabama, Alaska, Georgia, Louisiana, Mississippi, South Carolina, Virginia, and twenty-six counties in North Carolina and one in Arizona.

For now, that would be the extent of federal intervention in the South. Both Johnson and Katzenbach wanted to move cautiously; this was not going to be a second Reconstruction, with the South divided into military districts and troops enforcing civil rights laws. The president and his attorney general preferred cooperation, not conflict. The covered states and counties would be given the chance to comply with the law. If they resisted, then the federal government would send examiners. The Justice Department already had enough information to guide its actions; it had been filing lawsuits since 1961. The evidence compiled in these suits formed the basis of the "justification memoranda" in which the attorney general explained the government's actions. Katzenbach eventually sent these to 650 state election commissioners. No one could complain that the "Central Government," as George Wallace liked to call it, was suddenly and without warning taking over the South.[1]

Katzenbach and his aides spent a whole day choosing the first targets, which at one point numbered as many as twenty-four counties. But in the end only nine made the final cut: four in Alabama (including both Dallas and Lowndes Counties), three in Louisiana, and two in Mississippi. The total percentage of registered blacks in those three states was somewhere between 2 and 10 percent, whereas the figures for whites were astronomically higher, between 65 and 100 percent. These simple statistics were clear indications that black citizens of these counties were being systematically disenfranchised, most likely through poll taxes, literacy tests, or some other well-worn institutional obstacle. Armed with the new provisions of the Voting Rights Act, the federal examiners would make sure that nothing would obstruct black registration in these nine locales. The examiners, selected from the Civil Service Commission, were chosen on the basis of maturity and judgment, but many of them, not coincidentally, were also southern. Nearly all who were finally chosen hailed from such Southwest cities as San Antonio, Dallas, Fort Worth, Oklahoma City, and Little Rock. Employees connected to the civil rights movement were prohibited from volunteering. "Our business will be to register voters," said the Commission's executive director. "We're not in the business of integrating." Still, a few black employees—former postmen—were selected, and they were sent to Selma. The examiners expected to begin their work on Tuesday, August 10.[2]

Their first day on the job would be a busy one. That historic Tuesday morning, three hundred black citizens, many well dressed and all excited, lined up to register at the Federal Building in Selma. Across the street was the courthouse where registrars had fought them eight months earlier when Martin Luther King came to town. "I went down there so much," said one elderly man, "it began to seem like home. But I never got inside to register." Today would be different. One of the first things they saw was a new poster: "IT IS A FEDERAL CRIME TO DEPRIVE, OR ATTEMPT TO DEPRIVE, ANY PERSON OF ANY RIGHTS SECURED BY THE VOTING RIGHTS ACT OF 1965. VIOLATORS ARE SUBJECT TO A MAXIMUM PENALTY OF FIVE YEARS IN PRISON AND/OR A $5,000 FINE."

Many of the hopefuls were in their seventies and even eighties. They had to be helped up the fifty-two steps to the building's third floor, where the examiners waited to serve them. Registration started an hour late due to interruptions by reporters and photographers taking pictures. Some of the applicants still felt afraid or uncertain about the outcome or were just tired from standing in the stuffy, windowless hall. But the examiners were invariably polite, and the sight of Nathanial Phillips Jr., a well-known Selma postman, reassured them. "Would you like to register, sir? [or] ma'am?" they asked, putting them at ease. "Do you think you can fill out this form yourself, or would you like me to help you?" the examiners inquired—a tactful way of determining whether the applicant could read and write. If they were illiterate, the examiners would help them complete the form.[3]

Gone were the old tests used to trip applicants up. Now there was only a form titled "Application to be Listed Under the Voting Rights Act of 1965." If they were unable to fill out the form, the examiner asked them fourteen questions and wrote down their answers: What was their name? Age? Address? And how long had they lived there? Had they ever been convicted of a crime? (Traffic citations didn't count.) Had they ever been dishonorably discharged from the armed forces or declared insane? The only question the applicant answered without help was party affiliation; here no coaching was allowed.

Once the questions were answered, the applicant was asked to stand, raise their right hand, and swear or affirm that their answers were true and that they would abide by the law and be "well disposed to the good order and happiness of the state of Alabama." When the applicants answered, "I do," and signed or marked the form, they received "a certificate of eligibility to vote." The registration process was complete. "When you go to vote, vote for the best man," one enthusiastic examiner told a freshly minted voter. "Who is that?" the woman asked. "It's who you think is best. Not who somebody tells you." She agreed. It was an extraordinary moment for the newly registered voters, not least because the examiners addressed them as Mr. or Mrs., and this was probably the first time in their adult lives many of the registrants had been given that particular form of respect.[4]

First to emerge from the building was a smiling Ardies Mauldin, a gray-haired practical nurse at Selma Hospital, whose third attempt to register had finally succeeded. Her children had urged her to register early, and as it turned out, she became the first black southerner registered under the Voting Rights

Act. "It didn't take but a few minutes," she said. "I don't know why it couldn't have been like that in the first place." By the end of the day 107 new voters were registered, and the others were invited to return tomorrow when they could be accommodated. Unlike the discredited registrars of the past, the examiners worked every day, all day, from nine to five. Examiners working in eight other counties in Alabama, Mississippi, and Louisiana recorded 937 registrants, for a first-day total of 1,144. On Friday that number grew to almost 7,000. "The turnout far exceeded expectations," said a Justice Department official.[5]

Sheriff Jim Clark, wearing his "NEVER" button, was present at Selma's Federal Building, but on that day no one needed to fear him. Reporter Gene

A CORE activist reassures an impoverished citizen of Canton, Mississippi, that it is now safe to register to vote. © 1976 MATT HERRON/TAKE STOCK/THE IMAGE WORKS

Mrs. Jane Jackson, another resident of Canton, Mississippi, accompanied by her son, takes the voter's oath. "I had to register," she later said. "Got to do something. They cut off my pension." © 1976 MATT HERRON/TAKE STOCK/THE IMAGE WORKS

Roberts of the *New York Times* asked Clark how he was feeling. "I'm nauseated," he said. "The whole thing's so ridiculous I haven't gotten over laughing at it yet."[6]

The examiners registered black voters in great numbers and without major difficulties during that first week, although they often faced annoying problems. Some had difficulty obtaining office space because owners refused to participate in the endeavor, forcing them to work out of local post offices or other federal buildings. When neither was available, the General Services Administration condemned motel rooms, which were then hurriedly transformed into offices. In Lowndes County authorities set up trailers for the same purpose, but those were considered vulnerable to attack by the Ku Klux Klan. The examiners encountered other obstacles as well. In some counties local officials obtained injunctions prohibiting the addition of the new registrants to the voting lists, but Justice Department lawyers, who sometimes accompanied the examiners to their posts, were able to get federal judges to dismiss the orders. The state of South Carolina, meanwhile, was trying to bring the entire operation to a halt immediately petitioning the US Supreme Court to declare the Voting Rights Act unconstitutional.[7]

However, nobody interfered with the process of registration itself, although various officials, like Sheriff Clark, expressed their unhappiness to reporters. Mississippi's governor, Paul B. Johnson, called the examiners "federal snoopers," whereas Leander Perez, the racist boss of Louisiana's Plaquemine Parish, hoped his citizens would be peaceful because violence would only "aid Federal propaganda efforts." When six examiners came to Clinton, Louisiana, local businessmen complained about a second Reconstruction. "The Feds are fixing it so the Negroes can take over," the district attorney told Fred L. Zimmerman of the *Wall Street Journal,* and the sheriff thought "maybe it will be alright, as long as they leave our schools and little malt shops alone, and don't marry our daughters." Examiners who lunched at Louisiana's Clinton Café were treated like outcasts. But the registrations continued.[8]

IN ALABAMA THE MAJOR TEST OF THE VOTING RIGHTS ACT WOULD COME when the state held its first primary election in May 1966. In the one-party South nomination was tantamount to election, so the primary was a major event in state politics. It also represented the first opportunity for newly registered black voters to vote. The schedule, however, left little time for new candidates to organize and campaign for office between registration and election. And there were other problems as well. Would those who had registered actually vote? After all, many risks remained. If people had lost their jobs or had been physically abused because they *wanted* to apply, was not the danger even greater now that they could? There were no troops or FBI agents available to protect individual voters once they left the polls; they were on their own. And that's how Attorney General Katzenbach wanted it. His plan was "to take as limited action with these elections as possible," he wrote the president on April 26. "I am attempting to do the least that I can safely do without upsetting civil rights groups." Observers would be sent only "to the most difficult counties." Johnson did not disagree. Although he had signed the Voting Rights Act with great fanfare, he still feared alienating the South by strongly enforcing the Act.[9]

Martin Luther King returned to Alabama on Sunday, April 29, 1966, to encourage blacks to vote in the primary. It had been thirteen months since the triumphant march from Selma to Montgomery, and much had changed, both good and bad. There were numerous signs of positive change, of course.

Federal examiners had registered 235,348 new voters, almost 49 percent of those eligible. Fifty-four blacks, from fifteen counties throughout the state, were seeking both local and state offices. Among them were seven men hoping to become sheriff of their counties, and this was theoretically possible for five because they ran in areas that were predominately African American. In February and March two federal courts in Texas and Alabama had eliminated the poll tax, and the Supreme Court also heard South Carolina's case. On March 7, the anniversary of Bloody Sunday, the US Supreme Court ruled that the Act was constitutional. Congress, it said, had responded correctly in redressing a historic grievance when it enforced the Fifteenth Amendment by passing the Voting Rights Act. "Hopefully, millions of non-white Americans will now be able to participate for the first time on an equal basis in the government under which they live," wrote Chief Justice Earl Warren. (The Court, in *Katzenbach v. Morgan,* reaffirmed that stand in April.)[10]

If King's nonviolent revolution seemed to have triumphed in Selma, however, events in California indicated otherwise. On the night of August 11, 1965, just five days after Johnson signed the Voting Rights Bill into law, a riot erupted in Watts, a black district in Los Angeles, after a white police officer stopped a black motorist for driving drunk. A crowd gathered, rocks were thrown, and within hours, thousands were rampaging, looting, or burning stores and businesses that they believed exploited them. It took police and the California National Guard six days to restore order. Thirty-four people died, more than one thousand were injured, and four thousand were arrested—all at a cost of $200 million in property damage. The faces of berserk young men screaming "Burn, baby, burn" replaced the photographic image of Selma's courageous black protestors. And again television broadcast their pictures around the world. King feared that more long, hot summers were in store for the urban East and that similar outbreaks of violence there would threaten support for his own movement nationally, and especially in Washington, DC.[11]

King's relationship with the president was strained not only by Watts, but also by King's increasing criticism of Johnson's decision to expand American involvement in Vietnam. Combat troops were sent there in April 1965, followed by Operation Rolling Thunder, the continual bombing of North Vietnam. As antiwar sentiment increased in 1966, King felt morally compelled to add his voice to the chorus of criticism. "The bombs in Vietnam explode at home," King said. "They destroy the hope and possibilities of a decent America." Other civil rights groups such as SNCC had attacked the president earlier than King had and went further, publicly supporting those who evaded the draft and accusing the United States of committing "aggression in the name of freedom" in Vietnam. SNCC's proclamations and King's own words weakened his hand with the president and increased the tensions inside the movement.[12]

King's problems with SNCC had also worsened. Not only had SNCC opposed the marches that won blacks the Voting Rights Act, but some of its members also wished to create a new kind of African American politics, one that was more insular and defiant than what the more moderate SCLC and NAACP leaders envisioned. The divisions their message created among the black electorate along with the resistance it generated from many white voters now threatened to weaken black political influence, thereby undercutting many of the hard-won gains of King's SCLC and other civil rights groups.

Foremost among these advocates of a new politics was a twenty-three-year-old veteran activist named Stokely Carmichael, who chose Lowndes County as the place to build a new political party. Its symbol was the black panther, its slogan "Power for Black People." Carmichael was born in Trinidad to parents sympathetic to those who fought against British rule there. He grew up in New York, where he had been drawn to the city's radical politics, from Marxism and Socialism to the black nationalism of Harlem's street preachers. Eventually he joined the civil rights movement, helped organize the Student Nonviolent Coordinating Committee, and took part in sit-ins, freedom rides, and demonstrations. For his activism Carmichael was repeatedly arrested and incarcerated in numerous jails as well as in Mississippi's infamous Parchman Penitentiary, where guards beat him daily. Under such conditions King's nonviolence made no sense to Carmichael as well as others in the civil rights trenches. "I'm not going to let somebody hit me up the side of my head for the rest of my life and die," he said in 1961. "You got to fight back!"[13]

When King's voting rights march ended on March 25, Carmichael, ignoring his blistered feet, grabbed a sleeping bag and took off for Lowndes County, hoping to create a movement in that tortured place. Although 80 percent of Lowndes's approximately seventeen thousand people were black, white families were the ones who owned the land and controlled the life of the county. Almost six thousand black residents of Lowndes were eligible to vote, but none was registered before civil rights workers came to Alabama, and no one participated in the voting rights march. The reason was not apathy but rather fear. County Solicitor Carleton Perdue once said publicly that "We got ways to keep Nigras in their place if we have to use them. We have the banks, the credit. . . . We could force them to their knees if we so choose." If economic intimidation didn't work, there was always force. Almost half of all Alabama's lynchings occurring between 1880 and 1930 took place in Lowndes County.[14]

Carmichael's experiences in Lowndes only strengthened his conviction that black southerners would need to be more aggressive about defending themselves and claiming their rights. In disguise he traveled the county's back roads at night and met with local blacks brave enough to organize the Lowndes County Christian Movement for Human Rights. Carmichael tried to persuade people that their lives would be transformed if Lowndes had a black sheriff who would not beat them or a tax assessor who would give them better schools. It was tough going. Rallies, mass meetings, and voter workshops were no match for the county registrars, who rejected almost half of the applicants they saw in July 1965. This changed after federal registrars arrived on August 14, but even then the obstruction didn't cease. Within a few months approximately two thousand blacks were on the voting rolls in Lowndes County, but they continued to face economic intimidation. New voters were immediately fired from jobs they had held for decades, and there was murderous violence. On August 20, 1965, Tom Coleman, a volunteer deputy sheriff, killed divinity student Jonathan Daniels and seriously injured his coworker Richard Morrisroe, a Roman Catholic priest. An all-white jury later found Coleman innocent. "We're going to tear this county down," a saddened and angry Carmichael said following the tragedy. "Then we're going to build it back brick by brick, until it's a fit place for human beings."[15]

Carmichael's radicalization was representative of the growing rift between SCLC and SNCC, a division that became public on January 15, 1966. On that day there was a meeting called by King's aide Hosea Williams to discuss how to prepare for the spring election. Carmichael quickly used the forum to propose that Alabamians boycott the traditional two-party system and create their own independent parties. "Yesterday we marched," he said. "Today we need political power. . . . We are going to take it and we are going to keep it." He showed his audience the logo of Alabama's Democratic Party—a white rooster, its chest puffed out. Above it floated a banner bearing the words "WHITE SUPREMACY." "If you're registered in the Democratic Party, you back this," he said, with obvious scorn. "We pull no punches. We don't trust white folks." Asking blacks to support Democrats, he had said on more than one occasion, was "like asking Jews to join the Nazi Party."

Now Carmichael proudly unveiled the logo of the Lowndes County Freedom Organization, depicting a black panther ready to spring at any foe. "You ever see a panther?" he asked them excitedly. "He can't be tamed, and once he gets going, ain't nothing going to stop him. He's a MEAN cat!"

Albert Turner, a veteran of Bloody Sunday and head of the Perry County Voters League, quickly disagreed with Carmichael. "I still don't believe in a separate party," he told the group, "and I won't for a long time." After Turner spoke Carmichael left without responding. Williams, who was also bloodied that March day, was very angry at his proposal. "If any Negro is crazy enough to talk about a third party, he's out of his mind," he said. Racism was the enemy they had fought for a century; its black version must be rejected too. "Will they hate the white folks like the white folks hated them?" asked Williams. "We are only 35 percent of the people in Alabama, and ten percent in the nation. We can't go pitting race against race."[16]

But Carmichael had clearly captured the imagination of SNCC veterans, and many black residents of areas beyond Lowndes County were also attracted to his vision, which some called Black Power. Locals organized their own chapters in Wilcox, Greene, and even Dallas County. They selected their own slates of candidates to run in the forthcoming elections. A few months later SNCC ejected Jim Forman and unceremoniously dumped its leader John Lewis, replacing him with Carmichael. It also became clear that whites were no longer welcome in the organization's ranks. The civil rights movement, which had until recently relied on racial harmony to strengthen its numbers and generate national support, was rapidly splintering.[17]

Fighting to hold his movement together, King preached unity during his preelection visit to Alabama. "If we are to use the ballot well, we have to vote together," he told his audiences on April 29 as he raced from city to city—nine in all—at times driving at speeds of over eighty miles an hour. He saw almost five thousand people, but he avoided Lowndes County, which by then was indisputably Carmichael country. Further, the Klan's presence made it the most dangerous spot in the state. (Asked around this time how a film about his life would end, King replied, "It ends with me getting killed.") "Put aside your fears," he told hundreds of would-be voters who crowded into a broken-down church in Choctaw County. "I understand some of the white bosses have said they'll do something to you if you don't vote the way they want you to vote.

Once you put that ballot in the box, there is no way anyone can check up on you." Again and again, under a brutally hot sun in Wilcox County and a driving rain in Marengo County, he repeated his message: "Stick together, work together, vote together." Although they would be voting for a host of candidates from tax assessor in local counties to the state's governor, congressmen, and a US senator, most in Selma were especially interested in the contest for sheriff of Dallas County. King asked his audience at Brown Chapel to "nonviolently retire [Jim Clark] forever and evermore." To the many who approached him to shake his hand or just touch him, he asked, "Are you going to vote?" Their answer was always "yes" or "I'll be there, Doctor."[18]

It was a political season unlike any that had come before. For Alabamians of both races it brought surprise, bewilderment, and fear. It was as if the world had turned upside down. And indeed, it had. Mrs. Valester Russell, a resident of one of Birmingham's most rundown areas, was sitting on her front porch enjoying a bit of snuff when a group of white and black men suddenly approached. She leapt up, frightened.

"It's all right, honey," said one of the black men, who she now recognized as a minister. "All we're after is your vote. That white man there is Attorney General Richmond Flowers. He's running for Governor, and if you help elect him he'll get you out of this slum."

Mrs. Russell calmed down. Shaking the candidate's hand, she said, "I ain't never seen anything like this before. I thought he was gonna do something to me 'cause I registered. But God bless him ... and help him."

For Flowers, a Democrat and a racial moderate, becoming the governor of Alabama was an uphill battle. George Wallace remained as popular as ever with the state's white majority, and only the law prevented him from running for a third term. His handpicked successor was his wife, Lurleen, a quiet woman secretly suffering from cancer who had never before sought political office and did so now only because her husband demanded it. Her candidacy seemed acceptable to white Alabamians who, like their black counterparts, had registered in record numbers in the run-up to the primary. But if enough black voters supported Flowers, he might be able to force Mrs. Wallace into a runoff and possibly secure a victory.

For the first time in anyone's memory, a Democratic candidate for governor was vigorously campaigning for black votes. If elected, he promised to remove the Confederate flag that flew proudly atop the state capitol as well as the words "White Supremacy" from the party emblem. And he said he would appoint blacks to positions in his administration—men and women active in the civil rights movement, he assured voters, not "just a few Uncle Toms." Flowers campaigned mostly in black communities and joined them in singing "We Shall Overcome." In return, he received the support of Martin Luther King and Alabama's two largest black political groups, the Confederation of Alabama Political Organizations and the Alabama Democratic Conference.[19]

One might have expected such behavior from Flowers, but as the 1966 primary approached, other, less moderate candidates were uncharacteristically beginning to follow his lead. Al Lingo, one of the chief architects of Bloody Sunday, was now running for sheriff of Jefferson County. He also sought black votes. "I am not a racist," he told a reporter for the *Southern Courier*. "I have many Negro friends. A lot of good colored people here are actively working for my campaign." As for Bloody Sunday, he claimed that he had wanted to let the marchers proceed, but the governor overruled him, making him the "scapegoat" for what occurred. "I want the support of everybody, white or colored," he said. In that spirit he attended an SCLC rally in Birmingham and had his picture taken as he grandly added five dollars to the collection plate. If elected, he promised that the sheriff's office would include black deputies.[20]

Lingo's last-minute conversion did not persuade his audience, just as Jim Clark's invitation to a picnic on April 24, where beer and barbeque were served, did not win over Dallas County blacks. Clark was seeking reelection as Selma's sheriff, and finally acknowledging the new political realities in Alabama, he removed the NEVER button he always wore and attempted to woo black voters. The turnout, however, was disappointing. Fred Shuttlesworth had perhaps the final word on Clark's pursuit of black votes: "A man can't beat us in 1964 and 1965 and expect us to vote for him in 1966."[21]

Clark's opponent was Wilson Baker, who visited Selma's first black attorney, J. L. Chestnut, one day that spring. "J. L.," he said, "you can be of great help to me. We're going to clean Clark out of the courthouse and y'all need to go to work." In return Chestnut asked for black deputies and an end to the violent intimidation they had experienced under Clark. Baker was receptive. With black help he felt he could beat Clark, although he expected Clark to try to steal the election. "I'm going to help your people," he told Chestnut.

Baker's chances looked good; after all, he had the backing of Amelia Boynton and Frederick Reese, president of the Dallas County Voters League. Some other activists, however, wanted to run a black candidate for sheriff.

Carmichael was among these activists, but Boynton, Reese, and Chestnut feared that this would only split the vote and facilitate Clark's election. "Baker wasn't our liberator," Chestnut later wrote, "but he was a hell of a lot better than Clark and, without us, he would lose." Baker's visit left Chestnut feeling confident; it was another sign that because of the Voting Rights Act, black votes now counted.[22]

Because they did, reporters covering the campaign noted that certain words, long used in speeches and leaflets, had disappeared. One veteran Alabama journalist had attended a month's worth of rallies without ever hearing the word "nigger." George Wallace, accustomed to saying "Nigra," now struggled to remember it should be pronounced "Negro." "Segregation" was replaced with "states' rights" as the politicians' rallying call, and the governor removed the charged word from his wife's speeches. Racial epithets no longer blighted Alabama political discourse.[23]

White officials who had ruled Alabama since the end of Reconstruction were startled by the appearance in their offices of black men who now felt free to participate fully in the state's political life. For instance, on February 7 a tall, slim, black man entered the red brick courthouse in Camden, the Wilcox County seat, searching for Probate Judge Bill Dannelly. Finding him, he announced that he wanted to run for sheriff in the next election. Dannelly could barely speak but replied that it would cost fifty dollars to file for that office. The man pulled the cash from his pocket and put it on the counter. The judge gave him a receipt and a form to fill out. Later he learned that the man was Walter J. Calhoun, a thirty-year-old Army veteran with a wife and infant daughter as well as the owner of a small grocery store in Lower Peachtree, a tiny hamlet in southwest Alabama.

More shocks were in store for Judge Dannelly. Over the next few days four more black men stopped by his office to declare their candidacy for offices traditionally reserved for whites. Reverend Lonnie Brown wanted to be an Alabama state senator; James Robinson, the tax assessor; and Donnie Irby and James Perryman sought two seats on the County Road Commission. Although Wilcox County was 78 percent black, that had never been reflected in the county's political offices because not a single black had registered in more than half a century. But times had changed. After civil rights workers came to the county in March 1965 and the Voting Rights Act became law in August, thirty-six hundred blacks were registered, a thousand more than their white counterparts. This meant that the next sheriff might very well be black. Black candidates were also running for sheriff in six other counties: Bullock, Hale, Mercer, Green, Perry, and Lowndes.[24]

Walter Calhoun's candidacy terrified many of the white citizens of Wilcox County. No other office was more important than that of sheriff, a position that for most people was a "towering Big Daddy figure," according to southern-born journalist Marshall Frady. Nobody was bigger than P. C. "Lummie" Jenkins, who had been sheriff for twenty-seven years and was now seeking his eighth term. Tall and heavyset, he claimed never to carry a gun and handcuffs or chase after suspects: "I just send out word to the niggers and they generally come on in," he once said. Black citizens knew otherwise, however, having observed the sheriff once pulling his gun on a man trying to protect his young son who Jenkins thought had insulted him. To white residents of Wilcox County, Jenkins seemed like a typical good ol' boy, a pipe smoker and storyteller. But to black locals he was a dangerous man.

With Calhoun in the race, Jenkins's friends worried about Lummie's future—and theirs. People began stockpiling pistols, rifles, and shotguns, leaving them in their cars for everyone, especially black citizens, to see. One man remarked, "If they elect . . . a negro sheriff, they'd better elect 52 of them—one for each week in the year—because they just aren't going to last long."[25]

Jenkins wasn't worried, though. In fact, he expected to win *with* black votes. He believed that he'd always treated black people fairly and kindly, initialing their checks so they could be cashed in Camden or making sure they got their money back if some crooked used-car dealer sold them a truck that fell apart as soon as it left the lot. He was sure they'd back him again.[26]

But Jenkins's new opponents were confident too. With movement support, Calhoun launched his campaign, which was limited to black homes, farms, and businesses. He distributed cards with his photograph and the message, "Put Honesty And Dependability Back Into Law Enforcement and Take Fear Out." On the stump he told his listeners: "We need a colored sheriff. If I'm elected, I'll give you good, honest . . . law enforcement. But the only way I can be elected is for you to vote. Don't be afraid. Just get out there and vote on election day."

With Calhoun nipping at his heels, Jenkins stepped up his appeals to black voters. He kept mostly to the white side of the street, but if he saw a black man or woman he knew, he wasn't afraid to approach them, shake their hands (a first for Lummie), and make his pitch. "You know I always been fair to everybody in this county, now ain't I?" he would say. He passed out his own campaign card, on which he compared himself to a "Faithful Old Mule."

Despite such belated overtures from white incumbents, Wilcox County's black candidates were cautiously optimistic. They had never before run for office, but they knew what it would take to win: car pools to get black voters to the polls, people to help illiterate voters understand the procedures, and lawyers to make sure their opponents didn't steal the election. Voter turnout and black unity would be crucial to their success, but so too would the new election laws. The federal government provided poll watchers at seven places with a history of obstructionism; Wilcox County was among them. Win or lose, the new candidates felt it was worth the effort, regardless of the consequences. "We ran . . . to let younger people understand that you can do it," said Reverend Brown, running for the state Senate. But although the federal government could help ensure that the elections themselves proceeded smoothly, there were indeed consequences for the black candidates. A few days after filing for office, for instance, Walter Calhoun's landlady evicted him and his family from their home and store.[27]

Despite all their gains, many candidates and voters felt mixed emotions as election day approached. They enjoyed the happiness of doing something long denied from their parents and grandparents, something that had cost so much: physical pain from nightsticks and cattle prods, lost jobs and reduced income, the deaths of people they knew and admired. But there was fear too, especially among the elderly who couldn't read or write. They attended special classes, where their choices were printed on flashcards that they memorized. No jubilation or precautions, however, could fully prepare the 230,000 new voters or the many black candidates to commit an act that was completely unprecedented and still opposed by the white community that dominated their lives.[28]

The polls opened at 8:00 a.m., but voters started to line up hours before. In Selma, Marie Foster, who almost lost her life on the Edmund Pettus Bridge, happily provided car service from people's homes to the polls. People waiting in line at the courthouse were reminded of the voting rights campaign: the line stretched all the way back to Brown Chapel. Mrs. May Reese, although elderly, did not mind waiting or telling a reporter why she was there that day. "I'm going to vote . . . against Jim Clark," she said. "I been wanting him out for a long time, a LONG time." In Birmingham a blistering sun caused one older man to faint, but when an ambulance arrived, he refused to go to the hospital until he voted. "This is the first time I'm voting," he said. "It might be my last."[29]

Voting continued far into the night. In Montgomery the polls were supposed to close at 6:00 p.m., but at 8:30 eleven hundred people were still waiting at the Cleveland Avenue Fire Station, where unhappy white firemen watched them. The first-timers refused to leave until they had voted. At that same hour in Birmingham seven hundred stood in a long line at the Hill Elementary School. They started small fires in the parking lot to keep warm. The same kinds of problems—and lack of federal support—that had marred previous efforts to vote had caused at least some of the delays. Although officials at every level of government knew that the turnout was going to be far in excess of past elections, there was a significant shortage of voting machines, and generally nothing was done to improve conditions to make voting quicker and more efficient. Some reported waiting more than five hours before they were able to vote. Nevertheless, the new voters remained until they had done their duty. "It made me think I was sort of somebody," said Willie Bolden, eighty-one, the grandson of slaves.[30]

There were deliberate efforts to interfere with black voting. Officials in Selma marked black ballots with black stickers, which made discarding them easier. In Wilcox County hundreds set out for the polling place and discovered it was gone. Instead of just going home, they searched the countryside until they found it, and although it had been changed to a grocery store where Klansmen sometimes hung out, they got in line to vote anyway. Robert Crawford, a black poll watcher in Pine Apple, was turned away by state officials until federal monitors intervened on his behalf. In Choctaw County, where Reverend Linton I. Spears was running for commissioner, a black poll watcher observed a white official asking voters, "Why do all you niggers want to vote for Spears?" At another polling place in the same county, a site run by white officials, black voters waiting in line were forbidden from talking to one another and were treated harshly. After they filled out their ballots, an official who was related to Spears's opponent prevented them from placing their ballots in the box themselves. He deposited their ballots instead, giving him an opportunity to know who voted for or against his cousin. There were also a number of complaints in Bullock, Barbour, Greene, and Dallas Counties that illiterates or people having difficulty operating the cumbersome machinery were denied the assistance required by law. And when local election officials in Green, Sumter, and Marengo Counties did provide assistance, they would not let federal observers watch them.[31]

Nor had violence disappeared as a form of political intimidation. Poll watcher Andrew Jones, a quiet man who was passionate about voting, was struck in the back of the head while on duty in Fort Deposit, a Klan bastion. Stokely Carmichael went ballistic and, with a California friend named Huey Newton, organized a group of armed blacks to search for Jones's attacker. But they never found him.[32]

When the election returns began to come in, some must have wondered if their efforts and sacrifices had been worth it. Lurleen Wallace won a smashing victory, receiving 399,024 votes, almost twice as many as her husband had received in 1962. She triumphed in every section of the state, freeing her from having to face a challenger in the May 31 runoff. Richmond Flowers was left far behind with only 142,665 votes. He did win 90 percent of the black vote, but some of the new voters later admitted that they too had voted for the governor's wife. Political observers concluded that "it may now be years . . . before any serious Alabama politician will risk a close political identification with the Negro" and that other southern politicians would read the moderates' defeat as a reason to toughen their own positions against civil rights.[33]

No one doubted that Mrs. Wallace would win, but it was the size of her victory that was truly surprising. Analysts later discovered that although they had focused on the historic enfranchisement of Alabama's black citizens, they had missed an equally important development: the even greater expansion of the white vote. By eliminating the literacy test and other impediments, the Voting Rights Act gave many poor whites the opportunity to register and vote. Moreover, the voting rights march, protected by federal troops, alienated many Alabamians. "It's rubbing salt in our wounds," said one unhappy citizen. "I've become George Wallace's man." A skillful get-out-the-vote campaign by Wallace's staff added 110,000 new white voters to the white majority. By 1967 it had grown to 276,622, or 90 percent of those registered, thereby decreasing black influence even as the number of black voters grew exponentially. Nor was this phenomenon limited to Alabama. Throughout the South, whether because of race or demographic changes, most of the new registrants were white.[34]

Especially disappointing was the fate of Alabama's fifty-four black candidates seeking office for the first time. None won a decisive victory, and the twenty-three who qualified for the runoff faced tough opponents. Of the seven candidates for sheriff, only four won the chance to run again. Among the defeated was Wilcox County's Walter Calhoun. "It was too early for us to have a colored sheriff," Leo Taylor, a black house painter whose secondary employment as a school bus driver depended on the sufferance of whites, told a reporter. "The white folks wouldn't have liked that a bit and it would have caused us some trouble." Taylor had voted for Lummie. Such fear and dependence explained why candidates in Wilcox, Greene, and Barbour Counties failed to win the support of their fellow blacks. A black clergyman told Greene County sheriff candidate Thomas Gilmore: "If I vote for you and you win, they'll kill you. It's a nail in your coffin. I'm not gonna help kill you."[35]

Fraud was another possible reason for the many black defeats. A Barbour County businessman told Fred Gray, a veteran black attorney whose clients included Rosa Parks and Martin Luther King and who was now a candidate for the Alabama House of Representatives, that he'd probably be "a good legislator but you're not going to win it." Why? Gray asked. "We have been stealing elections from each other down here for years," the businessman answered, "and you can imagine what will happen to you." He was right. Gray was declared the winner until white election officials informed him that the absentee ballots, which were supposed to be counted first, had been counted last, giving the margin of victory to his opponent. Gray was convinced that his election had been stolen.[36]

Wilcox County had similar problems. When the Jenkins and Calhoun votes, 3,460 and 2,738 respectively, were tallied, the numbers "just didn't add up," said Albert Gordon, director of the Civic League. If correct, the figures meant a turnout of 98 percent of the county's eligible voters, which seemed unlikely. Furthermore, the county voter rolls had not been purged of those who had died or had moved, raising the possibility that former residents had returned and thus had voted twice, once in their new precincts and again in the old. There were also cases of missing write-in ballots suddenly appearing when the incumbent needed them. Gordon planned to file a formal complaint with the Justice Department.[37]

Still, black voters could take some pleasure in what became of their most vicious foes. Al Lingo, running for sheriff of Jefferson County, received less than one-tenth of the votes cast for his opponent, Mel Bailey, the incumbent. In Selma, Wilson Baker and Jim Clark fought about a group of uncounted ballots that would either give Baker a clear victory or allow Clark another chance in the May 31 runoff. By the end of the day Baker led by ninety-four votes with all ballots counted except for those in six boxes from black precincts, which were expected to go to him. So Clark turned to his friends on the Dallas County Democratic Executive Committee, headed by the founder of the White Citizen's Council. He argued that the uncounted ballots were mishandled and that the committee, which was charged with certifying the returns, should eliminate them. The committee's pro-Clark majority agreed. It appeared that Baker would again have to face Clark in the forthcoming runoff—that is, until John Doar, the assistant attorney general for civil rights, intervened.[38]

Doar, accompanied by five hundred federal monitors, had come to Dallas County "determined that the black citizens . . . not be disillusioned with their first actual participation in a local election," he later wrote. He had spent the day traveling from Selma to Orville, a tiny town eighteen miles away in rural Dallas County. There he found five hundred enthusiastic first-time voters waiting to drop their ballots in the four boxes provided for them. Everything seemed to be functioning correctly, but when Doar learned of the outcome of the Clark-Baker race, it aroused his suspicions. He had no confidence in the Executive Committee, whose members he considered "40 lily-white men," and after learning of its action Doar immediately prepared a lawsuit, the first one to charge a violation of the 1965 Voting Rights Act in Mobile's federal court. Judge Daniel Thomas, who often sided with the segregationists, was away, so Doar approached Judge Frank Johnson in Montgomery. Johnson ordered the boxes impounded until Judge Thomas's return.[39]

Jim Clark was furious. He had expected a challenge to his effort but thought it would end up in Judge James Hare's court, where he would receive a sympathetic hearing. Furious at the news of Doar's action, he lashed out at his critics in the national press corps. When *Los Angeles Times* reporter Jack Nelson approached him in the courthouse, Clark exploded. "Why don't you go to hell, you lyin' son of a bitch," he yelled. The *Baltimore Sun*'s Adam Clymer tried to interview Clark later that afternoon, but a deputy cried, "Why don't you leave him alone?" and then elbowed Clymer in the stomach. Some expected Clark's supporters to react even more violently if the sheriff was defeated, but Baker's black supporters were not afraid. About one hundred of them marched from Brown Chapel to the courthouse to protest the Executive Committee's action.[40]

Doar and his staff prepared for the hearing as if they were appearing before the Supreme Court. Each tally sheet was examined, and ballots were carefully counted. The six boxes contained a total of 1,600 ballots. Only 92 were cast for Clark, and 21 for two other candidates. Baker received an additional 1,487 votes and, therefore, won the election with a clear majority—if Judge Thomas disagreed with the committee and permitted the votes to count. Intentionally eliminating ballots cast by black voters was now a crime under the Voting Rights Act.[41]

When Thomas eventually returned in mid-May the hearing proved contentious. Sheriff Clark did not attend, fearing that his presence might enflame both sides. Clark's attorney, Frank Mizell, asked that the lawsuit be dismissed, arguing that the Thomas court had no jurisdiction and that the federal government only had the right to register blacks and could not obstruct local elections. Judge Thomas rejected his motion and ruled that the Voting Rights Act permitted the government "to intervene in local elections to insure that Negro votes were counted fairly." Therefore, Mizell must show cause as to why the ballots should be discarded.[42]

Attorney Mizell's main witness was Jesse W. Pearson, a pro-Clark member of the Executive Committee. He testified that the black poll watchers who had supervised the counting were incompetent and had mangled the ballots. Mizell accused the Justice Department of arrogance for bringing this frivolous case to the court. However, both the law and the facts were on Doar's side. Although his lawyers' examination of the records found some irregularities, more importantly it revealed how quickly the Executive Committee fastened on to the most minor errors in order to cast aside Baker's votes. For example, 264 citizens had signed the poll list attached to Box 45, but when Jesse Pearson counted its ballots, he found 263. Based on this he recommended that the box be excluded, and the committee agreed. For no obvious reason the committee eliminated Box 43, although there were 267 names on the poll list and the same number of ballots in the box.[43]

In closing, Doar argued that those truly guilty of arrogance were "the small group of men who—because they do not like the results of an election and the free expression of the will of the people of Dallas County—swept all the votes out and into a basket. That isn't what America is all about, and it's time every one of us stands up and tells them . . . it has to stop!"[44]

On May 24 Judge Thomas ruled for the government. He found no evidence of fraud or misconduct and determined that whatever irregularities occurred were accidental and insignificant. Both state and federal law required that the disputed ballots be counted in the election, which gave the victory to Wilson Baker. Clark attacked Thomas's decision, calling it yet another example of federal domination, and he announced that he would launch a write-in campaign to defeat Baker in the final election on November 8.[45]

Although Clark's defeat depended on the intervention of the Justice Department, white Alabamians still feared a black takeover in Selma and throughout the state. Their fears, however, proved unfounded, for such a sweeping change had become impossible. Only five black candidates survived the runoff and won election on November 8. A funeral director became the first black coroner in Sumter County, and a clergyman and civil rights activist won a seat on the Greene County school board. And in predominately black Macon County, an undertaker became tax collector, a retired teacher joined the county commission, and, most important, Lucius Amerson, a thirty-two-year-old postman and Korean War veteran, became Alabama's first black sheriff since Reconstruction. The "Black Power" slates in both Lowndes and Dallas Counties were defeated by wide margins. In Selma, Jim Clark campaigned not as a man who picnicked with blacks but as his old self, the sheriff who "will never be Overcome by Khrushchev, Johnson, Katzenbach, King or Baker nor any man quoting the Communist slogan, 'We Shall Overcome.'" His campaign, or some surreptitious intimidation, apparently changed some voters' minds, because Baker won by only 507 votes, a continuing sign of the city's racial polarization.[46]

The results of midterm elections outside Alabama were slightly more promising. Georgia, Tennessee, and Texas now had a total of twenty black legislators, including SNCC activist Julian Bond. Bond, first elected to the Georgia legislature in 1965 but denied admission due to his anti–Vietnam War stance, won reelection and was allowed to take his seat. Black votes may also have contributed to the victories of racial moderates in the governors' races in Maryland and Arkansas. Edward Brooke of Massachusetts became the first black US senator since Reconstruction. Although his election could not be directly attributed to the Act, many Bay State citizens had participated in the Selma campaign, which perhaps made the state's citizens more aware of the symbolic importance of Brooke's candidacy.[47]

The first election under the Voting Rights Act was a preview of the struggles to come over the next forty years. Over the decades, obstruction and intimidation continued, but in more subtle ways. Unable to prevent blacks from registering and voting, southern states attempted to make their votes worthless by employing what Congressman Emanuel Celler called "legal dodges and subterfuges," many of which harkened back to the days of southern resistance during Reconstruction and after. Offices that were once filled by electoral competition now became appointive by white leaders. Running for office became more expensive. In Lowndes County, for example, the cost of filing for office was raised to $500, a prohibitive amount for most blacks politicians wishing to become candidates. Some offices were simply eliminated or their terms extended to keep white men in office. Congressional districts were eliminated or redrawn to exclude black residents, thereby decreasing their political influence, or conversely, territory was annexed to increase the power of its white population. In place of a district system of election in which black citizens were better represented, southern states created at-large districts that placed black voters in a crippling minority position.[48]

The struggle to overcome these obstacles also continued, but activists found that the liberal mood so necessary for their success was fading. More important than the modest black successes in the 1966 midterm elections were the major Republican gains that swept the nation that November. Johnson's great political victory in 1964, which had made possible Medicare and the Voting Rights Act, was dealt a near-fatal blow. Republicans won forty-seven seats in the House, nine new governorships, and control of twelve state legislatures, all in the West. Among the losers was veteran California governor Edmund G. "Pat" Brown, who was defeated by onetime actor turned conservative politician Ronald Reagan. Brown could not understand what had happened to him and his Democratic colleagues. "Maybe [people] feel Lyndon Johnson has given them too much," Brown told a reporter. "People can only accept so much and then they regurgitate."[49]

Others thought Johnson's support of Martin Luther King's nonviolent revolution had actually led to more violent episodes of civil disorder. "The more civil rights legislation is piled onto the statute books, the more Federal money poured into attempts at Negro betterment . . . the more the anger rises," the *Wall Street Journal* editorialized shortly before the election. "Every legislative enactment seemed to incite more mob activity, more riots, more demonstrations, and bloodshed." That summer had been among the bloodiest in recent years; riots erupted in cities and towns in California, Ohio, Michigan, Wisconsin, and Nebraska. They seemed to please only Stokely Carmichael, who had said in September that "When you talk of Black Power, you talk of bringing this country to its knees . . . you talk of building a movement that will smash everything Western civilization has created."[50]

The Republicans had successfully exploited these events by calling on Americans, as one placard put it, to

> VOTE STRAIGHT REPUBLICAN IF YOU ARE:
> *AGAINST—violence, riots, and marches in the streets;*
> *AGAINST—disregard for law and order;*
> *AGAINST—The 3 Rs of today—Riots, Rape, & Robbery.*[51]

A group of British politicians, who had toured the United States during the midterm election, told White House aide Ted Van Dyke that the "backlash was far more important than it might appear to be. In district after district, and city after city, they found an undercurrent of resentment concerning civil order and gains made by the black population." America, after a decade of agitation for equal rights, seemed further away from becoming the "Beloved Community" of King's dreams.[52]

No one knew this better than King himself. After the Watts riots in August 1965, which he called "the language of the unheard," he began to think about taking the movement north to Chicago. There he would organize one hundred thousand people into the greatest nonviolent army the nation had ever seen. Their target would be the city's black ghettos, where so many were trapped in poverty and living in substandard housing without jobs, education, or hope. "The reality of equality will require extensive adjustments in the life of the White majority," King insisted. He also demanded open housing laws that would threaten the segregated suburbs, where the streets were paved and homes were beautiful.[53]

But the Chicago Freedom Movement failed. King himself was struck in the head by a rock during a march in a suburb as crowds of whites yelled, "You monkeys! . . . Kill 'em!" and "White Power." The depth of white fury shocked King. "I have never seen so much hatred and hostility on the faces of so many people . . . as I've seen here today," he later told reporters. Allowing black Americans to have a seat on a bus, a table in a restaurant, or the ability to vote was something that most white Americans were willing to accept; allowing them to live nearby in the white suburbs was something they were then unwilling to even imagine, much less allow.[54]

King's tactics that had worked so well in the South—the creation of morality plays with distinct heroes and villains—proved less successful in the North, where the problems were more complex and the villains less easy to identify and demonize.

By 1967 King had become isolated, at odds with the Black Power advocates who now controlled both SNCC and CORE ("Don't be trying to love that honky to death," said SNCC chairman H. Rap Brown, "Shoot him to death.") as well as alienated from a president waging a far-off war that King openly opposed with the kind of passion he had displayed in his fight for civil rights. According to an aide, Johnson, after reading one of King's antiwar speeches, went into a rage. *Life* magazine, whose photographs of Bull Connor's police dogs and Jim Clark's cattle prods had accelerated the passage of the two greatest civil rights acts of the 1960s, now called King a spokesman for "Radio Hanoi," and the *Washington Post* dismissed him as a relic of the past who had lost the respect and confidence of both white and black Americans. And J. Edgar Hoover's FBI was still watching his every move, its reports calling him "a traitor to his country and to his race." King's denunciations of the war so distressed even King's black allies—the UN's Ralph Bunche, the National Urban League's Whitney Young, and the NAACP's Roy Wilkins— that they urged him to renounce his leadership of the civil rights movement before he destroyed it.[55]

Chicago and Vietnam transformed King, as did the violent riots in the summer of 1967 that struck America's cities—Boston, Cincinnati, and, worst of all, Newark, where forty-three died. He was radicalized in a way that shocked those who had once seen him as merely a moderate reformer, well within the mainstream of American liberalism. "For years I labored with the idea of reforming the existing institutions of the South, a little change here, a little change there," he told the journalist David Halberstam in April 1967. "Now I feel quite differently. I think you've got to have a reconstruction of the entire society, a revolution of values." Such a reconstruction, he explained, entailed many of the characteristics long associated with Socialism, such as a guaranteed national income for the poor and government control of major industries. Although King became increasingly despondent about America's ability to save itself from the poisons of war and racism, he still believed that a better America could be achieved: "I can't lose hope," he once said, "because when you lose hope, you die."[56]

Although Coretta Scott King saw her husband imprisoned by a despair "greater than I had ever seen before," he persevered. In October 1967 he announced that he would soon launch a "Poor People's Campaign." A march on

Washington, where the impoverished of all races—black, white, brown, and red—would set up shelters on the Washington Mall and "cripple the operations of a repressive society" until the federal government granted them an "Economic Bill of Rights." King's own staff was skeptical about the campaign. Hosea Williams wanted to continue registering black voters in the South, Jim Bevel wanted King to make Vietnam his primary focus, and a young Jesse Jackson, then a Chicago organizer, warned King that "If we don't get some results, we'll lose face." King would certainly get no help from Lyndon Johnson: news of King's plans angered the president, who was already trapped by the Vietnam quagmire and facing a growing rebellion within the Democratic Party that threatened his reelection hopes. He pleaded with King to cancel his plans. J. Edgar Hoover told the president that King had now become "an instrument in the hands of subversive forces seeking to undermine our nation," and because of this, he ordered his agents to step up the campaign to discredit him.[57]

King refused Johnson's request and ignored the increased FBI surveillance as well as reports of impending assassination attempts, which grew daily. He asked Bernard Lafayette, who had "planted the first seed" in Selma, to organize the campaign, and as King set out on a tour to raise money, SCLC emissaries visited more than half a dozen cities that had experienced Watts-like rebellions. They hoped to persuade the poorest people to join their cause. But from the first, the campaign faltered. The money didn't come in, drained away by people already contributing to anti–Vietnam War protests. Nor were the urban poor much interested in traveling to Washington, where they would live in tent cities until Congress or the president came to their rescue. King had hoped to re-create Selma: organize the masses, demonstrate, touch the conscience of the nation, and thus force the government to act. It had happened in Birmingham in 1963 and in Selma two years later, so surely it could happen again. But it didn't. The response King was receiving from former donors and past supporters so discouraged him that he spoke openly of his disappointments. "We're in terrible shape with this . . . campaign," Williams later remembered him saying. "It just isn't working. People aren't responding." But his plans to occupy the capital went forward.[58]

King's closest friends grew increasingly worried about his physical and emotional health. He was chain-smoking, eating too much unhealthy food, sleeping too little, and suffering from migraine headaches. Sometimes he broke into tears during public events. His appearance shocked those who had known him in his glory days. One person thought him "a profoundly weary and wounded spirit" and chronically sad. His speeches now often seemed to be self-delivered eulogies, as when he told an audience at Atlanta's Ebenezer Baptist Church—his father's church—how he wished to be remembered after he was gone. "Say that I was a drum major for justice," he cried. "Say that I was a drum major for peace. That I was a drum major for righteousness. And all of the other shallow things will not matter. . . . I just want to leave a committed life behind."[59]

Only one thing might lift King's spirits: a call for help. It came in March 1968 from James Lawson, who a decade earlier had introduced nonviolent resistance to so many of King's future lieutenants. Now a pastor at a Memphis church, Lawson was supporting the city's mostly black sanitation workers, thirteen hundred strong, who had walked away from their jobs after the city government refused to allow them to unionize. Police wielding nightsticks interrupted their marches for better wages and working conditions, and a local judge issued an injunction forbidding future protests. Lawson hoped that King's presence would help them win their rights. Once again King's aides opposed the trip; they thought it a costly distraction from the floundering Washington campaign due to start in April. King again disagreed. This was both a worthy crusade—a fight for fundamental rights against a city government determined to deny them—and good preparation for what was to come in the capital. To his critics he said, "These are poor folks. If we don't stop for them, then we don't need to go to Washington. These are part of the people we're going there for."[60]

King's first march on Memphis City Hall on March 28, 1968, was a disaster. Among the six thousand people following him were a group of Black Power advocates—teenage gang members who called themselves The Invaders. They seemed more interested in breaking windows and looting stores along the route. King borrowed a bullhorn from Lawson and told the crowd, "I will never lead a violent march, so, please, call it off." King and Ralph Abernathy quickly fled the scene, but later chaos occurred, as police fired tear gas, then bullets at marchers. Even innocent citizens were caught up in the melee. By day's end downtown Memphis looked like a battlefield of burned buildings and injured people, sixty in all. One, a sixteen-year-old, lay dead. The mayor ordered a curfew, and three thousand National Guardsmen were soon patrolling the streets. (Andrew Young later learned that some of the rioters had been paid, perhaps by the FBI.)[61]

King was despondent. A policeman checked him into the Holiday Inn, and when King entered his room he got into bed, fully dressed, and pulled up the covers. He blamed himself for the tragedy that had occurred. "Martin Luther King is dead, he's finished," he would later tell his friend Stanley Levison about how he felt that day. "His nonviolence is nothing, no one is listening to it. . . . Martin Luther King is at the end of his rope." Young, accustomed to King's bouts of melancholy, had never seen him so downcast. King endured a very restless night; he "was greatly, greatly disturbed," Abernathy later said. But the next morning King was able to speak with reporters. He announced that he would lead another march, "a massive nonviolent demonstration," early in April. King's quick recovery thrilled Abernathy, but again, it vanished in an instant. "Get me out of Memphis," he begged Abernathy. "Get me out of Memphis as soon as possible." The next day they returned to Atlanta.[62]

King's moods remained volatile. He briefed his staff on the Memphis debacle and told them of his plan to return. Most opposed this. Jim Bevel reported that the Poor People's campaign was still going badly: "I don't even know how to preach people . . . into the campaign," he confessed—a first for the loquacious Bevel. Suddenly, King became angry. He "just jumped on everybody," Young later told the journalist Marshall Frady. "I can't take all this on myself," King said. "I need you to take your share of the load." Then he stormed out of the room with Jesse Jackson in pursuit, yelling, "Doc? Doc? Don't worry, everything's going to be all right." King turned around, shouting, "Everything's not going to be all right if things keep going the way they're going." When Jackson tried to reply, King yelled, "Jesse, don't bother me. . . . [F]or God's sake, don't bother me." Young was shocked by King's sudden rage. "Nobody had ever seen him mad like that before," he later said.[63]

King's mood improved slightly on March 31 after learning of President Johnson's decision not to seek another term as president. A new president— perhaps Robert Kennedy—would end the war and seek racial justice, he hoped. Now he thought it was even more necessary for the Poor People's campaign to succeed, and he planned to devote more energy to it after his return from Memphis.

King's plane arrived late in Memphis on Wednesday, April 3, delayed because of a bomb scare and inclement weather. King seemed more relaxed, less haunted by the many threats he faced. To Abernathy, who was always with him, King seemed "in good spirits," he later recalled. When local police offered their protection, he rejected it and hurried to check into the Lorraine Motel before the storm broke. The day was spent preparing for the forthcoming march, now scheduled for Friday, April 5. The meetings kept King focused on the kinds of logistical problems he and his aides were accustomed to solving. A Memphis judge had issued yet another injunction prohibiting their march, and King's lawyers were instructed to lift it. King was defiant: "We are not going to be stopped by Mace or by injunctions," he said. By nightfall King was tired, and fearing the onset of a cold and fever, he was reluctant to go out into a rain-filled night to speak at a mass meeting. He asked Abernathy to take his place at the Bishop Charles Mason Temple Church of God in Christ. Abernathy agreed, and King put on his pajamas and looked forward to a quiet evening. This was perhaps the final irony in a history replete with them: King's last and perhaps most poignant speech, "I've Been to the Mountaintop," was almost never delivered.[64]

Despite the rain's torrential downpour, Abernathy and Young found the hall filled with two thousand restless people waiting for Martin Luther King. They would accept no substitute, so at 8:30, Abernathy telephoned King, urging him to come. King refused. "Can't you talk to them?" King asked. "Won't they listen to you?"

Abernathy promised to deliver the major speech; King would only have to speak briefly. "This is your crowd," Abernathy emphasized, offering up the magic words that led King to get dressed and hurry to the temple. Without a single note in hand, he spoke eloquently of the plight of the sanitation workers and urged the crowd to join their march on Monday, despite the judge's injunction forbidding it. "Somewhere I read that the greatness of America is the right to protest for right," he said, and the people applauded. "We aren't going to let any dogs or water hoses turn us around, we aren't going to let any injunction turn us around. We are going on."

The dogs and fire hoses triggered something in his memory, and he began to speak about the long struggle for equal rights. He recalled being knifed at a book signing in New York City and later learning that if he had sneezed, the knife would have cut into his aorta. When that happens, he said, "you drown in your own blood—that's the end of you." But that grim event reminded him that among the letters he had received following the assault was one from a young, white high school girl who said, he told the crowd, "I'm so happy that you didn't sneeze." The applause was as loud as the thunder that shook the building as the storm raged outside.

"I want to say tonight . . . that I too am happy that I didn't sneeze," he continued.

> Because if I had sneezed, I wouldn't have been around here in 1960, when students all over the South started sitting-in at lunch counters. And I knew that as they were sitting in, they were really standing up for the best in the American dream. . . . If I had sneezed, I wouldn't have been around here in 1961 when we decided to take a ride for freedom and ended segregation in interstate travel. . . . If I had sneezed, I wouldn't have been here in 1963, when the black people of Birmingham, Alabama, aroused the conscience of this nation, and brought into being the Civil Rights Bill. If I had sneezed, I wouldn't have had a chance . . . in August, to try to tell America about a dream that I had had. If I had sneezed, I wouldn't have been down in Selma, Alabama, to see the great movement there. If I had sneezed, I wouldn't have been in Memphis to see the community rally around those brothers and sisters who are suffering. I'm so happy that I didn't sneeze.

He was growing tired now and was sweating profusely, whether from a fever or from the room's sweltering heat. He knew it was time to finish. "Well, I don't know what will happen now," he said.

> We've got some difficult days ahead. But it really doesn't matter with me now. Because I've been to the mountaintop. And I don't mind. Like anybody, I would like to live a long life. Longevity has its place. But I'm not concerned about that now. I just want to do God's will. And He's allowed me to go up to the mountain. And I've looked over. And I've *seeeen* the promised land! I may not get there with you. But I want you to *know* tonight, that we, as a people, *will* get to the promised land! And so I'm happy tonight! I'm not worried about *any*thing. I'm not fearing *any* man! Mine eyes have seen the glory of the coming of the Lord!

As the crowd clapped and cheered, he stumbled backward and fell into a chair. King's friend Benjamin Hooks thought he saw tears streaming down his face, but both Abernathy and Young believed King felt exhilarated and joyful. Before leaving for Memphis, Abernathy had asked a discouraged King, "Tell me, what is bugging you?" and King had replied, "Ralph, I'll snap out of it. . . . I'll pull through it." That night it seemed like he had.[65]

The storm passed, and Thursday, April 4, dawned clear and cool. King slept late, lunched happily and voraciously on catfish and salad, and met with his aides. Chauncy Eskridge, SCLC's lawyer, and Andy Young arrived after a long day in court bearing good news. After listening to the testimony of Young and Jim Lawson, the Memphis judge rescinded his injunction: the march could go forward, now on Monday, April 8. King was overjoyed, grabbed Young, and the two wrestled like young boys.

King was still in a happy mood as evening approached. He and his aides were to dine at Reverend Samuel Kyles's home, then attend another rally. King had inquired what the menu would be and learned that it was everything he liked: prime rib and good, old-fashioned "soul food," including black-eyed peas and pigs feet. Kyles arrived at 5:30, but King wasn't ready to leave. Leaning over the Lorraine Motel's third-floor balcony not far from his room, King bantered with his aides, who were in a playful mood in the parking lot below. King spied Jesse Jackson and Ben Branch, a bandleader, watching Hosea Williams and James Orange, two big, stocky men, tusseling with a thinner, weaker Jim Bevel. King warned Bevel to protect himself. Forgetting his spat with Jackson in Atlanta, King invited the young man—who adored King—to join them for dinner. But he would have to "dress up a little tonight," he told Jackson with a smile. "No blue jeans, all right?" Then King asked Branch to play one of his favorite tunes that night: "Precious Lord, Take My Hand." "Sing it *real* pretty," King said. Branch assured him that he would.

The car—a limousine owned by a local funeral home—that was to take King and his staff to dinner finally arrived. King's driver, Solomon Jones, suggested that he get a topcoat, as the evening had grown cold. As King turned to go back to the room, Young, shadowboxing with his friends in the parking lot, heard a loud noise that sounded, to him, "like a car backfiring or a firecracker." Looking up, he saw that King was now lying on the balcony floor. "Still clowning," was Young's first thought, then pandemonium erupted. Young raced up the stairs to find Abernathy kneeling over his old friend, saying, "Martin, this is Ralph. Can you hear me? . . . Don't be afraid. Everything will be all right." But Young could see that King had been mortally wounded. The assassin's high-velocity .30–06 bullet had opened a massive wound in his neck and right jaw, and blood poured from his head. "Oh God, Ralph," Young cried. "It's over." Abernathy would not accept it: "Don't you say that, Andy. It's not over. He'll be all right." Soon police arrived, and an ambulance rushed King to St. Joseph's Hospital where, a short time later, he died.[66]

Looking back on King's life and career, some would say that he had died at the right moment, that martyrdom rescued him from an equally serious blow: irrelevancy. The Selma campaign had clearly been his greatest achievement and, as it turned out, his last. But the 1964 Civil Rights Act and the 1965 Voting Rights Act are a testament to his leadership and commitment to achieving change through nonviolent protest. Nearly fifty years after his death it is King's words and deeds that live on in the American memory—not that of the racists who hated him or the Black Power advocates who scorned him.

In 1968, however, King's death was a major blow to the civil rights movement. It signaled to many the end of the strategy of nonviolence that King had championed throughout his life. Stokely Carmichael called for African Americans to arm themselves in response to King's murder; riots erupted in over one hundred American cities. The outpouring of anger terrified many white Americans and helped to polarize along racial lines a nation that King had so badly wanted to bring together.[67]

Other events that year would also shake the country. In June, Senator Robert Kennedy, winning the California Democratic presidential primary, which boosted his chances of winning his party's nomination, was shot to death in Los Angeles. In August, the Democratic Party's convention, meeting in Chicago, was torn by strife as police battled antiwar protestors in the streets. Lyndon Johnson's heir, Vice President Hubert Humphrey, won the Democratic presidential nomination, but it seemed to be worthless. America had not experienced such a sustained period of disorder since the Civil War. Two other candidates emerged, both promising to return America to its former greatness: George C. Wallace and Richard M. Nixon. The latter, defeated by John F. Kennedy in 1960, returned from political oblivion to win the Republican Party's presidential nomination. He told voters that he had a secret plan to end the Vietnam War, and if elected, he would create a new era of "law and order" at home.[68]

More threatening to America's future political well-being was former Alabama governor George Wallace. Running on the American Independent Party ticket, he exploited America's fears for political gain. His views on race were already well known, and they now appealed to some northerners as well as to southern segregationists. He promised to jail antiwar protestors, fight for states' rights, and represent "the workin' folk fed up with bureaucrats in Washington [and] the pointy headed intellectuals . . . tellin' 'em how to live their lives." Nixon, employing a "Southern Strategy" that played to

Wallace's audience and disenchanted Democrats, narrowly defeated Hubert Humphrey, but Wallace received ten million votes nationwide and carried five southern states.[69]

Civil rights activists were now very worried. In 1964 Johnson had won 61 percent of the vote. Now, just four years later, the combined total vote for Nixon and Wallace was almost 57 percent. The nation seemed to want an end to big-government liberalism, one of the beneficiaries of which had been civil rights. Surely Nixon, looking ahead to 1972, would move in Wallace's direction to recruit his constituency. With Martin Luther King gone and the movement in disarray, activists feared that the Voting Rights Act, due for reenactment in 1970, might now be doomed and that the "Second Reconstruction" would end as quickly as the first.[70]

EIGHT

WHERE THE VOTES ARE

RICHARD NIXON'S 1968 CAMPAIGN AND THE EARLY DAYS OF HIS PRESIDENCY gave the civil rights community every reason to be suspicious of him. His closest southern ally was South Carolina senator Strom Thurmond, the rabid segregationist and onetime Democrat who had recently switched to the Republican side out of disgust over the 1964 Civil Rights Act. It was also rumored that Nixon had made a number of promises to Thurmond and other southerners. When it came to voting rights law Nixon had agreed to "treat the South like the rest of the nation," Thurmond later claimed. Nixon, according to Thurmond, would also appoint sympathetic judges and select a running mate acceptable to the South. He kept those promises. Nixon named as his vice president former Maryland governor Spiro Agnew, known for his tough law-and-order stand during Baltimore's summer riots. And the president's first Supreme Court nominee was Clement F. Haynesworth Jr., a South Carolina appeals court judge and a favorite of Thurmond's.[1]

Underlying these early decisions of Nixon's was his desire to recruit those who resented black gains, namely, George Wallace's followers in the South and disaffected blue-collar Democrats everywhere. No African Americans served in his cabinet or were appointed to his White House staff, which now included Thurmond's former assistant, Harry Dent, who said that he wanted to get the voting rights "monkey . . . off the backs of the South." Twenty other Thurmond associates also became members of the Nixon administration. Nixon strongly opposed "forced busing" to achieve racial integration in schools and recommended that it be banned by constitutional

amendment. Nor did he encourage the Justice Department to enforce existing civil rights laws strongly. Narrowly elected in 1968, these measures were
designed to create an electoral majority in 1972. Would the Voting Rights
Act, due for renewal in 1970, be the first casualty in Nixon's campaign to win
a second term?[2]

Ironically Nixon realized that continuing the Voting Rights Act in some
form might serve his own political interests. He saw that the Act had profoundly alienated many white voters from the Democratic Party, presenting
Republicans with a golden opportunity to grow their political power. In 1970
one of Nixon's chief strategists, Kevin Phillips, explained the president's
thinking to the *New York Times*. "Republicans would be shortsighted if they
weakened enforcement of the Voting Rights Act," Phillips said. "The more
Negroes who register as Democrats in the South, the sooner the Negrophobe
whites will quit the Democrats and become Republicans. That's where the
votes are." Johnson had worried that the Voting Rights Act would destroy
the Democrats' control of the South, and the Republicans had begun to make
inroads there as early as 1968. By the mid- to late 1990s, excepting southern
Democrats like Jimmy Carter and Bill Clinton, the South would belong to the
Republicans for the rest of the twentieth century and beyond.[3]

As it turned out, civil rights activists were justified in fearing for the future
of the Voting Rights Act. On June 26, 1969, Attorney General John Mitchell
called for a three-year renewal of the Act, but one that would contain changes
that would significantly weaken it. First, he called for a *national* ban on literacy tests until 1974 (fourteen states outside the South still employed them).
This would please southerners who felt they were being exclusively stigma-
tized. Such a total ban, voting rights advocates believed, would be too difficult
for the Civil Rights Division's limited staff to enforce; it would be better to
focus on the South where their energies were still needed. Mitchell also tried
to undermine the Act by recommending the elimination of the triggering
mechanism—the 1964 presidential election returns—and the preclearance
provision. Instead of requiring the covered states or political subdivisions to
submit proposed changes in electoral practices to Washington, Justice Department lawyers would now have to challenge those practices in southern
courts, *after* the changes became law. It would be a return to the past, when
the Justice Department had to prove in courtrooms where southern judges
presided that electoral acts were discriminatory. The burden of proof would
be on the government rather than those seeking preclearance. Mitchell's an-

nouncement so enraged civil rights activists that a group from the South came to the capital, where they held a sit-in at the attorney general's office, the first such protest in four years.[4]

When the Mitchell Bill, as it was called, arrived in the House, a fight broke out between southern supporters who yearned to be free of federal supervision and critics, like the pro–civil rights Republican congressman from Ohio William McCulloch, who strongly denounced it. The Mitchell Bill, which nationalized the Voting Rights Act, would, McCulloch said, "sweep broadly into those areas where the need is the least and retreat from those areas where the need is greatest." But his strongest words were directed at the provision that eliminated preclearance "in the face of spellbinding evidence of . . . more sophisticated machinery for discriminating against the black voter." In short, the congressman concluded, "the Administration creates a remedy for which there is no wrong and leaves grievous wrongs without adequate remedy. . . . [W]hat kind of civil rights bill is that?"[5]

The critics won the first battle when Congressman Emanuel Celler's liberal-dominated House Judiciary Committee voted on July 17 to recommend a simple five-year extension of the 1965 Act, which became known as the Celler Bill. But the fight continued in the House Rules Committee, where its segregationist chairman, Mississippi Democrat William Colmer, who called the legislation "the annual civil wrongs bill," refused to release the Celler Bill for four months. He finally agreed to send the bill to the floor on November 18, 1969, only for the purpose of amending it to reflect the proposals embodied in the Mitchell version. Nixon's aides in the White House and Justice Department lobbied intensely for these amendments. "They covered this place like a carpet," said one disheartened Democrat. "And our people didn't realize what was happening until it was too late." Liberals found it difficult to attack a bill that appeared to be just; no one section of the country would be singled out for past injustices that now, with blacks voting in greater numbers than ever before, appeared to have been eliminated. When an amendment to replace the House bill with the administration's version came up for a vote on December 11, it won by a vote of 208 to 203—a margin of only 5 votes. A second vote was more decisive—the Mitchell Bill was approved by a vote of 234 to 179. The winning votes came from southern Democrats, a contingent that included every congressman from the covered states, and northern and midwestern Republicans. It was the worst defeat for the Voting Rights Act in its legislative history. When journalist Richard Harris asked a pro–voting rights

Republican, "What has happened to the party of Lincoln?" the congressman replied, "It has put on a Confederate uniform."[6]

Now the battle shifted to the Senate, where the Mitchell Bill first went to the Judiciary Committee's subcommittee, chaired by Sam Ervin Jr., the North Carolina Democrat who had opposed the 1965 Act. He began to hold hearings on the bill on February 18, 1970, and was in no hurry to complete them, hoping to slow down the legislative process until the 1965 Act expired in August. But Senate liberals, led by Michigan Democrat Philip Hart and Pennsylvania Republican minority leader Hugh Scott, both committed to voting rights, were able to require a March 1 deadline for the completion of the Judiciary Committee's work. Hart and Scott won another small victory when President Nixon announced the appointment of G. Harold Carswell, a conservative Florida federal judge, to be an associate justice of the US Supreme Court. Southern senators, strongly in support of Carswell, now called for an earlier decision on voting rights, and Majority Leader Mike Mansfield obliged them by placing the Voting Rights Act first on the Senate's calendar, before the Carswell nomination could be voted on. This change in schedule also made a time-consuming southern filibuster less likely.[7]

While the Senate debated the future of the Voting Rights Act, Senator Edward Kennedy, who had led the liberal fight to ban the poll tax in 1965, now saw an opportunity to broaden the American franchise by lowering the voting age from twenty-one years old to eighteen. This caused some consternation among both liberals and moderates in the Senate. They believed that such a change was possible only through a constitutional amendment. But an article in the *Harvard Law Review*, written by former solicitor general Archibald Cox, persuaded Kennedy. Cox argued that if Congress had the power to give voting rights to those who could not read English, then "Congress would seem to have the power to make a similar finding about state laws denying the franchise to eighteen, nineteen, and twenty year olds." And because the Supreme Court had ruled in *Katzenbach v. Morgan* that the Voting Rights Act was constitutional, it seemed to Kennedy that it was appropriate to go forward. Kennedy's plan did not please everyone; adding such a provision to the embattled Voting Rights Act, they feared, might sink the entire bill. But Kennedy, as he had in 1965, defied his reluctant colleagues. He won the help of Majority Leader Mansfield and Washington State's Democratic senator Warren Magnuson, who introduced the proposal on March 4. Surprisingly, the Senate approved the measure the next day by a vote of sixty-four to seventeen.

Most senators had probably found it difficult denying young people the right to vote while many were fighting and dying in Vietnam; indeed, Kennedy, campaigning for the measure, had noted that "one half of the deaths in Vietnam are of young Americans under twenty-one." Democrats were especially hopeful that the new voters would join their party, and others thought that giving young people a chance to fully participate in American politics would close the generation gap that had opened during the tumultuous 1960s. The success of the measure was another indication of the Voting Rights Act's power to expand the American franchise, in this case to eleven million young Americans—the greatest expansion since women received the right to vote in 1919.[8]

Meanwhile, Senators Hart and Scott had been working hard to craft a bill they hoped the Senate would approve rather than the one the House passed. Their bill extended the Act for another five years but, like the House bill, provided for a national ban on literacy tests, although it did not permit the Justice Department to monitor elections nationwide. A serious problem arose, however, when Senator Ervin proposed that the 1964 electoral returns standard be scrapped in favor of 1968, when the newly enfranchised black voters brought southern states up to 50 percent of its voting population. The liberals thought this a serious threat. If 1968 became the basis to define which states should be covered, those states with the worst record of discrimination—Alabama, Mississippi, Louisiana, Virginia, and North Carolina (Ervin's home state)—would be freed from coverage. "My state has been trying to get back into the Union for 100 years," Ervin proclaimed. "The Civil War is over. I wish I could say the same thing about Reconstruction."[9]

Kentucky Republican John Sherman Cooper found a way to avoid an impasse by adding an amendment that made the 1968 electoral returns the new standard but retained coverage of the original southern states. Therefore, it did not free the worst offenders on the basis of only one election and also now covered several northern counties that failed to meet the required 50 percent. Although the liberal forces were not happy with this addition, the Senate passed the amendment on March 10. Three days later, on March 13, the Senate voted sixty-four to twelve to substitute the Hart-Scott Bill for the administration's measure. Six southern senators joined the majority, and there was no filibuster. "I'm not going back to my state and explain a filibuster against black voters," South Carolina's Senator Ernest Hollings told an aide. Southern politicians no longer had any option: although some of them might pander predominately to white voters, they now had to at least consider the black vote.[10]

When the amended bill was returned to the House it encountered some resistance from those who thought that lowering the voting age to eighteen could be done only through a constitutional amendment. But a greater number supported it as well as the Hart-Scott version that, to southerners, was preferable to extending the original Act unchanged. They had won a partial victory: the South was no longer the only region covered by the Voting Rights Act. On June 17 the House approved the new Voting Rights Act by a vote of 272 to 132.[11]

The final version of the Act extended it for another five years. The literacy test was now prohibited nationally and the triggering mechanism was updated to reflect the 1968 election returns. This meant that now the Act covered three New York boroughs and jurisdictions in Arizona, California, and Wyoming. Section 5, the preclearance provision, was also continued unchanged. Residency requirements to vote in a presidential election were now reduced from generally one year (there were various exceptions) to thirty days, which permitted millions of Americans to vote who had heretofore been penalized simply for having moved recently to a new location. And eighteen-year-olds could now vote too.[12]

Nixon's choices were limited. He too thought that the voting age could be altered only through a constitutional amendment, but vetoing the bill was not a realistic prospect. It might please the South, but it would do so at the cost of alienating the many Republicans who had supported it in the House and Senate. Ever the pragmatist, Nixon signed the extended Act into law on June 22, 1970. Although the Act differed greatly from the one he preferred, he could at least tell southerners that they no longer had to wear a scarlet letter, and they were no doubt pleased when the president, unlike Johnson, did not hold an elaborate signing ceremony—in fact, there was no public ceremony at all—publicizing the Act's renewal.[13]

Although the Voting Rights Act survived its first renewal test, the experience left many civil rights activists concerned. The Act's five-year life span made it vulnerable to future congresses and presidents who might undermine it in some fundamental way. However, they were somewhat encouraged by the continuing support received from the Supreme Court and certain lower courts like the Fifth Circuit Court of Appeals in New Orleans. While the Nixon administration, from its first days in office, had been considering ways to weaken the Act, the US Supreme Court ruled in March 1969 in *Allan v. State Board of Elections* that a state could not change electoral practices in a way that might affect minority voting without first undergoing preclearance, which required submitting those potential changes to either the Justice Department or the US District Court in Washington, DC. Chief Justice Earl Warren, in one of his last decisions before retiring, sent a strong message to those who wished to subvert the new law: "The Voting Rights Act was aimed at the subtle, as well as the obvious, state regulations which have the effect of denying citizens their right to vote because of their race." This meant that Section 5 could not only combat efforts that affected black attempts to vote but also block those laws that many southern legislatures were now enacting that were designed, as one Mississippi legislator put it, "to preserve our way of doing business." Doing business the southern way meant electoral practices— gerrymandering and the like—that might allow blacks to run for office but would put them in white-dominated districts where they could not win. Such a broad definition of the Act's Section 5 preclearance provision boded well for the Act's survival.[14]

In 1973 the Court went after multimember districts in Alabama and Texas in *White v. Regester*, arguing that they denied black and Latino voters a chance to freely participate in American politics. That same year the Fifth Circuit assisted civil rights plaintiffs in *Zimmer v. McKeithen* by ruling that it was the *effect* of an electoral law rather than its *intent* that mattered. This decision gave activists even more weapons with which to fight disenfranchisement, as it was easier for a litigant to show that a law unfairly injured minority involvement or prevented the election of minority candidates than to prove racial bias in those who created it. From 1973 to 1980 lawyers from the ACLU, the NAACP, and other civil rights organizations filed forty lawsuits in eight covered states looking to prohibit at-large elections for city councils, county commissions, and school boards.[15]

Slowly but surely a pro–voting rights consensus emerged in Congress. When the Act came up for renewal again in 1975 the debate was less acrimonious than it had been in 1970. Nixon had been reelected by a stunning majority in 1972 (the attempted assassination of George Wallace left him paralyzed and removed him from the presidential race), only to resign two years later in the face of almost-certain impeachment following the Watergate scandal. His successor, President Gerald Ford, attempted to heal the nation's wounds after Watergate and the fall of Vietnam by dismantling Nixon's imperial presidency, with its enemies lists, break-ins, and illegal wiretaps. Although the former Republican House minority leader was not an enthusiastic supporter of civil rights and had tried to amend the Act in both 1965 and 1970, as president he was determined to reach out to the black community, who Nixon detested. In a private tape-recorded conversation with his aides, Nixon remarked that black Americans lived "like a bunch of dogs."[16]

Unlike Nixon, Ford worked hard to improve relations with African Americans. He met with the Congressional Black Caucus during his third day as president, an event that New York congressman Charles Rangel later called "absolutely, fantastically good." On January 15, 1975, King's forty-sixth birthday, he told the American people that "we must not let [Dr. King's] work die," and he praised the Voting Rights Act for opening "our political process to full participation." At the same time he called for another five-year extension of the Act "to safeguard [the] gains" that had been made.[17]

Prospects of renewal looked good. Liberals in Congress were so optimistic that they hoped to extend the Act for ten years so that it would still be in force when the 1980 census occurred, a time when state legislatures would be carving out new districts in their states. The Act would prevent southerners from damaging black chances of winning local and state offices. Some resistance came, of course, from southerners, but this time they chose a more low-key strategy. Instead of opposing the entire Act, they went after those sections they found the most objectionable. In particular, they tried to weaken the bailout provision so that covered states had a better chance to free themselves from the Act. But they were no match for their opponents, who, for the first time since Lyndon Johnson was president, had the support of the administration and the Justice Department. Assistant Attorney General J. Stanley Pottinger told the House Judiciary Committee that despite black gains, "More needs to be done."[18]

One congressperson in particular was encouraged by Ford and Pottinger's statements: Texas representative Barbara Jordan. The journalist William Broyles Jr. once called Jordan "the Jackie Robinson of Texas politics," and the description was no exaggeration. Although born in Houston's impoverished black ghetto in 1939 and the daughter of an evangelical Baptist minister who wanted her to become a music teacher, the fiercely determined Jordan eventually entered law school at Boston University and graduated in 1959, the only black student in her class. Returning to Houston, she practiced law briefly (her first office was her parents' dining room) before entering Texas politics and, in 1966, became the first black—male or female—elected to the Texas state Senate since Reconstruction. Her political and intellectual brilliance coupled with an eloquence and deep Churchillian-like voice brought her to the attention of President Lyndon Johnson, who invited her to attend White House meetings. She again broke the color line in 1972 when she was elected to the US Congress, joining King's lieutenant Andy Young as the first black representatives from the South since Reconstruction.

As a freshman congresswoman, she achieved another first. With Johnson's help, she secured a seat on the House Judiciary Committee. In 1974, from her seat on that committee, she won fame for arguing cogently and without rancor that Nixon deserved impeachment for violating the Constitution. Her great ability, achievements, charm, and large physical presence led to comparisons to Johnson, and some thought that she would eventually become the first black and female president.[19]

So after hearing Ford and Pottinger's remarks, Jordan proposed an extraordinary revision of the Act. As the congresswoman representing Texas's 18th congressional district, which encompassed Houston's poorest sections and the city's environs, she became concerned about the difficulties her black and Mexican American constituents faced when voting. For the Hispanic community it was especially challenging because the ballots were written in English. With the help of her two chief aides, Bob Alcock and Bud Myers, and supported by the US Civil Rights Commission, which found widespread voter intimidation in the Southwest, Jordan developed an argument that she presented to her colleagues on the Judiciary Committee. Because there were no bilingual ballots available to Mexican Americans in Texas, New Mexico, Florida, California, and parts of five other states, she asserted, the English-language ballot was the equivalent of a literacy test, which the Voting Rights Act banned. Eventually, Jordan, Alcock, and Myers, aided by Census Department officials, developed a formula based on low voter turnout and the presence of a sizable non-English-speaking population that would bring several new states and counties under the Act's protection.[20]

Jordan's proposal created a furor within the civil rights community and angered Texas state legislators opposed to having their state become subject to the Voting Rights Act's preclearance provision. Dr. Aaron Henry, a legendary figure in the NAACP's fight for black equality in Mississippi, spoke for many of his colleagues when he expressed the fear that expanding the Act would threaten its passage. "I do not want to give anybody an excuse to vote against what we have got now under the ruse of trying to extend it," he told the House Judiciary Committee. "If we have the votes for it, I am completely supportive of the idea. But I do not want to amend the Act to perfection and then lose the whole thing." Jordan, however, working with an energy reminiscent of Johnson when he was at the top of his game, was able to corral the votes, which included two-thirds of the Texas delegation even though their action would now bring their home state under federal scrutiny. When the full House began to consider the bill and its new provisions on June 2, its opponents proposed seventeen hostile amendments. Among them was one that would have excluded Texas entirely. But the bill's supporters were able to defeat them all, and on June 3 the House passed the Act by a vote of 341 to 70. Joining the majority were sixty-six southern Democrats.[21]

When the bill arrived in the Senate only two months were left before the Act expired on August 6. Senate supporters faced a number of obstacles and little time to overcome them. First, there was the Judiciary Committee, controlled by the archsegregationist Mississippi Democrat James Eastland, who refused even to hold hearings on the bill. And there was always the possibility of a southern filibuster. Majority Leader Mike Mansfield finally decided to intervene by using a parliamentary maneuver that forced the Senate to take up the House bill unchanged. The Act's supporters were also able to invoke cloture to defeat a possible filibuster. By mid-July a vote looked promising before too much longer.[22]

Then President Ford decided to reverse course. Fearing a conservative challenge from former California governor Ronald Reagan in 1976, Ford decided to court southerners in Congress and their constituents by urging that the Voting Rights Act now cover the entire country. Alabama Democrat James Allen thanked the president for what he called "the greatest stroke that he has made yet toward fairness and toward the promotion of unity in this country." Ford's behavior resulted only in confusing Republican supporters of the Act and angering its Democratic advocates. Quickly realizing his mistake, Ford told Minority Leader Hugh Scott that "he didn't want to mess up this bill" and reverted to his earlier position. But he was able to win one concession for southerners: the pro-Act coalition agreed to a seven- rather than a ten-year extension. The next day, July 24, the Senate voted 77 to 12 to pass the House bill. Among the majority were a record thirteen southerners. That modification sent the bill back to the House, which accepted it, thus leading to its passage on July 28 by a vote of 346 to 56.[23]

The Act's sweeping victory in both houses of Congress indicated that it was more acceptable in the South than it had been a decade before, primarily because southern politicians now had to seek black votes to win election. The original version of the Voting Rights Act had been intended primarily to safeguard the voting rights of African Americans, but ten years later politicians extended its promise to citizens outside the black community. The most striking reform in the 1975 version of the Act was that it now banned literacy tests of every kind, covered "language minorities," and required that states and local governments prepare bilingual ballots and registration materials. Southerners could rejoice that they were no longer the exclusive target of the Act; it now also covered Alaska's Native Americans, South Dakota's American Indians, and Hispanics living in Texas, Arizona, California, Florida, and New York. Signing the bill into law in the White House Rose Garden on August 6, 1975, the tenth anniversary of the original enactment, President Ford said, "There must be no question whatsoever about the right of each eligible American to participate in our political process."[24]

Invited to attend the ceremony was Barbara Jordan, who asked President Ford if she could have the index cards from which he had just read. Smiling,

August 6, 1975. Congresswoman Barbara Jordan (D-TX) watches President Gerald Ford sign the 1975 extension of the Voting Rights Act, which, thanks to her efforts, now protected Hispanic and Native American voters. COURTESY GERALD R. FORD LIBRARY

the president autographed the cards and Jordan took them home, a memento, she later said, of her "first big legislative victory." It would also be one of her last. She retired from the House in 1979, a victim of multiple sclerosis, which prevented her from battling to protect the Voting Rights Act when it again was threatened with extinction.[25]

THE VOTING RIGHTS ACT HAD SURVIVED TWO RENEWALS UNDER TWO different presidents, one notably hostile to it. But seven years later it would find itself facing a perfect storm of opposition that threatened it as never before. When the temporary provisions of the Act expired in 1982, triggering another renewal debate, America had again experienced a convulsive change in its politics. A rocky economy, the embarrassment of the yearlong Iran hostage crisis, and President Jimmy Carter's political ineptness brought to the White House in 1980 the most conservative Republican since Barry Goldwater. President Ronald Reagan was notably less supportive of the Act than Ford and perhaps even Nixon had been. He had opposed the original Act because he believed it unconstitutional, and fifteen years later he still called it "humiliating to the South." There were also signs that Reagan was anything but sympathetic to the underlying principles that had brought the Act into being. He had opposed making Martin Luther King's birthday a national holiday and had appointed only one black official to his cabinet—and when he later saw the man at a social function, didn't even recognize him.[26]

The other branches of government in 1982, like the executive, seemed newly unfriendly to the Act. The Senate had a Republican majority, and the chairman of the judiciary committee was Strom Thurmond, still a committed segregationist. The judicial branch had also started changing its tune on civil rights in the years leading up to the renewal debate. In 1980 the Supreme Court had ruled by a vote of five to four in *City of Mobile v. Bolden* that although the Fifteenth Amendment prohibited the denial of voting because of race, it did not guarantee the election of black candidates. Such a guarantee amounted to a quota system for blacks, the justices believed. Once again *intent* rather than *effect* guided courts when deciding a voting rights case. Not every member of the Court agreed with its decision, however. Justices Thurgood Marshall and William Brennan strongly dissented, with the former calling the Court "an accessory to the perpetuation of racial discrimination."[27]

The Court's ruling had shocked the civil rights community and its allies in the press. The *New York Times* called the decision "the biggest step backward in civil rights to come from the [Supreme] Court," and liberal lawyer Joseph L. Rauh Jr. predicted that the next time the Act came up for renewal, it would provoke "one of the toughest civil rights fights of all time."[28]

Congressman Don Edwards, who led the fight for the Act's renewal in the House, shared Rauh's fears. "We were in real trouble," he later recalled. The Republicans controlled the presidency and the Senate, and although the Democrats controlled the House, many southern representatives—the so-called "boll weevils"—were defecting to Reagan, and a number of able House Republicans were also opposed to the Act. But Edwards was equal to them all. A graduate of the Stanford University Law School, Edwards had served as a gunnery officer during World War II and was a former FBI agent. Originally a Republican, he had become a liberal Democrat in the late 1940s. Three years after his election to Congress the Californian strongly supported the 1965 Voting Rights Act, and now, as chair of the House Judiciary Subcommittee on Civil and Constitutional Rights, he became its floor manager. In that role he was responsible for seeing that the Act made its way safely through the House to a successful conclusion. With the support of committee chairman Peter Rodino, the two men were the chief defenders of the embattled Act.[29]

Among Edwards's and Rodino's tasks was revising Section 2, which prohibited imposing any "standard, practice or procedure" that denied the right to vote because of race or color. They needed to do this in order to deal with *City of Mobile v. Bolden,* whose impact had been devastating. Before the case the Justice Department had sued South Carolina because the state, despite a population that was 30 percent black, had never elected a black candidate to its state Senate in the twentieth century. Now, after *Mobile,* the suit was dropped. Even worse, the Justice Department's Voting Section stopped filing Section 2 lawsuits completely because of the new intent standard.[30]

Rodino and Edwards called for help in defending the Voting Rights Act, and the Leadership Conference on Civil Rights came to their aid. The conference, an umbrella group of 165 progressive organizations, had been expecting another conservative challenge, so even before Ronald Reagan was elected in November 1980 they began discussing how to again extend the Act. Realizing the importance of the campaign that lay ahead, the conference now appointed their first full-time executive director who would be charged with spearheading the effort to renew the Act. He was Ralph Neas, thirty-six, once chief counsel to former senator Edward Brooke and a civil rights specialist. He established a steering committee of twenty-five people to oversee the group's activities. They met every Friday in Edwards's office, where they plotted strategy in sessions that sometimes lasted fifteen hours. The Mexican American League supervised efforts in the Southwest; the National Urban League and the NAACP were responsible for the South; and the AFL-CIO's territory was the Northeast. Five of the best civil rights lawyers in the country—Frank Parker, Barbara Phillips, Armand Derfner, Laughlin McDonald, and Lani Guinier of the NAACP's Legal Defense Fund, who had fought for equal rights in Georgia, Mississippi, South Carolina, and Washington, DC—came to Washington to provide legal advice and develop congressional strategy. Every state had someone working: distributing literature, setting up phone banks to contact congressional offices (one congressman complained of receiving four thousand letters supporting preclearance and not a single one opposed), preparing eloquent witnesses for hearings, and alerting the media to major developments.[31]

On April 7, 1982, Congressman Rodino introduced his version of the bill, which had been drafted with the help of the Leadership Conference's lawyers. The most important change was to Section 2, and Rodino hoped this would resolve the problem that *City of Mobile* posed. The section now explicitly prohibited any "qualification," "prerequisite," or "practice" that resulted in the denial of any citizens' right to vote because of their race or skin color. By returning to the effects standard, the Voting Rights Act would not only guarantee the right to vote but also give activists greater latitude to defend that right.[32]

The bill went first to the House Judiciary Subcommittee on Civil and Constitutional Rights, chaired by Edwards. There it faced opposition from the ranking Republican, Henry Hyde of Illinois. The fifty-seven-year-old Hyde was politically conservative, but he had supported the Act's extension in 1975 when he was a freshman congressman from Chicago's western suburbs. Now, however, he had second thoughts, especially about Section 5, the Act's preclearance provision. He was angry that states had to experience what he thought was a demeaning experience. It was, he said, "like sitting in the back of the bus." Hyde introduced his own revised version of the Act, which eliminated Section 5's preclearance procedures and replaced it with a national plan that allowed the attorney general or anyone with a grievance to sue in federal court; if evidence indicated systematic voting rights abuses, then the government could require preclearance for four years. Hyde believed that his approach provided equal treatment to all citizens as it also freed from the burden of preclearance those places that no longer practiced discrimination.[33]

Hyde's argument struck many politicians as reasonable, and there were statistics to support it. In 1981 60 percent of Mississippi's black citizens were registered to vote, more than eleven times the number that had been registered in 1960. The number of elected black officials in the South had grown to more than 1,800 since the Act's original passage. Robert C. Henry had become the first black mayor of Springfield, Ohio, in 1966, and many more African Americans had followed his lead—in Cleveland, Ohio; Gary, Indiana; Chapel Hill, North Carolina; Fayetteville, Mississippi; Newark, New Jersey; Dayton, Ohio; and Tallahassee, Florida. In 1973 alone three black candidates were elected mayor across the country: Coleman Young in Detroit, Michigan; Maynard Jackson in Atlanta, Georgia; and Tom Bradley in Los Angeles, California. The dominant political figure in Birmingham was no longer Bull Connor but rather a black PhD, Richard Arrington, elected mayor in 1979. Harold Washington, the only black member of Edwards's subcommittee, would soon leave Congress to run successfully for mayor of Chicago.

The sudden appearance of so many black officials in American politics was a testament to the power of the Voting Rights Act, but it also represented the Achilles' heel of this historic piece of legislation. Commenting on these victories, Senator Edward Kennedy observed, "The most successful civil rights law in history is in danger of falling victim to its own success." If there no longer seemed to be a pressing need for the Act, then politicians might cease to safeguard its strongest provisions and might even fail to renew it at all.[34]

Yet the Act's success was incomplete. Mississippi had never elected a black to any statewide office, although blacks composed 37 percent of its population. Half of the state's majority black counties still had county boards without a black member. In Jackson County, Georgia, where an at-large electoral system existed, no black had ever served on the county commission or as sheriff, clerk of the court, probate judge, or tax commissioner. With the exception of a single justice of the peace, no other black had sought county office in ten years. The same problem existed in Opelika, Alabama, and in many other places in the Deep South. No black had ever been elected to the three-member city commission; the four who ran for seats between 1969 and 1978 were defeated primarily because they ran in at-large districts.[35]

To assess the South's progress for themselves, in June the subcommittee held hearings in Austin, Texas, and Montgomery, Alabama, where its members listened to Hispanic and black residents of the two states, both of which were covered by the Voting Rights Act. In Austin witnesses reported that in nearby Medina County white politicians had tried to limit Hispanic influence through gerrymandering; the tactic had been used four times in the past seven years. Jim Wells County, with a 67 percent Mexican American population, had similar problems and had not been able to draft a redistricting plan acceptable to the Justice Department. At present there was only one Mexican American on the four-person county commission. The most macabre testimony described how a Hispanic candidate running unopposed seemed assured of victory until another candidate's name appeared on the ballot, that of a white man, who was elected even though he could not serve because he was dead. This did not seem to bother the racists, who had entered him in the running. The federal government's presence, the witnesses insisted, was still necessary to protect the democratic process from such grotesque efforts to undermine it.[36]

The hearing at the Montgomery courthouse produced testimony that Edwards later called "shocking and sad." It emerged, for instance, that Choctaw County forced its citizens to register every year, ostensibly to remove from the rolls those who had died or moved, but the county's registration hours ran from 9:00 a.m. to 4:00 p.m., when most poorer citizens (who in Choctaw were disproportionately nonwhite) were working, often far from the courthouse. "How can we . . . look at that," Edwards asked Montgomery's mayor, "and say that it . . . does not reduce the number of black people who can vote?" Another witness complained that polling places were often located in stores owned by hostile whites, who frightened black voters, especially when the sheriff was present at the sites. In one town the registration book was located under the judge's desk. In another a black woman challenging the incumbent mayor was notified that her mortgage was due in three days. The bank officer responsible for her account was her opponent, the mayor.[37]

These stories had one immediate and positive effect. Henry Hyde was especially troubled to learn that voting rights violations were, in some places in the country, every bit as rampant as they were in 1965. So he abruptly changed course. He withdrew his bill and called for an indefinite extension of Section 5. "I was wrong, and now I want to be right," he told a reporter. But he still sought a more liberal bailout provision to free from preclearance those covered states that were not discriminating as well as to encourage those that were to do better.[38]

The subcommittee returned to Washington, where the hearings continued until 120 witnesses had testified and thousands of pages of testimony had been compiled. Some conservative critics later charged that the civil rights lobby had unduly influenced the hearings and that although the witnesses may have been inconvenienced by distant polling places and irritable sheriffs in their home districts, the subcommittee could not produce anyone who had actually been denied the opportunity to vote. But a few months later the Civil Rights Commission issued a report entitled "The Voting Rights Act: Unfulfilled Goals," which documented numerous cases in which black citizens had declined to register or vote because of intimidation. In Johnson County, Georgia, for example, the presence of the white sheriff at the registration office caused many blacks to stay away. In Wrightsville, Georgia, a woman drove two elderly blacks to the courthouse to register, and while waiting for them in her parked car, the sheriff appeared and was so menacing that she was "scared . . . to death." "I ain't going back there anymore," she testified. "I'm too old to be beaten up."[39]

Hyde's conversion led him to revise the bill to protect Section 5 but offered the bailout provision he had desired. To free themselves from preclearance, Hyde required that a state or political subdivision meet three requirements. They had to provide evidence that they had not used "a biased test or device" to obstruct voting during the past ten years, that the Justice Department had not blocked any previous changes requested because of "substantial" violations, and that they had made "constructive efforts" to encourage minorities to seek public office.[40]

The subcommittee submitted the bill, with Hyde's additions, to the full House Judiciary Committee on July 21, 1981. There the battle over the bailout continued. Edwards wanted stricter criteria to achieve bailout than Hyde would accept, and the Illinois congressman finally broke off negotiations. That left Edwards free to draft an even tougher provision than would have existed had Hyde not walked away. Chairman Rodino added a paragraph to reassure those who feared that the effects standard might lead to proportional representation, a form of the hated affirmative action that the administration was pledged to destroy in education, employment, and civil rights.

On July 31 the committee voted twenty-three to one to send the revised bill to the House, which would not consider it until after its August recess.

Even then the prognosis for the bill was not good, despite the House's generally Democratic makeup. Defections to the Republican Party continued, and
an unhappy Henry Hyde promised to fight for a better bailout when they
returned. Losing Hyde's support troubled the civil rights community. "The
Democrats have incurred the wrath of some Republicans," said Arnoldo S.
Torres of the League of United Latin American Citizens. "A lot of amendments will be offered later out of anger or frustration."[41]

THAT SUMMER RONALD REAGAN ENTERED THE DEBATE; THIS CAUSED
confusion rather than clarification. In June, Reagan had asked Attorney General William French Smith to draft a report that would determine if the Act
was still the best way to protect the right to vote. Subsequent statements from
the White House said only that a decision on reauthorization would not be
forthcoming until Reagan heard from the attorney general. His latest statements suggested that he was no longer opposed to the Act but preferred to
see it broadened to cover the entire nation. Nevertheless, nobody knew for
certain whether this was still his position—perhaps not even Reagan himself.
The president seemed to be withholding final judgment pending the input of
his top law enforcement official.[42]

Then Reagan reversed himself. During meetings with black Republicans
on July 9 and 10, he said that he had recently learned that broadening the
Voting Rights Act to cover the entire nation would weaken the Act, and he
"didn't want to do [that]." Reagan also promised that his decision, once it was
announced, would make them "very happy." But when word of the president's
remarks appeared in the New York Times and other major media, the White
House again changed its position. Reagan's visitors had misunderstood him,
said a senior official; the national alternative was still under consideration.[43]

Reagan's administrative style in part caused the confusion. Though a conservative through and through, the president was essentially pragmatic and
was willing to compromise his polices when it served his interests. His top
political aides, like Lynn Nofziger, tried to encourage the president's political
flexibility. Nofziger urged him to support renewal of the Voting Rights Act to
improve his standing among blacks, who were badly hurt by Reagan's budget
cuts and were convinced, unfairly but not without cause, that the president
was a racist. Even Hyde told Reagan that "If you move quickly, you may be
able to broaden your constituency by eliminating a fear which plagues the

black community most: that the time will soon return when they [are] literally unable to vote."[44]

But Reagan was also surrounded by ideologues who felt that to compromise on the Voting Rights Act would betray conservative principles. William Bradford Reynolds, assistant attorney general for civil rights, wanted to end preclearance because philosophically it was consistent with Reagan's economic deregulation policies; freeing the eight hundred counties in twenty-four covered southern states from federal bondage was the judicial counterpart of eliminating those federal laws that interfered with the free-market economy. The Reynolds-Reagan policies were profoundly disturbing to many Civil Rights Division lawyers, who were now on the verge of open rebellion. Robert Plotkin, chief of the division's litigation section, resigned on Friday, July 31, and three days later charged, in an article in the *New York Times,* that the Reagan administration had an intense "antipathy toward civil rights." He could no longer work for a Justice Department in which political appointees (who had no experience working civil rights cases) made policy without consulting the department's veteran lawyers. The result, Plotkin argued, was that "tough laws" were being "replace[d] with toothless tigers."[45]

On August 5 the president finally publicly rejected the national option. In an interview with the *Washington Star,* he announced that he supported a ten-year extension of the Voting Rights Act, including its preclearance provision. Applying the Act nationally, he had learned, "might make it so cumbersome as to not be effectively workable." He again expressed his belief that everyone should be able to vote. As for the other controversial issues— whether to define discrimination by intent or effects, or how a covered state or county could free itself from government supervision—the president was silent.[46]

It appeared that the president would not mount a major effort to destroy the bill after all; however, the civil rights community remained fearful that the Act was in serious danger. "I think we are at a crossroads," said John Lewis, who was running for a seat on the Atlanta city council. "We have made progress but if we lose this law, we stand to lose nearly everything we've gained." Even if they won in the House, the Senate—a Republican bastion where Strom Thurmond had called the Act "faulty and unfair"—might force serious changes in the law. Even Democrat Griffin Bell, Jimmy Carter's former attorney general, opposed extension so far as the current version of the bill was concerned. "I still think you need to protect the right to vote," he told a reporter that summer, "but the preclearance argument is poppycock. I'd let it all go down if they couldn't correct this. . . . The Voting Rights Act is no longer required in that area."[47]

House debate on the bill began on Friday, October 2, 1981. Louisiana Republican W. Henson Moore denounced his "sanctimonious brethren" who, he claimed, easily passed laws that didn't affect their constituents but hurt his. "We want to be treated like everybody else," he yelled. Although some representatives, like Moore, were against the bill, the majority of the House was staunchly for it and refused to accept changes that would weaken voting rights' safeguards. One by one, the House overwhelmingly defeated the more than ten amendments designed to relax bailout requirements or shift jurisdiction from Washington, DC, to local federal courts or eliminate bilingual ballots. The final vote, on Monday, October 5, was 389 to 24 in favor of extending the Voting Rights Act for another decade, the greatest margin of victory in its sixteen-year history. "It was just like old times," said a jubilant Don Edwards. "We creamed 'em."[48]

In fact, the results of the 1981 House debate were better than they had been in the old times. Gone were the Howard W. Smiths and L. Mendel Rivers, those representatives who had called the original Act "abominable." They had been defeated for reelection or chosen to retire. This time no one in the House questioned the legitimacy of the Act or the need to extend it. Among those representatives voting in favor of extension were seventy-one southerners, including some "boll weevils" who had supported Reagan's budget cuts but, recognizing the power of black voters, found it politically necessary to follow Don Edwards's lead. When a reporter asked Savannah's Ronald "Bo" Ginn, a staunch conservative who planned to run for governor of Georgia in 1982, why he voted for the bill, he replied, "It means little to whites. It means a whole lot to blacks."[49]

But this particular success of the bill had paradoxically put it in jeopardy yet again. The House bill had everything the Reagan administration disliked: preclearance for covered areas would continue for another decade, bailing out would not be easy, and assistance to bilingual voters would also last for at least another decade. And Section 2, which explicitly prohibited any voting discrimination based on race, now contained a *results* test, thereby allowing minorities to challenge more easily electoral practices that prevented them from winning elections. Attorney General Smith, though supporting a general extension of the Act, had opposed most of these specific provisions in his report, which the president received on October 2, three days before the House voted. The report was marked "Confidential" and buried. Few people ever saw it, not even the attorneys in the Civil Rights Division. But it would have a profound effect on Reagan's thinking in the weeks ahead.[50]

Once again the Reagan administration pondered its options. The president was growing concerned in light of two recent elections that had raised red flags for the Republicans. In a Mississippi district that was 45 percent black, the Democratic candidate explicitly supported extending the Voting Rights Act. The resulting turnout of black voters was so impressive that it was likely the factor that won him the election. And in Virginia Democrats swept statewide offices for the first time since 1966. At a cabinet meeting early in November, Reagan's advisers noted that Governor-elect Charles Robb received almost 97 percent of the black vote, whereas his Republican opponent couldn't break 4 percent. The lesson seemed clear. "[Blacks] are distrustful of us," said the Republican national chairman. "If we don't do better, we're going to lose time after time."

Several members of Reagan's cabinet recommended supporting the extension of the Voting Rights Act as a way to attract black voters. Initially, the president agreed. He had enough economic and diplomatic problems to contend with and didn't want to add a fight over voting rights to his troubles. Reagan's political aides, sensitive to the same concern, recommended that he announce his support for a ten-year extension of the Act regardless of its eventual content. William French Smith was livid, and an argument erupted between the attorney general and the president's staff.[51]

Reagan decided to follow Smith's advice and oppose preclearance and other specific provisions in the bill, but the president chose to couch his opposition in decidedly soft language. Disappointed aides leaked the story of the spat to the *New York Times*. The paper reported on November 7 that the president had earlier been willing to sign anything Congress approved, but after a quarrel between the more conservative Smith and White House aides, Reagan had decided to issue a definite statement. "To protect all our citizens, I believe the Voting Rights Act should be extended for 10 years," Reagan said, "either through a direct extension of the Act or through a modified version of the new bill recently passed by the House of Representatives." It was clear that the president preferred the latter. He called for retaining the intent test rather than the effects standard as well as easing the criteria required for states and localities to rid themselves of preclearance.[52]

Reagan's statement annoyed both the civil rights lobby and the southerners. Ralph Neas, executive director of the Leadership Conference on Civil Rights, announced that only the House bill was acceptable to his organization. White southerners weren't very happy either. They were hoping for a national expansion of the coverage provision that would free them from being the exclusive target of government lawyers: "Local officials have to go to Washington, get on their knees, kiss the ring and tug their forelock to all these third-rate bureaucrats," said Mississippi Republican Thad Cochran. But despite the fallout from both sides of the controversy, Reagan seemed blissfully unaware of what he had done. To a group of black reporters invited to the White House, he insisted that he was "doing just what the civil rights groups insisted we do." In truth, however, the president had effectively removed himself from the debate over the Voting Rights Act by so alienating voters and his fellow politicians. If the House bill was to be modified, it would be done by Smith and Reynolds working with the Senate as the president watched from the sidelines.[53]

Despite their triumph in the House, Ralph Neas and his colleagues in the Leadership Conference on Civil Rights were still anxious as the Senate took up the Voting Rights Bill early in 1982. The Republican-controlled Senate's Judiciary Committee waited three months to start their work, which worried Neas. His greatest concern was that the administration wanted the clock to run out so that the Act would simply expire on August 6. At the Leadership Conference's annual dinner in February its subject of discussion was "Civil Rights in Crisis," and the guests wondered if history was going to repeat itself. The Second Reconstruction, they feared, would pass away like the first, and the Reagan years would see the South again undermine all the great civil rights laws, as it had a century before.

The members of the Leadership Conference on Civil Rights viewed Strom Thurmond, president pro tempore of the Senate and chairman of the Judiciary Committee, as "the Brooding Omnipresence" of the coming ordeal. Some noted that recently he seemed to be reaching out to black voters, which—if true—might make the Senate debate much less arduous. Surprisingly, given his track record, Thurmond was one of the first of the southern senators to appoint a black man to his staff, and he also had arranged for South Carolina's black schools to be funded by federal dollars. But his record on the Voting Rights Act was clear and consistent. He had opposed it in 1965, and he opposed its extensions in 1970 and 1975. In 1982 Thurmond was eighty-one years old and quickly running out of opportunities to destroy the Act once and for all.

The conference members also worried about Utah's Oren Hatch, just a freshman but already chairman of the Judiciary's Subcommittee on the Constitution, which would first consider the bill. During his five years in the Senate he had introduced ten bills that would have weakened civil rights laws. Hatch was also a passionate opponent of results-test legislation, which, he thought, promoted affirmative action. The stress of facing off against such hostile Republicans as Thurmond and Hatch was taking a toll on Neas and his comrades. "Running scared" was the way one journalist described the civil rights lobby as the battle began again.[54]

The subcommittee began its hearings in late January 1982. Attorney General Smith testified that the Act should be extended for ten more years in its present form without the changes made by the House and desired by Senate Democrats. Senator Edward Kennedy, who had introduced the bill in the Senate with Republican Charles Mathias and sixty-one bipartisan cosponsors, quickly challenged Smith. Because of the administration's attitudes and policies, he said, there existed grave uncertainty that caused minorities to doubt the president's commitment to civil rights. The changes the president was calling for would turn the sixteen-year-old Act, supported by both Democratic and two Republican presidents, into "an empty shell."

"The President doesn't have a discriminatory bone in his body," Smith retorted, which caused the crowded hearing room to erupt in laughter. Senator Hatch gaveled the room into silence and threatened to clear it if such disrespectful behavior continued.

It quickly became clear that Smith's opposition to the Senate bill stemmed from a single source. The attorney general continued to disagree with the way in which Section 2 determined that discrimination had occurred: by results, undefined, rather than intent, which Smith believed should be the standard to guide courts that heard voting rights cases. By arguing that Section 2 smacked of quotas, the Reaganites hoped to exploit the conservative opposition to affirmative action. Smith called Section 2 "a hastily devised smokescreen" that would inevitably lead to proportional representation. He ignored the bill's explicit statement that the amended Section 2 did not endorse such an outcome. For Smith and many other Republicans opposed to the bill, political ideology continued to serve as the yardstick by which civil rights legislation was measured.[55]

AS THE SENATORS JOUSTED THAT JANUARY, CIVIL RIGHTS LEADERS DECIDED to take matters into their own hands. Led by the Reverend Joseph Lowery, now head of King's SCLC, they decided to re-create the historic march to Montgomery in the hopes that it would push Washington to pass the Voting Rights Act just as it had seventeen years earlier. But this time the march would begin in Carollton, Alabama. It was there, in 1979, that an all-white jury had convicted two local voting rights activists of mishandling absentee ballots on evidence that one judge later called "confusing and conflicting." Julia Wilder, sixty-nine, and Maggie Bozeman, fifty-one, received the stiffest sentences for voter fraud in modern Alabama history, five and four years, respectively, and were sent to the state penitentiary for women. (Judge Clatus Junkin had only recently sentenced a white police officer to six months in jail for a similar crime, then suspended the sentence.)[56]

Civil rights organizations believed that Wilder and Bozeman's prosecution was an effort by the segregationists who dominated Pickens County to suppress the black vote. Jack Greenberg, head of the NAACP's Legal Defense Fund, immediately sent Lani Guinier, one of his lawyers assigned to the voting rights fight, to help Wilder and Bozeman. The sentence was considered so outrageous that Alabama governor Fob James quickly transferred the women to Tuskegee, where they would serve out their sentences on a work-release program until they were eligible for parole. However, the women were still not shown anything like the sort of leniency given to the white police officer who had been convicted of a similar crime. During their time in the work-release program they were forbidden from returning to their homes and families in Pickens County. The SCLC's marchers left Carollton on February 6, 1982, hoping to bring the activists' case to the attention of the nation and also, as their signs put it, "Save The Voting Rights Act."[57]

Unlike King's journey, however, the second march had little impact. There were several reasons for its failure: fewer people participated (when Lowery decided to extend the march to Washington, DC, only eighty people followed him); the march lacked a dramatic beginning, such as Bloody Sunday, and a tragic end, like the Liuzzo murder; and, most importantly, it did not receive major, daily television coverage. The Lowery march did, however, succeed in alerting the nation to the plight of Bozeman and Wilder, but here too it failed to arouse the anger that the murder of Reverend James Reeb produced. As a result, it took Guinier and other lawyers eleven months to win parole for the women and an additional two years of hard work before a judge overturned the charges against them in April 1984.[58]

However ineffectual the march had been, it still reminded Americans that the Voting Rights Act had sailed through a Democratic House and was now barely moving through the Republican Senate. This possible public relations disaster worried the president's political aides and even some Republican senators, since it risked further alienating black voters. The most recent poll indicated that only 7 percent of black voters approved of Reagan's presidency, though this was a slight improvement over an earlier one that found that *none* of those sampled thought Reagan cared about them. Results like these, said pollster Robert Teeter, would threaten Republicans running in the 1982 midterm elections.

The president's budget cuts, his approval of tax exemptions for segregated schools, and, most of all, the administration's attack on the Voting Rights Act had seriously injured the Republican Party. The root cause was not racism, anonymous senators told reporters, but the White House's "insensitivity and incompetence." A Reagan aide was unusually candid: "The most unconscionable mistake we've made as a party was not to be out front on the Voting Rights Act."[59]

For Republicans, extending the Voting Rights Act had become a struggle between the party's pragmatists and its ideologues, who, in the case of Oren Hatch, chaired the Senate's Judiciary Subcommittee on the Constitution. Hatch, whose home state of Utah had few black voters, let the members of his committee spend six weeks discussing Section 2 while giving less attention to the other provisions. It was no accident. Hatch thought the best way to defeat the bill was to argue that the House's revision of Section 2, which restored the effects test, could be used to rally those who opposed what Bradford Reynolds called "preferential treatment for minorities," a favorite theme of George Wallace and now a staple of Republican rhetoric. In this Hatch was following the president's lead. Perhaps influenced by Justice Department officials William French Smith and Bradford Reynolds (who called the effects test "a quota system for politics"), the president, at a news conference the previous December, condemned the House's action, saying that it would create a situation "where all of society had to have an actual quota system."[60]

On the hearings' last day, Hatch predicted an apocalypse if the results standard of the bill's voting discrimination provision was not eliminated. America, he said, would become "a country in which considerations of race and ethnicity intrude into each and every public policy decision. Rather than continuing to move toward a constitutional color-blind society, we will be moving toward a totally color-conscious society." Few observers missed the irony that it was now those who had either opposed or been indifferent to civil rights laws who were embracing Martin Luther King's dream of a country where people would be judged not by the color of their skin but by the content of their character.[61]

Hatch's subcommittee eventually settled on a compromise, albeit one that many activists argued went too far in diluting the House version of the bill. On March 24 the subcommittee voted to accept amendments that extended Section 5 for ten years but, as Attorney General Smith recommended, eliminated the House's revised Section 2. The intentional discrimination test remained unchanged. The subcommittee's bill was then sent to the full Judiciary Committee, and when it became public, civil rights advocates declared that it "severely jeopardized the voting rights of millions."[62]

When the Judiciary Committee finally took up the bill on April 27, it found itself almost deadlocked. Nine senators (seven Democrats and two Republicans) supported the House version whereas seven—all Republican—were opposed. Undecided were Kansas Republican Bob Dole and Alabama's Howell Heflin, a conservative Democrat but one proud of his earlier support of civil rights. Before the committee members could start resolving their differences, North Carolina's Jesse Helms, last of the diehard segregationists, brought their session to a sudden halt by invoking a rarely used Senate rule prohibiting the Judiciary Committee from meeting while the Senate was in session. They adjourned. Democrats grumbled and called for evening meetings.[63]

It was Kansas's Bob Dole who broke the logjam. "The works around here get gummed up pretty easily," he later said. Wishing to rescue the Republican Party by broadening it to include blacks and Hispanics (whose support he would need should he ever seek the presidency), Dole met privately with Senators Kennedy and Mathias as well as civil rights lawyers associated with Neas's group (who had also been working the Senate) in order to fashion a compromise. It was quickly achieved, and on May 3 the president approved it and urged Congress to pass the bill swiftly.

The "Dole Compromise" extended Section 5, the bill's preclearance provision, for twenty-five years—shorter than the permanent status it had enjoyed in the House bill but longer than the ten years that Hatch's subcommittee had recommended. Bailout was still difficult (the covered states had to have a record free of discriminatory practices for at least ten years and also encourage minorities to participate in politics), but the provision could be reconsidered in fifteen years or earlier if Congress desired. And assistance to non-English-speaking voters would continue until 1992. Further, the most divisive issue in Section 2, the continued admissibility of results tests in efforts to determine instances of voter discrimination, remained; however, courts could also examine all circumstances in a voting case to determine if discrimination had occurred. This had been standard before the Supreme Court's *City of Mobile* decision. To alleviate the concerns of the Reagan administration and Senator Hatch, the amended bill specifically stated that it did not establish "a right for minority group members to be elected to public office in numbers equal to their proportion of the population."

The Judiciary Committee approved the compromise by a fourteen-to-four vote. Voting no were Senators Hatch, North Carolina's John East, Alabama's Jeremiah Denton, and South Carolina's Strom Thurmond. In the past Thurmond would have tried to block the new measure, but now, even in opposition, he voted to refer the amended bill to the Senate.[64]

The usual suspects, now greatly reduced, attacked the bill when the Senate began its debate on June 9. Helms threatened a filibuster that, he promised, would last "until the cows came home." This time, however, even southerners challenged Helms's assertion that because of Section 5, the good people of North Carolina had become "second class citizens." Louisiana's Russell Long, who voted against the 1965 Act, admitted that the South had been guilty of past violations, and "we have to pay for that."

The diehards—Helms, North Carolina's John East, and Virginia's Harry F. Byrd—didn't stand a chance. They offered eighteen amendments, all of which were soundly defeated. Helms wanted to go on filibustering for another month, but his colleagues had had enough of what one called Helms's "verbal sit-in." So on June 15, by a vote of eighty-six to eight, the Senate invoked cloture, paving the way for a vote on the bill.[65]

The Senate finally voted on June 18, and although its outcome was predictable—eighty-five for and eight against—there were a few historic surprises. Among the eighty-five senators who voted aye were two famously obstructionist southerners who had never before cast an affirmative vote for civil rights. One was Mississippi's John Stennis, who had fought against every modern civil rights bill as well as the original Voting Rights Act and its subsequent extensions. Now, in his thirty-fourth year in the Senate and planning to run again in 1984 with black support, he joined the majority in approving the Voting Rights Act.[66]

The other was Strom Thurmond, the longest-serving senator whose opposition to integration went back decades. In 1948 Truman's civil rights programs had led Thurmond to bolt the Democratic National Convention and run for president as a Dixiecrat. He carried four states and won over a million votes. Elected to the Senate in 1954, he wrote the first draft of the Southern Manifesto and launched a historic filibuster against the 1957 Civil Rights Act. He had called the Freedom Riders "Red pawns," dubbed the use of federal troops to integrate the University of Mississippi in 1962 "abominable," and denounced the 1964 Civil Rights Act as "vicious . . . and unconstitutional." That same year Thurmond had become a Republican and rejoiced as Barry Goldwater won Mississippi, Alabama, Louisiana, and South Carolina (which backed Thurmond in 1948), thus beginning the political transformation of the South from staunchly Democratic to reliably Republican.[67]

Now, in June 1982, 30 percent of Thurmond's constituency was black, leaving the oldest defender of southern traditions little choice but to vote for the Act. In doing so he wanted to make it clear that although he supported the current bill, he intended in the future to work to change those provisions he opposed, like the preclearance coverage to which his own home state was, he believed, unfairly subjected. Most importantly, he did not want to fall victim to "the common perception that a vote against the bill indicates opposition to the right to vote and, indeed, opposition to the group of citizens who are protected under the Voting Rights Act." The latter was an oblique way of saying that now black votes counted too.[68]

Opposed to the bill were seven Senate Republicans and one Independent, Virginia's Harry Byrd. Four of these naysayers were southerners from the states of the Old Confederacy: Byrd, Jesse Helms, and John East of North Carolina as well as Alabama's Jeremiah Denton. The others were among the Senate's most conservative and quirky members: New Hampshire's Gordon Humphrey, who served two terms and eventually became a radio broadcaster; S. I. Hayakawa of California, who was too far to the right even for

Ronald Reagan, who asked Hayakawa not to seek reelection in 1982; and both of Idaho's senators, James McClure and Steven Symmes, both of whom boasted of being prototypical westerners, "the kind of people," McClure once said, "who say, 'I may do it but you're not going to make me do it.'"[69]

On June 29, 1982, a smiling President Reagan signed the Voting Rights Act extension bill into law. Among the 350 guests in the White House's East Room were NAACP executive director Benjamin Hooks and other black leaders like SCLC's Joseph Lowery, whose pilgrimage to witness the renewal of the Voting Rights Act had brought him to Washington after the Senate voted but in time for this occasion. They were invited, said one presidential aide, as "part of a White House effort to portray Mr. Reagan as sensitive to minorities." That effort failed. Those who remembered President Johnson's elaborate ceremony in 1965 were troubled by the swiftness with which Reagan handled that day's events. Reagan's remarks were brief and uninspiring, and whereas Johnson used fifty pens, Reagan used only one to sign the document, after which he remarked, "It's done." The entire ceremony took four minutes. "I . . . congratulate the President . . . for belatedly at least coming along with the civil rights act," said Hooks, as if the president was merely a passenger on a train driven by others. The characterization was not far off the mark.[70]

The civil rights community received more good news a few days later. On July 1 the Supreme Court, following Congress's strong rejection of *Mobile* in the reauthorization act, upheld by a six-to-three vote lower-court rulings in *Rogers v. Lodge,* a case in which blacks had never been able to elect a county commissioner in Burke County, Georgia, because the at-large electoral system was disadvantageous to black voters. The lower court ordered the end of at-large voting and created five new districts. The Supreme Court's ruling stated that no smoking gun was needed as evidence to prove intentional discrimination but rather that circumstantial evidence was sufficient. The Court seemed to be no longer wedded to the standard found in *City of Mobile.* That and the Voting Rights Act's amended Section 2, which allowed a results test, suggested that it would be easier in the future to eliminate those practices that diluted the black vote.[71]

"Victory has a hundred fathers," John F. Kennedy once observed, "while defeat is an orphan." So it was with the successful extension of the Voting Rights Act in 1982. There were a multitude of fathers *and* mothers, chief among them the men and women of the Leadership Conference on Civil

Rights, whose energetic lobbying had led to overwhelming success in the House. No civil rights group was better at mobilizing its forces, networking with congressmen, arranging hearings, and finding the best witnesses to testify. Opponents of the Act lacked such strong organizational support, and the emerging anti-Act intellectuals like Abigail and Stephan Thernstrom, who argued that the original Act had been perverted to protect the outcome of minority voting, had little impact on the debate.[72]

Finally, the perfect storm of resistance that had so worried the civil rights community was no match for the power of the Act itself. As one of its critics noted, "Voting rights is the most difficult area of civil rights law in which to reverse policies; the right to vote retains an apple pie and motherhood image." The Act's almost iconic status had now brought even John Stennis and Strom Thurmond to support it, however grudgingly. More importantly, the Act had succeeded in doing what it was created to do: create millions of new black voters. No politician, North or South, could ignore that. The new reality had been clear to Thurmond as early as 1970, when Republican congressman Albert Watson ran for governor against Democratic lieutenant governor John West. Both opposed integration of the state's schools, but Watson campaigned as if he was South Carolina's George Wallace. Thurmond worked hard for Watson, and even President Nixon and Vice President Spiro Agnew campaigned for him, but he lost. Three blacks were elected to South Carolina's state House, no doubt helped by a 17 percent increase in black registration since 1964. Strom Thurmond tried to console the defeated Watson but at the same time gave him some advice, which all southerner politicians ignored at their peril: "Well, Albert," Thurmond said, "this proves we can't win elections any more by cussin' Nigras."[73]

THE WIDENING OF THE AMERICAN POLITICAL LANDSCAPE WAS OLD NEWS TO most politicians when the Voting Rights Act once again came up for renewal two decades later, but the power of black voters would continue to shape the Act's future. In 2006 George W. Bush was halfway through the second term of his presidency, and his popularity among African Americans—never strong—had declined to all-time lows. In the 2000 presidential campaign he had campaigned as a "compassionate conservative," and when addressing the NAACP's annual convention, he stated that he regretted that "the party of Lincoln has not always carried the mantle of Lincoln." That would change if he became president, Bush insisted: "Strong civil rights enforcement will be a cornerstone of my administration." But Bush had won only 9 percent of the black vote in the 2000 election, and his strongest supporters were conservative white men, so he had no political reason to keep such promises about civil rights. And as it turned out, other issues would take priority after Bush became president, namely, the War on Terror following the September 11 attacks, the invasion and occupation of Iraq, and the attempt to legitimize a presidency created by the Supreme Court.[74]

The gulf between Bush and the black community had widened in his second term. On January 27, 2005, the president had a tense meeting with the Congressional Black Caucus. "In that room, you had 43 individuals whose whole life [has been spent] . . . trying to uplift . . . Black America," Illinois representative Bobby Rush later said. "We came [to do] business." Among the issues discussed was the 1965 Voting Rights Act that was due to be reauthorized in 2007. "I don't know anything about . . . the . . . Act," Bush remarked. "When the legislation comes before me, I'll take a look at it but I don't know about it to comment any more than that." The president's "unfamiliarity" with the most important civil rights law in American history so shocked Congressman Jesse Jackson Jr. that he later contacted other members of the group to see if he had heard the president correctly. Congresswomen Maxine Waters and Sheila Jackson Lee told him that his hearing was fine, as did Congressman Rush, who later told the *Chicago Defender* that he too was "surprised and astounded" by Bush's ignorance.[75]

But during his second term Bush found it necessary to court black voters. The president's slow response to the devastation caused by Hurricane Katrina, which hurt blacks disproportionately and revealed again the presence of widespread poverty in the South, damaged Bush's standing. In an attempt to recoup his political fortunes as congressional elections approached in 2006, Bush turned to the black community. On a trip to Memphis, Bush visited the Lorraine Motel and stood on the balcony where Martin Luther King was assassinated in 1968. He also agreed to address the NAACP's annual convention, which he had ignored for six years. There Bush was received coolly but won a standing ovation when he expressed his support for the Voting Rights Act, urging Congress to enact it then, one year before it was due to expire. This was not simply rhetoric. Behind the scenes Bush's staff encouraged Republicans, who now controlled both houses of Congress, to extend the Act. And this time the Republican congressional leadership in both the House and Senate were receptive to such appeals because if you weren't a southerner, there was no political payoff for attacking the now-iconic Voting Rights Act.[76]

Although the Act was all but guaranteed passage in Congress, southern Republicans were still opposed. Once again they attacked Section 5 as well as Section 203, which provided for multilingual assistance to voters. Georgia's Republican congressman Lynn Westmorland asserted that "Congress is declaring from on high that states with voting problems forty years ago can simply never be forgiven—that Georgians must eternally wear the scarlet letter because of the actions of their grandparents and great-grandparents. We have repented and reformed." House conservatives briefly delayed the bill—named for Fannie Lou Hamer, the Mississippi activist, Rosa Parks, and Coretta Scott King, all now deceased—but the body eventually passed it, 390 to 33.

On July 21 the Senate, like the House, approved the measure unanimously. Preclearance and minority-language provisions were continued for another twenty-five years. The Act was also amended to overturn earlier Supreme Court decisions like *Reno v. Bossier Parish School Board* (2000) and *Georgia V. Ashcroft* (2003), both of which had significantly weakened the power of the Voting Rights Act to prevent states from altering electoral practices and engaging in redistricting that affected minority voting and electoral participation.[77]

Observing the debate and voting from the gallery were Congressman John Lewis and Jesse Jackson Sr., father of Congressman Jackson and an activist who had run unsuccessfully for the Democratic Party's nomination for president in both 1984 and 1988. They later joined Senator Edward Kennedy to reminisce about the past. "I recall watching President . . . Johnson sign the 1965 act just off the Senate chamber," Kennedy said. "We knew that day we had changed the country forever, and indeed we had." Now, over forty years later, Congress and the president were firmly behind the Voting Rights Act once again.[78]

The signing ceremony on July 27, 2006, was a celebration, rivaling that of Lyndon Johnson's in 1965. Over six hundred guests were invited to gather on the White House's South Lawn, a venue usually reserved for Easter egg hunts and visiting heads of state. Those attending included relatives of Fannie Lou Hamer, Rosa Parks, and Martin Luther King. Unlike President Reagan, who had devoted four minutes to his event, Bush took his time, greeting and thanking almost everyone who was there. "Today, we renew a bill that helped bring a community on the margins into the life of American democracy," said the president. "My administration will vigorously enforce the provisions of this law, and we will defend it in court." The crowd applauded enthusiastically. He continued, "I am proud to sign the Voting Rights Reauthorization and Amendments Act of 2006." Then he moved to the table and signed the document, becoming the fourth Republican president to extend the Voting Act, this time for twenty-five years.[79]

The Voting Rights Act had flown through Congress, but some of the Act's supporters weren't pleased with its swift passage. Distinguished academic supporters like historian and voting rights specialist J. Morgan Kousser and legal scholars Nathan Persily and Richard Pildes later argued that both Democrats and Republicans failed to consider whether the Act needed to be strengthened to meet the needs of the twenty-first century. Kousser, Persily, and Pildes argued that Republicans feared criticizing the Act would leave them vulnerable to charges of racism, whereas Democrats were cautious because African Americans were such an important part of their political constituency. It seemed that the Voter Rights Act, like Social Security, had become the "third rail" of American politics; any politician who suggested changing it would be discredited. Furthermore, as Kousser later noted, congressional advocates missed an opportunity to "update" the coverage and bailout provisions and, through a vigorous debate in both houses, provide additional evidence to prove both the continuing "necessity and constitutionality of the law." In the future the enemies of the Voting Rights Act would look to a conservative-dominated Supreme Court to take up the fight they were too cowardly to risk in Congress.[80]

That challenge came swiftly. On August 4, 2006, only eight days after Bush signed the twenty-five-year extension of the Voting Rights Act, Gregory Coleman, an ultraconservative Texas attorney and a former state solicitor general, filed a lawsuit in Washington's US District Court on behalf of a Texas municipal utility district (the Northwest Austin Municipal Utility District Number One, or NAMUDNO). The suit argued that Section 5 was unconstitutional because it required too much from the area under its coverage, and Coleman therefore requested that NAMUDNO be freed from coverage. The *Legal Times*'s Emma Schwartz called NAMUDNO's suit "the most significant assault on the Voting Rights Act in a quarter of a century."

Coleman was not surprised when the district court panel ruled against NAMUDNO on May 28, 2008. Two of the three judges were Clinton appointees and therefore likely to accept the legitimacy of the Act. The majority rejected the plaintiff's claims largely because it did not believe that the municipal district, which did not register voters, met the Act's definition of what constituted a "political subdivision." Going even further, the judges stated their belief that Section 5 was a proper response to a legitimate problem—the presence of racial discrimination. They based their finding on *South Carolina v. Katzenbach* (1966), the Supreme Court's first decision on the constitutionality of the Voting Rights Act.

Coleman then decided to appeal the court's ruling to the US Supreme Court. The Court agreed to hear the case, but when the justices finally rendered their decision in 2009, an unprecedented occurrence in American history almost certainly guided their ruling. The election of Barack Obama, the first African American president of the United States, had transformed the American political landscape. Ironically, that glorious moment in American history became perhaps the gravest threat yet to the survival of the Voting Rights Act.[81]

NINE

THE STRUGGLE
OF A LIFETIME

JOHN LEWIS WAS NOT A MAN WHO COULD BE EASILY SHOCKED, BUT DURING the inaugural weekend of 2009 he found everything "bewildering." "It's almost too much," he told the *New Yorker*'s David Remnick, "too emotional," too unreal. The idea that an African American would be elected president in his lifetime struck Lewis as simply "crazy." As January 20 approached, so many memories assaulted him: the sit-ins, the Freedom Rides, the arrests, the beatings (none of them worse than those he received on Bloody Sunday), and the final triumphant march to Montgomery. But it was the Edmund Pettus Bridge that stood out in Lewis's mind during the preinaugural festivities. Barack Obama, who was about to become president of the United States, "is what comes at the end of that bridge in Selma," he told Remnick.[1]

Obama's unprecedented election gave rise to the hope that America had become a postracial society—a hope that led many, including John Roberts, the chief justice of the US Supreme Court, to wonder if perhaps the Voting Rights Act had outlived its usefulness. On June 22, 2009, the Supreme Court issued its ruling in *Northwest Austin Municipal Utility District Number One v. Holder.* By a vote of eight to one, the justices favored the plaintiff on technical grounds, broadening the definition of what constituted a "political subdivision" under the law, thus allowing the municipal district to take advantage of the law's bailout provision. But the ruling left Section 5 intact, avoiding a major decision that would have severely weakened the Act. Chief Justice Roberts expressed the post-Obama conventional wisdom: "We are now a very different nation," he said. "Things have changed in the South. Voter turnout and registration rates approach parity. Blatantly discriminatory evasions of federal decrees are rare. And minority candidates hold office at unprecedented levels. Whether conditions continue to justify such legislation," he concluded, "is a difficult constitutional question we do not answer today." Justice Clarence Thomas, the sole dissenter, believed that Section 5 was unconstitutional and recommended its elimination.[2]

Both liberals and conservatives claimed victory. "This case was brought to tear the heart out of the Voting Rights Act," argued the NAACP's Debo P. Adegbile, "and today that effort failed." But Hans A. von Spakovsky, a former member of the Civil Rights Division whose advocacy of voter ID laws made him a controversial figure, expressed his support for Chief Justice Roberts's view that Section 5 "raises serious constitutional concerns" in an article written for the *National Review*. He also looked forward to more lawsuits, one of which, he anticipated, would undoubtedly lead to the elimination of the hated provision.[3]

The question for many Americans was whether the chief justice was correct in asserting that America was "now a very different nation" in the Age of Obama. Even before Obama's election there was evidence to support the view that race was no longer a relevant factor in American political life. In 1965 there were only five black members in Congress; in 2011 there were forty-four. In 1965 there were approximately fourteen hundred black officeholders in America; in December 2009 there were ten thousand. Among them were many elected from white-majority districts or states, including those in the South. In all, about two hundred black Americans have been elected to offices once held by whites in New Hampshire, Iowa, Kentucky, Minnesota, Missouri, North Carolina, and Tennessee—all white-majority states.[4]

A 2009 survey of seven southern states originally covered by Section 5 as well as two, Texas and Florida, added in 1975 also reveals significant improvement in the political status of African Americans. Whether one looks at Mississippi, where in 2009 more African Americans held public office than in any other state, or at Georgia, which that year had four African Americans in Congress and fifty-five in its statehouse, or at Texas and Florida, where large numbers of blacks and Latinos serve in their legislatures, it seems beyond dispute that America is a changed nation.[5]

But the nation is not as different as it may seem. History reveals that improved conditions come less from a revolution in white attitudes toward African Americans than from the Act's effectiveness in altering electoral conditions that had prevented blacks from winning elections. In other words, if the Act had never existed, there is no guarantee that Mississippi would have so many black public officials or, for that matter, any at all. Furthermore, although the Voting Rights Act has given black citizens the opportunity to enter the American political arena, their prospects are still limited. In towns and cities they can become county commissioners, sheriffs, tax assessors, mayors, and congresspersons. But statewide offices, especially in the South, still seem reserved for whites only. Occasionally, there has been a breakthrough—Douglas Wilder was narrowly elected governor of Virginia in 1969 but, because of term limits, served just one term. No other southern state has sent a black man or woman to its governor's mansion since Reconstruction. The North and West have not done much better. Deval Patrick, a former assistant attorney general for civil rights under President Bill Clinton, was comfortably elected governor of Massachusetts in 2006 and reelected in 2010. David Patterson succeeded to the governorship of New York State after Elliot Spitzer resigned in 2008, but he withdrew from the next gubernatorial race because of scandals and personal problems. To be sure, other people of color—Hispanic Americans (Governor Bill Richardson of New Mexico), Indian Americans (Governors Bobby Jindal of Louisiana and Nikki Haley of South Carolina), and Asian Americans (Governor Gary Locke of Washington State) have won statewide office, but their successes have not opened any doors for black politicians.[6]

Some federal offices also still seem off-limits to black candidates. African Americans have been able to win seats in the US House of Representatives, but only three have been elected to the US Senate since Reconstruction. Massachusetts's Edward Brooke served two terms after his election in 1966 but was defeated in 1980. Illinois's Carole Moseley-Braun won in 1992 but lost in 1998. A brief presidential campaign in 2004 was a dismal failure. That same year Illinois sent state senator Barack Obama to the US Senate, and when he resigned in 2008 after assuming the presidency, his elected successor, a Republican, returned the upper chamber to its all-white status.[7]

And ironically it was Obama's election itself that indicated that race, for many, remained a divisive issue. If southern racial attitudes had been transformed since 1965, Obama should have done well in the covered states in

2008. He did not. In Alabama he received 10 percent of the white vote, his worst showing anywhere in the country. Next was Mississippi, where only 11 percent of white voters chose Obama. Louisiana was third worst: 14 percent of the white population voted for him. In these three states Senator John Kerry, the 2004 Democratic presidential nominee, fared better than Obama by 9 percent in Alabama, 3 percent in Mississippi, and, in Louisiana, 10 percent. Obama won 23 percent of the white vote in Georgia and 26 percent in both South Carolina and Texas. North Carolina, now only partially covered, gave Obama 35 percent, and Virginia gave Obama 39 percent.[8]

These figures indicate that the racial polarization that has long characterized political life in the covered southern states still existed in 2008, especially when compared with Obama's showing among minorities. In Alabama, Mississippi, Georgia, and Texas, Obama won an incredible 98 percent of the black vote, whereas in Virginia and North Carolina, he scored 92 and 95 percent, respectively. Obama also did well with Latinos in the covered states (62 percent), noncovered states with some covered districts (68 percent), and states not directly affected by the Voting Rights Act (71 percent). The gulf separating southern white and minority voters was greater than ever before. Virginia was the only completely covered state that Obama won.[9]

A similar gulf existed between white voters in the covered and noncovered states. In the latter Obama received 47 percent of the white vote, a bit better than Kerry had in 2004, but more than 20 percent greater than in the covered states of the South. Although Obama's showing among white voters outside the South is encouraging, he won a majority of their vote only in eighteen states and the District of Columbia. Without an increase in minority turnout and decline in white participation (both of which characterized the 2008 election), Obama probably would have lost even though the conditions—an unpopular incumbent, a sinking economy, high unemployment, and two wars—favored the Democratic nominee.

Furthermore, scholars who examined the 2008 electoral results and other polling found that racial prejudice remained a significant factor in American life. Seth Stephens-Davidowitz, a Harvard doctoral candidate in economics, studied how often people searched the Internet for "racially charged material," principally jokes that denigrated African Americans. He found that most searches originated in places where Obama did poorly in 2008. He concluded that racial prejudice cost Obama "3 to 5 percentage points of the popular vote," essentially giving his white opponent "the equivalent of a home state advantage nationally." Michel Tessler, a political scientist, and David Walsh, a psychologist, agreed: they found "that public opinion and voting behavior [in 2008] . . . were considerably more polarized by racial attitudes than at any other time on record." The conclusion is inescapable: at the time of the 2008 election America was still a racially divided country, and the results of that election and the next one to come in 2010 indicated that the Voting Rights Act remained indispensable. Only because of the Act's protections could voters of all racial backgrounds be assured of casting their vote and, as a result, be able to level the political playing field.[10]

Just when it seemed that the democratic process had reached its apotheosis with the election of America's first black president, a political earthquake occurred in 2010 that threatened all that had been accomplished since 1965. Two years after Obama's election the midterm elections saw a conservative backlash that swept Republicans back into office in droves. As the media focused on the Republican takeover of the House of Representatives and increases in the Senate, more important developments were occurring closer to home. Republicans now controlled both legislative bodies in twenty-six states, and twenty-three won the trifecta: controlling the governorships as well as both statehouses. What happened next was so swift that it caught most observers off guard—and began surreptitiously to reverse the last half-century of voting rights reforms.

All across the country following the 2010 midterms Republican legislatures passed and governors enacted a series of laws designed to make voting more difficult for Obama's constituency—minorities, especially the growing Hispanic community; the poor; students; and the elderly or handicapped. These included the creation of voter photo ID laws, measures affecting registration and early voting, and, in Iowa and Florida, laws to prevent ex-felons from exercising their franchise. (Florida's governor, in secret, reversed the policies of his Republican predecessors Jeb Bush and Charlie Crist, policies that would have permitted one hundred thousand former felons, predominantly black and Hispanic, to vote in 2012.) Democrats were stunned. "There has never been in my lifetime, since we got rid of the poll tax and all the Jim Crow burdens in voting the determined effort to limit the franchise that we see today," said President Bill Clinton in July 2011. Once again the voting rights of American minorities were in peril.[11]

The newly elected Republican officials were able to act so quickly because they had the help of an ultraconservative organization known as the American Legislative Exchange Council (ALEC). Its founder was the late Paul Weyrich, a legendary conservative writer and proselytizer who founded both ALEC and the Heritage Foundation, a conservative think tank dedicated to limited government, an economy free of federal regulations, and the sanctity of traditional marriage. Backed by conservative corporations such as Coca-Cola, Philip Morris, AT&T, Exxon Mobil, and Walmart, among many others, and funded by right-wing billionaires Richard Mellon Scaife, the Coors family, and David and Charles Koch, ALEC provided services for like-minded legislators and lobbyists. ALEC wrote bills and created the campaigns to pass them. Its spokesmen boasted "that each year more than 1,000 bills based on its models are introduced in state legislatures, and that approximately 17% of those bills become law."[12]

High on ALEC's agenda were voter identification laws, which it hoped would have the effect of undercutting Obama's support base so that conservative politicians who supported ALEC's goals could be elected. Speaking to a convention of evangelicals in 1980, Paul Weyrich said, "Many of our Christians ... want everybody to vote. I don't want everybody to vote. ... As a matter of fact, our leverage in the elections quite candidly goes up as the voting populace goes down." Weyrich believed that America was suffering from what he called "a plague of unlawful voting" that the new laws would combat.[13]

But according to the best analyses, there was almost no evidence of illegal voting. Wisconsin's attorney general, a Republican, examined the 2008 election returns and discovered that out of three million votes cast, just twenty were found to be illegal. A wider study conducted by the Bush Justice Department had found similar results for the period 2002 to 2007. More than three hundred million people had voted, and only eighty-six were found guilty of voter fraud, and most of them were simply mistaken about their eligibility. "There is no evidence of widespread or systemic voter fraud occurring in the United States in recent history," reports Robert Brandon, founder and president of the nonpartisan Fair Elections Legal Network.[14]

Nevertheless, the Bush administration and Republicans, believing in the existence of widespread voter fraud, generally made its elimination a top priority. In 2007 the Bush Justice Department fired seven US attorneys supposedly for failing to prosecute cases of voter fraud that the attorneys claimed did not exist. To combat voter fraud, ALEC proposed a state voter ID for those citizens who lacked a driver's license or other means of identification that had once been acceptable, like a Social Security card. Among the many young politicians ALEC nurtured was Scott Walker, a future governor of Wisconsin, as well as both statehouse leaders. Walker was a faithful attendant at ALEC conventions since 1993, when he was a state legislator. So were the Fitzgerald brothers: Scott, the Senate majority leader, and Jeff, Speaker of the Assembly, along with many other legislators.

Wisconsin's voter photo ID law was one of the first pieces of legislation the new governor signed into law in 2011, and it became a model many other states followed. It required that potential voters show a current or expired driver's license, or some form of military identification, or a US passport, or a signed and dated student ID from an accredited state college or university, or a recent certificate of nationalization. If voters had none of these documents, they could present a birth certificate to receive a special photo ID issued by the Wisconsin Department of Transportation. Such requirements made voting extremely arduous for the very people who disproportionately supported Barack Obama in 2008, such as racial minorities, students, and the elderly.[15]

Among those who found complying with the new law difficult was Gladys Butterfield, who had voted in every local, state, and presidential election since 1932. She had stopped driving decades ago, so she had no license. Her birth certificate was also missing. She did have a baptismal record, but that document was not acceptable as proof of identity in her home state. Therefore, under Wisconsin's new law, she had to obtain a special government ID available only at an office of the Department of Transportation (DOT) before she could vote in the next presidential election. She was wheelchair bound so was dependent on a family member to drive her to the nearest DOT office. (She could not apply online because she lacked a current license.) A quarter of the offices were open only one day a month and closed on weekends. Sauk City's office was perhaps the hardest to visit; in 2012 it was open only four days that entire year. Many other states' DOT offices posed similar problems: odd schedules, distance from public transportation, and the like.[16]

With her daughter Gail's help, Butterfield applied for a state-certified birth certificate, costing twenty dollars, which she could show as proof of American citizenship. Next she had to visit the DOT. Transporting a wheelchair was a problem as was the inevitable wait in line to fill out the forms and have her picture taken. She was charged $28 because she did not know that it would not have cost her a cent if she had explicitly requested a free voter ID.

DOT officials were instructed not to offer applicants a free ID unless applicants requested one. (When an outraged government employee e-mailed friends of the news and encouraged them to "TELL ANYONE YOU KNOW!! ANYONE!! EVEN IF THEY DON'T NEED THE FREE ID, THEY MAY KNOW SOMEONE THAT DOES!!," he was abruptly fired for "inappropriately using work email," said an official.) "My mother is fortunate that she has someone to take her through this vote suppression procedure," Gail Butterfield Bloom told a journalist in 2011. "How many elderly or disabled residents do not? Are Scott Walker and his followers making it difficult for the elderly, disabled, poor and young to vote? My mother thinks so." So too, perhaps, did the 178,000 other Wisconsin seniors who did not have a driver's license or a state photo ID. They would have to go through similar efforts to exercise their constitutional rights.[17]

Like the elderly, students who wanted to vote in the next election would find new obstacles when they again tried to vote in Wisconsin and many other states. Under Wisconsin's new law student IDs would be accepted as proof of identity only if they contained a signature and an expiration date. But in 2011 the cards carried by Wisconsin's 182,000 students were not signed or dated and, therefore, would not be accepted at the polls. Some colleges hurriedly tried to manufacture an acceptable card at a cost of $1.1 million. South Carolina, Tennessee, and Texas would not accept any student ID whatsoever (although in the Lone Star State a concealed handgun license would suffice). New Hampshire's effort to limit student voting pleased William O'Brien, the Speaker of the Republican-dominated House, who, while speaking at a Tea Party function, called students "foolish" because they lacked "life experience [and] just vote their feelings." They voted, he said, "as a liberal. . . . [T]hat's what kids do."[18]

Before the Republican victory in the 2010 midterms only two states had rigorous voter ID requirements. By August 2012 thirty-four state legislatures had considered photo ID laws and thirteen had passed them; five more made it past state legislatures only to be vetoed by the Democratic governors of Montana, Minnesota, Missouri, North Carolina, and New Hampshire. By that same summer a number of states already had the new laws in place: Pennsylvania (where it was estimated that 9.2 percent of registered voters had no photo ID), Alabama, Mississippi (approved by referendum), Rhode Island, New Hampshire (whose state General Court overrode the governor's veto), and five whose sponsors were all ALEC members—Kansas, South Carolina, Tennessee, Texas, and Wisconsin. In Alabama, Kansas, and Tennessee people wishing to register or vote must show their birth certificate. To acquire that document they must pay a fee, which many believe is the equivalent of the poll tax, banned by the Constitution's Twenty-Fourth Amendment. Minnesota's citizens would vote on a state constitutional amendment in the 2012 election; if passed, voters could cast their ballot after showing a government-issued photo ID.

What these policies had in common, beside their connection to ALEC, was their negative impact on minorities. The nonpartisan Brennan Center for Justice at New York University's Law School estimated in October 2011 that the new voter ID laws could affect more than twenty-one million potential voters, predominately African Americans, Hispanics, students, the elderly, and the poor.[19]

Other voting laws passed in the wake of the 2010 midterms were just as injurious as the voter ID laws and threatened not merely minorities but also people likely to vote for Democratic candidates. Florida's new voter law turned Jill Cicciarelli, a thirty-five-year-old civics teacher, into a criminal. She inadvertently ran afoul of H.B.1355, which tightened the state's already strict regulations governing the registration of new voters. The 158-page bill became law twenty-four hours after it passed because Governor Rick Scott considered it essential to combat "an immediate danger to the public health, safety or welfare." Cicciarelli, who taught government and sponsored the Student Government Association at New Symrna Beach High School, was on maternity leave when the law went into effect in July 2011, so when she returned to school that fall she was unaware that she was about to commit a crime. In her senior government class she discussed the 2012 presidential election and, as she had many times before, organized a campaign to preregister those students who would turn eighteen before November. Eventually fifty students applied, and after a few days she sent the forms to the county election office. "I just want them to be participating in our democracy," she said later. "The more participation we have, the stronger our democracy will be."

The new law required that third-party registration organizations must register with the state election office, receive an identification number, undergo training, and turn in their application forms no later than forty-eight hours after their completion. (Previously registration was voluntary and the completion deadline was ten days, but it was rarely enforced.) Cicciarelli violated each of the new provisions and could be fined up to $1,000 for missing the due date and an additional $1,000 for failing to register. When Ann McFall, Volusia County Supervisor of Elections, learned of Cicciarelli's infractions in late

October, she reluctantly alerted the secretary of state's office that the teacher had violated the new law's requirements, potentially a third-degree felony if investigators determined that she was guilty of "willful noncompliance." "I was sick to my stomach when I did it," McFall later told a reporter, "but my job was on the line if I ignored it."[20]

The local press learned about Cicciarelli, the alleged felonious teacher, and sent reporters to interview her. The *Daytona Beach News-Journal* thought her story important enough to run on the paper's front page. Among its readers that Sunday morning was Florida senator Bill Nelson, a Democrat. He was appalled by what had happened and, after meeting with Cicciarelli and her students, urged US attorney general Eric Holder and Illinois senator Richard Durban, chair of the Judiciary Committee's Subcommittee on the Constitution, to investigate whether Florida's new law and others like it had been coordinated to suppress voter turnout. He found an unlikely ally in Ann McFall, the official who had turned in Cicciarelli and who subsequently wrote an editorial for the the *Daytona Beach News-Journal* calling the new law "egregious" and "unenforceable." The story went national when she appeared on MSNBC's *Rachel Maddow Show*. "I did catch some flak from the Division of Elections for speaking out," McFall later admitted. "It's bizarre. I haven't found one person who likes this law."[21]

Republican state representative Dorothy Hulkill, running for reelection in 2012, was one person who liked the Florida law. She believed it would limit voter fraud and stop people from "engaging in shady activities designed to give Democrats an unfair advantage." Who these people were, she did not say. McFall, also a Republican, responded quickly to defuse Hulkill's comments. "This is a partisan piece of legislation," she said. "It's not done to stop fraud. If someone was trying to register more than once, or register a bogus person, our system would catch it." A spokesman for the secretary of state announced that there was no plan to forward the Cicciarelli case to the attorney general for prosecution. Because this was her first offense, she would probably just receive a warning.[22]

The controversy over Florida's new voting law did not stop there, however. Soon five other teachers were accused of similar infractions. The entire group was dubbed the "Subversive Six" by an Internet blogger who had tired of criticizing the Florida schools' traditional preoccupations, evolution and sex education.[23]

By targeting a wide swath of American voters not because of race but rather because of their political sympathies, the legislators in these states had struck a serious blow to the suffrage of hundreds of thousands of citizens, all in ways that the creators of the Voting Rights Act had never imagined. Because of Florida's new law, the state chapter of the League of Women Voters announced that for the first time in seventy-two years, it would not register new voters in 2012. That time-honored job had become too risky. "It would . . . require our volunteers to have an attorney on one side and administrative assistant on the other," said League chapter president Diedre Macnab. She called the law "a war on voters." Other organizations like Rock the Vote, which registered 2.5 million new voters in 2008, and the Florida Public Interest Research Education Fund also ended their activities. It was not only the young who responded to such registrations drives and who now found a well-traveled route to the polls blocked: census figures indicated that in 2004 10 million new voters, among them many African Americans and Hispanics, registered with the help of community-based groups. Under the new voting laws many of these men and women would likely never make it to a voting booth.[24]

Some of these new efforts to restrict voters' access to the polls exposed significant racial biases on the part of the Republicans responsible for them. Colorado, Iowa, and Florida compiled lists of registered voters they thought ineligible and attempted to remove them from the voting rolls. Florida officials determined that 180,000 citizens were suspect; 74 percent of them were African American and Hispanic, groups more likely to be Democrats than Republicans. Governor Rick Scott became so concerned that illegal aliens could vote that he demanded access to the Department of Homeland Security's database, and they eventually granted his request. The Florida secretary of state found that thousands of registered voters could be considered "potential noncitizens" and removed them from the voting rolls. Further examination by more objective analysts concluded that significant errors had occurred: only 207 of the suspect 180,000 voters were judged unqualified. Among those caught in the net were elderly World War II veterans and many other longtime American citizens whose only offenses, in many instances, were being nonwhite. Florida's election supervisors refused to follow the governor's orders and stopped purging voters from the rolls. Nevertheless, Republican-dominated Lee and Collier Counties continued to remove those they considered suspicious. And on July 17, 2012, Homeland Security finally granted Florida officials the right to check the department's databases. "Our antennae are way up," declared the president of the Florida League of Women Voters, Debra McNab. "We will be watching very, very carefully to make sure that eligible voters are not removed from Florida voting lists."[25]

Florida's attempt at voter purging was not a new phenomenon. A more informal practice known as "caging" had been used mostly by Republican campaign officials for decades throughout America. It was simple: letters marked nonforwardable were sent to black citizens and those that came back unopened resulted in the addressee being removed from the voting lists. No less than the Republican National Committee was found guilty of caging in the 1980s, and a federal decree ordered them to desist at once, although Republicans still employed it decades later.[26]

Some states also attempted to suppress minority voting by curtailing early voting, which had avoided problems such as crowded polling places and voting machinery that often broke down from overuse. Early voting meant that more people could be accommodated over a longer period of time in, for example, Cleveland, Akron, Columbus, and Toledo, Ohio, cities with a heavy concentration of pro-Democratic black voters and a scarcity of voting machines. In the two years following the 2010 midterms, Georgia, Maine, Tennessee, West Virginia, Ohio, Florida, and Wisconsin all passed laws shortening the period during which citizens could cast their ballots. Ohio and Florida also eliminated voting on the Sunday before the election. This especially could have a profound impact on future minority voting. In 2008 54 percent of African Americans voted early, many on that Sunday, when churches held "Get Your Souls to the Polls" campaigns that brought blacks and Hispanics to the voting booths. Obama won Florida with 51 percent of the vote in 2008. In Ohio, another narrow victory for Obama, 30 percent of the state's total voters, 1.4 million people, voted during the early period, which was then thirty-five days before the election. Under each state's new law passed in 2011, it was shortened to sixteen days. Furthermore, people could vote only between 8 a.m. and 5 p.m., when many minorities as well as whites were at work. Because the Voting Rights Act covers five of Florida's sixty-seven counties—Hillsborough, Monroe, Collier, Hendry, and Hardell—voting officials had to submit their changes for preclearance. On August 17, 2012, a three-judge federal panel rejected their request on the grounds that the changes would discriminate against African Americans, who habitually vote early. The decision did not affect Florida's other sixty-two counties.[27]

Voters in Maine were so incensed that the new law had eliminated election day registration that a coalition of progressive organizations quickly collected seventy thousand signatures, enough to trigger the state's "People's Veto," putting the measure to a vote. On November 8, 2011, the law was repealed in a special election: "Maine voters sent a clear message: No one will be denied a right to vote," noted Shenna Bellows, head of the state's ACLU.[28]

Although Republicans continued to insist that the new laws were created solely to fight voter fraud, GOP officials twice revealed another motive. At a meeting of the Pennsylvania Republican State Committee in June 2012, Mike Turzai, the House majority leader, boasted openly that Pennsylvania's new law would affect the next presidential election. Proudly listing the GOP's achievements, Turzai said, "Voter ID, which is gonna allow Governor Romney to win the state of Pennsylvania: Done." Similarly, when, in August 2012, the *Columbia Dispatch* asked Doug Preise, a prominent Republican official and adviser to the state's governor, why he so strongly supported curtailing early voting in Ohio, Preise admitted, "I really actually feel that we shouldn't contort the voting process to accommodate the urban—read African American—voter turn-out machine." These admissions indicate that winning the presidency by suppressing the minority vote was the real reason behind the laws requiring voter IDs, limited voting hours, obstructed registration, and the like that Republican legislatures passed since the party's victory in 2010.[29]

Voter ID and similar laws tested voting rights' advocates as nothing had since the fight to extend the Act when Ronald Reagan was president. But in the twenty-first century, as in the twentieth, defenders of American suffrage were up to the challenge. The American Civil Liberties Union and the Lawyers Committee for Civil Rights Under Law, among others, filed lawsuits on behalf of minority voters affected by the new laws, and there were several important victories in 2012. They were successful in Wisconsin, the first state to pass such laws since the 2010 election. There, in October 2011, lawyers for the League of Women Voters argued that the new voter ID law violated the state's constitution, which barred from voting only those younger than eighteen, felons, and people judged "incompetent." The governor and state legislature could not on their own create a new class who could not vote—those who lacked a voter ID. In March 2012 Dane County circuit judge Richard Niess ruled in their favor. "A government that undermines the very foundations of its existence—the people's inherent, pre-constitutional right to vote," declared Judge Niess, "imperils its legitimacy as a government by the people, for the people, and especially of the people." In July 2012 a second Wisconsin judge, David Flanagan, also ruled that the law placed "an unconstitutional burden on the right to vote," and issued an injunction ordering the state to stop enforcing the voter ID requirement.[30]

Lawyers for the League of Women Voters won a second victory on May 31, 2012, when a Florida federal judge issued a temporary injunction that forbid state election officials from applying that part of the new law that obstructed the efforts of the League and Rock the Vote from registering new voters. "We're going to dust off our clip boards and pick up the forms and [get] into the business of registering people to vote," said Darden Race, president of the St. Petersburg chapter, on June 6, 2012.[31]

Judge Robert L. Hinckle's decision led to a similar action in Texas where, on August 2, 2012, US District Court judge Greg Costa ruled that the state had not produced sufficient evidence to prove that the restrictions on registration would solve the problem of voter fraud, and because of this, he struck down the new provisions and issued a preliminary injunction barring their use. "Texas now imposes more burdensome regulations on those engaging in third-party voter registration than the vast majority of, if not all, other states," Judge Costa noted in his ninety-six-page opinion. Texas state election officials immediately asked the judge to stay his injunction, but on August 14 Judge Costa denied their motion. "These drives are important to reaching millions of Texans, including three-quarters of a million African-Americans and 2 million Latinos, who are eligible but still not registered to vote," declared Chad Dunn, the attorney for Voting for America and Project Vote, who filed the lawsuit.[32]

On August 31, 2012, an Ohio federal judge restored early voting in the days prior to the 2012 presidential election, a time when almost one hundred thousand Buckeye State voters cast ballots in 2008. And in September the Pennsylvania State Supreme Court "sharply rebuked a lower court's approval of the law," noted journalist Elizabeth Drew, and asked Commonwealth court judge Robert Simpson "to block the law if it can't be implemented without disenfranchising voters." A few weeks later, on October 2, Judge Simpson ruled that Pennsylvania officials had not made enough progress in seeing that potential voters had the necessary ID card, and, therefore, he issued a temporary injunction barring their use in 2012. But the judge, who had previously called the ID "reasonable," also announced that he would convene a new trial to examine the issue in 2013.[33]

There were also efforts at the federal level to protect minority voting rights. Eric Holder, the first African American attorney general of the United States, promised to strictly enforce the Voting Rights Act and to use its power to thwart any efforts to subvert it. Per the preclearance requirement in Section 5 of the Act, South Carolina and Texas—both covered states—submitted their new voting laws to the Justice Department, which rejected both states' new legislation on December 23, 2011, and March 12, 2012, respectively.

As the presidential election approached, voter suppression efforts had been successfully blocked in Texas, Wisconsin, Florida, Ohio, and, temporarily, in Pennsylvania. Only Kansas, Indiana, Georgia, and Tennessee were left with rigid voter ID requirements, states not expected to be critical in the 2012 presidential election. Nevertheless, it was likely that one or more of these cases would eventually make its way through the appeals process and be heard by an unsympathetic Supreme Court. This is exactly what occurred in April 2008, when the Supreme Court upheld Indiana's two-year-old voter ID law, and in 2009, when the Court expressed its skepticism about the continued need for Section 5 in *Northwest Austin Municipal Utility District Number One v. Holder.*

Voter suppression laws like ID requirements and registration-drive bans offer yet another example of the crucial importance of the Voting Rights Act, but they also reveal its shortcomings. Although the preclearance provision in Section 5 has proven crucial for protecting voting rights, it covers only nine states completely—Alabama, Alaska, Arizona, Georgia, Louisiana, Mississippi, South Carolina, Texas, and Virginia—as well as counties in California, Florida, New York, North Carolina, and South Dakota as well as townships in Michigan and New Hampshire. It does nothing to protect the rights of minority voters in a number of states like Pennsylvania that have a troubling history of racial conflict but that are not covered by Section 5. If the Supreme Court succeeds in scaling back the advances that the Act has made, then there may also be places where American citizens never have a chance to enjoy the full extent of its benefits in the first place.[34]

IT IS MERCIFUL, PERHAPS, THAT SO MANY IN THE NONVIOLENT ARMY assaulted on the Edmund Pettus Bridge in 1965 did not live to see their cause threatened once again. Hosea Williams, winner of the coin toss that brought him to the confrontation with Major Cloud, died from cancer in 2000. Albert Turner, the movement's leader in Perry County, died of heart failure that same year. Marie Foster, whose clinics had prepared would-be voters for registration, died in 2003. Pancreatic cancer killed Jim Bevel in 2008, one year after his conviction on incest charges overshadowed all the good he had done as architect of the Birmingham and Selma campaigns.

Amelia Platts Boynton Robinson lived to celebrate her 101st birthday, but an association with political extremist Lyndon LaRouche tarnished her reputation. Bernard Lafayette was still active, teaching at Emory University and building nonviolence centers in America and abroad. Obama's election, he believed, "embodied King's principles of reaching out to one's enemies and seeking reconciliation."[35]

It was perhaps a blessing that ex-sheriff Jim Clark, for his part, did not live to see an African American president. In the decades after Bloody Sunday he remained an unrepentant racist. Chuck Bonner, one of Bernard Lafayette's young Selma acolytes who went on to become a lawyer in northern California, thought it might be interesting to see the former sheriff during a visit to Selma in 2005. He found him in Elba, Alabama, living in a nursing home. Confined to a wheelchair after a series of strokes and heart surgery left him an invalid, the eighty-two-year-old Clark was no longer the menacing figure he once was. In fact, he had never recovered after his defeat for sheriff in 1966. Almost unemployable, he and six other men were convicted of drug trafficking in the 1970s. Clark was sentenced to two years in a federal penitentiary and served nine months. His wife divorced him in 1980. He sold mobile homes until his health failed. Bonner asked him if he felt like apologizing for what he had done to Selma's blacks in the 1960s. "No," he said. "I was just doing my job and upholding the law."

Up until the very end of his life Clark refused to accept the changes that had overcome the country or to make peace with the civil rights movements' soldiers, past and present, who had made those transformations possible. To a Montgomery journalist in 2006 Clark said that Martin Luther King was "a liar" who "made sure he was nowhere around if there was a chance he might get hurt." The "bridge deal" that almost killed the marchers never really happened the way the media portrayed it, he claimed. "They all came and just flopped down . . . but they weren't knocked down." He'd done nothing wrong that day or ever, he insisted. It was Clark's last interview. He died on June 4, 2007.[36]

To have to fight for the right to vote all over again was intensely painful for Congressman John Lewis, the last surviving leader from the group of marchers who had been assaulted on Bloody Sunday, but he quickly joined the struggle against a new generation of politicians trying to return America to a darker time. Not long after Wisconsin passed its voter ID law in May 2011, Lewis addressed a nearly empty House chamber. "Mr. Speaker," he said, "Voting Rights are under attack in America by a deliberate and systematic attempt to prevent millions of elderly voters, young voters, students [and] minority and low-income voters from exercising their constitutional right to engage in the Democratic process." His voiced choked with emotion. He called voter IDs a poll tax, just like the one he fought against in the 1960s: "People who are already struggling to pay for basic necessities, cannot afford a voter ID." Voting must be made "simple, easy, and convenient."

Lewis departed from his text to speak of what he saw in the '60s—the long lines of registrants who waited patiently in summer and winter, the hostile clerks asking how many bubbles were in a bar of soap, how many jelly beans in a jar. "The history of the right to vote in America," he reminded his tiny audience, "is a history of conflict, of struggle, for that right. Many people died trying to [obtain] that right. I was beaten and jailed because I stood up for it. For millions like me, the struggle . . . is not mere history, it is experience. . . . We must not step backward."

For a moment it seemed like he *was* in Brown Chapel again, standing in a muddy raincoat, his head bleeding. "We must fight back," he cried. "We must speak up and speak out. We must never go back." Forever a movement man, Lewis understood how long it would take to achieve a multiracial society: "Our struggle is not a struggle that lasts one day, or one week, or one month, or one session of Congress, or one presidential term. Our struggle is the struggle of a lifetime."[37]

It was not just the struggle of one man's lifetime or even one race's but rather that of our nation as well. "Voter suppression" is as American as cherry pie and was often used to prevent immigrants from voting in both the nineteenth and twentieth centuries. New York officials attempted to prevent Jews from voting in 1908 by making Saturdays and even Jewish high holidays registration days. Also among the disenfranchised were New Jersey women who owned property and were allowed to vote until the state constitution limited the suffrage to "free white male citizen(s)" in 1807 as well as impoverished white men who had lost the property that once qualified them to vote. But the African American experience was unique: they were the only people to be first denied the right to vote, then, during Reconstruction, to receive it only to have it taken away again shortly thereafter. Although they won it yet again in 1965, it is perhaps not surprising that their achievement should again be endangered.[38]

February 15, 2011. President Barack Obama gives Congressman John Lewis (D-GA) the Medal of Freedom, America's highest civilian honor. Later Lewis tells reporters, "If somebody told me one day I would be standing in the White House and an African American president presenting me the Medal of Freedom, I would have said, 'Are you crazy?'" © RON SACHS/CNP/CORBIS

America's racial problems have endured and are likely to intensify as the country's population grows more diverse and the white majority continues to decline. As John Lewis notes, the history of the African American experience and that of the Voting Rights Act is one of continuing struggle, of reform and reaction, advance and retreat. Therefore, the Voting Rights Act remains in some form an essential tool for maintaining American democracy. "The power of the ballot we need in sheer self-defense," the scholar-activist W. E. B. Du Bois wrote in 1902, "else what shall save us from a second slavery?" Protecting that ballot requires the courage and determination to fight for the gains that the extraordinary generations who came before us paid for in blood. Without a similar commitment today and tomorrow, history may well repeat itself.[39]

Acknowledgments

ALTHOUGH WRITING HISTORY IS A SOLITARY ACT, I HAVE, TO PARAPHRASE Tennessee Williams, relied greatly on the kindness of strangers. First there are the many writers whose books and articles on the struggle for black equality inspired me and informed this work. They are, in alphabetical order, Taylor Branch, Charles Fager, Adam Fairclough, Frye Gaillard, David J. Garrow, Steven F. Lawson, Stephen Oates, Harvard Sitkoff, J. Mills Thornton, III, and, especially, Professor Richard M. Valelly of Swarthmore College, who generously took time from his busy schedule to review chapter 8 and alerted me to inadvertent factual errors. Any that remain are solely my own.

There are also several journalists who covered the events depicted in this book, giving me what Alan Barth called "the first rough draft of history": Renata Adler, Alvin Benn, the late Marshall Frady, John Herbers, the late Jack Nelson, Roy Reed, and Frank Sikora. I would especially like to thank John Fleming of the *Anniston Star,* who loaned me the FBI records on the murder of Jimmie Lee Jackson that he collected while researching this case. They enabled me to write with more authority about that tragedy. Thanks, too, to Frye Gaillard, who allowed me to examine the interviews he conducted while writing *Cradle of Freedom,* and Professor John H. Roper, who shared his interviews with Congressman Don Edwards with me.

The historians' unsung heroes are the many archivists whose labors provide us with the records that are essential to our work. Those who helped me are John F. Fox Jr., the FBI's resident historian; Maureen Hill at the Atlanta branch of the National Archives; Allen Fisher and Regina Greenwald at the Lyndon B. Johnson Presidential Library; John Fletcher and Jonathan Roscoe at the Richard

Nixon Presidential Library; and Tim Holtz at the Gerald R. Ford Presidential Library.

John W. Wright, my agent, brought me together again with Lara Heimert, who edited my third book while she was at Yale University Press and is now the publisher at Basic Books. Lara and her brilliant staff turned a long, unwieldy manuscript into a better book. Special thanks go to my editor, Alex Littlefield, whose hard work is evident on every page; the wonderful Melissa Veronesi, the book's project editor, who oversaw its progress through the various stages of production; Josephine Mariea, a brilliant copy editor; the gifted Nicole Caputo and Andrea Cardenas, who are responsible for the evocative cover design; and Editorial Assistant Katy O'Donnell, the Jacqueline of all trades.

George Watson, dean of the University of Delaware's College of Arts and Sciences, granted me sabbatical time that enabled me to complete this work. Associate Dean Ann Ardis was especially kind during a difficult period, and the department of history's Faculty Support Fund helped me acquire the photographs that illustrate the chapters. Others who helped me obtain photos were Elizabeth Partridge, author of *Marching for Freedom*, who recommended several excellent sources; Casey Anderson and Dana Caragiulo of Corbis; Tracy Martin, daughter and custodian of Spider Martin's superb collection; Matt Herron, a distinguished recorder of many of these events, and Lorraine Goonan of the Image Works, who made Mr. Herron's photos available to me; Michael Schulman of Magnum Photos; the LBJ Library's Christopher Banks; and Nancy Mirshah at the Gerald R. Ford Presidential Library.

Those closest to me are always the hardest to thank and deserve it the most. My daughter, Joanna, and son, Jeff, have been constant sources of pride and encouragement. And then there is Gail, who has shared my life for forty years and claims not to have regretted a single moment. I like to believe that's true, but I regret the too-many times she spent alone while I was writing; I marvel at how she managed to maintain her optimism when mine flagged. That's why this book belongs to her. Finally, although they'll never know it, two others have greatly enriched my life: Darcy, who left me in 2011, and Izzy, who arrived four months later to take her place. Only dog lovers will appreciate why these sentences, maudlin though they may be, are true.

—GM
Newark, Delaware
September 29, 2012

Notes

PROLOGUE: THE MOST POWERFUL INSTRUMENT

1. King's "Letter from a Birmingham Jail" is quoted in Stephen Oates, *Let The Trumpet Sound: The Life of Martin Luther King, Jr.* (New York: Harper and Row, 1982), 229, and the Theodore Parker quote is on 364. On King's use of Parker's quote, see Jamie Stiehm, "Oval Office Rug Gets History Wrong," *Washington Post*, September 4, 2010, http://www.washingtonpost.com/wp-dyn/content/article/2010/09/03/AR2010090305100.html.

2. Steven F. Lawson, "Civil Rights in America: Racial Voting Rights, A National Historic Landmarks Theme Story," National Park Service, US Department of the Interior, National Historical Landmarks Program (Washington, DC: 2007), 4.

3. Garrett Epps, *Democracy Reborn: The Fourteenth Amendment and the Fight for Equal Rights in Post-Civil War America* (New York: Henry Holt and Company, 2006), 142–44, 145–48, quote is on 148.

4. Lawson, "Civil Rights in America," 8; Eric Foner and Olivia Mahoney, *America's Reconstruction: People and Politics after the Civil War* (Baton Rouge: Louisiana State University Press, 1995), 80–81.

5. Lawson, "Civil Rights in America," 9–10.

6. Leon Litwack, *Trouble in Mind: Black Southerners in the Age of Jim Crow* (New York: Alfred A. Knopf, 1999), 223–26; Lawson, "Civil Rights in America," 13.

7. Litwack, *Trouble in Mind*, 223–27.

8. For invited guests, see White House Central Files (WHCF), Subject File, Box LE 66, Folder "Ex Hu 2–7, 6/1/65–9/3/65, Lyndon B. Johnson Library, Austin, Texas.

9. Danielle L. McGuire, *At the Dark End of the Street* (New York: Vintage Books, 2012), 12; Rosa Parks with Jim Haskins, *Rosa Parks: My Story* (New York: Puffin Books, 1992), 71–75, quote is on 75; Douglas Brinkley, *Rosa Parks: A Life* (New York: Penguin Books, 2000), 44–49.

10. Gilbert King, *Devil in the Grove: Thurgood Marshall, the Groveland Boys, and the Dawn of a New America* (New York: HarperCollins, 2012), 82–83; Charles L. Zelden, *The Battle for the Black Ballot: Smith v. Allwright and the Defeat of the Texas All-White Primary* (Lawrence: University of Kansas Press, 2005), 89–132.

11. John Dittmer, *Local People: The Struggle for Civil Rights in Mississippi* (Urbana: University of Illinois Press, 1994), 1–2, quote is on 2.

12. Ibid., 3–9.

13. Taylor Branch, *Parting the Waters: America in the King Years* (New York: Simon and Schuster, 1988), 410–11; Diane McWhorter, "Civil Lion," *California Magazine*, March/April 2007, 67; John Doar, "The Work of the Civil Rights Division in Enforcing Voting Rights Under the Civil Rights Acts of 1957 and 1960," *Florida State University Law Review* 25, no. 1 (1997): 1–13, http://www.law.fsu.edu/journals/lawreview/frames/251/doartext.html; Brian K. Landsberg, *Free at Last to Vote: The Alabama Origins of the Voting Rights Act* (Lawrence: University of Kansas Press, 2007), 155.

14. Testimony of Hon. Nicholas deB. Katzenbach, Voting Rights, Hearings before Subcommittee No. 5 of the Committee on the Judiciary House of Representatives Eighty-Ninth Congress First Session on H.R. 6400 (Washington, DC: Government Printing Office, 1965), 5–6.

15. John Lewis with Michael D'Orso, *Walking with the Wind: A Memoir of the Movement* (New York: Harcourt Brace, 1998), 360–61; David Halberstam, *The Children* (New York: Fawcett Books, 1998), 516–18.

16. David J. Garrow, "An Unfinished Dream," *Daily Beast*, January 18, 2009; Martin Luther King Jr., "Give Us the Ballot," Address Delivered at the Prayer Pilgrimage for Freedom, May 17, 1957, in *The Papers of Martin Luther King, Jr., Volume 1V: Symbol of the Movement, January 1957–December 1958*, Clayborn Carson et al., eds. (Berkeley: University of California Press, 2000), 208–15.

17. Eric Goldman, *The Tragedy of Lyndon Johnson* (New York: Alfred A. Knopf, 1969), 331–32; *New York Times*, August 7, 1965; Taylor Branch, *At Canaan's Edge: America in the King Years 1965–68* (New York: Simon and Schuster, 2006), 276–77.

18. *Alabama Journal*, quoted in Landsberg, *Free at Last to Vote*, 35.

19. *Time*, August 13, 1965; Oates, *Let The Trumpet Sound*, 370–71.

20. Stephen Pollak, interview by Thomas H. Baker, Part 111, 14–19, January 31, 1969, LBJ Library (hereafter cited as Pollak Interview); *New York Times*, August 7, 1965; Goldman, *The Tragedy of Lyndon Johnson*, 332.

21. *Daily Diary*, August 6, 1965, 2–3, LBJ Library; *Time*, August 13, 1965; Joseph A. Califano Jr., *The Triumph and Tragedy of Lyndon Johnson: The White House Years* (New York: Simon and Schuster, 1991), 57–58; Neil MacNeil, *Dirksen: Portrait of a Public Man* (New York: World Publishing Company, 1970), 260; "Text of Johnson's Statement on Voting Rights Law," *New York Times*, August 7, 1965.

22. Quoted in James Farmer, Transcript, James Farmer Oral History Interview II, 7/20/71, by Paige Mulholland, 2–4, Electronic Copy, LBJ Library; James Farmer, *Lay*

Bare the Heart: An Autobiography of the Civil Rights Movement (Fort Worth: Texas Christian University Press, 1990), 300.

23. Quoted in Oates, *Let The Trumpet Sound*, 370. See also "Protecting Minority Voters: The Voting Rights Act at Work 1982–2005," *A Report by The National Commission on the Voting Rights Act*, Lawyers Committee for Civil Rights Under Law, 2006.

24. Randall B. Woods, *LBJ: Architect of American Ambition* (New York: Free Press, 2006), 583; Frye Gaillard, *Alabama's Civil Rights Trail: An Illustrated Guide to the Cradle of Freedom* (Tuscaloosa: University of Alabama Press, 2009), 87.

25. Johnson is quoted in Xi Wang, "Building African American Voting Rights in the Nineteenth Century," in *The Voting Rights Act: Securing the Ballot*, Richard M. Valelly, ed. (Washington, DC: CQ Press, 2006). For a critical view, see Abigail Thernstrom and Stephen Thernstrom, "Racial Gerrymandering Is Unnecessary, *The Wall Street Journal*, November 11, 2008; *New York Times*, April 28, 2009; Edward Blum and Roger Clegg, "Color Inside the Lines," *Legal Affairs*, November 2003, http://www.legalaffairs.org/printerfriendly.msp?id=469; Maragret Edds, "Debating the Effects of the Voting Rights Act," *Washington Post*, September 27, 1987; Jeffrey Toobin, "Voter Beware," *New Yorker*, March 2, 2009; *New York Times*, June 23, 2009.

CHAPTER ONE: PLANTING THE FIRST SEED

1. For a portrait of Selma in 1962, see "Selma—Cracking the Wall of Fear," Civil Rights Movement Veterans, http://www.crmvet.org/tim/timhis63.htm#1963selma.

2. For Lafayette's early activities, see his testimony in *United States of America vs. Dallas County, Alabama, et al.*, Civil Action No. 3064–63, October 15, 1963, 46–47, National Archives, Atlanta branch (hereafter cited as *United States of America vs. Dallas County, Alabama*); Fred Powledge, *Free at Last: The Civil Rights Movement and the People Who Made It* (New York: Little, Brown, 1991), 204, 257–59.

3. Affidavit of Bernard Lafayette, June 24, 1963, 1, in *United States of America v. Dallas County, James G. Clark, Jr., et al.*, Civ. A. No. 3064–63, Accession #021–73B2029, Box 17, National Archives, Atlanta, GA (hereafter cited as Lafayette Affidavit); *Time*, May 26, 1961; Frye Gaillard, *Cradle of Freedom: Alabama and the Movement That Changed America* (Tuscaloosa: University of Alabama Press, 2004), 67; John Lewis with Michael D'Orso, *Walking with the Wind: A Memoir of the Movement* (New York: Harcourt Brace, 1998), 73–74; David Halberstam, *The Children* (New York: Fawcett Books, 1998), 53–56.

4. Gaillard, *Cradle of Freedom*, 70; Halberstam, *The Children*, 136.

5. Halberstam, *The Children*, 136–38.

6. Lafayette is quoted in Cheryl Lynn Greenberg, *A Circle of Trust: Remembering SNCC* (New Brunswick, NJ: Rutgers University Press, 1998), 88; Powledge, *Free at Last*, 614; Taylor Branch, *Pillar of Fire: America in the King Years, 1963–1965* (New York: Simon and Schuster, 1998), 63; Cynthia Griggs Fleming, *In the Shadow of*

Selma: The Continuing Struggle for Civil Rights in the Rural South (Lanham, MD: Rowman and Littlefield, 2004), 142–43; Clayborne Carson et al., eds., *The Eyes on the Prize: Civil Rights Reader: Documents, Speeches, and Firsthand Accounts from the Black Freedom Struggle, 1954–1990* (New York: Viking, 1991), 209–10; Halberstam, *The Children*, 411.

7. Alston Fitts III, *Selma: Queen City of the Black Belt* (Selma, AL: Clairmont Press, 1989), 1–10; Peter Applebome, *Dixie Rising: How the South Is Shaping American Values, Politics, and Culture* (New York: Harcourt Brace, 1996), 63.

8. Fitts, *Selma*, 54–61; Gay Talese, *A Writer's Life* (New York: Knopf, 2006), 128; Powledge, *Free at Last*, 612–13.

9. Turner is quoted in Applebome, *Dixie Rising*, 64. See also Richard Bailey, *Neither Carpetbaggers Nor Scalawags: Black Office Holders During the Reconstruction of Alabama, 1867–1879* (Montgomery, AL: NewSouth Books, 2010), 83–84; Eric Foner and Olivia Mahoney, *America's Reconstruction: People and Politics After the Civil War* (Baton Rouge: Louisiana State University Press, 1995), 93–137; Eric Foner, *Freedom's Lawmakers: A Directory of Black Officeholders During Reconstruction* (Baton Rouge: Louisiana State University Press, 1996), xi–xxxi. See also Philip Dray, *Capitol Men: The Epic Story of Reconstruction Through the Lives of the First Black Congressmen* (New York: Houghton Mifflin, 2008), passim; Howard N. Rabinowitz, *Southern Black Leaders of the Reconstruction Era* (Urbana: University of Illinois Press, 1982), passim.

10. The Confederate colonel is quoted in Applebome, *Dixie Rising*, 64.

11. "Voting: 1961 Commission on Civil Rights Report, Book 1," 26, University of Maryland School of Law, Baltimore, MD; J. Mills Thornton III, *Dividing Lines: Municipal Politics and the Struggle for Civil Rights in Montgomery, Birmingham, and Selma* (Tuscaloosa: University of Alabama Press, 2002), 392, 436–38; Margaret Price, *The Negro Voter in the South* (Atlanta, GA: Southern Regional Council, 1956), 32; Talese, *A Writer's Life*, 128; Jerry DeMuth, "Black Belt, Alabama," in *We Shall Overcome: The Civil Rights Movement in the United States in the 1950s and 1960s, Vol. 1*, David J. Garrow, ed. (Brooklyn: Carlson, 1989), 1.

12. Halberstam, *The Children*, 416; Gaillard, *Cradle of Freedom*, 176.

13. Amelia Platts Boynton Robinson, *Bridge Across Jordan* (Washington, DC: Schiller Institute, 1991), 109–56; J. L. Chestnut Jr. and Julia Cass, *Black in Selma: The Uncommon Life of J. L. Chestnut* (Tuscaloosa, AL: Fire Ant Books, 1990), 74.

14. Chestnut and Cass, *Black in Selma*, 51–54; Thornton, *Dividing Lines*, 416, 435, 439, 670n14; Robinson, *Bridge Across Jordan*, 174.

15. For the Supreme Court's decision, see *William Earl Fikes, Petitioner v. State of Alabama*, January 14, 1957, 352 U.S. 191 (77 S. Ct.281, 1 L. Ed. 2d 246); *Time*, January 28, 1957; Thornton, *Dividing Lines*, 391; Chestnut and Cass, *Black in Selma*, 40; Talese, *A Writer's Life*, 133–34.

16. Thornton, *Dividing Lines*, 390; Chestnut and Cass, *Black in Selma*, 78; Robinson, *Bridge Across Jordan*, 176–82.

17. Mary Francis Berry, *And Justice for All: The United States Commission on Civil Rights and the Continuing Struggle for Freedom in America* (New York: Knopf, 2009), 24–25.

18. *New York Times*, December 7, 9, 1958; *Time*, December 15, 1958; Berry, *And Justice for All*, 14–15.

19. "Hearings Before the United States Commission on Civil Rights, Voting, December 8, 1958," in *United States Commission on Civil Rights: Report on Voting, vol. 1*, Gabriel J. Chen and Lois Wagner, eds. (Buffalo, NY: William S. Hein and Co., 2005), 218–19, 225, 237–41.

20. Sara Bullard, *Free At Last: A History of the Civil Rights Movement and Those Who Died in the Struggle* (New York: Oxford, 1993), 40–43; Gene Roberts and Hank Klibanoff, *The Race Beat: The Press, the Civil Rights Struggle, and the Awakening of a Nation* (New York: Alfred A. Knopf, 2006), 80–82; John Dittmer, *Local People: The Struggle for Civil Rights in Mississippi* (Urbana: University of Illinois Press, 1994), 54.

21. For Guice's testimony, see "Hearings, United States Commission on Civil Rights, Montgomery, Alabama (December 8 and 9, 1958)" in *Debating the Civil Rights Movement, 1945–1968*, Steven F. Lawson and Charles Payne, eds. (Lanham, MD: Rowan and Littlefield, 1998), 65–73. For Sellers's testimony, see Gabriel J. Chen and Lois Wagner, eds., *United States Commission on Civil Rights: Report on Voting, vol. 1* (Buffalo, NY: William S. Hein and Co., 2005), 237–41, 267–81. For the Boyntons' testimony, see Chen and Wagner, *United States Commission on Civil Rights,* 212–27.

22. Branch, *Pillar of Fire*, 82; Gaillard, *Cradle of Freedom*, 224; Andrew Young, *An Easy Burden: The Civil Rights Movement and the Transformation of America* (New York: HarperCollins, 1996), 343.

23. Thornton, *Dividing Lines*, 447–48; Halberstam, *The Children*, 422; Gaillard, *Cradle of Freedom*, 175; *New York Times*, September 8, 2003; Chestnut and Cass, *Black in Selma*, 137, 149, 154–55; Powledge, *Free at Last*, 616.

24. Lafayette Affidavit, 3; Robinson, *Bridge Across Jordan*, 226; Chestnut and Cass, *Black in Selma*, 137; *Southern Courier*, December 10–11, 1966, 2; Branch, *Pillar of Fire*, 64; Lewis, *Walking with the Wind*, 213; Fry, "The Voter-Registration-Drive," in *We Shall Overcome: The Civil Rights Movement in the United States in the 1950s and 1960s, Vol. 1*, David J. Garrow, ed. (Brooklyn: Carlson, 1989), 6; Robert A. Caro, *The Years of Lyndon Johnson: Master of the Senate* (New York: Alfred A. Knopf, 2003), x.

25. Chestnut and Cass, *Black in Selma*, 153–54, 160; SAC, Mobile to Director, FBI, May 1963, 1, FBI File 157-6-61-180; Fry, "The Voter-Registration Drive," 6.

26. Applebome, *Dixie Rising*, 57–58; Charles Bonner Interview, Veterans of the Civil Rights Movement, 2005, http://www.crmvet.org/nars/chuckbet.htm (hereafter cited as Bonner Interview).

27. SAC, Mobile to Director, FBI, 5-13-63, 1–2, FBI File 157-6-61-184; Chestnut and Cass, *Black in Selma*, 148–49, 161–63; Branch, *Pillar*, 65; Halberstam, *The Children*, 419.

28. *United States of America vs. Dallas County, Alabama, et al.*, 80; SAC, Mobile to Director, FBI, 3; SAC, Mobile to Director, May 14, 1963, 1–2, FBI File 157-6-61–183; SAC, Birmingham to Director, FBI, May 15, 1963, 1–2, FBI File 157-6-61–185; "Racial Situation, State of Alabama, Selma," FBI Mobile Field Office memo, no file number; Gaillard, *Cradle of Freedom*, 224–25.

29. Lafayette Affidavit, 4; Halberstam, *The Children*, 424.

30. Lafayette Affidavit, 4; Chestnut and Cass, *Black in Selma*, 163–64; Halberstam, *The Children*, 423.

31. Clark's statement is in *United States of America vs. Dallas County, Alabama, et al.*, 28; Lafayette Affidavit, 4; *New York Times*, March 16, 1965; Halberstam, *The Children*, 423; *The Economist*, June 14, 2007; Chestnut and Cass, *Black in Selma*, 165; Gaillard, *Cradle of Freedom*, 225.

32. James Forman, *The Making of Black Revolutionaries* (Washington, DC: Open Hand, 1985), 3–54; Clayborne Carson, *In Struggle: SNCC and the Black Awakening of the 1960s* (Cambridge, MA: Harvard University Press, 1981), 42–43; Chestnut and Cass, *Black in Selma*, 164; *Washington Post*, January 11, 2005; *New York Times*, January 12, 2005.

33. *United States of America vs. Dallas County, Alabama, et al.*, 55, 66; SAC, Mobile to Director, FBI, May 15, 1963, 1–2, FBI File 157-6-61–187; Chestnut and Cass, *Black in Selma*, 164–65; Thornton, *Dividing Lines*, 450–51; Greenberg, *A Circle of Trust*, 92; Branch, *Pillar of Fire*, 84; Halberstam, *The Children*, 424.

34. Bonner Interview; Bernard Lafayette Interview, National Park Service, http://www.nps.gov/archive/semo/freedom/508/transcripts/P18-trns.html; Greenberg, *A Circle of Trust*, 92; Chestnut and Cass, *Black in Selma*, 166.

35. Bonner Interview; Thornton, *Dividing Lines*, 446.

36. *United States of America vs. Dallas County, Alabama, et al.*, 58; Lafayette Affidavit, 4–5; Halberstam, *The Children*, 425–26.

37. Lafayette describes the attack in a SNCC document, "A Report on Selma," reprinted in Forman, *The Making of Black Revolutionaries*, 318–26 (hereafter cited as "A Report on Selma"). See also Lafayette Affidavit, 5, and Greenberg, *A Circle of Trust*, 90–92. Bob Owen to John Doar, June 13, 1963, in *United States v. Dallas County*, Voting Investigation, Historical Documents, U.S. Justice Department, FOIA Electronic Reading Room. See also Halberstam, *The Children*, 426–27; Gaillard, *Cradle of Freedom*, 175–76; Fleming, *In the Shadow of Selma*, 149.

38. Halberstam, *The Children*, 427–28; Gaillard, *Cradle of Freedom*, 176. For the Evers murder, see Maryanne Vollers, *Ghosts of Mississippi: The Murder of Medgar Evers, the Trials of Byron De La Beckwith, and the Haunting of the New South* (Boston: Little, Brown, 1995).

39. Chestnut and Cass, *Black in Selma*, 166; Halberstam, *The Children*, 428; Bonner Interview.

40. "A Report on Selma," 322–23; Lafayette Affidavit, 5–6; Bosie's testimony is quoted in Fry, "The Voter-Registration Drive," 254.

41. SAC, Mobile to Director, FBI, June 17, 1963, 1, FBI File 157–6-61–200; SAC, Mobile to Director, FBI, June 19, 1963, 1–3, FBI File 157–6-61–214; "A Report on Selma," 323–24; Lafayette Affidavit, 6–7.

42. SAC, Mobile to Director, FBI, 6–19–63, 1, FBI File 157–6-61–213; Carl Gabel, Memo to the Files, June 19, 1963, in *U.S. v. Dallas County*, Voting Investigation; "A Report on Selma," 324; Lafayette Affidavit, 7–8.

43. "A Report on Selma," 324–25; Lafayette Affidavit, 8; Chestnut and Cass, *Black in Selma*, 93. See also *United States v. Dallas County*, Voting, 40–49, Transcripts, Justice Department records; Fry, "The Voter-Registration Drive," 6.

44. Chestnut and Cass, *Black in Selma*, 166–68.

45. Forman, *The Making of Black Revolutionaries*, 318, 326. For the FBI's reports on the summer rallies, see, for example, SAC, Mobile to Director, FBI, July 9, 1963, 1–4, FBI File 157–6-61–239; SAC, Mobile to Director, FBI, July 15, 1963, FBI File 157–6-61–242; SAC, Mobile to Director, FBI, July 23, 1963, FBI File 157–61–243; SAC, Mobile to Director, FBI, July 29, 1963, FBI File 157–61–6-252; SAC, Mobile to Director, FBI, August 5, 1963, 157–6-254; SAC, Mobile to Director, FBI, August 12, 1963, FBI File 157–6-61–259; SAC, Mobile to Director, FBI, August 19, 1963, FBI File 157–6-61–269; SAC, Mobile to Director, FBI, August 26, 1963, FBI File 157–6-61–278.

CHAPTER TWO: AN IDEAL PLACE

1. Taylor Branch, *Parting the Waters: America in the King Years* (New York: Simon and Schuster, 1988), 536–37, 548–49, 628–30; Stephan Oates, *Let the Trumpet Sound: The Life of Martin Luther King, Jr.* (New York: Harper and Row, 1982), 189–201, 211, 232–35, 240–41; Harvard Sitkoff, *King: Pilgrimage to the Mountaintop* (New York: Hill and Wang, 2008), 89–113; *Newsweek*, September 30, 1963; SAC, Birmingham to Director, et al., September 15, 1963, FBI File 157–352–1; Frank Sikora, *Until Justice Rolls Down: The Birmingham Church Bombing Case* (Tuscaloosa: University of Alabama Press, 1991), 9–19; Gary May, *The Informant: The FBI, the Ku Klux Klan and the Murder of Viola Liuzzo* (New Haven, CT: Yale University Press, 2005), 87–104, quote is on 88.

2. SA John Culpepper to SA John C. Newsom, September 15, 1963, 1–2, FBI File 157–352–44; SA Roy Osborn to SAC, September 15, 1963, FBI File 157–352–47; A. Rosen to Mr. Belmont, September 16, 1963, 2–3, FBI File 157–1025–28; SAC, Birmingham to Director, September 16, 1963, FBI File 157–205–45, 16th Street Church Bombing Records, Part I; *New York Times*, September 16, 1963; *Newsweek*, September 30, 1963; Sikora, *Until Justice Rolls Down*, 14.

3. Oates, *Let the Trumpet Sound*, 211, 232–35, 240–41; May, *The Informant*, 68–69. Kennedy is quoted in May, *The Informant*, 78.

4. Oates, *Let the Trumpet Sound*, 256–64. For Lewis's speech, see Lewis, *Walking with the Wind*, 218–31.

5. SAC, Mobile to Director, FBI, August 14, 1964, 25, FBI File 157–6–61–696; SAC, Mobile to Director, FBI, September 11, 1963, "Racial Situation," September 11, 1963, 1, FBI, no file number; Charles Bonner Interview, Veterans of the Civil Rights Movement, 2005, http://www.crmvet.org/nars/chuckbet.htm (hereafter cited as Bonner Interview); J. Mills Thornton III, *Dividing Lines: Municipal Politics and the Struggle for Civil Rights in Montgomery, Birmingham, and Selma* (Tuscaloosa: University of Alabama Press, 2002), 455; James Forman, *The Making of Black Revolutionaries* (Washington, DC: Open Hand, 1985), 348; Lewis, *Walking with the Wind*, 238; J. L. Chestnut Jr. and Julia Cass, *Black in Selma: The Uncommon Life of J. L. Chestnut* (Tuscaloosa, AL: Fire Ant Books, 1990), 168–69, 182; *Post-Herald* (Birmingham, AL), September 24, 1963, in FBI File 157–6–?A; *New York Herald Tribune*, October 31, 1963, FBI File 157–6–4-A, Bonner is quoted in Bonner Interview.

6. Lewis, *Walking with the Wind*, 60–61; David Halberstam, *The Children* (New York: Fawcett Books, 1998), 59, 145–47, 396–99; Lynne Olson, *Freedom's Daughters: The Unsung Heroines of the Civil Rights Movement from 1830 to 1970* (New York: Touchstone, 2002), 151–62, 211; David J. Garrow, *Bearing the Cross: Martin Luther King, Jr. and the Southern Christian Leadership Conference* (New York: W. Morrow, 1986), 294, 296; Taylor Branch, *Pillar of Fire: America in the King Years, 1963–1965* (New York: Simon and Schuster, 1998), 143; Diane Nash, Interview, Eyes on the Prize, November 12, 1985, Hampton Collection, Film and Radio Archive, Washington University (hereafter cited as Nash Interview); James Bevel, Interview, Eyes on the Prize, November 15, 1985, Hampton Collection, Film and Radio Archive, Washington University (hereafter cited as Bevel Interview); Frye Gaillard, *Cradle of Freedom: Alabama and the Movement That Changed America* (Tuscaloosa: University of Alabama Press, 2004), 204–6; Halberstam, *The Children*, 492–93.

7. Garrow, *Bearing the Cross*, 292–94.

8. Ibid., 294, 296; Branch, *Pillar of Fire*, 143; Nash quote is from Nash Interview; Bevel Interview; Gaillard, *Cradle of Freedom*, 204–6; Halberstam, *The Children*, 492–93; SAC, Mobile to Director, FBI, August 14, 1964, 25, FBI File 157–6–61–696; SAC, Mobile to Director, FBI, September 11, 1963, "Racial Situation," September 11, 1963, 1, FBI, no file number; Bonner Interview; Thornton, *Dividing Lines*, 455; Forman, *The Making of Black Revolutionaries*, 348; Lewis, *Walking with the Wind*, 238; Chestnut and Cass, *Black in Selma*, 168–69, 182; *Post-Herald* (Birmingham, AL), September 24, 1963, in FBI File 157–6–?A; *New York Herald Tribune*, October 31, 1963, FBI File 157–6–4-A.

9. *New York Herald Tribune*, ibid.; Lewis, *Walking with the Wind*, 238.

10. Lewis, *Walking with the Wind*, 238–39; Forman, *The Making of Black Revolutionaries*, 349; *New York Herald Tribune*, October 31, 1963, in FBI File 157–6–6A; *New York Times*, September 26, 1963.

11. Forman, *The Making of Black Revolutionaries*, 349; Branch, *Pillar of Fire*, 67, 71, 151.

12. Dick Gregory with Robert Lipsyte, *Nigger: An Autobiography* (New York: Pocket Books, 1964), 200–5; Howard Zinn, *SNCC: The New Abolitionists* (Cambridge, MA: South End Press, 2002), 150–52; Danny Lyon, *Memories of the Southern Civil Rights Movement* (Santa Fe, NM: Twin Palms Publishing, 2010), 98.

13. SAC, Mobile to Director, FBI, October 7, 1963, 1, FBI File 157–6-61–37?; Forman, *The Making of Black Revolutionaries*, 349–50; Zinn, *SNCC*, 153–55.

14. SAC, Mobile to Director, FBI, October 7, 1963, FBI File 157–6-61–38?; *New York Times*, October 8, 1963; Lyon, *Memories of the Southern Civil Rights Movement*, 99; Zinn, *SNCC*, 157–58.

15. SAC, Mobile to Director, FBI, October 11, 1963, 4, FBI File 157–6-61–399; *New York Times*, ibid.; Zinn, *SNCC*, 161–62.

16. Zinn, *SNCC*, 161–62.

17. SAC, Mobile to Director, FBI, October 7, 1963, 1–2, FBI File 157–6-382; A. Rosen to Alan Belmont, October 8, 1963, FBI File 157–6-61–397; SAC, Mobile to Director, FBI, October 9, 1963, 1, FBI File 157–6-61–406; Zinn, *SNCC*, 162–63.

18. Zinn, *SNCC*, 163; Neblett's report on his assault is in Lewis, *Walking with the Wind*, 240–43; *New York Times*, October 8, 1963.

19. SAC, Mobile to Director, FBI, October 7, 1963, 2, FBI File 157–6-382; Zinn, *SNCC*, 164.

20. "Racial Situation: Selma, Alabama," n.d., 4, no file number; Zinn, *SNCC*, 165; Forman, *The Making of Black Revolutionaries*, 352.

21. Forman, *The Making of Black Revolutionaries*, 354; Zinn, *SNCC*, 165–66; *New York Times*, October 13, 1963. For Lewis, see Henry Hampton and Steve Fayer with Sarah Flynn, *Voices of Freedom: An Oral History of the Civil Rights Movement from the 1950s Through the 1980s* (New York: Bantam, 1990), 213.

22. SAC, Mobile to Director, FBI, May 11, 1963, "Racial Situation, State of Alabama, Selma, Alabama," May 11, 1964, 1–2, no FBI File number; Thornton, *Dividing Lines*, 458–61. On black efforts to register, see, for example, SAC, Mobile to Director, FBI, October 18, 1963, FBI File 157–6-61–430; SAC, Mobile to Director, FBI, October 24, 1963, FBI File 157–6-61–460; SAC, Mobile to Director, FBI, October 28, 1963, FBI File 157–6-61–463; SAC, Mobile to Director, FBI, November 8, 1963, FBI File 157–6-61–497.

23. Robert A. Caro, *The Years of Lyndon Johnson: The Passage of Power* (New York: Alfred A. Knopf, 2012), 427–33.

24. *The Student Voice* 4, no. 10 (December 30, 1963), in *The Student Voice: 1960–1965*, Clayborne Carson, ed., unpaginated (Westport, CT: Meckler Publishers, 1990).

25. *U.S. v. Clark*; David J. Garrow, *Protest at Selma: Martin Luther King, Jr. and the Voting Rights Act of 1965* (New Haven, CT: Yale University Press, 1978), 33–34; Jerry DeMuth, "Black Belt, Alabama," in *We Shall Overcome: The Civil Rights Movement in the United States in the 1950s and 1960s, Vol. 1*, David J. Garrow, ed. (Brooklyn: Carlson, 1989), 3; Branch, *Pillar of Fire*, 391.

26. *New York Times*, July 7, 1964; Thornton, *Dividing Lines*, 462; see also SAC, Mobile to Director, FBI, July 21, 1964, 1–2, 157-6-61–677; *U.S. v. Clark*; Lewis, *Walking with the Wind*, 312; Thornton, *Dividing Lines*, 462; Branch, *Pillar of Fire*, 391; DeMuth, "Black Belt, Alabama," 184.

27. *U.S. v. Clark*; Lewis, *Walking with the Wind*, 312; "The Selma Injunction (July)," Veterans of Civil Rights Movement, http://www.crmvet.org/tim/tim64c .htm#1964selmainj; Thornton, *Dividing Lines*, 462–63.

28. Thornton, *Dividing Lines*, 463; Gaillard, *Cradle of Freedom*, 226; Chestnut and Cass, *Black in Selma*, 175; Branch, *Pillar of Fire*, 391.

29. *Time*, April 23, 1965; Thornton, *Dividing Lines*, 424–25; Halberstam, *The Children*, 494–95; Chestnut and Cass, *Black in Selma*, 173, 178–80; Howell Raines, *My Soul Is Rested: The Story of the Civil Rights Movement in the Deep South* (New York: Penguin, 1983), 382–83.

30. Thornton, *Dividing Lines*, 463; Gaillard, *Cradle of Freedom*, 226; Chestnut and Cass, *Black in Selma*, 175; Branch, *Pillar of Fire*, 391, 31; Adam Fairclough, *To Redeem the Soul of America: The Southern Christian Leadership Conference and Martin Luther King, Jr.* (Athens: University of Georgia Press, 1987), 211–12; Gaillard, *Cradle of Freedom*, 228–29.

31. Charles E. Fager, *Selma, 1965* (New York: Charles Scribner's Sons, 1974), 5–6; Branch, *Pillar of Fire*, 554; Thornton, *Dividing Lines*, 467–68.

32. For Smeltzer's work, see Stephen L. Longenecker, *Selma's Peacemaker: Ralph Smeltzer and Civil Rights Mediation* (Philadelphia: Temple University Press, 1987), 33–214; Thornton, *Dividing Lines*, 464–66.

33. Amelia Platts Boynton Robinson, *Bridge Across Jordan* (Washington, DC: Schiller Institute, 1991), 237–38; Fairclough, *To Redeem the Soul of America*, 211–12; *New York Times*, October 13, 1964.

34. Branch, *Pillar of Fire*, 523; David J. Garrow, *Bearing the Cross: Martin Luther King, Jr., and the Southern Christian Leadership Conference* (New York: W. Morrow, 1986), 358–59; Chestnut and Cass, *Black in Selma*, 188–89; Gaillard, *Cradle of Freedom*, 227.

35. Rowland Evans and Robert Novak, *Lyndon B. Johnson: The Exercise of Power* (New York: New American Library, 1966), 427–34.

36. Thornton, *Dividing Lines*, 475; Garrow, *Bearing the Cross*, 368–69; Ralph David Abernathy, *And the Walls Came Tumbling Down: An Autobiography* (New York: Harper and Row, 1989), 299; Gaillard, *Cradle of Freedom*, 227.

37. Garrow, *Bearing the Cross*, 359–60; Thornton, *Dividing Lines*, 476.

38. Sitkoff, *King*, 65; Peter J. Ling, *Martin Luther King, Jr.* (New York: Routledge, 2002), 60; Garrow, *Bearing the Cross*, 311.

39. Garrow, *Bearing the Cross*, 57–58; Sitkoff, *King*, 37–40; Ling, *Martin Luther King, Jr.*, 46.

40. Garrow, *Bearing the Cross*, 365; Marshall Frady, *Martin Luther King, Jr.: A Life* (New York: Penguin, 2005), 153.

41. Frady, *Martin Luther King, Jr.*, 225–26.

42. Adam Fairclough, *Better Day Coming: Blacks and Equality* (New York: Penguin, 2001), 129–30; Stephen G. N. Tuck, *We Ain't What We Ought To Be: The Black Struggle from Emancipation to Obama* (Cambridge, MA: Harvard University Press, 2010), 210.

43. King is quoted in William Chafe, *Private Lives/Public Consequences: Personality and Politics in Modern America* (Cambridge, MA: Harvard University Press, 2005), 79–80; Oates, *Let the Trumpet Sound*, 283–84.

44. Garrow, *Bearing the Cross*, 310, 312, 374–76; David J. Garrow, *The FBI and Martin Luther King, Jr.: From "Solo" to Memphis* (New York: W. W. Norton, 1981), 121; Frady, *Martin Luther King, Jr.*, 127, 198.

45. Garrow, *The FBI and Martin Luther King, Jr.*, 124–25; Nick Kotz, *Judgment Days: Lyndon Baines Johnson, Martin Luther King, Jr. and the Laws That Changed America* (Boston: Houghton Mifflin, 2005), 229–30.

46. Garrow, *Bearing the Cross*, 363; Ben Bradlee, *A Good Life: Newspapering and Other Adventures* (New York: Simon and Schuster, 1996), 272; Frady, *Martin Luther King, Jr.*, 199; Kotz, *Judgment Days*, 232–33, 239; James Farmer with Don E. Carleton, *Lay Bare the Heart: An Autobiography of the Civil Rights Movement* (Fort Worth: Texas Christian University Press, 1998), 269; Oates, *Let the Trumpet Sound*, 314.

47. Garrow, *The FBI and Martin Luther King, Jr.*, 125–26, Sitkoff, *King*, 145.

48. Stewart Burns, *To the Mountaintop: Martin Luther King, Jr.'s Mission to Save America, 1955–1968* (San Francisco: HarperOne, 2003), 260; Fairclough, *To Redeem the Soul of America*, 222; Oates, *Let the Trumpet Sound*, 321.

49. Oates, *Let the Trumpet Sound*, 321–22.

50. For the Johnson-Farmer relationship, see Paige Mulholland, James Farmer Oral History Interview II, Transcript, July 20, 1971, 2–4, Electronic Copy, LBJ Library; Farmer, *Lay Bare the Heart*, 300. For the formation of the Mississippi Freedom Democratic Party, see John Dittmer, *Local People: The Struggle for Civil Rights in Mississippi* (Urbana: University of Illinois Press, 1994), 272–302. Johnson is quoted in Michael E. Parrish, *Citizen Rauh: An American Liberal's Life in Law and Politics* (Ann Arbor: University of Michigan Press, 2010), 168–69.

51. Kotz, *Judgment Days*, 234–38, 243–46.

52. Garrow, *Protest at Selma*, 36; Mark Stern, *Calculating Visions: Kennedy, Johnson, and Civil Rights* (New Brunswick, NJ: Rutgers University Press, 1992), 216–17; Robert Mann, *The Walls of Jericho: Lyndon Johnson, Hubert Humphrey, Richard Russell, and the Struggle for Civil Rights* (New York: Harcourt, 1996), 444, 448; Oates, *Let the Trumpet Sound*, 322.

53. Michael Beschloss, ed., *Reaching for Glory: Lyndon Johnson's Secret White House Tapes, 1964–1965* (New York: Simon and Schuster, 2001), 314; Robert A. Caro, *The Years of Lyndon Johnson: Master of the Senate* (New York: Alfred A. Knopf, 2002), xv; Robert A. Caro, *The Years of Lyndon Johnson: Passage of Power* (New York: Alfred A. Knopf, 2012), 250–62.

54. Hugh Davis Graham, *The Civil Rights Era: Origins and Development of National Policy* (New York: Oxford University Press, 1990), 162; Theodore H. White, *The Making of the President 1964* (New York: Atheneum, 1965), 382; Stern, *Calculating Visions*, 211–12; Kotz, *Judgment Days*, 245.

55. Memorandum to the President, December 28, 1964, 1–2, in *Administrative History of the Civil Rights Division of the Department of Justice During the Johnson Administration, Vol. 17*, Michael R. Belknap, ed. (New York: Routledge, 1992), 169–170; Graham, *The Civil Rights Era*, 163; Garrow, *Protest at Selma*, 37; Steven F. Lawson, *Civil Rights Crossroads: Nation, Community, and the Black Freedom Struggle* (Lexington: Kentucky University Press, 2006), 66.

56. Memorandum to the President, ibid., 2–4, 170–72; Stephen Tuck, "Making the Voting Rights Act," in *The Voting Rights Act: Securing the Ballot*, Richard M. Valelly, ed. (Washington, DC: CQ Press, 2006), 89; Task Force Issue Paper, June 17, 1964, 2, 5, Lee C. White Papers, White House Central Files, LBJ Library; Graham, *The Civil Rights Era*, 163–64.

57. Garrow, *Protest at Selma*, 38–39; Steven F. Lawson, *Black Ballots: Voting Rights in the South, 1944–1969* (New York: Columbia University Press, 1976), 307.

58. Kotz, *Judgment Days*, 234–38, 243–46.

CHAPTER THREE: "GIVE US THE BALLOT!"

1. Ralph David Abernathy, *And the Walls Came Tumbling Down: An Autobiography* (New York: Harper and Row, 1989), 475–78; Taylor Branch, *Pillar of Fire: America in the King Years, 1963–1965* (New York: Simon and Schuster, 1998), 552.

2. For King's relationship with Dr. Sullivan Jackson, see Branch, *Pillar of Fire*, 552–54.

3. *New York Times*, January 3, 1965; Charles E. Fager, *Selma, 1965* (New York: Charles Scribner's Sons, 1974), 9–10; Stephan Oates, *Let the Trumpet Sound: The Life of Martin Luther King, Jr.* (New York: Harper and Row, 1982), 330; Branch, *Pillar of Fire*, 555; Harvard Sitkoff, *King: Pilgrimage to the Mountaintop* (New York: Hill and Wang, 2008), 150; Frye Gaillard, *Alabama's Civil Rights Trail: An Illustrated Guide to the Cradle of Freedom* (Tuscaloosa: University of Alabama Press, 2009), 103. For King's earlier speech entitled "Give Us the Ballot," see David Garrow, "An Unfinished Dream," *Newsweek*, January 21, 2009.

4. Oates, *Let the Trumpet Sound*, 330; Adam Fairclough, *To Redeem the Soul of America: The Southern Christian Leadership Conference and Martin Luther King, Jr.* (Athens: University of Georgia Press, 1987), 229.

5. Bevel is quoted in Fairclough, *To Redeem the Soul of America*, 230.

6. Fager, *Selma, 1965*, 23; Branch, *Pillar of Fire*, 558; David J. Garrow, *Protest at Selma: Martin Luther King, Jr. and the Voting Rights Act of 1965* (New Haven, CT: Yale University Press, 1978), 40.

7. Fager, *Selma, 1965*, 25; Branch, *Pillar of Fire*, 558–59.

8. Quoted in David J. Garrow, *Bearing the Cross: Martin Luther King, Jr., and the Southern Christian Leadership Conference* (New York: W. Morrow, 1986), 373.

9. Garrow, *Bearing the Cross*, 374–75; Andrew Young, *An Easy Burden: The Civil Rights Movement and the Transformation of America* (New York: HarperCollins, 1996), 328–29.

10. Sitkoff, *King*, 150; David J. Garrow, *The FBI and Martin Luther King, Jr.: From "Solo" to Memphis* (New York: W. W. Norton, 1981), 134–35; Abernathy, *And the Walls Came Tumbling Down*, 311; Young, *An Easy Burden*, 329–331.

11. Oates, *Let the Trumpet Sound*, 332.

12. *New York Times*, January 15, 1965; Fager, *Selma, 1965*, 26; Branch, *Pillar of Fire*, 559–60.

13. Michael Beschloss, ed., *Reaching for Glory: Lyndon Johnson's Secret White House Tapes, 1964–1965* (New York: Simon and Schuster, 2001), 159–63; Stephen Tuck, "Making the Voting Rights Act," in *The Voting Rights Act: Securing the Ballot*, Richard M. Valelly, ed. (Washington, DC: CQ Press, 2006), 77–78.

14. Gary May, *The Informant: The FBI, the Ku Klux Klan and the Murder of Viola Liuzzo* (New Haven, CT: Yale University Press, 2005), 68; Fager, *Selma, 1965*, 26; Oates, *Let the Trumpet Sound*, 335.

15. Coretta Scott King, *My Life with Martin Luther King, Jr.* (New York: Henry Holt, 1969), 236; Nick Kotz, *Judgment Days: Lyndon Baines Johnson, Martin Luther King, Jr. and the Laws That Changed America* (Boston: Houghton Mifflin, 2005), 257.

16. *New York Times*, January 19, 1965; Abernathy, *And the Walls Came Tumbling Down*, 314–15; Fager, *Selma, 1965*, 29–30; King, *My Life with Martin Luther King, Jr.*, 236; Fairclough, *To Redeem the Soul of America*, 230; Lewis, *Walking with the Wind*, 320–21.

17. Fager, *Selma, 1965*, 31–32.

18. Boynton is quoted in Frank Sikora, *The Judge: The Life and Opinions of Alabama's Frank M. Johnson, Jr.* (Montgomery, AL: NewSouth, 2007), 203; *New York Times*, January 20, 24, 1965.

19. Amelia Boynton Robinson Interview, Eyes on the Prize, December 6, 1985, Hampton Collection, Film and Radio Archive, Washington University (hereafter cited as Boynton Interview); James G. Clark Interview, Eyes on the Prize, February 19, 1986, Hampton Collection, Film and Radio Archive, Washington University; Frye Gaillard, *Cradle of Freedom: Alabama and the Movement That Changed America* (Tuscaloosa: University of Alabama Press, 2004), 230.

20. Fager, *Selma, 1965*, 34.

21. Fager, *Selma, 1965*, 38–39; Sheyann Webb-Christburg, Rachel West Nelson, and Frank Sikora, *Selma, Lord, Selma: Girlhood Memories of the Civil Rights Days* (Tuscaloosa: University of Alabama Press, 1997), 35.

22. Frederick D. Reese Interview, Eyes on the Prize, December 5, 1985, Hampton Collection, Film and Radio Archive, Washington University (hereafter cited as Reese

Interview); *New York Times*, January 23, February 3, 1965; Fager, *Selma, 1965*, 40; Gaillard, *Cradle of Freedom*, 230–31; J. Mills Thornton III, *Dividing Lines: Municipal Politics and the Struggle for Civil Rights in Montgomery, Birmingham, and Selma* (Tuscaloosa: University of Alabama Press, 2002), 482.

23. *New York Times*, January 26, 1965; Fager, *Selma, 1965*, 61; Garrow, *Protest at Selma*, 44–45.

24. Annie Lee Cooper Statement, Moments in History: Foot Soldiers for the Right to Vote in Alabama, http://www.scribd.com/19047236/Foot-Soldiers-for-the-Right -to-Vote-in-Alabama; Gaillard, *Cradle of Freedom*, 226.

25. Cooper, Statement; *New York Times*, January 26, 1965; Fager, *Selma, 1965*, 44–45; Gaillard, *Cradle of Freedom*, 231–32.

26. *New York Times*, February 2, 3, 1965; Fager, *Selma, 1965*, 47–49.

27. *New York Times*, ibid.

28. *New York Times*, February 5, 1965; Kotz, *Judgment Days*, 267.

29. *New York Times*, February 5, 1965.

30. Quoted in *New York Times*, February 5, 1965.

31. Fairclough, *To Redeem the Soul of America*, 234; Garrow, *Protest at Selma*, 55.

32. Quoted in Garrow, *Protest at Selma*, 52–53.

33. Beschloss, *Reaching for Glory*, 172; Kotz, *Judgment Days*, 269; Lyndon B. Johnson, *The Vantage Point: Perspectives on the Presidency, 1963–1969* (New York: Holt, Rinehart and Winston, 1974), 162.

34. *New York Times*, February 7, 1965; Branch, *Pillar of Fire*, 578–579; Kotz, *Judgment Days*, 270–71; Stewart Burns, *To the Mountaintop: Martin Luther King, Jr.'s Mission to Save America, 1955–1968* (San Francisco: HarperOne, 2003), 269–70; Gaillard, *Cradle of Freedom*, 233.

35. *New York Times*, February 10, 1965; Branch, *Pillar of Fire*, 583–84; Randall B. Woods, *LBJ: Architect of American Ambition* (New York: Free Press, 2006), 580; Robert Dallek, *Flawed Giant: Lyndon Johnson and His Times, 1961–1973* (New York: Oxford University Press, 1998), 214; Fairclough, *To Redeem the Soul of America*, 236; Steven F. Lawson, *Black Ballots: Voting Rights in the South, 1944–1969* (New York: Columbia University Press, 1976), 309.

36. Branch, *Pillar of Fire*, 587; Thornton, *Dividing Lines*, 484.

37. David Halberstam, *The Children* (New York: Fawcett Books, 1998), 500–1; James Bevel Interview, Eyes on the Prize, November 15, 1985, Hampton Collection, Film and Radio Archive, Washington University (hereafter cited as Bevel Interview); Branch, *Pillar of Fire*, 586–88.

38. Quoted in Sikora, *The Judge*, 206–7.

39. Halberstam, *The Children*, 500–1; Bevel Interview; Branch, *Pillar of Fire*, 586–88; Fager, *Selma, 1965*, 66–67; *New York Times*, April 27, 1965.

40. Garrow, *Bearing the Cross*, 388–90; Gaillard, *Cradle of Freedom*, 114, 246–47; May, *The Informant*, 150, 185.

41. *New York Times*, February 13, 1965 (emphasis in original photograph); Fager, *Selma*, 1965, 68–69.

42. Garrow, *Bearing the Cross*, 391; *New York Times*, February 17, 1965; Eyes on the Prize, "Bridge to Freedom" [VHS], 1992; Halberstam, *The Children*, 502; Gaillard, *Cradle of Freedom*, 233–34.

43. Albert Turner Interview, Eyes on the Prize, 1979, Hampton Collection, Film and Radio Archive, Washington University (hereafter cited as Turner Interview); *New York Times*, February 22, 1965; Jack Mendelsohn, *The Martyrs: Sixteen Who Gave Their Lives for Racial Justice* (New York: Harper and Row, 1966), 136–39; Howell Raines, *My Soul Is Rested: The Story of the Civil Rights Movement in the Deep South* (New York: Penguin, 1983), 187–89; John Fleming, "The Death of Jimmie Lee Jackson," *The Anniston Star*, March 6, 2005; Gaillard, *Cradle of Freedom*, 236–37; Dan T. Carter, *The Politics of Rage: George Wallace, the Origins of the New Conservatism, and the Transformation of American Politics* (New York: Simon and Schuster, 1995), 241–42.

44. Observations of SA Alvin Lee King, February 19, 1965, 11, in "Report of Robert L. Frye," March 9, 1965, 44–1226, FBI records in possession of Mr. John Fleming (hereafter cited as Frye Report). I am grateful to Mr. Fleming, who has done extensive reporting on the shooting of Jimmie Lee Jackson, for making these records available to me.

45. Halberstam, *The Children*, 503; Gene Roberts and Hank Klibanoff, *The Race Beat: The Press, the Civil Rights Struggle, and the Awakening of a Nation* (New York: Alfred A. Knopf, 2006), 384; Turner Interview; "Observations of S.A. Archibald Riley," February 18, 1965, Frye Report, 5.

46. Pete Fisher Interview, February 19, 1965, Frye Report, 82.

47. Vera Gooden Statement, February 22, 1965, Frye Report, 138; Edna Langford Statement, February 22, 1965, Frye Report, 137; *New York Times*, February 22, 1965.

48. Pete Fisher Interview; John Lynch Interview, February 19, 1965, Frye Report, 78; Reginald W. Smith Interview, February 21, 1965, Frye Report, 91; Carter, *The Politics of Rage*, 242–43; T. O. Harris Interview, February 22, 1965, Frye Report, 94.

49. Oral History: Richard Valeriani, 4; Civil Rights and the Press Symposium, April 25, 2004, "Killing Jim Crow: The 1964 Civil Rights Act," Syracuse University; John Herbers Interview, February 19, 1965, Frye Report, 76–77; Lynch Interview, 78–79; *New York Times*, February 22, 1965; Raines, *My Soul Is Rested*, 371–72; Carter, *The Politics of Rage*, 243. On Dozier, see "Assaults on News Media," March 8, 1965, Frye Report. On Valeriani's attack, see Richard Gerard Valeriani Interview, February 19, 1965, Frye Report, 80–81; John Herbers Interview, February 19, 1965, Frye Report, 76–77.

50. Quoted in Alvin Adams, "Young Man Tried to Register," *Jet*, March 18, 1965, 18; Mendelsohn, *The Martyrs*, 143.

51. Mendelsohn, *The Martyrs*, 144; Leandrew Benson Statement, March 10, 1965, Frye Report, 5; Dr. W. B. Dinkins Interview, February 20, 1965, Frye Report, 151;

Sister Michael Ann, SJJ, February 20, 1965, Frye Report, 149–50; James Bell Interview, February 22, 1965, Frye Report, 53; Statement of Dr. Arthur F. Wilkerson, March 8, 1965, Frye Report, 41; Statement of Robert Boise Tubbs, March 4, 1965, Frye Report, 30; Statement of Sheriff W. U. Loftis, February 26, 1965, Frye Report, 65; Fleming, "The Death of Jimmie Lee Jackson"; *New York Times*, February 27, 1965; Peter J. Ogniburn, "Jimmie Lee Jackson: The Death That Gave Life to Voting Rights," *Huffington Post*, February 18, 2010.

52. Memorandum for the Attorney General, February 19, 1965, 1–2, FBI Records, 44–17669–161; *New York Times*, February 20, 1965; Branch, *Pillar of Fire*, 593–94.

53. *New York Times*, February 23, 1965.

54. Certificate of Death, Alabama Center for Health Statistics, 3–16–65, Fleming Papers; Dr. William B. Dinkins Interview, February 23, 1965, Frye Report, 66; *New York Times*, February 27, 1965; on Fowler, see *New York Times*, November 15, 2010, and Jon Fleming Interview, November 17, 2010, "Democracy Now," Civil Rights Cold Case Project, http://coldcases.org/blog-author/15.

55. Turner Interview; Bevel Interview; *New York Times*, March 4, 1965; Garrow, *Bearing the Cross*, 394; Roberts and Klibanoff, *The Race Beat*, 384.

56. *New York Times*, February 22, 1965; Halberstam, *The Children*, 503–4; Gaillard, *Cradle of Freedom*, 241; Fairclough, *To Redeem the Soul of America*, 240; Branch, *Pillar of Fire*, 599.

57. *New York Times*, February 27, 1965.

58. Taylor Branch, *At Canaan's Edge: America in the King Years 1965–68* (New York: Simon and Schuster, 2006), 24–25.

59. Fairclough, *To Redeem the Soul of America*; Garrow, *Bearing the Cross*, 396; Branch, *At Canaan's Edge*, 40; Kotz, *Judgment Days*, 54; Andrew B. Lewis, *The Shadows of Youth: The Remarkable Journey of the Civil Rights Generation* (New York: Hill and Wang, 2009), 191.

60. Carter, *The Politics of Rage*, 246–47; Branch, *At Canaan's Edge*, 38–39.

61. Kotz, *Judgment Days*, 279–80.

62. *New York Times*, March 6, 1965; Garrow, *Protest at Selma*, 69; Kotz, *Judgment Days*, 280–81.

63. Young, *An Easy Burden*, 354–55.

64. Branch, *At Canaan's Edge*, 48–49; Lewis, *Walking with the Wind*, 337.

CHAPTER FOUR: NOTHING CAN STOP US

1. Sheyann Webb-Christburg, Rachel West Nelson, and Frank Sikora, *Selma, Lord, Selma: Girlhood Memories of the Civil Rights Days* (Tuscaloosa: University of Alabama Press, 1997), 83–84; Warren Hinckle and David Welsh, "Five Battles of Selma," *Ramparts*, June 1965, reprinted in *We Shall Overcome: The Civil Rights Movement in the United States in the 1950s and 1960s, Vol. II*, David J. Garrow, ed. (Brooklyn: Carlson, 1989), 428.

2. Charles E. Fager, *Selma, 1965* (New York: Charles Scribner's Sons, 1974), 37; David Halberstam, *The Children* (New York: Fawcett Books, 1998), 511; Henry Hampton and Steve Fayer with Sarah Flynn, *Voices of Freedom: An Oral History of the Civil Rights Movement from the 1950s Through the 1980s* (New York: Bantam, 1990), 227.

3. *Williams et al. v. Wallace*, Civil Action No. 2181-N. Vol. II, Lewis Testimony, 296, 300–1, National Archives, Atlanta, GA; *New York Times*, March 8, 1965; Albert Turner Interview, Eyes on the Prize, 1979, Hampton Collection, Film and Radio Archive, Washington University (hereafter cited as Turner Interview); Halberstam, *The Children*, 513; John Lewis with Michael D'Orso, *Walking with the Wind: A Memoir of the Movement* (New York: Harcourt Brace, 1998), 340; David Remnick, *The Bridge: The Life and Rise of Barack Obama* (New York: Alfred A. Knopf, 2010), 9–11; Amelia Platts Boynton Robinson, *Bridge Across Jordan* (Washington, DC: Schiller Institute, 1991), 255–56; Frye Gaillard, *Cradle of Freedom: Alabama and the Movement That Changed America* (Tuscaloosa: University of Alabama Press, 2004), 243; John Dittmer, *The Good Doctors: The Medical Community for Human Rights and the Struggle for Social Justice in Health Care* (New York: Bloomsbury Press, 2010), 89; Hinckle and Welsh, "Five Battles of Selma," 428–29.

4. Hinckle and Welsh, "Five Battles of Selma," 429; *New York Times*, March 8, 1965; Webb-Christburg, Nelson, and Sikora, *Selma, Lord, Selma*, 96; Howell Raines, *My Soul Is Rested: The Story of the Civil Rights Movement in the Deep South* (New York: Penguin, 1983), 385; J. Mills Thornton III, *Dividing Lines: Municipal Politics and the Struggle for Civil Rights in Montgomery, Birmingham, and Selma* (Tuscaloosa: University of Alabama Press, 2002), 488.

5. *Williams et al. v. Wallace*, 299; Hinckle and Welsh, "Five Battles of Selma," 430; Fager, *Selma, 1965*, 95.

6. Charles Bonner Interview, Veterans of the Civil Rights Movement, 2005, http://www.crmvet.org/nars/chuckbet.htm (hereafter cited as Bonner Interview).

7. *Williams et al. v. Wallace*, 300–1; Dittmer, *The Good Doctors*, 89; Gaillard, *Cradle of Freedom*, 243; Lewis, *Walking with the Wind*, 342.

8. Andrew Young Interview, Eyes on the Prize, October 11, 1985, Hampton Collection, Film and Radio Archive, Washington University (hereafter cited as Young Interview); Gaillard, *Cradle of Freedom*, 249.

9. Andrew Young, *An Easy Burden: The Civil Rights Movement and the Transformation of America* (New York: HarperCollins, 1996), 357; Taylor Branch, *At Canaan's Edge: America in the King Years 1965–68* (New York: Simon and Schuster, 2006), 57.

10. *New York Times*, March 8, 1965; Lewis, *Walking with the Wind*, 333–34; Remnick, *The Bridge*, 11.

11. Roy Reed Interview with T. Harri Baker, July 7, 2000, *Arkansas Gazette* Project, Pryor Center, University of Arkansas, 7 (hereafter cited as Reed Interview); Roger Mudd, *The Place to Be: Washington, CBS, and the Glory Days of Television News* (New York: PublicAffairs, 2008), 282; Gene Roberts and Hank Klibanoff, *The Race Beat: The*

Press, the Civil Rights Struggle, and the Awakening of a Nation (New York: Alfred A. Knopf, 2006), 377–78; Raines, *My Soul Is Rested*, 386. For Pierce's career, see Reese Schonfeld, "The Unsung Heroes of TV News," *Channels*, 1983, 58–60.

12. Dan T. Carter, *The Politics of Rage: George Wallace, the Origins of the New Conservatism, and the Transformation of American Politics* (New York: Simon and Schuster, 1995), 248; Mudd, *The Place to Be*, 282; Branch, *At Canaan's Edge*, 55–56.

13. Reed Interview, 26.

14. George B. Leonard, "Midnight Plane to Alabama," in *Reporting Civil Rights Part Two: American Journalism 1963–1973*, Clayborne Carson, ed. (New York: Penguin Putnam, 2003), 329. See also David J. Garrow, *Protest at Selma: Martin Luther King, Jr. and the Voting Rights Act of 1965* (New Haven, CT: Yale University Press, 1978), 84–85.

15. Leonard, "Midnight Plane to Alabama," 329; Roberts and Klibanoff, *The Race Beat*, 388; Branch, *At Canaan's Edge*, 56.

16. Leonard, "Midnight Plane to Alabama," 329, 331; *New York Times*, March 9, 1965; Branch, *At Canaan's Edge*, 60.

17. A. J. Decker to William C. Sullivan, March 10, 1965, 1–2, FBI File 157-6-61-792; *New York Times*, March 15, 1965.

18. *New York Times*, March 9, 1965; Nicholas deB Katzenbach, *Some of It Was Fun: Working with RFK and LBJ* (New York: W. W. Norton, 2008), 165; Fager, *Selma, 1965*, 99–100; Johnson is quoted in Michael Beschloss, ed., *Reaching for Glory: Lyndon Johnson's Secret White House Tapes, 1964–1965* (New York: Simon and Schuster, 2001), 222–23.

19. Hinckle and Welsh, "Five Battles of Selma," 51; Richard B. Stolley, "The Nation Joins the Negros' March," *Life*, March 26, 1965, 35; Wilkins is quoted in *LBJ: The American Experience* [VHS], 1999.

20. Robert Mann, *The Walls of Jericho: Lyndon Johnson, Hubert Humphrey, Richard Russell, and the Struggle for Civil Rights* (New York: Harcourt, 1996), 65; Michael Belknap, *Civil Rights, The White House and the Justice Department, 1945–1968* (New York: Garland, 1991), 17; "Constitutional Amendment, Draft 1/8/65," in *Administrative History of the Civil Rights Division of the Department of Justice During the Johnson Administration, Vol. 17*, Michael R. Belknap, ed. (New York: Routledge, 1992), 224–25; "An Act," in Belknap, *Administrative History of the Civil Rights Division*, 173–211; James L. Morison to Norbert Schlei, February 15, 1965, in Belknap, *Administrative History of the Civil Rights Division*, 226; Horace Busby to Bill Moyers, February 27, 1965, 1–4, Bill Moyers Files, Voting Rights Act of 1965, White House Central Files, LBJ Library; Nicholas Katzenbach to Honorable Bill D. Moyers, March 1, 1965, 1–2, Bill Moyers Files, Voting Rights Act of 1965, White House Central Files, LBJ Library.

21. Byron Hulsey, "Everett Dirksen: Master Legislator," The Dirksen Congressional Center, http://www.dirksencenter.org/print_emd_masterlegislator.htm; Nick Kotz, *Judgment Days: Lyndon Baines Johnson, Martin Luther King, Jr. and the Laws That*

Changed America (Boston: Houghton Mifflin, 2005), 115, 328; Neil MacNeil, *Dirksen: Portrait of a Public Man* (New York: World Publishing, 1970), 252; Charles W. Whalen and Barbara Whalen, *The Longest Debate: A Legislative History of the 1964 Civil Rights Act* (Washington, DC: Seven Locks, 1985), 153; *Time*, September 14, 1962, June 19, 1964.

22. Hulsey, "Everett Dirksen"; "A Conversation with Doris Kearns Goodwin," *The American Prospect*, December 19, 2007; Michael Beschloss, *Taking Charge: The Johnson White House Tapes, 1963–1964* (New York, Simon and Schuster, 1998), 109–10.

23. Beschloss, *Taking Charge*, 436; MacNeil, *Dirksen*, 253; Garrow, *Protest at Selma*, 63; Steven F. Lawson, *Black Ballots: Voting Rights in the South, 1944–1969* (New York: Columbia University Press, 1976), 309; Samuel Shaffer, *On and Off the Floor: Thirty Years as a Correspondent on Capitol Hill* (New York: Newsweek Books, 1980), 101–2; Byron C. Hulsey, *Everett Dirksen and His Presidents* (Lawrence: University of Kansas Press, 2000), 211; *Time*, September 14, 1962; *New York Times*, May 11, 1965.

24. Paula D. McClain, Michael C. Brady, Niambi M. Carter, Efren O. Perez, and Victoria M. DeFrancesco Soto, "Rebuilding Black Voting Rights Before the Voting Rights Act," in *The Voting Rights Act: Securing the Ballot*, Richard M. Valelly, ed. (Washington, DC: CQ Press, 2006), 69; Stephen Tuck, "Making the Voting Rights Act," in Valelly, *The Voting Rights Act*, 79; Brian K. Landsberg, *Free at Last to Vote: The Alabama Origins of the Voting Rights Act* (Lawrence: University of Kansas Press, 2007), 133; *Time*, March 26, 1965; Lawson, *Black Ballots*, 299; Mann, *The Walls of Jericho*, 245; Stephan Thernstrom and Abigail M. Thernstrom, *America in Black and White: One Nation Indivisible* (New York: Simon and Schuster, 1997), 117–18.

25. Tuck, "Making the Voting Rights Act," 90; Mark Stein, *Calculating Visions: Kennedy, Johnson and Civil Rights* (New Brunswick, NJ: Rutgers University Press, 1992), 223; Lawson, *Black Ballots*, 312–14; Landsberg, *Free at Last to Vote*, 109.

26. Stephan J. Pollak Interview with Thomas H. Baker, Part III, January 30, 1969, 6–8, LBJ Library (hereafter cited as Pollak Interview); Mann, *The Walls of Jericho*, 469; Eric F. Goldman, *The Tragedy of Lyndon Johnson* (New York: Alfred A. Knopf, 1969), 326.

27. MacNeil, *Dirksen*, 254; Hulsey, *Everett Dirksen and His Presidents*, 212; Pollak Interview; "Voting Rights Act of 1965," Congress Link, The Dirksen Congressional Center, http://www.congresslink.org/print_basics_histmats_votingrights_contents .htm; *New York Times*, March 18, 1965.

28. MacNeil, *Dirksen*, 168; Hulsey, *Everett Dirksen and His Presidents*, 148, 215.

29. Adam Fairclough, *To Redeem the Soul of America: The Southern Christian Leadership Conference and Martin Luther King, Jr.* (Athens: University of Georgia Press, 1987), 243–44; David J. Garrow, *Bearing the Cross: Martin Luther King, Jr., and the Southern Christian Leadership Conference* (New York: W. Morrow, 1986), 400–1.

30. *New York Times*, March 9, 1965; Fairclough, *To Redeem the Soul of America*, 244; Stephan Oates, *Let the Trumpet Sound: The Life of Martin Luther King, Jr.* (New York: Harper and Row, 1982), 350; Branch, *At Canaan's Edge*, 73.

31. Beschloss, *Reaching for Glory*, 219, 223.

32. Garrow, *Bearing the Cross*, 402–3; Branch, *At Canaan's Edge*, 68–69; Martin A. Dyckman, *Floridian of His Century: The Courage of Governor LeRoy Collins* (Gainesville: University Press of Florida, 2006), 229–30.

33. Gay Talese, "The Walk Through Selma," *New York Times*, March 10, 1965; "Turn-Around Tuesday," Oral History, Civil Rights Veterans Movement, http://www .crmvet.org/nars/bruce1.htm#bhtues; Fager, *Selma, 1965*, 102–3; Andrew Kopkind, "Selma: 'Ain't Gonna Let Nobody Turn Me Round,'" in Carson, *Reporting Civil Rights Part Two*, 341.

34. Dyckman, *Floridian of His Century*, 230; Fager, *Selma, 1965*, 103; Steven Mc-Nichols, e-mail, August 19, 2007, in Oral History, Veterans of the Civil Rights Movement, http://www.crmvet.org/disc/selma.htm#ala65turnaround (hereafter cited as McNichols e-mail); *New York Times*, March 12, 1965; *Time*, March 19, 1965.

35. Talese, "The Walk Through Selma"; Branch, *At Canaan's Edge*, 75; Ralph David Abernathy, *And the Walls Came Tumbling Down: An Autobiography* (New York: Harper and Row, 1989), 340.

36. *New York Times*, March 10, March 14, 1965; Talese, "The Walk Through Selma"; McNichols e-mail; Young, *An Easy Burden*, 360–61; Oates, *Let the Trumpet Sound*, 351–52; Abernathy, *And the Walls Came Tumbling Down*, 342; Branch, *At Canaan's Edge*, 76–78; *Time*, March 19, 1965.

37. Talese, "The Walk Through Selma"; McNichols e-mail. Frye is quoted in "Turn-Around Tuesday," Oral History, Veterans of the Civil Rights Movement, http://www .crmvet.org/disc/selma.htm#ala65turnaround; Orloff Miller Interview, Eyes on the Prize, November 18, 1985, Hampton Collection, Film and Radio Archive, Washington University (hereafter cited as Miller Interview); Garrow, *Bearing the Cross*, 405.

38. Kopkind, "Selma," 343; Andrew B. Lewis, *The Shadows of Youth: The Remarkable Journey of the Civil Rights Generation* (New York: Hill and Wang, 2009), 195.

39. *Jet,* March 25, 1965; *New York Times*, March 11, 1965; Miller Interview; Jack Mendelsohn, *The Martyrs: Sixteen Who Gave Their Lives for Racial Justice* (New York: Harper and Row, 1966), 168–69; Oates, *Let the Trumpet Sound*, 353.

40. *New York Times*, ibid; Mendelsohn, *The Martyrs*, 170–71.

41. Quoted in Hinckle and Welsh, "Five Battles of Selma," 48.

42. *New York Times*, March 12, March 14, 1965; *Time*, March 19, 1965; Jack Greenberg, *Crusaders in the Courts: How a Dedicated Band of Lawyers Fought for the Civil Rights Revolution* (New York: Basic Books, 1995), 358–60; Jack Bass, *Taming the Storm: The Life and Times of Judge Frank M. Johnson, Jr. and the South's Fight Over Civil Rights* (New York: Anchor Books, 2003), 241–42.

43. *New York Times*, ibid; Richard B. Stolley, "Inside the White House: Pressures Build Up to the Momentous Speech," *Life*, March 26, 1965, 34–35.

44. White House Daily Diary, March 11, 1965, 1, LBJ Library; *New York Times*, March 12, 1965; Lady Bird Johnson, *A White House Diary* (New York: Holt, Rinehart and Winston, 1970), 250; Goldman, *The Tragedy of Lyndon Johnson*, 312.

45. White House Daily Diary, ibid., 4; *New York Times*, March 14, 1965; Kotz, *Judgment Days*, 301.

46. White House Diary, ibid., 4; Kotz, *Judgment Days*, 301; Garrow, *Protest at Selma*, 93; Branch, *At Canaan's Edge*, 89; *New York Times*, March 14, 1965.

47. Branch, *At Canaan's Edge*, 89; Johnson, *A White House Diary*, 251; Garrow, *Protest at Selma*, 97.

48. Carter, *The Politics of Rage*, 250–51; Branch, *At Canaan's Edge*, 90.

49. *New York Times*, March 12, 1965.

50. Brown is quoted in H. Rap Brown, *Die Nigger Die!: A Political Autobiography* (New York: Lawrence Hill, 1969, 2002), 51–53, and in Hinckle and Welsh, "Five Battles of Selma," 51; *Time*, October 25, 1971.

51. *New York Times*, March 12, 1965; Stolley, "Inside the White House," 34.

52. *New York Times*, ibid., March 14, 1965; Stolley, "Inside the White House," 34–35.

53. Lady Bird Johnson is quoted in Beschloss, *Reaching for Glory*, 227. Johnson is quoted in Beschloss, *Reaching for Glory*, 226–27.

54. For Johnson's efforts to reach Wallace, see Beschloss, *Reaching for Glory*, 217–21, and Alice Anne Stephens, "The President, the Wildcard, and the Link: President Johnson, Governor Wallace, and Buford Ellington in Selma, Alabama," 1–9, Presidential Recording Program, Miller Center of Public Affairs, University of Virginia, http://whitehousetapes.net/print/264.

55. For the Johnson-Wallace conversation, see Carter, *The Politics of Rage*, 252–54; Stephen Lesher, *George Wallace: American Populist* (New York: Addison Wesley, 1994), 330–33; Branch, *At Canaan's Edge*, 95–98; Katzenbach is quoted in *LBJ: The American Experience* [VHS], 1999. See also Katzenbach, *Some of It Was Fun*, 166–67.

56. Kotz, *Judgment Days*, 306; *Time*, March 19, 1965.

57. *New York Times*, March 14, 1965; *Time*, ibid.; *Daily Diary*, March 13, 1965; Carter, *The Politics of Rage*, 254; Lesher, *George Wallace*, 333.

58. Kotz, *Judgment Days*, 306–8, 314; Stolley, "Inside the White House"; *Life*, March 26, 1965, 35; Beschloss, *Reaching for Glory*, 227–28; White House Daily Diary, March 13, 1965, 5–6, LBJ Library.

59. Johnson, *A White House Diary*, 163–64; Randall B. Woods, *LBJ: Architect of American Ambition* (New York: Free Press, 2006), 582–83; Kotz, *Judgment Days*, 299.

60. Beschloss, *Reaching for Glory*, 226; Garth E. Pauley, *LBJ's American Promise: The 1965 Voting Rights Address* (College Station: Texas A&M University Press, 2006), 95.

61. Richard N. Goodwin, *Remembering America: A Voice From the Sixties* (New York: Harper and Row, 1989), 326–28; Robert Schlesinger, *White House Ghosts: Presidents and Their Speechwriters from FDR to George W. Bush* (New York: Simon and Schuster, 2008), 117–18, 150, 151–52, 158–59; Kotz, *Judgment Days*, 313.

62. Goodwin, *Remembering America*, 13–16.

63. Johnson, *A White House Diary*, 252; Branch, *At Canaan's Edge*, 110–11; Carl T. Rowan, *Breaking Barriers: A Memoir* (Boston: Little, Brown, 1991), 249.

64. Robert A. Caro, *The Years of Lyndon Johnson: Means of Ascent* (New York: Alfred A. Knopf, 1991), xix; Rowan, *Breaking Barriers*, 249.

65. Goodwin, *Remembering America*, 336; Shaffer, *On and Off the Floor*, 100.

66. Shaffer, *On and Off the Floor*, 99–100.

67. *New York Times*, ibid.; *Life*, March 26, 1965, 34.

68. Branch, *At Canaan's Edge*, 114–15; Kotz, *Judgment Days*, 312; *Time*, March 26, 1965. For King's response, see *New York Times*, March 17, 1965; Katzenbach, *Some of It Was Fun*, 168.

69. Robert Caro, "When LBJ Said, 'We Shall Overcome,'" *New York Times*, August 28, 2008; Shaffer, *On and Off the Floor*, 100.

70. *Time*, March 26, 1965. Johnson's speech "An American Promise" is available online at the LBJ Library at http://www.lbjlibrary.org/about-lbj/voting-rights-speech .html. For Lady Bird Johnson's comment, see Johnson, *A White House Diary*, 253.

CHAPTER FIVE: TO THE PROMISED LAND

1. J. L. Chestnut Jr. and Julia Cass, *Black in Selma: The Uncommon Life of J. L. Chestnut* (Tuscaloosa, AL: Fire Ant Books, 1990), 212; Frye Gaillard, *Cradle of Freedom: Alabama and the Movement That Changed America* (Tuscaloosa: University of Alabama Press, 2004), 256.

2. *New York Times*, March 17, 1965; Gaillard, *Cradle of Freedom*, 257.

3. *New York Times*, March 17, March 18, 1965; Gaillard, *Cradle of Freedom*, 257–58. For photographs of the Montgomery assault, see Michael S. Durham, *Powerful Days: The Civil Rights Photography of Charles Moore* (Tuscaloosa: University of Alabama Press, 1991), 168–77.

4. Mobile (Selma) to Director, March 18, 1965, 5–6, FBI File 44–12831–656, FBI; *New York Times*, March 18, 20, 1965.

5. The conversation is quoted in Frank Sikora, *The Judge: The Life and Opinions of Alabama's Frank M. Johnson, Jr.* (Montgomery, AL: NewSouth, 2007), 222–23. See also Taylor Branch, *At Canaan's Edge: America in the King Years 1965–68* (New York: Simon and Schuster, 2006), 122.

6. Sikora, *The Judge*, 203–18; John Lewis with Michael D'Orso, *Walking with the Wind: A Memoir of the Movement* (New York: Harcourt Brace, 1998), 351; Jack Bass, *Taming the Storm: The Life and Times of Judge Frank M. Johnson, Jr. and the South's Fight Over Civil Rights* (New York: Anchor Books, 2003), 248.

7. Bass, *Taming the Storm*, 248–49; Sikora, *The Judge*, 223, 228. For the plan of the march, see *New York Times*, March 17, 1965.

8. *New York Times*, March 18, 1965; Bass, *Taming the Storm*, 249–52; Dan T. Carter, *The Politics of Rage: George Wallace, the Origins of the New Conservatism, and the Transformation of American Politics* (New York: Simon and Schuster, 1995), 255; Sikora, *The Judge*, 223–25.

9. Lewis, *Walking with the Wind*, 354–55; David J. Garrow, *Bearing the Cross: Martin Luther King, Jr. and the Southern Christian Leadership Conference* (New York: W. Morrow, 1986), 409; Gaillard, *Cradle of Freedom*, 248–49.

10. *New York Times*, March 22, 1965; Adam Fairclough, *To Redeem the Soul of America: The Southern Christian Leadership Conference and Martin Luther King, Jr.* (Athens: University of Georgia Press, 1987), 249; Garrow, *Bearing the Cross*, 410.

11. The Wallace-Johnson conversation is in Michael Beschloss, ed., *Reaching for Glory: Lyndon Johnson's Secret White House Tapes, 1964–1965* (New York: Simon and Schuster, 2001), 231–35, LBJ is quoted on 235.

12. Wallace is quoted in *Birmingham News*, March 21, 1965, FBI File 44–28541A; *New York Times*, March 19, March 22, 1965; Carter, *The Politics of Rage*, 255–56.

13. Randall B. Woods, *LBJ: Architect of American Ambition* (New York: Free Press, 2006), 584–85; *Washington Daily News*, March 20, 1965, FBI File 44–28544-A.

14. *New York Times*, March 22, 1965; Stephan Oates, *Let the Trumpet Sound: The Life of Martin Luther King, Jr.* (New York: Harper and Row, 1982), 356.

15. Quoted in Renata Adler, "Letter from Selma," in *Reporting Civil Rights Part Two: American Journalism 1963–1973*, Clayborne Carson, ed. (New York: Penguin Putnam, 2003), 368–69. For a partial list of the marchers, see *New York Times*, March 22, 23, 1965. Letherer is quoted in Simeon Booker, "50,000 March on Montgomery," *Ebony*, May 1965, 58. Lee is quoted in Paul Good, "It Was Worth the Boy's Dying," in Carson, *Reporting Civil Rights Part Two*, 353; on Liuzzo, see Gary May, *The Informant: The FBI, the Ku Klux Klan and the Murder of Viola Liuzzo* (New Haven, CT: Yale University Press, 2005), 138–41.

16. Sheyann Webb Interview, Eyes on the Prize, December 6, 1985, Hampton Collection, Film and Radio Archive, Washington University (hereafter cited as Webb Interview); Sheyann Webb-Christburg, Rachel West Nelson, and Frank Sikora, *Selma, Lord, Selma: Girlhood Memories of the Civil Rights Days* (Tuscaloosa: University of Alabama Press, 1997), 96–98; Howell Raines, *My Soul Is Rested: The Story of the Civil Rights Movement in the Deep South* (New York: Penguin, 1983), 204.

17. Webb-Christburg, Nelson, and Sikora, *Selma, Lord, Selma*, 95–98.

18. King is quoted in *New York Times*, March 22, 1965; *New York Times*, March 22, 1970; Adler, "Letter from Selma," 370; Webb-Christburg, Nelson, and Sikora, *Selma, Lord, Selma*, 124.

19. Adler, "Letter from Selma," 370–71; *New York Times*, March 22, 1965; *Birmingham Post-Herald*, March 22, 1965, FBI File 44–28544-A; Memo by SA M. A. Alexander, November 24, 1965, FBI File BH 44–1236–751 2A; Report by M. L. Alexander, November 24, 1965, FBI File BH 44–1236–751; Ralph David Abernathy, *And the Walls Came Tumbling Down: An Autobiography* (New York: Harper and Row, 1989), 352.

20. Elizabeth Partridge, *Marching for Freedom: Walk Together Children and Don't You Grow Weary* (New York: Viking, 2009), 38; Good, "It Was Worth the Boy's Dying," 354.

21. Adler, "Letter from Selma," 371; *New York Times*, March 22, 1965; *Birmingham Post-Herald*, March 22, 1965, *Washington Daily News*, March 22, 1965, both in FBI File 44–28544-A; SAC, Birmingham to Director, SAC Selma, March 20, 1965, 1–2, FBI File 157–920–8; Webb-Christburg, Nelson, and Sikora, *Selma, Lord, Selma*, 125–25; Partridge, *Marching for Freedom*, 28.

22. *New York Times*, March 23, 1965; Booker, "50,000 March on Montgomery," 75; Lewis, *Walking with the Wind*, 358.

23. Webb Interview; Webb-Christburg, Nelson, and Sikora, *Selma, Lord, Selma*, 125–26.

24. *Washington Evening Star*, March 22, 1965, FBI File 44–28544-A; *New York Times*, March 23, 1965; Charles E. Fager, *Selma, 1965* (New York: Charles Scribner's Sons, 1974), 152–53; Adler, "Letter from Selma," 371–74, 384. Lewis is quoted in Harris Wofford, *Of Kennedys and Kings: Making Sense of the Sixties* (New York: Farrar, Strauss and Giroux, 1980), 194.

25. Adler, "Letter from Selma," 372; Abernathy, *And the Walls Came Tumbling Down*, 353; Partridge, *Marching for Freedom*, 40–41.

26. Adler, "Letter from Selma," 373; *New York Times*, March 23, 1965; *Washington Post*, March 23, 1965.

27. *Washington Post*, ibid; Adler, "Letter from Selma."

28. *Washington Post*, March 23, 1965; Adler, "Letter from Selma," 382; Oates, *Let the Trumpet Sound*, 360–61.

29. Oates, *Let the Trumpet Sound*, 359; Branch, *At Canaan's Edge*, 147–48.

30. Gaillard, *Cradle of Freedom*, 261–62.

31. For King's speech, see *New York Times*, March 24, l965; Fager, *Selma, 1965*, 155; UPI-33, March 24, 1965, FBI File 44–28544-A; Oates, *Let the Trumpet Sound*, 361.

32. Bruce Hartford, Veterans of the Civil Rights Movement, 3–4, http://www.crmvet.org/nars/bruce1.htm; *New York Times*, March 24, 1965.

33. *New York Times*, March 24, 1965; Howard Zinn, *Howard Zinn on Race* (New York: Seven Stories, 2011), 121; Fager, *Selma, 1965*, 157–58.

34. Branch, *At Canaan's Edge*, 153; Oates, *Let the Trumpet Sound*, 361.

35. *New York Times*, March 24, 1965; Hartford, Veterans of Civil Rights Movement, 4, http://www.crmvet.org/nars/bruce1.htm.

36. UP-12, March 25, 1965, in FBI File 44–28544-A; *New York Times*, March 25, 1965; Oates, *Let the Trumpet Sound*, 362.

37. Andrew Young, *An Easy Burden: The Civil Rights Movement and the Transformation of America* (New York: HarperCollins, 1996), 366.

38. Jimmy Breslin, "Changing the South," in Carson, *Reporting Civil Rights Part Two*, 362–63.

39. *New York Times*, March 25, 1965; Gaillard, *Cradle of Freedom*, 263; Adler, "Letter from Selma," 37, 40, 391, 393.

40. Burns, *To the Mountaintop*, 281; Marshall Frady, *Martin Luther King, Jr.: A Life* (New York: Penguin, 2005), 163–64; Wofford, *Of Kennedys and Kings*, 199–200; Oates, *Let the Trumpet Sound*, 363–64; Branch, *At Canaan's Edge*, 38.

41. Partridge, *Marching for Freedom*, 53; Webb-Christburg, Nelson, and Sikora, *Selma, Lord, Selma*, 126–27; Gaillard, *Cradle of Freedom*, 263.

42. *New York Times*, March 26, 1965.

43. Adler, "Letter from Selma," 394; Amelia Platts Boynton Robinson, *Bridge Across Jordan* (Washington, DC: Schiller Institute, 1991), 270–71.

44. Beschloss, *Reaching for Glory*, 242; Young, *An Easy Burden*, 367–68.

45. Douglas Linder, "Bending Toward Justice: John Doar and the Mississippi Burning Trial," *Mississippi Law Journal* 9 (2002–2003), 72.

46. May, *The Informant*, 146–47.

47. Ibid., 148–49, 154–55, 162, 166, 171, 172.

48. On Rowe's career, see ibid., 1–124.

49. Hoover is quoted in ibid., 169.

50. Murphy is quoted in ibid., 190. For the trials of the Klansmen, see ibid., 184–272.

51. Ibid., 175–80.

52. Truman is quoted in *New York Times*, March 21, 1965; Adler, "Letter from Selma," 367–68.

53. Branch, *At Canaan's Edge*, 183–84.

CHAPTER SIX: THE DIE IS CAST

1. Samuel Shaffer, *On and Off the Floor: Thirty Years as a Correspondent on Capitol Hill* (New York: Newsweek Books, 1980), 100–1; Merle Miller, *Lyndon: An Oral Biography* (New York: Putnam, 1980), 434; *New York Times*, March 18, March 19, 1965.

2. Eric F. Goldman, *The Tragedy of Lyndon Johnson* (New York: Alfred A. Knopf, 1969), 323; David J. Garrow, *Protest at Selma: Martin Luther King, Jr. and the Voting Rights Act of 1965* (New Haven, CT: Yale University Press, 1978), 36; Robert Mann, *The Walls of Jericho: Lyndon Johnson, Hubert Humphrey, Richard Russell, and the Struggle for Civil Right* (New York: Harcourt, 1996), 448; Mark Stern, *Calculating Visions: Kennedy, Johnson and Civil Rights* (New Brunswick, NJ: Rutgers University Press, 1992), 216–17.

3. Talmadge and Thurmond are quoted in Bernard Grofman and Chandler Davidson, eds., *Controversies in Minority Voting: The Voting Rights Act in Perspective* (Washington, DC: Brookings Institution, 1992), 18. See also *New York Times*, March 17, 1965.

4. *New York Times*, March 19, 1965; Neil MacNeil, *Dirksen: Portrait of a Public Man* (New York: World Publishing, 1970), 254; Mann, *The Walls of Jericho*, 466; Goldman, *The Tragedy of Lyndon Johnson*, 325.

5. Keith M. Finley, *Delaying the Dream: Southern Senators and the Fight Against Civil Rights, 1938–1965* (Baton Rouge: Louisiana State University Press, 2008), 41–49, 90; Robert A. Caro, *The Years of Lyndon Johnson: Master of the Senate* (New York: Alfred A. Knopf, 2003), 164–202; Mann, *The Walls of Jericho*,193, 464–66; Stephen Tuck, "Making the Voting Rights Act," in *The Voting Rights Act: Securing the Ballot*, Richard M. Valelly, ed. (Washington, DC: CQ Press, 2006), 89; *New York Times*, May 21, 22, 1965. For the campaign to pass the 1964 Civil Rights Act, see Charles W. Whalen and Barbara Whalen, *The Longest Debate: A Legislative History of the 1964 Civil Rights Act* (Washington, DC: Seven Locks, 1985), and Mann, *The Walls of Jericho*.

6. Finley, *Delaying the Dream*, 286–90, 294; Mann, *The Walls of Jericho*, 466–67.

7. *New York Times*, April 9, 1965; Tuck, "Making the Voting Rights Act," 88–89; Mann, *The Walls of Jericho*, 465; Steven F. Lawson, *Black Ballots: Voting Rights in the South, 1944–1969* (New York: Columbia University Press, 1976), 421n96; Nick Kotz, *Judgment Days: Lyndon Baines Johnson, Martin Luther King, Jr. and the Laws That Changed America* (Boston: Houghton Mifflin, 2005), 314.

8. Adam Clymer, *Edward M. Kennedy: A Biography* (New York: William Morrow, 1999), 65–66; Goldman, *The Tragedy of Lyndon Johnson*, 325–26; Tuck, "Making the Voting Rights Act," 90; *New York Times*, April 5, 1965.

9. *New York Times*, March 24, 25, 1965; Mann, *The Walls of Jericho*, 468.

10. *New York Times*, April 9, 1965; Goldman, *The Tragedy of Lyndon Johnson*, 326; Michael Beschloss, ed., *Reaching for Glory: Lyndon Johnson's Secret White House Tapes, 1964–1965* (New York: Simon and Schuster, 2001), 267.

11. Nicholas deB Katzenbach, *Some of It Was Fun: Working with RFK and LBJ* (New York: W. W. Norton, 2008), 171–72. Katzenbach's 2008 memoir published forty-three years after the events it describes is often incorrect. He states that the bill was reported out of the Committee just as it had been submitted, which was clearly not the case. MacNeil, *Dirksen*, 255–56. For executive session meetings of the Senate Judiciary Committee, see "Report of Proceedings Meeting Held before Committee on Judiciary S.1564 to Enforce the Fifteenth Amendment to the Constitution of the United States," 4 vols., April 7–9, 1965.

12. Edward L. Schapsmeier and Frederick H. Schapsmeier, *Dirksen of Illinois: Senatorial Statesman* (Urbana: University of Illinois Press, 1985), 183; MacNeil, *Dirksen*, 306–7.

13. "Voting Rights: The Consent of the Governed," Notebooks, f.162, Everett McKinley Dirksen Papers, The Dirksen Congressional Center; *New York Times*, April 23, 1965.

14. Mann, *The Walls of Jericho*, 472.

15. *New York Times*, March 29, April 23, 1965; Karl E. Campbell, *Senator Sam Ervin: Last of the Founding Fathers* (Chapel Hill: University of North Carolina Press, 2007), 148; Lawson, *Black Ballots*, 317. Javits is quoted in Lawson, *Black Ballots*, 318.

16. *New York Times*, ibid; Mann, *The Walls of Jericho*, 471; Lawson, *Black Ballots*, 317; *Time*, March 8, 1971; *Washington Post*, April 24, 1985.

17. Campbell, *Senator Sam Ervin*, 148; *New York Times*, May 7, 1965; Garrow, *Protest at Selma*, 125; Mann, *The Walls of Jericho*, 471–72. See also Sam J. Ervin Jr., *Preserving the Constitution: The Autobiography of Senator Sam Ervin* (Charlottesville, VA: The Michie Company, 1984), 170.

18. Taylor Branch, *At Canaan's Edge: America in the King Years 1965–68* (New York: Simon and Schuster, 2006), 253.

19. *New York Times*, April 25, 27, 29, 1965.

20. *New York Times*, April 30, May 2, 1965.

21. *New York Times*, May 4, 5, 10, 1965.

22. *New York Times*, May 4, 5, 9, 10, 1965; Arthur Krock, "In the Nation," *New York Times*, May 11, 1965; Beschloss, *Reaching for Glory*, 313.

23. Edward M. Kennedy, *True Compass: A Memoir* (New York: Twelve-Hachette, 2009), 232; *New York Times*, May 5, 10, 13, 15, 16, 1965; *Time*, May 7, 21, 1965; Clymer, *Edward M. Kennedy*, 65; MacNeil, *Dirksen*, 256; Katzenbach, *Some of It Was Fun*, 173.

24. *Time*, May 21, 1965.

25. *Time*, May 10, 21, 1965; *New York Times*, May 12, 1965; Clymer, *Edward M. Kennedy*, 66–67.

26. *New York Times*, May 16, 17, 20, 1965; Mann, *The Walls of Jericho*, 472–73.

27. *New York Times*, May 21, 1965; Jeff Shesol, *Mutual Contempt: Lyndon Johnson, Robert Kennedy, and the Feud That Defined a Decade* (New York: W. W. Norton, 1997), 238.

28. Mann, *The Walls of Jericho*, 473; *New York Times*, May 26, 1965; *Time*, June 4, 1965.

29. *New York Times*, May 5, 15, 22, 24, 1965; Mann, *The Walls of Jericho*, 473; Goldman, *The Tragedy of Lyndon Johnson*, 328.

30. MacNeil, *Dirksen*, 257–58.

31. "Voting Rights Act of 1965," The Dirksen Congressional Center; *New York Times*, May 22, 24, 1965; *Time*, June 4, 1965; MacNeil, *Dirksen*, 259; Goldman, *The Tragedy of Lyndon Johnson*, 328.

32. *New York Times*, May 26, 1965; "Revolution in Civil Rights," 80, *Congressional Quarterly Service*, 3rd ed. (Washington, DC: 1967); Garrow, *Protest at Selma*, 126; Lawson, *Black Ballots*, 318.

33. *New York Times*, May 27, 1965; Mann, *The Walls of Jericho*, 473–74; Garrow, *Protest at Selma*, 283n58; Stern, *Calculating Visions*, 227.

34. For those who testified, see Voting Rights: Hearings Before Subcommittee No. 5 of the Committee on the Judiciary House of Representatives Eighty-Ninth Congress, First Session on H.R. 6400 and Other Proposals to Enforce the 15th Amendment to the Constitution of the United States, March 18, 1965, Serial No. 2 (Washington, DC:

1965), 369; Tuck, "Making the Voting Rights Act," 555; Wilkins, in Voting Rights: Hearings, 377–78; *Dallas Express*, November 3, 1963; *New York Times*, April 2, 1965.

35. *New York Times*, April 10, May 13, 1965; Lawson, *Black Ballots*, 318.

36. On McCulloch, see Katzenbach, *Some of It Was Fun*, 120, 121–28, 295; James M. Oda, Biography of William M. McCulloch, 1–3, Friends of William M. McCulloch, http://www.williammcculloch.org/.

37. *New York Times*, May 13, 27, 1965; "Revolution in Civil Rights," 81.

38. Quoted in Branch, *At Canaan's Edge*, 253.

39. Goldman, *The Tragedy of Lyndon Johnson*, 329; Garrow, *Protest at Selma*, 128; Katzenbach, *Some of It Was Fun*, 173; *New York Times*, July 6, 9, 1965.

40. *New York Times*, July 6, 1965; Mann, *The Walls of Jericho*, 475; "Revolution in Civil Rights," 81.

41. *New York Times*, July 7, 1965; Goldman, *The Tragedy of Lyndon Johnson*, 329.

42. "Revolution in Civil Rights," 81; *New York Times*, July 9, 1965; Goldman, *The Tragedy of Lyndon Johnson*, 330; Garrow, *Protest at Selma*, 129.

43. Oral History of the US House of Representatives—Cokie Roberts Interview 1, August 28, 2007, http://oralhistory.clerk.house.gov/interviewee.html?name=roberts -cokie&view=docs; Lindy Boggs, *Washington Through a Purple Veil: Memoirs of a Southern Woman* (New York: Harcourt Brace, 1994), 202–4; "Revolution in Civil Rights," 81; Lawson, *Black Ballots*, 320; *New York Times*, July 9, 1965. On Boggs's career, see *New York Times*, January 4, 1973.

44. *New York Times*, July 10, 1965; Mann, *The Walls of Jericho*, 375, 474; Goldman, *The Tragedy of Lyndon Johnson*, 330n66; Lawson, *Black Ballots*, 320; Garrow, *Protest at Selma*, 129; Goldman, *The Tragedy of Lyndon Johnson*, 330–31.

45. *New York Times*, July 30, 1965; Garrow, *Protest at Selma*, 130.

46. Beschloss, *Reaching for Glory*, 416; *New York Times*, July 30, 1965; Garrow, *Protest at Selma*, 130–31.

47. Branch, *At Canaan's Edge*, 270; Mann, *The Walls of Jericho*, 475.

48. Garrow, *Protest at Selma*, 132; Mann, *The Walls of Jericho*, 475; *New York Times*, July 30, 1965.

49. Tuck, "Making the Voting Rights Act," 91; "Voting Rights Act, August 6, 1965," in Valelly, *The Voting Rights Act*, 259–67; Alexander Keyssar, *The Right to Vote: The Contested History of Democracy in the United States* (New York: Basic Books, 2000), 263–64.

50. For Califano's remark, see Joe Califano to Bill Moyers, August 6, 1965, White House Central Files (WHCF) Subject File, Box LE 66, Folder "Ex Hu 2–7, 6/1/65– 9/3/65," Lyndon B. Johnson Library, Austin, Texas.

51. For King's 1957 speech, see Martin Luther King, "Give Us the ballot, We Will Transform the South," May 17, 1957, available at "Why Vote?" PBS, www.pbs.org/pov /pov 2008/election/wvote/king.html; Garrow, "An Unfinished Dream," *Newsweek*, January 21, 2009.

52. John Lewis with Michael D'Orso, *Walking with the Wind: A Memoir of the Movement* (New York: Harcourt Brace, 1998), 361–62.

CHAPTER SEVEN: BREAKING DOWN INJUSTICE

1. White House Diary, August 6, 1965, 7, Lyndon B. Johnson Library; *New York Times*, August 8, 1965; John Doar, "The Work of the Civil Rights Division in Enforcing Voting Rights Under the Civil Rights Acts of 1957 and 1960," *Florida State University Law Review* (1997), 9; Steven F. Lawson, *In Pursuit of Power: Southern Blacks and Electoral Politics, 1965–1982* (New York: Columbia University Press, 1985), 17.

2. Stephen J. Pollak, Interview with Thomas H. Baker, Part III, January 30, 1969, 6–8, LBJ Library (hereafter cited as Pollak Interview); *New York Times*, August 7, 8, 1965; *Time*, August 20, 1965; Lawson, *In Pursuit of Power*, 21; *Wall Street Journal*, August 27, 1965; J. L. Chestnut Jr. and Julia Cass, *Black in Selma: The Uncommon Life of J. L. Chestnut* (Tuscaloosa, AL: Fire Ant Books, 1990), 234.

3. *Southern Courier*, August 13, 1965, 1; Chestnut and Cass, *Black in Selma*, 234.

4. *Wall Street Journal*, August 27, 1965; Pat Watters and Reese Cleghorn, *Climbing Jacob's Ladder: The Arrival of Negroes in Southern Politics* (New York: Harcourt, Brace and World, 1967), 275n2.

5. *New York Times*, August 11, 1965; *Time*, August 20, 1965; Steven F. Lawson, *Black Ballots: Voting Rights in the South, 1944–1969* (New York: Columbia University Press, 1976), 329–30; David J. Garrow, *Protest at Selma: Martin Luther King, Jr. and the Voting Rights Act of 1965* (New Haven, CT: Yale University Press, 1978), 181–82; Eric F. Goldman, *The Tragedy of Lyndon Johnson* (New York: Alfred A. Knopf, 1969), 332. On Mrs. Mauldin, see *Jet*, January 2, 1969, 14; *Jet*, August 27, 1981, 24; Chestnut and Cass, *Black in Selma*, 234.

6. *New York Times*, August 11, 1965; *Time*, August 20, 1965; "The Voting Rights Act . . . the First Months," 21, US Commission on Civil Rights, 1965, Thurgood Marshall Law Library, University of Maryland, Baltimore. For a discussion of how the examiners were selected, see "The Voting Rights Act . . . the First Months," 14–22; Lawson, *Black Ballots*, 329–30; Goldman, *The Tragedy of Lyndon Johnson*, 332.

7. Pollak Interview, 17–18.

8. *Wall Street Journal*, August 27, 1965; *Time*, August 27, 1965.

9. David J. Garrow, *Bearing the Cross: Martin Luther King, Jr. and the Southern Christian Leadership Conference* (New York: W. Morrow, 1986), 471.

10. *New York Times*, April 17, 1966; *Time*, May 13, 1966; *South Carolina v. Katzenbach*, 383 U.S. 301 (1966), 271–80, in *The Voting Rights Act: Securing the Ballot*, Richard M. Valelly, ed. (Washington, DC: CQ Press, 2006); Colin D. Moore, "Extensions of the Voting Rights Act," 97, in Valelly, *The Voting Rights Act*; Armand Derfner, "Racial Discrimination and the Right to Vote," *Vanderbilt Law Review* 26 (1973), 551–52, 567–68.

11. *Southern Courier*, August 20, 1965, 1; Stephan Thernstrom and Abigail M. Thernstrom, *America in Black and White: One Nation Indivisible* (New York: Simon and Schuster, 1997), 158–59, 165; Milton Viorst, *Fire in the Streets: America in the 1960s* (New York: Simon and Schuster, 1980), 309–41; Stephan Oates, *Let the Trumpet Sound: The Life of Martin Luther King, Jr.* (New York: Harper and Row, 1982), 377.

12. Harvard Sitkoff, *The Struggle for Black Equality, 1954–1992* (New York: Hill and Wang, 1993), 205–6; James Forman, *Sammy Younge, Jr.: The First Black College Student to Die in the Black Liberation Movement* (Washington, DC: Open Hand, 1986), 223; Lewis, *Walking with the Wind*, 375.

13. Gary May, *The Informant: The FBI, the Ku Klux Klan and the Murder of Viola Liuzzo* (New Haven, CT: Yale University Press, 2005), 228–29; Viorst, *Fire in the Streets*, 347–61; Stewart E. Tolnay and E. B. Beck, *A Festival of Violence: An Analysis of Southern Lynching, 1882–1930* (Urbana: University of Illinois Press, 1995), 27.

14. Perdue is quoted in May, *The Informant*, 186; Tolnay and Beck, *A Festival of Violence*, 27.

15. May, *The Informant*, 230; Viorst, *Fire in the Streets*, 362, 367–68; *Southern Courier*, January 1–2, 1966, 1; Sara Bullard, *Free at Last: A History of the Civil Rights Movement and Those Who Died in the Struggle* (New York: Oxford University Press, 1993), 86–87. On Daniels, see Charles W. Eagles, *Outside Agitator: Jon Daniels and the Civil Rights Movement in Alabama* (Chapel Hill: University of North Carolina Press, 1993), 185–94; *Southern Courier*, October 3–4, 1965, 1; Hasan Kwame Jeffries, *Bloody Lowndes: Civil Rights and Black Power in Alabama's Black Belt* (New York: New York University Press, 2009), 59–60, 78–79, 81–82; Stokely Carmichael and Charles Hamilton, "Black Belt Election: New Day A'Coming," in *The Eyes on the Prize: Civil Rights Reader*, Clayborne Carson, ed. (New York: Penguin, 1991), 265: Frye Gaillard, *Cradle of Freedom: Alabama and the Movement That Changed America* (Tuscaloosa: University of Alabama Press, 2004), 277–82. On those fired for registering, see *New York Times*, January 1, 1966; *Southern Courier*, January 8–9, 1966, 1; Jeffries, *Bloody Lowndes*, 72, 106.

16. *Southern Courier*, January 22–23, 1966, 1, 6; *Time*, April 29, 1966.

17. Jeffries, *Bloody Lowndes*, 165; Gaillard, *Cradle of Freedom*, 291–92; Jack Nelson, "2 Veteran Rights Leaders Ousted by SNCC," *Los Angeles Times*, May 17, 1966, reprinted in Clayborne Carson, ed., *Reporting Civil Rights Part Two: American Journalism 1963–1973* (New York: Penguin Putnam, 2003), 491–94; *New York Times*, May 17, 1966; Lewis, *Walking with the Wind*, 381–92; Lewis, *The Shadows of Youth*, 202–6.

18. *New York Times*, April 30, May 1, 1966; *Capital Times*, April 30, 1966; Taylor Branch, *At Canaan's Edge: America in the King Years 1965–68* (New York: Simon and Schuster, 2006), 458–59; Garrow, *Bearing the Cross*, 470–71.

19. *New York Times*, April 14, 18, 1966; *Southern Courier*, March 5–6, 1966, 1; *Time*, May 13, 1966; Dan T. Carter, *The Politics of Rage: George Wallace, the Origins of the New Conservatism, and the Transformation of American Politics* (New York:

Simon and Schuster, 1995), 275–76, 277–81, 285; Branch, *At Canaan's Edge*, 459; Gaillard, *Cradle of Freedom*, 308; Garrow, *Protest at Selma*, 187.

20. *Southern Courier*, April 9–10, 1966, 6; *New York Times*, April 14, 18, 1966; Charles E. Fager, *Selma, 1965* (New York: Charles Scribner's Sons, 1974), 209; Oates, *Let the Trumpet Sound*, 371; Watters and Cleghorn, *Climbing Jacob's Ladder*, 277n12; Garrow, *Protest at Selma*, 187.

21. *New York Times*, April 20, May 3, 1966; Gene Roberts and Hank Klibanoff, *The Race Beat: The Press, the Civil Rights Struggle, and the Awakening of a Nation* (New York: Alfred A. Knopf, 2006), 398; Oates, *Let the Trumpet Sound*, 371; Chestnut and Cass, *Black in Selma*, 240; Garrow, *Protest at Selma*, 187.

22. *Jet*, March 10, 1966, 18, 20; Fager, *Selma, 1965*, 210; Chestnut and Cass, *Black in Selma*, 236–39.

23. *New York Times*, April 17, May 3, 1966; *Southern Courier*, April 9–10, 1966, 1, 5; Fager, *Selma, 1965*, 209–10; Garrow, *Protest at Selma*, 187.

24. *New York Times*, April 17, 1966; *Southern Courier*, March 26–27, 1966, 1, 5; Branch, *At Canaan's Edge*, 19–20; Cynthia Griggs Fleming, *In the Shadow of Selma: The Continuing Struggle for Civil Rights in the Rural South* (Lanham, MD: Rowman and Littlefield, 2004), 17, 246.

25. *New York Times*, April 17, May 8, 1966; Marshall Frady, *Southerners: A Journalist's Odyssey* (New York: New American Library, 1980), 157; Fleming, *In the Shadow of Selma*, 22–23, 31.

26. *New York Times*, ibid.

27. *New York Times*, April 17, May 2, 3, 7, 1966; *Southern Courier*, February 19–20, 1966, 1; Fleming, *In the Shadow of Selma*, 246.

28. *New York Times*, May 2, 3, 1966; *Southern Courier*, April 9–10, April 30–May 1, May 7–8, 1966, 1.

29. *Southern Courier*, May 7–8, 1966, 1; *New York Times*, May 4, 1966; Chestnut and Cass, *Black in Selma*, 241.

30. John Beecher, "Sword in the Heart of Dixie," *Nation*, May 23, 1966, 612; *New York Times*, May 5, 1966.

31. "Political Participation," *A Report of the United States Commission on Civil Rights, 1968*, 67–190, Thurgood Marshall Law Library, The University of Maryland School of Law, Baltimore, MD; *New York Times*, May 4, 1966; Susan Youngblood Ashmore, *Carry It On: The War on Poverty and the Civil Rights Movement in Alabama, 1964–1972* (Athens: University of Georgia Press, 2008), 181–82; Branch, *At Canaan's Edge*, 462–65.

32. Frye Gaillard, "Notes and Quotes: The Interviews for *Cradle of Freedom*, 2000–2002," 45, Frye Gaillard Papers, Alabama State University; *Southern Courier*, November 12–13, 1966, 2.

33. *New York Times*, May 4, 5, 1966; *Southern Courier*, May 7–8, 1966, 1; *Southern Courier*, June 4–5, 1966, 6; Carter, *The Politics of Rage*, 287; Branch, *At Canaan's Edge*, 464.

34. Earl Black and Merle Black, *Politics and Society in the South* (Cambridge, MA: Harvard University Press, 1987), 138–40; Peyton McCrary, Jerome A. Grey, Edward Still, and Huey L. Perry, "Alabama," 39, in *Quiet Revolution in the South: The Impact of the Voting Rights Act, 1965–1990*, Chandler Davidson and Bernard Grofman, eds. (Princeton, NJ: Princeton University Press, 1994); Garrow, *Protest at Selma*, 190; Carter, *The Politics of Rage*, 287.

35. *Jet*, May 19, 1966, 16–24; *Time*, May 13, 1966; *New York Times*, May 8, 29, 1966; *Southern Courier*, May 7–8, 1966, 6. For Gilmore's candidacy, see Frady, *Southerners*, 157–66, and Gaillard, *Cradle of Freedom*, 313–25, clergyman's quote is on 319.

36. *Time*, May 13, 1965; *New York Times*, May 5, 1966; Fred Gray, *Bus Ride to Justice: The Life and Works of Fred Gray* (Montgomery, AL: NewSouth Books, 2002), 242.

37. *Jet*, May 19, 1966, 14–17; *Jet*, May 26, 1966, 8–9; *New York Times*, ibid. For similar problems in Greene County, see Gaillard, *Cradle of Freedom*, 319–20.

38. *Southern Courier*, May 7–8, 1966, 2; *Southern Courier*, May 21–22, 1966, 1, 6; *New York Times*, May 6, 1966.

39. Doar, "The Work of the Civil Rights Division," 10; Fager, *Selma, 1965*, 210–11; *New York Times*, ibid.

40. *New York Times*, May 6, 7, 1966; Roberts and Klibanoff, *The Race Beat*, 398.

41. Doar, "The Work of the Civil Rights Division," 10.

42. Anne Permaloff and Carl Grafton, *Political Power in Alabama: The More Things Change . . .* (Athens: University of Georgia Press, 2008), 112; *Southern Courier*, May 21–22, 1966, 1.

43. *Southern Courier*, May 21–22, 1966, 1, 6; *United States v. Executive Com. of Dem. P. of Dallas Co.*, ALA. 254 F. Supp. 537 (1966).

44. Doar is quoted in *Time*, June 3, 1966; *Southern Courier*, ibid.

45. *New York Times*, May 25, 1966; *Southern Courier*, May 28–29, 1966, 1; *Time*, ibid.; Fager, *Selma, 1965*, 211; *U.S. v. Executive*.

46. *Big Spring Herald* (Texas), June 1, 1966; *New York Times*, May 29, 31, November 9, 10, 1966; *Southern Courier*, May 28–29, 1, 5, November 5–6, 1966, 1, 5, November 12–13, 1965, 2; Alston Fitts III, *Selma: Queen City of the Black Belt* (Selma, AL: Clairmont, 1989), 157–58; Chestnut and Cass, *Black in Selma*, 237.

47. *New York Times*, November 10, 1966; *Time*, November 18, 1966. On Bond, see Frady, *Southerners*, 167–83; Garrow, *Protest at Selma*, 188–89; Earl Black and Merle Black, *The Rise of the Southern Republican* (Cambridge, MA: Harvard University Press, 2002), 99.

48. Chandler Davidson, "The Voting Rights Act: A Brief History," in *Controversies in Minority Voting: The Voting Rights Act in Perspective*, Bernard Grofman and Chandler Davidson, eds. (Washington, DC: Brookings Institution, 1992), 22–23, Celler is quoted on 22; Peyton McCrary, Jerome A. Gray, Edward Still, and Huey A. Perry, "Alabama," 39–40, in Grofman and Davidson, *Controversies in Minority Voting*; Gaillard, *Cradle of Freedom*, 291–92; Lawson, *In Pursuit of Power*, 171–72.

49. Rick Perlstein, *Nixonland: The Rise of a President and the Fracturing of a Nation* (New York: Scribner, 2008), 163–65, Brown is quoted on 165.

50. Ibid., 123–24; Sitkoff, *The Struggle for Black Equality*, 186–87.

51. Quoted in Perlstein, *Nixonland*, 151.

52. Ibid., 165; David Greenberg, "It's a Reprieve, Not a Pardon," *Washington Monthly*, December 2006, http://www.washingtonmonthly.com/features/2006/0612.greenberg.html.

53. King is quoted in Frady, *Southerners*, 262; Oates, *Let the Trumpet Sound*, 387–419.

54. Frady, *Southerners*, 254–68; Adam Fairclough, *Martin Luther King, Jr.* (Athens, University of Georgia Press, 1995), 107–9.

55. Frady, *Southerners*, 262–63, 278–79; Fairclough, *Martin Luther King, Jr.*, 108, 113, King quote is on 114; Brown quoted in Sitkoff, *The Struggle for Black Equality*, 203; Oates, *Let the Trumpet Sound*, 438.

56. The King-Halberstam conversation is quoted in Oates, *Let the Trumpet Sound*, 441–42, 445; Frady, *Southerners*, 281–82.

57. Oates, *Let the Trumpet Sound*, 449–54. Hoover is quoted in Frady, *Southerners*, 278; Fairclough, *Martin Luther King, Jr.*, 120.

58. Oates, *Let the Trumpet Sound*, 457–58; Frady, *Southerners*, 293.

59. King is quoted in Oates, *Let the Trumpet Sound*, 458; Frady, *Southerners*, 296.

60. Frady, *Southerners*, 296–97; Oates, *Let the Trumpet Sound*, 469–70, King is quoted on 470.

61. Garrow, *Bearing the Cross*, 610–11; Frady, *Southerners*, 297–98; Oates, *Let the Trumpet Sound*, 477–78; Andrew Young, *An Easy Burden: The Civil Rights Movement and the Transformation of America* (New York: HarperCollins, 1996), 460.

62. Garrow, *Bearing the Cross*, 614; Frady, *Southerners*, 298; Oates, *Let the Trumpet Sound*, 447–49.

63. Oates, *Let the Trumpet Sound*, 481; Frady, *Southerners*, 299.

64. Oates, *Let the Trumpet Sound*, 482; Garrow, *Bearing the Cross*, 619.

65. Oates, *Let the Trumpet Sound*, 484; Frady, *Southerners*, 299; Branch, *At Canaan's Edge*, 756–59; Young, *An Easy Burden*, 463. Hook's comment can be found in Martin Luther King Jr., "I've Been to the Mountaintop," April 3, 1968, American Radio Works, http://www.americanradioworks.publicradio.org/features/sayitplain/mlking.html. For King's speech, see also Clayborne Carson and Kris Shephard, eds., *A Call To Conscience: The Landmark Speeches of Dr. Martin Luther King, Jr.* (New York: Grand Central, 2002), 207–23.

66. For King's last day, see Young, *An Easy Burden*, 463–66; Oates, *Let the Trumpet Sound*, 487–93; Frady, *Southerners*, 302–6; Branch, *At Canaan's Edge*, 759–66; Garrow, *Bearing the Cross*, 622–24.

67. Perlstein, *Nixonland*, 255–59; Charles Kaiser, *1968 in America: Music, Politics, Chaos, Counterculture, and the Shaping of a Generation* (New York: Grove, 1988), 145–49.

68. Kaiser, *1968 in America*, 167–89, 230–44; Perlstein, *Nixonland*, 307–27, 329–54.

69. Perlstein, *Nixonland*, 223–24, Wallace is quoted on 234. On the Wallace campaign, see also Stephen Lesher, *George Wallace: American Populist* (New York: Addison Wesley, 1994), 387–41. On Nixon, see Elizabeth Drew, *Richard M. Nixon* (New York: Times Books, 2007), 18–21.

70. Carter, *The Politics of Rage*, 335.

CHAPTER EIGHT: WHERE THE VOTES ARE

1. Elizabeth Drew, *Richard M. Nixon* (New York: Times Books, 2007), 20, 44; Steven F. Lawson, *Civil Rights Crossroads: Nation, Community, and the Black Freedom Struggle* (Lexington: University of Kentucky Press, 2005), 127.

2. Drew, *Richard M. Nixon*; Lawson, *Civil Rights Crossroads*, 127, 320n37.

3. Phillips is quoted in James Boyd, "Nixon's Southern Strategy: 'It's All in the Charts,'" *New York Times Magazine*, May 17, 1970, 215; Charles M. Blow, "The G.O.P.'s 'Black People' Platform," *New York Times*, January 6, 2012.

4. Steven F. Lawson, *In Pursuit of Power: Southern Blacks and Electoral Politics, 1965–1982* (New York: Columbia University Press, 1985), 134–38; *Time*, June 29, 1970; Richard Harris, *Justice: The Crisis of Law, Order, and Freedom in America* (New York: E. P. Dutton, 1970), 213–14, 218–19; Colin D. Moore, "Extensions of the Voting Rights Act," in *The Voting Rights Act: Securing the Ballot*, Richard M. Valelly, ed. (Washington, DC: CQ Press, 2006), 98–99.

5. McCulloch is quoted in Harris, *Justice*, 215–16; Lawson, *In Pursuit of Power*, 137.

6. The unnamed Republican is quoted in Harris, *Justice*, 219–21.

7. Moore, "Extensions of the Voting Rights Act," 99; Lawson, *In Pursuit of Power*, 145–46.

8. Adam Clymer, *Edward M. Kennedy: A Biography* (New York: William Morrow, 1999), 163–66; Edward M. Kennedy, *True Compass: A Memoir* (New York: Twelve, 2009), 319–20; Burton Hersh, *Edward Kennedy: An Intimate Biography* (Berkeley, CA: Counterpoint, 2010), 396–99; Lawson, *In Pursuit of Power*, 151–52; *Time*, June 29, 1970.

9. Lawson, *In Pursuit of Power*, 146–47, 149–50, Ervin is quoted on 150.

10. Moore, "Extensions of the Voting Rights Act"; David J. Garrow, *Protest at Selma: Martin Luther King, Jr. and the Voting Rights Act of 1965* (New Haven, CT: Yale University Press, 1978), 194–97; Steven F. Lawson, *Running for Freedom: Civil Rights and Black Politics in America Since 1941*, 3rd ed. (Malden, MA: Blackwell, 2009), 142–43. For the "Voting Rights Act Extension," June 22, 1970, see Richard M. Valelly, ed., *The Voting Rights Act: Securing the Ballot* (Washington, DC: CQ Press, 2006), 286–90.

11. Moore, "Extensions of the Voting Rights Act," 100.

12. Alexander Keyssar, *The Right to Vote: The Contested History of Democracy in the United States* (New York: Basic Books, 2000), 275–77; *Time*, June 29, 1970; Moore, "Extensions of the Voting Rights Act."

13. Lawson, *Civil Rights Crossroads*, 127–29; Lawson, *In Pursuit of Power*, 154–55. An examination of President Richard M. Nixon's Daily Diary for June 1970 reveals no indication that the president signed the Act or held any public ceremony indicating that he did. For the Daily Diary for June 1970, see http://www.nixonlibrary .gov/virtuallibrary/documents/PDD/1970/023%20June%201970.pdf. However, on June 22, 1970, he issued a statement in which he expressed his reservations about the provision of the Act that allowed eighteen-year-olds to vote, but he indicated that he had signed the Act on that day. See "Statement on Signing the Voting Rights Act Amendments of 1970," June 22, 1970, American Presidency Project, http://www .presidency.ucsb.edu/ws/index.php?pid=2553&st=&st1=. How or under what circumstances he signed the Act remains a mystery.

14. Chandler Davidson, "The Recent Evolution of Voting Rights Law Affecting Racial and Language Minorities," in *Quiet Revolution in the South: The Impact of the Voting Rights Act, 1965-1990*, Chandler Davidson and Bernard Grofman, eds. (Princeton, NJ: Princeton University Press: 1994), 32; Armand Derfner, "Voter Dilution and the Voting Rights Act Amendments of 1982," in *Minority Vote Dilution*, Chandler Davidson, ed. (Washington, DC: Howard University Press, 1989), 150. For *Allen v. State Board of Elections*, see Valelly, *The Voting Rights Act*, 280–85; Lawson, *In Pursuit of Power*, 161–62.

15. Lawson, *In Pursuit of Power*, 219–20.

16. Nixon is quoted in *New York Times*, December 10, 2010; Eugene Robinson, "Needed: Competition for Black Votes," *Real Clear Politics*, October 8, 2010.

17. Sean Wilentz, *The Age of Reagan: A History, 1974-2008* (New York: Harper-Collins, 2008), 45–46; Douglas Brinkley, *Gerald R. Ford* (New York: Times Books, 2007), 67. Rangel is quoted in Lawson, *In Pursuit of Power*, 226; Lawson, *Running for Freedom*, 186–87, Rangel is quoted on 187. For Ford's remarks, see Gerald Ford, "Remarks on the Anniversary of the Birth of Martin Luther King, Jr., January 14, 1975," American Presidency Project, http://www.presidency.ucsb.edu/ws/index.php?=4927 &st=&st.

18. For Pottinger's comments, see *New York Times*, March 6, 1975; Lawson, *In Pursuit of Power*, 236–44.

19. William Broyles, "The Making of Barbara Jordan," *Texas Monthly* (October 1976), http:www.texasmonthly.com/cms/printthis.php?file=feature6.php&issue =1976-10-01; *New York Times*, January 18, 1996; Mary Beth Rogers, *Barbara Jordan: American Hero* (New York: Bantam, 1998), 3–227.

20. Rogers, *Barbara Jordan*, 241–244; Moore, "Extensions of the Voting Rights Act," 103–4. For Jordan's testimony, see *Hearings Before The Subcommittee on Civil and Constitutional Rights of the Committee on the Judiciary, House of Representatives, 94th*

Cong., 1st Sess., Part 1 (Washington, DC: US Government Printing Office, 1975), 75–93.

21. Rogers, *Barbara Jordan*, 244–46; Moore, "Extensions of the Voting Rights Act," 204; Lawson, *In Pursuit of Power*, 243–44.

22. Moore, "Extensions of the Voting Rights Act," 104; Lawson, *In Pursuit of Power*, 246.

23. Lawson, *In Pursuit of Power*, 247–50; Moore, "Extensions of the Voting Rights Act," 104–5.

24. Gerald R. Ford, "Letter to the Senate Minority Leader Urging Extension of the Voting Rights Act of 1965," July 23, 1975, American Presidency Project, http://www.presidency.ucsb.edu/ws/?pid=5097; Thomas M. Boyd and Stephan J. Markman, "The 1982 Amendments to the Voting Rights Act: A Legislative History," *Washington and Lee Law Review* 40, no. 4 (1983), 1351; Lawson, *Running for Freedom*, 186–91; Lawson, *In Pursuit of Power*, 235–53, Ford is quoted on 253; Moore, "Extensions of the Voting Rights Act," 102–5. For the Act, see "Voting Rights Act Extension," August 6, 1975, in Valelly, *The Voting Rights Act*, 297–302.

25. Rogers, *Barbara Jordan*, 247; Craig Hines, "Jordan Gets Both Her Wishes—Voting Act and Ford Cards," *Houston Chronicle*, August 7, 1975.

26. On Carter, see Julian E. Zelizer, *Jimmy Carter* (New York: Times Books, 2010), 53–150, and Wilentz, *The Age of Reagan*, 73–126; Lou Cannon, *President Reagan: The Role of a Lifetime* (New York: Simon and Schuster, 1991), 104, 458–63.

27. *New York Times*, May 9, July 26, 1981; *New York Times*, April 14, 1982; Raymond Wolters, *Right Turn: William Bradford Reynolds, the Reagan Administration, and Black Civil Rights* (New Brunswick, NJ: Transaction, 1996), 27; Wilentz, *The Age of Reagan*, 181. On *City of Mobile v. Bolden,* see Peyton McCrary, "History in the Courts: The Significance of *City of Mobile v. Bolden*," in Davidson, *Minority Vote Dilution* (Washington, DC: Howard University Press, 1984), 47–63; Lawson, *In Pursuit of Power*, 276–81; Kiron K. Skinner, "Ronald Reagan and the African American," *National Review*, February 21, 2011; David Remnick, *The Bridge: The Life and Rise of Barack Obama* (New York: Alfred A. Knopf, 2010), 480.

28. Rauh is quoted in *Time*, May 11, 1981; *Washington Post*, April 23, 1980; *New York Times*, April 23, 1980.

29. John Hebert Roper, "The Voting Rights Extension Act of 1982," *Phylon* 45, no. 3 (1984), 193.

30. *Time*, May 11, 1981; *New York Times*, August 22, 1982; Don Edwards, "The Voting Rights Act of 1965, As Amended," 6, in *The Voting Rights Act: Consequences and Implications*, Lorn S. Foster, ed. (New York: Praeger, 1985), 6; Howard Ball, "Racial Vote Dilution: Impact of the Reagan DOJ and the Burger Court on the Voting Rights Act," 42, *Publius: The Journal of Federalism* 16, no. 4 (Fall 1986), 42; Armand Derfner, "Vote Dilution and the Voting Rights Act Amendments of 1982," in Davidson, *Minority Vote Dilution*, 149.

31. Boyd and Markman, "The 1982 Amendments to the Voting Rights Act," 1351–52, 1358n61; Lorn S. Foster, "Political Symbols and the Enactment of the 1982 Voting Rights Act," in Foster, *The Voting Rights Act*, 88–89; Wolters, *Right Turn*, 33; Barton Gellman, "The New Old Movement," *New Republic*, September 6, 1982, 10–13; *New York Times*, October 6, 1981; Michael Pertschuk, *Giant Killers* (New York: W. W. Norton, 1986), 156–58; Lani Guinier, *Lift Every Voice: Turning a Civil Rights Setback into a New Vision of Social Justice* (New York: Simon and Schuster, 1998), 75–86.

32. Boyd and Markman, "The 1982 Amendments to the Voting Rights Act," 1356–57; Lawson, *In Pursuit of Power*, 283; Moore, "Extensions of the Voting Rights Act," 106.

33. Boyd and Markman, "The 1982 Amendments to the Voting Rights Act," 1357–58, 1358n63; *New York Times*, July 19, 1981.

34. Minion K. C. Morrison, ed., *African Americans and Political Participation: A Reference Handbook* (Santa Barbara, CA: ABC Clio, 2003), 352; Kennedy is quoted in *Time*, May 11, 1981.

35. *Time*, ibid.; US Commission on Civil Rights, *The Voting Rights Act: Unfulfilled Goals*, September 1981, 43–44.

36. Roper, "The Voting Rights Extension Act of 1982," 192; Boyd and Markman, "The 1982 Amendments to the Voting Rights Act," 1360–61; US Commission on Civil Rights, *The Voting Rights Act*, 52.

37. Boyd and Markman, "The 1982 Amendments to the Voting Rights Act," 1362–63n85; Wolters, *Right Turn*, 28; Lorn S. Foster, ed., *The Voting Rights Act: Consequences and Implications* (New York: Praeger, 1985), 7; Roper, "The Voting Rights Extension Act of 1982," 191–92; *New York Times*, June 13, July 2, 19, 1981.

38. Boyd and Markman, "The 1982 Amendments to the Voting Rights Act," 1363–64n85; Roper, "The Voting Rights Extension Act of 1982," 191–92; *New York Times*, June 13, July 2, 19, 1981; Wolters, *Right Turn*, 33–35; Lawson, *In Pursuit of Power*, 284–85.

39. US Commission on Civil Rights, *The Voting Rights Act*, 24, see also 25–63. For criticism of the subcommittee hearings, see Wolters, *Right Turn*, 34; *New York Times*, September 10, 1981; Foster, *The Voting Rights Act*, 6.

40. Lawson, *In Pursuit of Power*, 284; Roper, "The Voting Rights Extension Act of 1982," 194–95.

41. Boyd and Markman, "The 1982 Amendments to the Voting Rights Act," 1369–75; Moore, "Extensions of the Voting Rights Act," 107; Nadine Cohodas, *Strom Thurmond and the Politics of Southern Change* (New York; Macon, GA: Mercer University Press, 1993), 466–68; *New York Times*, August 1, 1981.

42. Boyd and Markman, "The 1982 Amendments to the Voting Rights Act," 1364–65; Foster, *The Voting Rights Act*, 8; *New York Times*, June 16, 1981; Ronald Reagan, "Remarks in Denver, Colorado, at the Annual Convention of the National Association for the Advancement of Colored People," June 29, 1981, American Presidency Project, http://www.presidency.ucsb.edu/ws/?pid=44016.

43. *New York Times*, July 16, 21, 1981.

44. *New York Times*, July 16, 1981. Hyde's letter to Reagan is quoted in Boyd and Markman, "The 1982 Amendments to the Voting Rights Act," 1369n106.

45. Robert Plotkin, "Injustice Department," *New York Times*, August 3, 1981; *New York Times*, July 16, 21, 1981; Wilentz, *The Age of Reagan*, 180–83; Roper, "The Voting Rights Extension Act of 1982," 188.

46. *New York Times*, August 6, 1981.

47. Boyd and Markman, "The 1982 Amendments to the Voting Rights Act," 1375, 1379; *New York Times*, August 6, September 27, 1981; Moore, "Extensions of the Voting Rights Act," 107.

48. *Time*, October 19, 1981; Boyd and Markman, "The 1982 Amendments to the Voting Rights Act," 1375–79; Derfner, "Voter Dilution and the Voting Rights Act Amendments of 1982," 152–54; Hyde is quoted in Lawson, *In Pursuit of Power*, 285.

49. *Time*, ibid.; *New York Times*, October 6, 1981; Steven Suitts, "Amended Act Passes," *Southern Changes* 4, no. 1 (1981); Moore, "Extensions of the Voting Rights Act," 107.

50. *New York Times*, November 1, 1981; Suitts, "Amended Act Passes," 7; Boyd and Markman, "The 1982 Amendments to the Voting Rights Act," 1385–86.

51. *New York Times*, July 6, 9, October 20, November 5, 1981; Larry Sabato, "The 1981 Gubernatorial Election in Virginia," *Newsletter*, Institute of Government, University of Virginia, February 1982, 24–25; Lawson, *In Pursuit of Power*, 287.

52. *New York Times*, November 7, 10, 13, 1981; Derfner, "Voter Dilution and the Voting Rights Act Amendments of 1982," 154; Boyd and Markman, "The 1982 Amendments to the Voting Rights Act," 1386–87.

53. *New York Times*, November 7, 8, 13, 1981; Lawson, *In Pursuit of Power*, 287.

54. Boyd and Markham, 1382–83, 1388–89; Gellman, "The New Old Movement," 10; Barton Gellman, "Voting Wrongs," *New Republic*, June 27, 1981, 10; Cohodas, *Strom Thurmond and the Politics of Southern Change*, 468; *New York Times*, December 18, 22, 1981; *New York Times*, January 22, 1982.

55. Norman C. Amaker, *Civil Rights and the Reagan Administration* (Washington, DC: Urban Institute Press, 1988), 145; Boyd and Markman, "The 1982 Amendments to the Voting Rights Act," 1393–94; *New York Times*, January 27, 1982.

56. *New York Times*, February 7, 1982; *Washington Post*, February 18, 1982; *Maggie S. Bozeman v. State*, 2 Div. 262 (Ms. March 31, 1981); Walter Leavy, "The Old South Refuses to Die," *Ebony*, May 1982, 147; Ron Nixon, "Turning Back the Clock on Voting Rights," *Nation*, October 28, 1999.

57. *New York Times*, ibid.; Guinier, *Lift Every Voice*, 88–89; Kelly Dowe, "Paying the Price in Pickens County," *Southern Changes* 4, no. 3 (1982), 13–14.

58. *New York Times*, November 10, 1982; *News Courier/Evening Post* (Charleston, SC), April 14, 1984; Guinier, *Lift Every Voice*, 204; Gary May, *The Informant: The FBI, the Ku Klux Klan and the Murder of Viola Liuzzo* (New Haven, CT: Yale University Press, 2005), 336–60.

59. *New York Times*, March 20, April 14, May 7, 1982.

60. Reynolds and Reagan are quoted in Lawson, *In Pursuit of Power*, 288–89.

61. Boyd and Markham, 1411–12; Derfner, "Voter Dilution and the Voting Rights Act Amendments of 1982," 154.

62. Boyd and Markham, 1411–12; Cohodas, *Strom Thurmond and the Politics of Southern Change*, 472; *New York Times*, April 19, 1982.

63. Boyd and Markman, "The 1982 Amendments to the Voting Rights Act," 1415; *New York Times*, April 30, 1982; *New York Times*, March 30, 2005.

64. Boyd and Markman, "The 1982 Amendments to the Voting Rights Act," 1414–17; Cohodas, *Strom Thurmond and the Politics of Southern Change*, 474–75; Jack Bass and Marilyn W. Thompson, *Strom: The Complicated Personal and Political Life of Strom Thurmond* (New York: PublicAffairs, 2005), 295; *New York Times*, May 4, 5, 1982; *New York Times*, June 6, 16, 1982; Lawson, *In Pursuit of Power*, 290–91; Moore, "Extensions of the Voting Rights Act," 107–8.

65. Boyd and Markman, "The 1982 Amendments to the Voting Rights Act," 1421–24; Lawson, *In Pursuit of Power*, 292; Cohodas, *Strom Thurmond and the Politics of Southern Change*, 475–79; *New York Times*, June 16, 18, 1982; *Time*, June 28, 1982.

66. Robert Mann, *The Walls of Jericho: Lyndon Johnson, Hubert Humphrey, Richard Russell, and the Struggle for Civil Right* (New York: Harcourt, 1996), 161, 165, 397, 400, 401, 473; *New York Times*, June 13, 24, 1982.

67. Robert A. Caro, *The Years of Lyndon Johnson: Master of the Senate* (New York: Alfred A. Knopf, 2002), 998; Cohodas, *Strom Thurmond and the Politics of Southern Change*, 294–97, 332, 350, 356–62; Bass and Thompson, *Strom*, 190.

68. Cohodas, *Strom Thurmond and the Politics of Southern Change*, 12, 480; Abigail M. Thernstrom, *Whose Votes Count? Affirmative Action and Minority Voting Rights* (Cambridge, MA: Harvard University Press, 1987), 109.

69. Boyd and Markman, "The 1982 Amendments to the Voting Rights Act," 1424n398–1425; *New York Times*, March 2, 2011. For information on the eight, see *Biographical Directory of the United States Congress, 1774–Present*, http://bioguide .congress.gov.

70. Boyd and Markman, "The 1982 Amendments to the Voting Rights Act," 1425; *New York Times*, June 24, 30, 1982; *Washington Post*, June 24, 1982. For "Remarks on Signing the Voting Rights Act Amendments of 1982," and Public Law 97–205, see Valelly, *The Voting Rights Act*, 307–11.

71. *New York Times*, July 2, 1982; Lawson, *In Pursuit of Power*, 358n28.

72. For Thernstrom's views, see Thernstrom, *Whose Votes Count?*, passim, and Thernstrom and Thernstrom, *America in Black and White*, 462–92.

73. Cohodas, *Strom Thurmond and the Politics of Southern Change*, 41–42; Abigail Thernstrom, "Voting Rights Trap," *New Republic*, September 2, 1985, 21.

74. *New York Times*, July 11, 2000. On Bush, see Wilentz, *The Age of Reagan*, 408–58.

75. *Chicago Defender*, January 27, 2005, posted on Hungry Blues blog, http:// hungryblues.net/2005/01/31/bush-tells-cbc-hes-unfamiliar-with-voting-rights-act/;

Roland S. Martin, *Black America Today*, January 27, 2005, http://www.blackamerica-today.com/article.cfm?Article ID=735.

76. Lawson, *Running for Freedom*, 322; J. Morgan Kousser, "The Strange, Ironic Career of Section 5 of the Voting Rights Act, 1965–2007," *Texas Law Review* 86, no. 4 (March 2008), 752, http://www.texaslrev.com/issues/vol/86/issue/4/kousser; *Los Angeles Times*, July 18, 2006; *New York Times*, July 21, 2006. For Bush's address, see "President Bush Addresses NAACP Annual Convention," July 20, 2006, http://georgewbushwhitehouse.archives.gov/news/releases/2006/07/print/20060720.html.

77. Kousser, "The Strange, Ironic Career of Section 5," 753. Katherine Tate, "Black Politics, the GOP Southern Strategy, and the Reauthorization of the Voting Rights Act," *Forum* 4, no. 2 (2006), 1–9; Pei-te Lien, Dianne M. Pinderhughes, Carol Hardy-Fanta, and Christine M. Sierra, "The Voting Rights Act and the Election of Nonwhite Officials," *PS: Political Science and Politics*, July 2007, www.apsanet.org/imgtest/PSJuly07LienPinderhughesEtal.pdf, 489; *Washington Post*, June 22, 2006; *New York Times*, June 22, July 21, 2006. For a discussion of the Supreme Court's impact on the Act, see Lawson, *Running for Freedom*, 282–85, 336.

78. Kennedy is quoted in *New York Times*, July 21, 2006.

79. Associated Press, "Bush Signs Voting Rights Act Extension," MSNBC, July 27, 2006, http://www.msnbc.msn.com/id/14059113/; "President Bush Signs Voting Rights Act Reauthorization and Amendments Act of 2006," Office of the Press Secretary, July 27, 2006, http://georgewbush-whitehouse.archives.gov/news/releases/2006/07/print/20060727.html.

80. Kousser, "The Strange, Ironic Career of Section 5," 762–63; Nathaniel Persily, "The Promise and the Pitfalls of the New Voting Rights Act," *Yale Law Journal* 117, no. 2 (2007), 174; Richard H. Pildes, "Political Avoidance, Constitutional Theory and the VRA," *Yale Law Journal* 117 (2007), 148, http://thepocketpart.org/2007/12/10/pildes.html; *New York Times*, March 29, 2006.

81. "First Challenge to Voting Rights Act Amendment Rejected in D.C. District Court," *BLT: The Blog of Legal Times*, June 2, 2008, http://www.legaltimes.typepad.com/blt/2008/06/first-challenge.html; Christopher F. Moriarity, "The Demise of the Voting Rights Act? A Preview of *Northwest Austin Municipal Utility District Number One v. Holder*," *Duke Journal of Constitutional Law and Public Policy Sidebar* 4 (2009), 459, 462.

CHAPTER NINE: THE STRUGGLE OF A LIFETIME

1. David Remnick, *The Bridge: The Life and Rise of Barack Obama* (New York: Alfred A. Knopf, 2010), 6, 75.

2. Jeffrey Toobin, "Voter Beware," *New Yorker*, March 2, 2009. See also Toobin, "Holder's Legacy, Daily Comment," *New Yorker*, December 27, 2011.

3. Adegbile is quoted in *New York Times*, June 23, 2009; Hans A. von Spakovsky, "Interpreting *Northwest Austin Municipal Utility District Number One v. Holder*," *Na-*

tional Review Online, June 22, 2009, http://www.nationalreview.com/corner/183737 /interpreting-i-northwest-austin-municipal-utility-district-i-v-i-holder-i/hans-von-spa. On Spakovsky's tenure at the Justice Department, see *Washington Post*, June 8, 2007.

4. For the percentage of African Americans by state, see US Department of Commerce, US Census Bureau, http://quickfacts.census.gov/qfd/states/21000.html. Janai S. Nelson, "Defining Race: The Obama Phenomenon and the Voting Rights Act," *Albany Law Review* 72, no. 4 (July 2010), 892–93; Rachel L. Swarns, "Quiet Political Shifts as More Blacks Are Elected," *New York Times*, October 13, 2008.

5. Charles S. Bullock III and Ronald Keith Gaddie, *The Triumph of Voting Rights in the South* (Norman: University of Oklahoma Press, 2009), 56–57, 64–67, 77, 109–10, 139–40, 162–63, 250–52, 280–82; Chandler Davidson and Bernard Grofman, eds., *Quiet Revolution in the South: The Impact of the Voting Rights Act, 1965–1990* (Princeton, NJ: Princeton University Press, 1994), passim.

6. On Wilder, see Margaret Edds, *Free at Last: What Really Happened When Civil Rights Came to Southern Politics* (Bethesda, MD: Adler and Adler, 1987), 212–38, and Edds, *Claiming the Dream: The Victorious Campaign of Douglas Wilder of Virginia* (Chapel Hill, NC: Algonquin, 1990), passim. On Patrick, see Gwen Ifill, *The Breakthrough: Politics and Race in the Age of Obama* (New York: Doubleday, 2009), 179–204. On Patterson, see *New York Times*, February 26, 2010.

7. Steven F. Lawson, *Running for Freedom*: *Civil Rights and Black Politics in America Since 1941*, 3rd ed. (Malden: Blackwell, 2009), 145–46, 189, 205, 273, 311. See also Wayne D'orio, *Carole Moseley-Braun: African American Leaders* (New York: Chelsea House, 2003), passim. On Obama's election to the Senate, see Remnick, *The Bridge*, 370–83.

8. On white support for Kerry in 2004 compared to Obama's in 2008, see Polster.com at http://www.pollster.com/blogs/white_vote_for_obama_in_the_st_1 .php?nr=1; Laughlin McDonald, "The Voting Rights Act: Still Needed in Obama's America," *Jurist*, January 4, 2012; Stephan Ansolabehere, Nathaniel Persily, and Charles Stewart III, "Race, Region, and Vote Choice in the 2008 Election: Implications for the Future of the Voting Rights Act," *Harvard Law Review* 123 (April 2010), 1414, 1422, 1432; "Amici Curiae on Behalf of Neither Party," Brief for Nathaniel Persily, Stephen Ansolabehere, and Charles Stewart III, *Northwest Austin Municipal Utility District Number One v. Eric H. Holder, Jr., Attorney General of the United States of America*, et al., February 26, 2009, 11–12.

9. "Amici Curiae on Behalf of Neither Party."

10. Ibid., 8–9; Toobin, "Voter Beware"; Seth Stephens-Davidowitz, "How Racist Are We? Ask Google," *New York Times*, June 9, 2012. For a fuller explication of Stephens-Davidowitz's views, see "The Effects of Racial Animus on a Black Presidential Candidate: Using Google Search Data to Find What Surveys Miss," http://www.people.fas .harvard.edu/~sstephen/papers/RacialAnimusAndVotingSethStephensDavidowitz .pdf; Michael Tessler and David Walsh, *Obama's Race: The 2008 Election and the Dream of a Post-Racial Society* (Chicago: University of Chicago Press, 2010), 5.

11. Wendy R. Weiser and Lawrence Norden, "Voting Law Changes in 2012," 1, Brennan Center for Justice at New York University School of Law; *St. Petersburg Times*, July 6, 2011. On changes in felon rights, see *Washington Post*, March 9, 2011. Clinton is quoted in Ari Berman, "GOP Voting Laws Could Swing the 2012 Election," *Nation*, October 3, 2011.

12. Weiser and Norden, "Voting Law Changes in 2012," 1; *New York Times*, December 19, 2008; Tony Newmyer, "The Big Political Player You've Never Heard Of," *Fortune*, January 10, 2011; Jerry Landay, "The 'Patriots' Are Suppressing the 2012 Voter Turnout," *Nation of Change*, January 16, 2012, http://www.nationofchange .org/blog/jerrylanday; Tobin Van Ostern, "Conservative Corporate Advocacy Group ALEC Behind Voter Disenfranchisement Efforts," Campus Progress, March 8, 2011, http://www.campusprogress.org/articles.

13. Paul Weyrich, "A National Plague of Unlawful Voting," *Townhall*, October 17, 2008. Weyrich's remarks on voting are available at "Paul Weyrich—'I Don't Want Everybody to Vote,'" YouTube, www.youtube.com/watch?v=8GBAsFwPglw.

14. Brandon is quoted in Van Ostern, "Conservative Corporate Advocacy Group ALEC Behind Voter Disenfranchisement Efforts." See also Ari Berman, "The GOP War on Voting," *Rolling Stone*, August 30, 2011, http://www.rollingstone.com/politics/news/the-gop-war-on-voting-20110830.

15. Elizabeth Drew, "Voting Wrongs," *New York Review of Books*, October 12, 2012, http://www.nybooks.com/blogs/nyrblog/2012/sep/21/voting-wrongs/?utm _medium=email&utm_campaign=September+25+2012&utm_content=September +25+2012+CID_96d06f4761e5910c3bc1f601fe3e530c&utm_source=Email%20 marketing%20software&utm_term=Voting%20Wrongs; Voter ID Information, City of Madison, WI, n.d., http://www.cityofmadison.com/clerk/PhotoIDDetails.cfm.

16. Keesha Gaskin and Sundeep Iyer, "The Challenge of Obtaining Voter Identification," Brennan Center for Justice at New York University School of Law, 2012, 6; Testimony of Judith A. Browne-Dianis, codirector, Advancement Project, Hearing on "New State Voting Laws: Barriers to the Ballot?," Before the Subcommittee on the Constitution, Civil Rights, and Human Rights, Senate Committee on the Judiciary, Washington, DC, Thursday, September 8, 2011, 3, 8 (hereafter cited as Browne-Dianis Testimony).

17. Dave Zweifel, "Plain Talk: 101-Year-Old Disgusted with Walker's Voter ID Law," *Capitol Times*, July 22, 2011; Jessica Vanegeren and Shawn Doherty, "Top DOT Official Tells Staff Not to Mention Free Voter ID Cards to the Public—Unless They Ask," *Capitol Times*, September 7, 2011. For information on Oneida County DOT procedures, see www.dot.state.wi.us. See also Hearing of the US House Committee on the Judiciary, "Protecting the Right to Vote," 2, Demos: Ideas and Action to Promote the Common Good, November 14, 2011, http://www.demos.org/publications /protecting-right-vote; Browne-Diannis Testimony, 8, 9; John Pawasarat, "The Driver License Status of the Voting Age Population in Wisconsin," Employment and Training Institute, University of Wisconsin-Milwaukee, June 2005; *Wisconsin Journal Sentinel*, September 8, 2011.

18. *New York Times*, December 26, 2011; Weiser and Norden, "Voting Law Changes in 2012," 8; "Youth Vote Faces Challenge with Voter ID Legislation," *Nation*, July 21, 2011.

19. Scott Keyes, Ian Millhiser, Tobin Van Ostern, and Abraham White, "Voter Suppression 101: How Conservatives Are Conspiring to Disenfranchise Millions of Americans," Center for American Progress, April 4, 2012, 7, http://www.americanprogress.org/issues/progressive-movement/report/2012/04/04/11380/voter-suppression-101/; Ari Berman, "The GOP War on Voting"; Megan Donovan, "Voter Suppression Update: Taking Stock of 2011, Planning for 2012," Campus Progress, December 20, 2011, http://campusprogress.org/articles; Browne-Dianis Testimony, 3.

20. Berman, "The GOP War on Voting." For the statute, see Title IX, Chapter 97.0575, http://www.leg.state.fl.us/Statutes/index; *Daytona Beach News-Journal*, October 27, 2011; *Palm Beach Post*, October 27, 2011; *Florida Independent*, October 31, 2011; *THINKPROGRESS*, October 25, 2011; 2012 Summary of Voting Law Changes Analysis, August 3, 2012, Brennan Center, 1–2, "Statement of Wendy R. Weiser," director, Democracy Program, Brennan Center for Justice at NYU School of Law before Subcommittee on the Constitution, Judiciary Committee, House of Representatives, April 18, 2012, 3.

21. *Daytona Beach News-Journal*, November 3, 2011. McFall's editorial is in *Daytona News Journal*, October 23, 2011.

22. Huellkill's statement can be found in *Central Republican News*, November 6, 20011; *Palm Beach Post*, October 27, 2011; Associated Press, "Teacher May Face Fine Under Fla. Election Law," October 29, 2011.

23. Rick Outzen, "In Defense of Florida's 'Subversive Six' Teachers," *Florida Voices*, December 20, 2011, http://www.floridavoices.com/columns; *Florida Independent*, December 13, 2011; "Nel's New Day," November 6, 2011, http://nelsnewday.com.

24. Weiser and Norden, "Voting Law Changes in 2012," 17, 20; *Los Angeles Times*, October 30, 2011; *Time*, November 7, 2011; "League of Women Voters, Rock the Vote, and Florida PIRG Ask Federal Court to Block Florida Voter Registration Restrictions," December 15, 2011, Common Dreams, http://www.commondreams.org/newswire. Macnab is quoted in Jonathan Wiseman and Carol E. Lee, "Obama Aims at Election Laws," *Wall Street Journal*, November 2, 2011.

25. Marc Caputo, "How Rick Scott's Noncitizen Voter Purge Started Small and Then Blew Up," *Miami Herald*, June 12, 2012; Rachel Weiner, "Florida's Voter Purge Explained," *Washington Post*, June 18, 2012; Ari Berman, "Florida Voter Purge Is Unlikely to Resume," *Nation*, July 3, 2012, http://www.the nation.com/blog/168714/florida-voter-purge-unlikely-resume#; Rachel Weiner, "Florida Voter Purge Fight Isn't Over," *Washington Post*, July 17, 2012; Elizabeth Drew, "Voting Wrongs."

26. Brenton Mock, "The Growing Debate Over the Voting Rights Act," *ColorLines: News for Action*, May 24, 2012; Timothy Noah, "Art of War," *New Republic*, August 2, 2012; Wiseman and Lee, "Obama Aims at Election Laws"; *New York Times*, November 16, 2011.

27. "Court Rejects Florida's Efforts to Curtail Early Voting," People for the American Way, August 17, 2012, http://blog.pfaw.org/content/court-reejcts-floridas-effforts-curtail-early-voting; Dan Froomkin, "Republican Voter Suppression Campaign Rolls Back Early Voting," *Huffington Post*, August 28, 2012, http://www.huffington-post.com/2012/08/18/republican-voter-suppression-early-voting_n_1766172.html; Gene Demby, "Black Pastors Group Criticizes Ohio for New Rules That Limit Early Voting," *Huffington Post*, Black Voices, August 14, 2012, http://www.huffingtonpost.com/2012/08/14/black-pastors-early-voting_n_1776585.html.

28. *Washington Post*, December 23, 2011; *New York Times*, December 23, 2011; Wendy Weiser and Nhu-Y Ngo, "Voting Rights in 2011: A Legislative Round-Up," July 15, 2011, 2, Brennan Center for Justice at New York University School of Law; "Editorial," *Texas Star Telegram*, December 28, 2011. For the Supreme Court's decision, see *New York Times*, April 29, 2008; *San Antonio Express*, March 13, 2012; *Nation*, March 15, 2012.

29. Turzai and Preiss are quoted in Ari Berman, "Ohio GOP Admits Early Voting Cutbacks Are Racially Motivated," *Nation*, August 28, 2012, http://www.thenation.com/blog/169454/ohio-gop-admits-early-voting-cutbacks-are-racially-motivated.

30. *Huffington Post*, October 21, 2011, March 12, 2012; *Jurist*, July 18, 2012. For Judge Niess's decision, see *League of Women Voters of Wisconsin Education Network vs. Scott Walker, et al.*, Case No. 11 CV 4669, http://media.jsonline.com/documents/voteridruling.pdf. For Judge Flanagan's decision, see *Milwaukee Branch of the NAACP, et al. vs. Scott Walker, et al.*, Case No. 11 CV 5492, at http://media.jsonline.com/documents/Voter+ID+injunction.pdf.

31. *New York Times*, May 31, 2012; *Miami Herald*, June 6, 2012. For Judge Hinckle's decision, see *League of Women Voters of Florida, et al. vs. Kurt Browning, etc., et al.*, Case No. 4:11cv628-RH/WCS, US District Court of the Northern District of Florida, Tallahassee Division, http://www.scribd.com/doc/95458735/Florida-Voter-Registration.

32. For Judge Costa's decision, see http://docs.google.cm/open?id=0BxeOfQQn UrgenJ1T2tERDNuMTQ.

33. *Huffington Post*, October 21, 2011, March 12, 2012; *Jurist*, July 18, 2012; *Los Angeles Times*, August 31, 2012; Elizabeth Drew, "Voting Wrongs," *Wall Street Journal*, September 18, 2012. On Pennsylvania judge Robert Simpson's decision, see *Politico*, October 2, 2012, http://www.politico.com/news/stories/1012/81905.html; *Washington Post*, October 2, 2012; *New York Times*, October 2, 2012; *Austin Post*, August 3, 14, 28, 2012.

34. Abby Rapoport, "What's the Deal with the Pennsylvania Voter-ID Law?" *American Prospect*, July 25, 2012. See also "Section 2 of the Voting Rights Act," Civil Rights Division, Department of Justice, http://www.justice.gov/crt/about/vot/sec_2/about_sec.2.php; *ColorLines: News for Action*, June 14, 2012; *New York Times*, July 19, 2012; Reuters, July 23, 2012; Section 5 Covered Jurisdictions, Civil Rights Division, US Department of Justice, http://www.justice.gov/crt/about/vot/sec_5/covered.php.

35. *New York Times*, November 17, 2000 (Williams); *New York Times*, April 15, 2000 (Turner); *Los Angeles Times*, September 11, 2003 (Foster); *Los Angeles Times*, December 24, 2008 (Bevel); Ruth C. Bryant, "Amelia Boynton Robinson," February 2, 2009, *Encyclopedia of Alabama*; Lyndon H. LaRouche Jr., "In the Garden of Gethsemane," in Amelia Platts Boynton Robinson, *Bridge Across Jordan* (Washington, DC: Schiller Institute, 1991), xix–xxiv; Andrea Shalal-Esa, "Activist Spreads King's Teachings on Nonviolence," Reuters, January 19, 2009 (Lafayette).

36. Charles Bonner Interview, Veterans of the Civil Rights Movement, 2005, http://www.crmvet.org/nars/chuckbet.htm; Alvin Benn, "1960s Sheriff Won't Back Down," *Montgomery Advertiser*, March 3, 2006; *Washington Post*, 2007; *New York Times*, June 7, 2007.

37. John Lewis, "Voter ID Laws Are a Poll Tax," July 21, 2011, Online Office of Congressman John Lewis, johnlewis.house.gov; John Lewis, "A Poll Tax by Another Name," *New York Times*, August 20, 2011; *THINKPROGRESS*, November 3, 2011; "What I've Learned: Representative John Lewis (D, Ga.)," Politics Blog, *Esquire*, October 22, 2010, http://www.esquire.com/blogs/politics/john-lewis-interview-1110.

38. Alexander Keysar, "Voter Suppression Returns," *Harvard Magazine*, July–August 2012, htttp:harvardmagazine.com/2012/07/voter-suppression-returns. See also Alexander Keysar, *The Right to Vote: The Contested History of Democracy in the United States* (New York: Basic Books, 2000), 54.

39. Richard M. Valelly, *The Two Reconstructions: The Struggle for Black Enfranchisement* (Chicago: University of Chicago Press, 2004), 1–5; W. E. B. Du Bois, *The Souls of Black Folk* (New York: Penguin, 1996), 27.

Index

303